PROMISED LAND

PROMISED LAND
Competing Visions of Agrarian Reform

Edited by Peter Rosset, Raj Patel, and Michael Courville

A project of the Land Research Action Network (LRAN)

FOOD FIRST BOOKS • *Oakland, California*

Text design by BookMatters, Berkeley
Cover design by BookMatters
Cover photograph: "Amazon, Brazil. Squatters occupy unproductive estate" by J.R. Ripper/ Social Photos.

Library of Congress Cataloging-in-Publication Data

     Promised land : competing visions of agrarian reform / edited by Peter Rosset, Raj Patel, and Michael Courville.
     p. cm.
     "This book represents the first harvest in the English language of the work of the Land Research Action Network (LRAN). LRAN is an international working group of researchers, analysts, nongovernment organizations (NGOs), and representatives of social movements"— Pref.
     Includes bibliographical references and index.
     ISBN-13: 978-0-935028-28-7 (pbk.)
     ISBN-10: 0-935028-28-5 (pbk.)
     1. Land reform. 2. Land use, Rural. 3. Minorities — Land tenure. 4. Economic development. 5. Distributive justice. I. Title: Competing visions of agrarian reform. II. Rosset, Peter. III. Patel, Raj. IV. Courville, Michael.
     HD1332.P76   2006
     333.3'1–dc22   2005033784

Food First Books are distributed by
CDS
425 Madison Avenue
New York, NY 10017
(800) 343-4499

Printed in Canada

This book is dedicated to all those who struggle for land that has been promised, yet never delivered, to the hundreds of peasant women and men who are assassinated every year for daring to claim their right to land, and to the hundreds of indigenous people who are murdered for defending their ancestral territories.

Thanks to your struggle and sacrifice, a better world *is* possible.

Contents

Foreword

Only two decades ago, land redistribution appeared to be dead, along with the state-led model of industrialization that had motivated most agrarian reform efforts. The structural adjustment programs of the 1980s once again focused attention on external markets. In this context, land redistribution lost its primary economic rationale since enhancing rural incomes to support an expanding internal market for the industrialization effort was no longer a priority.

The issue of the pressing need for land redistribution was resurrected in the 1990s by two contending forces: the rural social movements contesting their exclusion under neoliberalism, and the World Bank. Despite their differences, they share a recognition of the centrality of the land question for rural livelihoods.

The World Bank now associates the continued concentration of land in less-developed countries with intractable rural poverty and, in a departure from its previous analyses, also with the disappointingly low economic growth rates in many regions. The solution is to put land into the hands of those who can work it most productively, ostensibly small farmers. This should be done via the market, it contends, which can distribute land more efficiently than the state and with less conflict.

For the rural social movements that have joined together to form Vía Campesina (an international association of peasant, landless, indigenous, and women's organizations), the market, rather than being part of the solution, is part of the problem. Increased reliance on market forces in the context of neoliberal economic restructuring has led to the demise of peasant farming. Under these conditions, market-led land reform is destined to fail. Market-led land reform is also unjust, they argue, since it rewards those who in the past have usurped and concentrated land.

Most of the essays in this volume—whose scope includes Africa, Asia, and Latin America—demonstrate either the shortcomings of previous agrarian reform efforts or the limited nature of market-led land reform in those countries where it has been implemented. The authors, most of whom are researchers closely associated with the rural social movements, place power relations center-stage in their analyses. They show that the limited agrarian reform efforts of the past failed, not because of intrinsic problems of peasant agriculture but because of the lack of political will among elites in the face of entrenched resistance from the landlord class. Similarly, decentralizing land distribution efforts to the local level, including the sale and purchase of land, exacerbates the power differences between those who control land and those who do not in favor of the former.

Several factors favor redistributionary agrarian reform in the current period. Somewhat ironically, among them is hyper-urbanization. The lack of correspondence between urbanization and industrialization has meant that in a number of the countries discussed in this volume, the majority of the poor now reside in urban areas. High rates of urban under- and unemployment, and the attendant crime and squalor, have made the cities increasingly unlivable. In this context, a rural solution to urban problems has gained support among social movements and some sectors of the urban middle class and the elite, particularly in contexts where it is cheaper to redistribute land than to create urban jobs.

Another factor favoring redistributionary agrarian reform in the current period is the pressing need for sustainable agricultural systems. The industrial model of agriculture, based on the intense use of natural resources (particularly water and hydrocarbons), while successful in the short run to generate export revenues, is simply not sustainable on a global scale.

The most important factor, however, in placing redistributionary agrarian reform back on the agenda has been the agency of peasants, rural workers, and their organizations. The 1990s brought a resurgence of rural organizing, particularly among sectors that had not been previously organized, such as rural women, indigenous groups, and the landless. Moreover, these national organizations are increasingly linked at the regional and global levels. Vía Campesina has taken a leading role in the World Social Forums, which have been held annually since 2001, and in the case of Latin America, the hemispheric-level Social Summits and anti-FTAA meetings.

The essays in this volume argue that redistributionary agrarian reform could be the pillar of an alternative model of development to neoliberalism, one built on food sovereignty—favoring national agriculture over imports— and sustainable development—prioritizing small farmers over corporate agriculture. They outline the main elements required for successful agrarian reform efforts: they must be massive in scale, based on the intense mobilization and participation by the landless, and comprehensive, which requires a supportive state. As the rural social movements remind us, "Another World Is Possible!" This volume is an important contribution to defining this vision.

Carmen Diana Deere
Director, Center for Latin American Studies
University of Florida

Preface: A History and Overview of the Land Research Action Network

This book comes at a key moment in the history of the age-old struggle for land. Agrarian reform is back at the center of the international debate over rural development, after a long hiatus during which it was virtually a forbidden topic. Fair and equitable access to land and other resources like water, forests, and biodiversity is perhaps the most fundamental prerequisite for the kind of inclusive, broad-based development that would allow nations to provide all of their citizens with a decent standard of living and make possible more ecologically sustainable management of natural resources. This book proposes a model of development that focuses on the redistribution of land through agrarian reform and through supportive policies for small farmers, an alternative paradigm, that has been called "food sovereignty" by La Via Campesina, the global alliance of peasant, family farm and landless peoples' movements, and which is described on the final chapter of this volume.

In the immediate post–World War II period, there was a flurry of land reform efforts across the Third World, some successful and some relatively unsuccessful, for reasons addressed in this volume. Yet in the 1970s and 1980s, the topic of agrarian reform became taboo in official development circles—one would be labeled a communist or a dinosaur, stuck in the past, if one raised agrarian reform as a serious option. But recently, a combination of factors has put it squarely back at the center of the development debate.

The 1990s saw the coming of age of well-organized movements of landless peasants and rural workers in much of the Third World. While the landless have always engaged in sporadic invasions of property belonging to absentee landlords, there has been a qualitative change in the cohesion, organization, and political savvy demonstrated by contemporary groups—the undisputed leader of which is Brazil's Landless Workers' Movement (Movimento dos Trabalhadores Rurais Sem Terra [MST])—though very significant, organized land occupations have also taken place in recent years in countries as diverse as Indonesia, Paraguay, Zimbabwe, Honduras, Thailand, South Africa, and Nicaragua, among others.

These organizations press for access to land for their landless or land-poor members, and they increasingly speak with an international voice through La Via Campesina, which also sponsors the Global Campaign for Agrarian Reform (GCAR). GCAR seeks to build cooperation among landless movements and to build support for them so they can bring effective pressure to bear on governments and in international forums.

Landless movements have put the struggle for land reform back on the agenda of national policy debates—often at tremendous cost in terms of arbitrary arrests and lives lost. At the opposite end of the spectrum, economists at the World Bank have finally come to accept a key point that activists and social scientists alike have been making for decades: after examining their own data on countries around the world, World Bank economists have come to the conclusion that extremely inequitable access to productive resources, such as land, is a major obstacle to economic development and even to economic growth. The Bank itself has now placed its version of land reform at the center of the policy packages it pushes on Third World governments.

While what the Bank calls land reform—essentially privatization, the promotion of markets in land, and "market-led" mechanisms of access—is a far cry from what La Via Campesina and other grassroots movements call for, this change in Bank policy has had the salutary effect of making legitimate again the call for land reform and the struggle over its definition. In fact, as highlighted in this book, we are witnessing a period of intense struggle over the content of the "agrarian reform" that is back on the development agenda. There are at least four general visions that define the key positions in this debate. On the one hand, the Bank and other international agencies, as well as governments, favor a market-based approach born of neoliberal thinking, which is examined by the authors in part II of this volume; while grassroots movements and progressive governments lean toward redistributive models that involve expropriation, some of which are reviewed in part III. Other crucially important viewpoints are those of indigenous peoples' organizations, which emphasize the importance of "territory" over "land," as well as autonomy and self-determination; and a gender perspective that is highly critically of biases favoring men, both in current land tenure arrangements and in many agrarian reform programs, while women often lack titles or other guarantees of access to land. These perspectives are also examined in this volume.

This book represents the first harvest in the English language of the work of the Land Research Action Network (LRAN). LRAN is an international working group of researchers, analysts, nongovernment organizations (NGOs), and representatives of social movements. LRAN's aim is to provide research and analytical support to movements that are struggling for land, as part of the Global Campaign for Agrarian Reform (GCAR). We offer this volume as an informational and analytical tool to those movements, and to those researchers, policy makers, activists, academics, analysts, students, and others who are interested to learn more about issues of agrarian reform in the early twenty-first century. In this book we begin with a historical perspective on agrarian reform and land issues, using case studies of representative countries. We then devote the bulk of the book to an examination of the different viewpoints in the struggle to define agrarian reform, and to an evaluation of the results to date of the policies and strategies that emerge from these contrasting perspectives.

Financial support for much of the research presented in the volume and for the publication of this book was provided by the Ford, C. S. Mott, and Pond Foundations; by the Kaplan Fund; and by the Evangelischer Entwicklungsdienst (EED) of Germany. We are grateful for their support. We express special thanks to the peasants and landless people of La Via Campesina and other social movements for the constant inspiration that they give us.

Shalmali Guttal,
Focus on the Global South, Thailand

Maria Luisa Mendonça,
Social Network for Justice and Human Rights (Rede Social), Brazil

Peter Rosset,
Center for the Study of Rural Change in Mexico (CECCAM), Mexico

Co-coordinators,
Land Research Action Network (LRAN)
www.landaction.org

PART ONE

Land and Agrarian Reform: Historical Perspectives

The Resurgence of Agrarian Reform in the Twenty-first Century

Michael Courville and Raj Patel

We have a real problem with land tenancy; land distribution—
mucho tierra en pocos manos (much land in few hands)—not
everyone has land and everyone needs some!
—*Honduran small-scale farmer*

Although more people now live in cities than in rural areas, a significant pro-portion of the world's poor still live in the countryside. For them, no less than for their homeless counterparts in towns and cities, landlessness remains a pervasive social problem. From the dawn of modern capitalism in sixteenth-century Britain (Wood 2000) to contemporary land claims in Zimbabwe (Moyo 2000; Moyo and Yeros 2005) land has been, and continues to be, at the center of rural conflict.[1]

A constant theme in conflicts over land is control, both of the land itself and of material resources and uses associated with it, such as water, wood, min-erals, grazing and gathering. This control hinges on property rights. The abil-ity to own and transfer possession of land through private property, in turn, has invariably been predicated on other forms of economic, social, and cultural power. At the same time, the development and concentration of private prop-erty rights have typically been mechanisms for entrenching and consolidating the power of some groups over others. Perhaps the starkest example of the inequities propagated through the privatization of property is seen through the lens of gender: while they produce the majority of the world's food, for exam-ple, women in the Global South[2] own only 1 percent of the land. The domi-nance of the private property model has allowed landownership to become increasingly concentrated along existing lines of power in the hands of fewer and fewer people, usually men. Exceptions to this rule are hard won.

Private property ignores need in favor of the demands of rule and order. As

Wood notes (2000), the instantiation of such property rights has involved nothing less than the birth of our modern capitalist world. The transformation of the relationship that farmers, producers, and, indeed, landlords had with the land, turning it into an entity that can be traded and mediated by the market, changed the character of rural life forever. The expansion of land markets had the effect of dislocating the peasantry economically, physically, and socially, first in England and then, within an astonishingly short period of time, in the rest of the world.

> This pattern would be reproduced in the colonies, and indeed in post-Independence America, where the independent small farmers who were supposed to be the backbone of a free republic faced, from the beginning, the stark choice of agrarian capitalism: at best, intense self-exploitation, and at worst, dispossession and displacement by larger, more productive enterprises. (Wood 2000)

The inequality resulting from this dislocation brought radical social change across the world (Polanyi 1944; Williams 1994, 41–103). Thousands of peasants and smallholders were pushed off the land toward new cities and towns. Once there, they became integrated into a new set of social relations that no longer depended upon a primary relationship to the land (Brown 1988, 28–31). During the early colonial period in the United States, in a nation that had little actual peasantry[3] and that championed free market liberalism, the swift and uneven concentration of land was widely thought to foment social unrest. Led by Thomas Paine, a demand for "agrarian justice" was advanced, calling for an equal distribution of land or for just compensation to small farmers, to avoid the ill effects observed during England's feverish land grab of the eighteenth century (Paine 1925). This call for justice fell on deaf ears as the United States moved toward industrial expansion and did not look back.

The increased concentration into fewer hands of agricultural land around the world continues to this day, with little regard for the overwhelming evidence of the landlessness[4] and inequality it has caused (Herring 2000; Thiesenhusen 1995, 159–62; Umehara and Bautista 2004, 3–18). The extent of this concentration of control undoubtedly would be more severe were it not for persistent and ongoing resistance, with new agrarian struggles commanding the attention of millions worldwide. The struggles of the landless in Africa, Asia, and Latin America have brought a renewed demand for agrarian and land reform around the world. This book provides an overview of these struggles, the issues and policies they confront, and the links that bind them together.

The Shifting Demands for Agrarian Change

Early nineteenth-century land tenure reforms were often taken up, particularly in Latin America, by fledgling states as they struggled to break free from their colonial past. More often than not, the catalyst for land tenure reform and early agrarian change during this era was the liberation of a new merchant class and the emancipation of national elites from the vestiges of colonial power and religious rule. The consideration of the small farmer rarely, if ever, figured into this burgeoning expansion of colonial relations. The importance of the small farmer, however, would come to the fore as national development projects of the late nineteenth century began to confront the obstacle posed by feudal land relations.

The agrarian question of the late nineteenth century pivoted on the role of the small-farm sector and the pace of capitalism's movement into agricultural production. By the early twentieth century, a now-classic debate emerged in the Soviet Union, between those who championed the inevitability of large-farm dominance and efficiency, as argued by Karl Kautsky (1988, reprint), and the family farm economy as a viable alternative path to development, championed by Alexander Chayanov (1966). The former positioned the small farmer as transitory, a shrinking class in the transition to capitalist development in the countryside. The latter viewed the small producer as a central actor in the economic activity of the countryside, destined to maintain an integral position within the rural class structure. Kautsky's analysis and argument for a more efficient, modernized agricultural sector helped move the peasantry off the land and toward industrialized cities. The Kautskian view of agrarian change shared much of the optimism found in classic theories of industrialization and capitalist transition at the turn of the twentieth century; it was a vision that captured the imaginations of most world leaders struggling for independence, and it shaped the policies of revolutionary nations aiming for rapid, large-scale conversion of the agricultural sector. The small-farm path to development was, conversely, often viewed as reactionary, anachronistic, and romantic.

Twentieth-century industrial production biases directed the practice of most national rural development schemes toward input-intensive, monocultural production that, crucially, required large contiguous areas of land in order to be successful. Sowing the seeds of a new "national agriculture" along these lines, governments turned away from the rural poor, who had their own vision for agrarian change. The Chayanovian view of a different rural vision, based on family farms and peasant cooperatives, has its echoes today in peasant movement struggles for agrarian reform (see the conclusion in this volume).

The national reorganization of the countryside in favor of industrial agriculture was made possible, paradoxically, by struggles for national liberation, which drew heavily on ideas of land being for the people. From the end of the Second World War until the fall of the Berlin Wall, efforts for independence from colonialization were suffused with the rhetoric of democracy, equality, and rights, while they bore differing visions of land and agrarian reform for national change. The extent to which this rhetoric matched reality depended on a complex amalgam of domestic and international circumstances and choices, with highly variable outcomes in different countries (as we detail below). With the end of the Cold War, however, the debate over land redistribution has narrowed dramatically. Formerly a central point in a program of postcolonial independence, agrarian and land reform programs are now framed by considerations of equity and production efficiency arbitrated by the World Bank, with the full support of international finance institutions and their network of local elites.

This shift in focus differs dramatically from the original understanding of agrarian reform as a means to a range of outcomes including dignity, justice, and sovereignty, and as a platform in a broader process of national enfranchisement and democracy. Today, it is possible to see a convergence of agrarian policies in different countries, shaped by each nation's domestic political considerations but tending toward a common set of features: property, scale, technology, and the market. This is the neoliberalization of agrarian policy— a process that has its analogues across a range of other domains, from trade to the role of the state (Magdoff, Foster, and Buttel 2000).

Neoliberal agrarian reforms diagnose, and prescribe policies for, rural areas in ways that differ significantly from the national liberation projects of the twentieth century. Through this analytical paradigm shift, the policies to which the term "land reform" refers have altered beyond recognition from their mid–twentieth century counterparts. Most centrally, redistributive state-led agrarian reform is unthinkable within this new paradigm. Instead, policy discussions now highlight considerations of efficiency, making issues of equality and distributive justice secondary, if they are considered at all. Many of the most prominent and recent arguments for and against land reform since the Cold War have come to pivot on economic questions (de Janvry and Sadoulet 1989; de Janvry et al. eds. 2001; Kay 2002a; Deininger et al. 2003; Griffin, Khan, and Ickowitz 2002). Along the way, an interest in small farmer efficiency has reemerged as a legitimate debate and policy concern. Many World Bank development economists have come around to the view that the redistribution of land to small farmers would lead to greater overall productivity and economic dynamism (Deininger 1999; Binswanger, Deininger, and Feder 1995), a view long since arrived at by others (see Barret 1993; Berry and Cline 1979; Cornia 1985; Ellis 1993; Feder 1985; Lappé et al. 1998; Prosterman and Riedinger 1987; Rosset 1999; Sobhan 1993; Tomich, Kilby, and Johnston 1995).

It is a measure of the success of this neoliberal reframing of policy that even those scholars and policy makers who side with arguments for redistributive land reform find themselves doing so on terms of economic growth—as increased Gross Domestic Product (GDP)—and not on terms of justice, food sovereignty,[5] equality, or rural transformation. Nonetheless, it is useful to see, for example, as Griffin, Khan, and Ickowitz (2002) have demonstrated, using what they term a "heterodox economic framework" (though see Byres 2004a, b), that without a redistribution of land in the Global South, economic growth will continue to evade the best efforts at top-down development, and the chasm between poverty and wealth will continue to deepen. Griffin, Khan, and Ickowitz (2004, 362–63) offer a theoretical model that allows for consideration of the political dimensions of resource distribution—land in this case— by considering the socially sanctioned dimensions of property law and the ways in which property rights change over time.

When and how property is defined and regulated reflects the struggle for power in any given place and is subject to change usually in alignment with the needs of large property owners and the goals of the state (Kerkvliet and Selden 1998, 50–53). The case of Guatemala is helpful for illustrating this process (see chapter 1 in this volume). The definition of public lands, or *economiendas*, in colonial Guatemala was sufficient to maintain the colonial lords' power and access to land, but it stood in the way of the desires of the new merchant class upon independence. Land law was reconfigured to facilitate land seizure from the Church and taxes were brought upon the old *latifundistas* who left so much land idle (Scofield 1990, 161–65; Williams 1994, 58–60). Agrarian reform can be and has always been a political as well as an economic demand, and it is the political aspect of redistributive reform—who calls for the reforms and on what terms—that has been so caustic throughout the twentieth century, and even more so in the beginning of the twenty-first century. While it has become somewhat less controversial to call for land reform on economic grounds (as Griffin, Khan, and Ickowitz [2002] have done), economically based arguments for land alone will not be sufficient to change the structured inequalities of the rural sector. As the logic of neoliberalism continues to unfold across the globe, a suffocating economism[6] continues to choke off any demands for increased resource equality (Amin 2004).

The rise of neoliberalism has come to be associated with an antiauthoritarianism that exacerbates the decline of an already weakened state and a concomitant promise of "democratization." Many liberal scholars, citizens, and activists currently celebrate the opportunity they see for marginalized groups to now mobilize, and for civil society, more generally, to flourish. The declining ability of the state to regulate and direct a domestic development project has, to some eyes, created this welcome opportunity for resistance and grassroots empowerment. Yet, most grassroots movements find themselves struggling to be effective political forces in an age of free-market politics in which access to the state is now mediated by direct economic power.

While it is true that the marginalized are increasingly allowed to make demands and to organize within civil society, the reconfigured neoliberal state stops them short of bringing their demands to fruition through government. Through a combination of decentralization and an increased privatization of public services, the state comes to function as an organizational tool for market expansion, and less a vehicle for representative democracy or resource distribution. Thus neoliberal populism creates a force that empowers people to act without ever providing any actual mechanism to help movements realize their goals: it has led to an era of both more political voices and increasing state quiescence (Petras and Veltmeyer 2003; Teichman 1995). This reorganization of the state thus forces any current demand for agrarian reform firmly within the parameters of a depoliticized (market-oriented) project. In this way, an emphasis on land reform alone as a means to boost agricultural productivity avoids addressing the other dimensions of power and historical inequity that in the current agenda have marginalized both the rural sector and the rural poor. Similarly, a populist struggle for land that does not take into consideration power, social rights, and the historical struggle of small farmers[7] and the landless could quickly become part of the neoliberal project and lead to increased political exclusiveness.

A Call for Agrarian Reform from Below:
The Small Farmer and the Landless

In many nations rural dwellers still rely on the land to grow their own food and to provide sustenance for their families (Ghimire 2001b, 17–18). Land in rural communities is the central component ensuring the well-being and longevity of families, much as Chayanov saw it. In this context land is not a commodity, it is a source of life and society. Yet this foundation of life for the world's poorest is systematically denied to them. The exclusion from this life-giving resource is what drives the call for land and agrarian reform from below. Basic statistics on landholding and farm size from around the world can help to underscore this point. In Honduras, for example, the rural population was 64 percent in 2002. A 2003 agricultural census calculated that 2.4 million hectares, or 62 percent of the nation's agricultural land, were under the ownership of the largest farmers (those with 50 or more hectares), yet these farms made up only 10 percent of the total number of farms (Courville 2005, 62–63). The total landholding of the smallest farmers (those with less than 5 hectares) accounted for a little more than 3.5 thousand hectares, or 9 percent of the total farmland in the nation. It is the smallest farmers, however, who account for over 72 percent of the total farms in the nation (Courville 2005, 62–63). The most recent data also show a 28 percent increase in landholding concentration for the largest farmers since the implementation of neoliberal reforms, while the smallest farmers faced a 4 percent decline in overall landholding area.[8]

This is by no means a Latin American phenomenon. Uneven land concentration has created persistent landlessness in the Philippines. Population statistics from 2000 show that 48 percent of the Philippine population live in rural areas and that three-quarters of the rural poor depend on farming and agriculture for their livelihood (Balisacan 2002; Economist Intelligence Unit [EIU] 2004, 16). Yet at the same time, official estimates during the preceding decade report that between 58 and 65 percent of all agricultural workers were considered to be landless at any given time (Riedinger 1990, 17–18). Landholding in the Philippines has favored the largest landholders, who are often linked to positions of political power and prominence, as in the case of former president (1986–1992) Corazon Aquino. Aquino's administration endorsed land reform policy during her presidential tenure, but it effectively avoided major confiscations that would have dismantled the largest landholdings, including her own family's 6,000-hectare estate (de Guzman, Garrido, and Manahan 2004). The 2002 Philippine agricultural census found that while the total number of farms since the 1991 census had increased by 4.6 percent, the average landholding of small farmers fell from 2.5 to 2 hectares. The limited data on land tenure makes this change hard to interpret, but the ineffectiveness of past reforms and the questionable actions of past administrations suggest a continued trend toward the erosion of small-farm landholdings. This, in part, has mobilized small farmers across the nation to call for agrarian reform that is more transparent and that is designed not by the landed and political elites, but by those who seek land for subsistence (Borras 2003a; Llanto and Ballesteros 2003, 3–5).

The trend of land concentration and exclusion has also shaped the fate of small producers and indigenous people in Africa. Take, for instance, the case of Tanzania, which struggled to escape a colonial legacy of large coffee farms and plantation agriculture established under German and English rule. In the late 1960s, shortly after independence, the Tanzanian government removed the Masai people from their ancestral territory in an effort to collectivize agriculture, dismantle colonial land-tenure patterns, and abolish plantation agriculture (Hyden 1980). The reform relied on the invocation of a fictive Masai collectivity, which was supposed to provide the necessary dynamism for socialized village agriculture. The reform effort failed in large part. A decline in agricultural production followed. This brought increased private investment and a voracious land grab from foreign developers that continued to keep the Masai from their ancestral lands (Williams 1996, 218). Forty years after Tanzanian independence, food security is still elusive, and the country's agricultural export production remains under the control of foreign investors (Mihayo 2003; Ponte 2004, 622–25; Skarstein 2005, 334). Furthermore, 48 percent of Tanzania has been designated as wildlife preserve, even though as recently as 2001, 63 percent of the population still relied on agriculture and fishing for subsistence (Economist Intelligence Unit 2004, 15). The land squeeze has increased the number of Masai employed in the newly established safari tourist industry, which continues to funnel the lion's share of GDP into foreign pockets (ole Ndaskoi 2003a, 2003b). Many landless Masai struggle to survive, earning meager wages while trying to maintain some of their traditional hunting and gathering rights on state lands, to feed themselves and their families (ole Ndaskoi 2003a).

How such uneven land concentration arises—whether in Honduras, the Philippines, or Tanzania—is no mystery. Though varied, the agents that account for these examples of uneven land concentration are invariably acting within a broad macroeconomic climate that privileges large-scale industry. Modern production schemes such as logging, dam construction, tourism, large-scale agricultural export, and cattle ranching are hungry for land, and their land consumption pushes rural communities to the margins in almost every case (Williams 1986). Rather than being protected by the state, small farmers, indigenous communities, and peasants have been forced by governments, under the banner of "broad-based rural development," to work within the demands of the market. The agricultural modernization championed by governments and other global elites does not necessarily lead to new opportunities for rural people, who are, if they were not already, marginal to the increased GDP of national development (Bryceson 2001; Carter and Barham 1996; Kay 1997). International financing of the agricultural sector builds a very uneven playing field that is tilted against small producers, and the net economic gains of world competition invariably involve vast gain for a few and devastating loss for many.

Though part of a profoundly political project, neoliberal land policy tries to smother its own politics, couching its interventions as purely "technical" or expedient (Ferguson 1990). Through this "technicalized" policy, small producers and the rural poor around the world continue to be squeezed out of national development schemes. The landless have, however, fought back. Indeed, despite efforts to depoliticize the claims of landless people for agrarian reform, there is ample evidence that the failure of the neoliberal project is what has fueled the repoliticization of the very people it has excluded (Patel 2006). They have fought back not by adopting the language of technical efficiency or expediency, but by means of political struggle, direct action, or strategic linkages with international support systems or nongovernmental organizations (NGOs).

Demonstrating that neoliberalism will fail in theory is one thing; showing how it fails in fact is quite another. Listening to the experiences of those who have endured the onslaught of modern agrarian reform policies, not only do we see the theoretical deficiencies of the agrarian reform program, we learn how this program, at best, willfully ignores existing power relations, thus compounding them and exacerbating the inequalities that result. This is important because, although the attempt to paper over historical inequalities has been successful—to the extent that a range of government policies in the Global South are premised on their irrelevance—the on-the-ground experience of power persists and, with it, the possibility of other approaches to agrarian politics. At the time this book goes to press, for example, the South African government has taken a stern line in opposing any further expansion of its land program on the grounds that such a move would endanger "investor confidence." Yet even within the ruling African National Congress (ANC), many grassroots party members remain convinced of the necessity for broader powers of land confiscation and of their wider implementation. Still, the belief that land reform should happen within a paradigm of "willing buyer–willing seller" is pervasive within most development circles. Indeed, South Africa is one of many "success stories" that the World Bank has attempted to spin in the Global South, with the explicit aim of furthering its policies. In this book, we consider these policy experiments and their failings—the Bank's "success" stories are demonstrably inefficient, failing on the Bank's own terms (see chapter 5 in this volume). But the issue of the success or failure of a land reform policy is even subtler than just World Bank policy failure, and has to do with the fact that the terms for understanding land reform success and failure have shifted over the last few decades.

There are currently at least two competing frameworks for establishing "success" in agrarian reform. The first, rooted in the World Bank, sees efficiency and effectiveness[9] as the defining characteristics of successful land reform. This framework holds much of the politics, and the allocation of resources having to do with agriculture, as a constant. Over the past decade, during which land reform has existed under these parameters, this mode of agrarian reform has established itself as, at best, a palliative approach, maintaining the *status quo* while tinkering on the margins in order to address the most prominent and acute symptoms of rural dispossession. Before the (as yet incomplete) capture of policy options by neoliberalism, land reform was, to a greater or lesser extent, part of a broader series of interventions in agrarian and national reform projects, encompassing considerations of nationhood, identity, employment, history, the Cold War, decolonization, and the provision of food. In these circumstances, metrics of success were far more ambiguous and varied.

A second contemporary framework for posing "the land question" is offered by La Via Campesina, the international peasant movement,[10] whose framework is inherently plural. It demands a democratic process in which a range of people not only "participate," that is, play a central role in setting the agenda, but also shape and dictate the contours of agrarian policy (Patel 2006). The terms of reference for this kind of land reform are not written in Washington, but in the fields—and defining its success or failure is in itself a democratic project, informed by a history of struggle. Successful land reform, under this rubric, depends on the political and historical context at the time reform is implemented, but it invariably involves a mass democratic engagement and will result in systemic, widespread redistribution, requiring a deep commitment from the state. In most cases, though not all, the poorest need the state to protect them, to fund their projects, and to engage in the radical redistribution that will ensure that the reform involves more than simply a cosmetic change. Successful land reform will be, in a word, political. The emphasis on the political is important to bear in mind, when contrasting it with the current crop of supposed Bank successes.

Land and Agrarian Reform after World War II

A first step toward understanding the neoliberalization of agrarian reform and the World Bank model is to look more closely at the historical variance of agrarian reforms worldwide since World War II. This period (1945–2000) covers the process of decolonization and a reconfiguration of the international trading system. This reconfiguration (Friedmann 1982) had the effect, after their nominal independence, of leaving many nations in the Global South shackled to their preindependence economic roles as producers of agricultural exports and natural resources for their former colonizers. The entrenchment of colonial economic relations, within the emerging nation-states of the then-designated "third world," was a design feature of the postwar settlement (Hobsbawm 1994). Toward the end of the Second World War, the Allied powers held a landmark conference at Bretton Woods in New Hampshire, at which the architecture for many of today's international financial institutions was laid out. The web of world markets became more binding through these organizations as lending and credit became new carrots for shaping the development policies of the emergent nations, and these nations assumed mostly dependent positions within this nexus.

A major outcome of this conference was the establishment and development of the International Monetary Fund (IMF) and the World Bank (WB). These international financial institutions were developed by the victors of the war in an attempt to maintain international economic stability. In many ways, these institutions have worked to shape the function of land within developing nations, and they have a longstanding relationship to national banking systems that have continued to finance large-scale agricultural modernization and expansion in the Global South (Bello 1994). Indeed, it is possible to view the considerable resources—political and military, as well as financial—invested in these institutions' success as a sign of the threat posed by agrarian reform to the core nations after World War II. To understand this situation, it is essential to explore how the meaning of land reform has changed through the latter half of the twentieth century up to now. A brief look at a few nations from the Global South will help illustrate the variance in the conceptualization of land reform.

At the beginning of the twentieth century, four nations had already engaged

in varying degrees of land reform efforts as part of their plans for independence, national development, and change. As early as 1910 Mexico, China,
Guatemala, and the former Soviet Union all made direct efforts to alter the
relationship between land and peasantry. Different assumptions about the role
of the peasantry in these four nations became the impetus for the redistribution of land and the reorganization of relationships in the agricultural sector
(Enríquez 2003, 2004; Kerkvliet and Selden 1998; Lewin 1968; Thiesenhusen
1995). These early efforts ranged from the peasant revolution–driven land
reforms in China and the rather more anti-peasant transformations of the
Soviet Union, to the reorganization of export agriculture coupled with the rise
of popular struggle in Guatemala[11] and the radical agrarian struggle of Mexico.
Each of these nations successfully moved land into the hands of the landless,
but that alone did not correct persistent, uneven distribution of wealth and
power in the countryside.

In the case of Mexico, peasants have fought and struggled for land both
before and after the implementation of larger revolutionary movements for
independence. The hacienda system was weakened through the revolutionary
transitions, and land was redistributed to *campesinos*, but securing social
equality for campesinos has been an ongoing and increasingly frustrated project (Henriques and Patel 2003; Thiesenhusen 1995, 29–49). In the Soviet
Union, peasants reluctantly participated in land reform efforts, and in most
instances faced violence, murder, and increased rural conflict throughout the
process (Lewin 1968, 107–31). Land tenure in the Soviet Union was mostly
reshaped through efforts at collectivization and the establishment of large state
farms, changes driven primarily not by the needs of rural producers, but by
urban demands for cheap food, a Kautskian view of the peasantry, and an inaccurate analysis of rural society by party elites.[12] In China, by contrast, the needs
of rural populations were foremost, and many of the beneficiaries of land
reform participated in the revolutionary transformation of power relations in
rural areas (Hinton 1996).

On the other end of the distributive continuum is the case of Guatemala.
Early colonial relationships to export markets brought about some limited,
but notable, land tenure reforms prior to the twentieth century (Williams
1994, 61–69). This early demand for land tenure reform emerged in
response to the conflicting interests of indigenous communities, political
elites, and large-scale domestic coffee producers. The latter saw some
benefit in extending the small producers' tenure—allowing them to grow
food for their own consumption, thusrequiring less income to sustain their

families—while maintaining reliance on seasonal peasant labor at very low wages on large coffee *haciendas*. It wasn't until the period from 1944 to 1952, however, that the nation pursued an official program of land and agrarian reform. With this formal state commitment to agrarian reform came much social upheaval that, on first glance, would suggest a redistributive success— a case of increased smallholder beneficiaries and the reorganization of rural social relations. Yet, despite the upheaval and international attention brought about by these official efforts at reform, the impact of the land redistribution that occurred during the period was quickly reversed. (see chapter 1 this volume)

This brief consideration of the four countries that saw significant land reform before World War II point to the implications of the larger structural (i.e., political, economic, historical) dimensions of agrarian change. These cases also helped to stamp in the minds of policy elites elsewhere the very real possibility of radical land reform implementation through violence, carried out perhaps by those most oppressed under current regimes. Following the interruption of World War II, these examples informed the thinking of those on both sides of the Cold War. Communism, or the Cold War fear of its expansion, fueled a number of post–World War II land reform efforts promoted by the United States and its allies to deter unwieldy revolutions from below. And behind these ideologically charged efforts remained the questions—summed up in the refrain with which we began the chapter—of who controls the land, who is entitled to use it, and for what ends. It would be an exaggeration to say that land reform shaped the Cold War, but it is useful to see the struggle for land as part of a broader struggle over the meaning of and limits to property. While the contours of power and the mechanisms through which land reform was effected shaped the ultimate success or failure of land reform efforts in every country experiencing such reforms after World War II, the question of property burned at the heart of agrarian reform.

With the above framework in mind, a team of researchers[13] from the Land Research Action Network (LRAN) compared historical data on formal land reform efforts[14] in twenty countries since World War II (see figure 1).[15] Though varied, the impetus for land redistribution in these nations often reflected significant efforts to address economic stagnation, to acquire independence, to build political solidarity, and/or to "develop" national agricultural export production. Figure 1 lists the twenty countries chronologically by date of land reform implementation and by period of comparison.[16] From these historical experiences, the authors identified four distinct categories of land reform implementation: Cold War proxy, endogenous social revolution, postwar allied consolidation, and endogenous political compromise.

Group 1: Cold War Proxies (Cases: El Salvador, Honduras, Philippines, South Vietnam). Reforms in these countries were pursued in the effort to quell peasant unrest, stave off larger revolutionary action, and/or comply with the US and/or Eastern Bloc foreign and economic policies. Formal land reform polices were a mix of expropriation and redistribution of public lands.

Group 2: Endogenous Social Revolution (Cases: China, Cuba, Mexico, North Vietnam, former Soviet Union, Kerala state [India]). These reforms emerged in response to social pressures and revolutionary platforms or national struggles for independence. In these cases land reform was implemented along with more comprehensive agrarian reforms aiming to address longstanding inequalities regarding access to land and to reduce persistent rural poverty. Here the state played an active role in instituting and carrying out reform policies. Large amounts of land were expropriated from large landholders and redistributed to landless beneficiaries.

Group 3: Postwar Allied Consolidation (Cases: South Korea, Japan, Taiwan, Germany). These land reforms were carried out in concert with industrial expansion and other economic reforms by the state, with the support of the major post–World War II political players, and aimed to avoid persistent inequality in land tenure before engaging in industrial expansion. Land was expropriated from large landholders and redistributed to landless beneficiaries by fiat.

Group 4: Endogenous Political Compromise (Cases: Brazil, Guatemala, India, South Africa, Zimbabwe). These reforms emerged largely in response to a combination of pressures exerted by large social movements, landless organizing and government policy making that aimed to meet new demands of export-oriented agricultural production. Limited amounts of land were expropriated from large landholders and redistributed to a limited number of landless beneficiaries.

While these typologies are not hard and fast—many countries fell simultaneously under the categories of Cold War proxies and post–World War II allied consolidation efforts in the attempt to build bulwarks against communism— they reveal that among the most sweeping land reforms (i.e., swift, state-backed reforms, involving a large number of families and leaving little quar-

FIGURE 1 Periods of land reform in select countries, 1945–2004

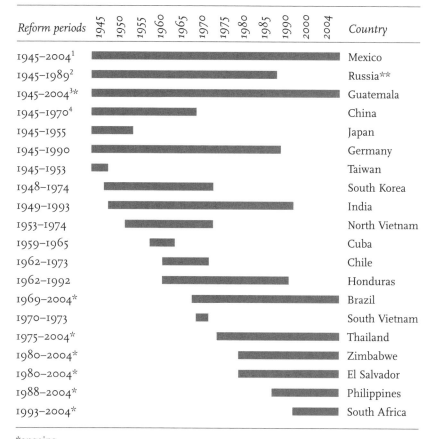

Reform periods	1945	1950	1955	1960	1965	1970	1975	1980	1985	1990	2000	2004	Country
1945–2004[1]													Mexico
1945–1989[2]													Russia**
1945–2004[3]*													Guatemala
1945–1970[4]													China
1945–1955													Japan
1945–1990													Germany
1945–1953													Taiwan
1948–1974													South Korea
1949–1993													India
1953–1974													North Vietnam
1959–1965													Cuba
1962–1973													Chile
1962–1992													Honduras
1969–2004*													Brazil
1970–1973													South Vietnam
1975–2004*													Thailand
1980–2004*													Zimbabwe
1980–2004*													El Salvador
1988–2004*													Philippines
1993–2004*													South Africa

*ongoing

**former Soviet Union

[1] (1917); [2] (1923); [3] (1944); [4] (1910).

ter for existing elites) were those preemptively imposed by capitalists—notably under the postwar allied consolidation category. A measure of the success of these land reforms has been the extent to which all the countries that experienced them have developed strong and robust internationally linked economies (though only after a prolonged period of growth fueled by domestic industrial protection) (Hart 2002). A little less robust have been the compromises forged through endogenous social revolution, and more fissiparous still have been the settlements agreed through endogenous political compromise, with the most extreme cases of land injustice residing in those states that were Cold War battle grounds. Yet the Cold War affected all land reforms, whether directly, through endogenous struggles between capitalism and communism, or by the perceived threat of communism in "frontline states."

The end of the Cold War heralded at least the temporary end of the possibility of radical land reform programs. While it was inconceivable that land could be redistributed through a willing buyer–willing seller approach at the beginning of the Cold War, by the Cold War's end it was inconceivable that it could be done any other way. By the early 1970s land reform policy making had already began to shift to a "one-size-fits-all" market-assisted land reform (MALR) imposed by the IMF, the United States Agency for International Development (USAID), and the World Bank. A general shift from the state-led agrarian reforms of the earlier part of the century to a demand-driven, MALR process ensued (Borras, chapter 5 in this volume; Kay 2002a). The proponents of this kind of reform claimed that the state-led reforms failed to distribute land adequately to the landless and resulted, for the most part, in a distortion of land markets, and they argued that this prevented efficient producers from acquiring land and encouraged inefficient farmers to continue farming. Borras (chapter 5) provides an exemplary treatment of the substance of these arguments. The issue of whether or not there was any truth to these arguments was almost irrelevant to their reception. As Kelsey (1995) notes in a different context, a great part of the successful adoption of the neoliberal regime comes through its ability to claim that "there is no alternative." In many instances, it certainly feels as if there is none. Under neoliberal agrarian reform, there has been a concerted effort to disparage people living in rural areas, de-skill farmers, and demobilize their organizations to remove the possibility of an alternative. Yet the alternative persists.

The tragedy of neoliberal land policy, as each of the chapters in this book shows, is that it prevents successful land reform—reform that lifts people out of poverty, increases levels of resource equality, raises living standards, ensures the subsistence of the rural dweller, and, in some cases, even increases agricultural export production (de Janvry and Sadoulet 1989; Herring 2000; Sobhan 1993). Successful land reform can also result in the improved environmental protection of land when stewardship is granted to those who depend directly on the land for their own well-being and survival (Holt-Giménez 2002; Ghimire 2001b). Land reform programs, however, are necessary but not sufficient to accomplish these goals. They require integration into a broader strategy for rural development that also considers the landless and the small producer as the focus of several coordinated efforts (Patel 2003).

The promarket argument fails to acknowledge not only the noncommodity nature of food production, but also the falsity of the assumption that rising GDP inevitably leads to decreased poverty for rural dwellers. Conceptualizing agriculture as a commodity-oriented system of production, the World Bank's MALR models and the neoliberal economic models that spawned it avoid any direct consideration of the relationship between the land and the majority of the world's poor.

About the Cases in Part I

The first part of this book consists of four case studies representing nations from each region in which LRAN has focused its efforts. Guatemala, Zimbabwe, South Africa, and India serve as exemplars of reform efforts categorized as endogenous political compromise in group 4, above. Regardless of the specifics in each case, all four countries have experienced one or more historical periods of land reform that fell short of the hopes and demands of the most resource-poor agents in each nation. These shortcomings are not surprising, of course, given that compromise was required for the implementation of any land reform policy at all. As such, compromise is one of the few attributes common to all these national cases. The African cases share some regional similarities as well, but even with the regional overlap there is quite a bit of variance among these countries. Yet, despite the national differences described by each of the authors of these four studies, all four nations have strangely found themselves facing similar policy options at the turn of the twenty-first century.

It is this common point of arrival that leads these four authors to take stock and raise important research and policy questions with regard to the homogenized land and agrarian reform policy being imposed upon their nations. Through brief historical review, demographic comparison, and general policy analysis, the four cases in this section begin to highlight failures and problems associated with the received neoliberal model that has unfolded before them. The remainder of the book will explore in more depth and with greater analysis the themes, criticisms, and alternatives introduced throughout part I. A brief overview of each chapter in part I will help to direct the reader toward some of the more salient challenges now facing these nations, on their path toward implementing a land reform that will more directly benefit the landless and resource poor.

The first chapter, by Wittman and Saldivar-Tanaka, focuses on the long, contradictory agrarian reform policies of Guatemala. The Guatemala case highlights the changing role of the state with regard to the land question in general, and the implementation of agrarian reform policy, in particular. The state played a crucial role in shaping land policy both before and after the World War II era, while it has also implemented formal policies of repression—enlisting military force when necessary—to stop any demands that have threatened the power of landed elites tied to export production. The history of agrarian reform in Guatemala is a violent one. Past and present efforts at agrarian change have been accompanied by much hardship and loss throughout the countryside. The authors delve into the outcomes of earlier attempts at land reform and find them mostly hollow. A brief review of landholding shows that the beneficiaries of past efforts have largely been those who sought compromise, via the state, with landless peasants and indigenous peoples: the landed elite and agribusiness holders. Wittman and Saldivar-Tanaka emphasize the limitations of these earlier gains and briefly explore the ways that peace and human rights movements in the 1990s began to impact the breadth and depth of popular political participation. The role of the 1996 peace accords is considered in this chapter, as is the ongoing impact of a century of agricultural export on the nation's land tenure system. Finally, the author highlights the ways in which political and landed elites—often one and the same—continue to use the rhetoric of land reform to appease foreign interests, both political and economic, as new land market conversions have become the emphasis of state policy.

In chapter 2 Tom Lebert chronicles the Zimbabwe case, one of the most recent cases of high-profile land seizure. Lebert provides a brief historical sketch of the ways colonial rule and the issue of race have shaped a struggle for land that is tied to the need for both productive resources and political power. The relationship of Africa to its former colonial powers (Britain in this case) has not dissolved easily. The Zimbabwe case points to the significant ways in which legislation and legal codes play a part in determining who is considered landless at any point in history, and, further, who is deserving of land and full land tenure at any time. Zimbabwe poses critical questions about race and power that are often overlooked in general discussions of economic or technical reform programs. Lebert's contribution to this section provides some new vantage points from which to reassess the struggle for land and agrarian reform in that nation and across Africa more generally, even as the situation deteriorates for an increasing numbers of Zimbabweans.[17]

Positing an interesting regional comparison, South Africa is considered in chapter 3. Though close to Zimbabwe geographically, it shares a quite different historical and post-colonial relationship. Wellington Thwala's consideration of South Africa examines the legacy of apartheid on the nation through codified legal mandates, which used categories of race to determine definitions of property, citizenship, and personhood. Thwala argues that this practice has left an indelible mark on the agrarian question in South Africa, and he discusses how the legacy of racialized land policy persists well into the twenty-first century under new World Bank–directed reform programs.

Increasingly, the political landscape of South Africa is being shaped by an ongoing struggle between rural and urban dwellers for land and resource allocation. This demographic split between urban and rural dwellers in South Africa has presented new dilemmas for political organizing around questions of land distribution. Shifts toward industrial expansion, increased direct foreign investment in agriculture, and national policies of modernization have further marginalized the rural sector, with poverty rates in rural areas systematically higher, and human development indicators systematically lower, than in urban areas (United Nations Development Programme 2003). This gap between the needs of rural dwellers and the dictates of an urban policy bias is considered with relation to both national land redistribution policies and recent land market conversion efforts in South Africa. Thwala closes the chapter by exploring alternatives to the World Bank's national agenda, calling for a "people-centered land reform" and discussing the necessary components of a successful alternative to land privatization in South Africa.

The case of India, Manpreet Sethi explains, is a history of broken promises and of encroachment on many resources fundamental to farming communities and ecological preservation: water, forests, and common property. India is the only case that offers a compelling regional example of expropriative land reform within a larger comprehensive national reform policy. The Kerala state reforms would easily fit in group 2 (endogenous social revolution), as landless farmers and poor rural dwellers in that region persisted in their efforts to elect a socialist government in their state and then to press for agrarian reform. Yet most Indian states have not seen large-scale, comprehensive agrarian reforms that have benefited large numbers of landless dwellers. In this way, India serves as a persuasive example of why land reform alone, without a comprehensive agrarian reform project, can quickly become part of the popular neoliberal project to accommodate market expansion under the guise of poverty reduction, which use the poor as justification for, but not a direct beneficiary of, neoliberal policy making.

A recent period of urban migration in India has also posed several new challenges for rural households, and Sethi draws attention to the question of gender and the historical relationship of women to land and agrarian social structure. This final chapter of part I leaves us to consider not only the issues of historical variance, regional differences, race, gender, and property relations, but also the appeal of neoliberal populism to mobilize support for projects that ultimately confound efforts for equitable resource distribution, food sovereignty, and self-sufficiency.

Together these cases paint a varied historical picture of land reform. While each nation has been brought closer to world markets by neoliberal interventions, their trajectories are still deeply weighed down by the ghosts of their pasts. In part II, we analyze the themes of these different histories, and in part III, we investigate the alternative trajectories that, as ever, continue to be fought for in the parliaments, policy rooms, streets, and fields of the Global South.

CHAPTER 1

The Agrarian Question in Guatemala

Hannah Wittman with Laura Saldivar-Tanaka

On May 6, 1996, the Guatemalan government, the general command of the Unidad Revolucionaria Nacional Guatemalteca, and a United Nations representative signed the Guatemalan Peace Accords, marking an official end to the thirty-six-year civil war. Since the beginning of the war, one out of every four Mayans—the largest group of indigenous peoples in the nation—had been displaced, more than 200,000 Guatemalans had been killed or disappeared, and more than 1,000,000 Guatemalans had been designated as internal refugees. The 1996 peace accords recognized that both the historical social exclusion of Guatemala's indigenous and *campesino* rural populations and the unequal distribution of land were not only root causes of the civil conflict, but also primary obstacles to long-term national development and a lasting peace.

The peace accords included agreements on socioeconomic and agrarian issues, resettlement, and ethnic identity and rights of indigenous peoples. These agreements emphasized the Guatemalan government's duty to restore land to indigenous communities, to eliminate gender discrimination in land allocation, and to promote measures to regularize the legal codification of communal landholdings. All three agreements obligate the Guatemalan government to enact rural development programs, solve land disputes generated during the war and identify land for resettlement for displaced communities and landless indigenous and campesino families, and address longstanding inequalities in land distribution and rural welfare.

While the 1996 accords represented a landmark attempt to address Guatemala's longstanding agrarian problems, little progress has been made in changing current practices of rural land distribution, and agrarian conflicts continue throughout the Guatemalan countryside. Today's extremely high levels of rural poverty and landlessness continue, products of one of the most historically inequitable systems of land distribution and tenure in the world. To provide a framework for understanding the potential for the 1996 peace accords to truly enact agrarian reform, this chapter analyzes the historical roots of Guatemala's agrarian situation and compares previous land administration policies to current programs outlined in the accords. While the reasons previous attempts at agrarian reform have failed in Guatemala are complex and historically contingent, it is important to ascertain whether the fundamental power dynamics governing the Guatemalan economy and society have changed sufficiently to allow the 1996 agreement to foster a meaningful redistribution of land. Caution is warranted, given the ongoing dependence on the agro-export sector, which is supported by the rural elite, the military, and foreign institutions. This dependence has conditioned the implementation of agrarian policies that benefit larger and more capitalized[1] owners, who have taken advantage of previous attempts at land reform to achieve further consolidation of both land and political power in Guatemala.

Exclusion in the Countryside

Guatemala has one of the most unequal land distribution patterns in the world. It also has one of the most historically stable rural sectors in Latin America, currently comprising 69 percent of the population. Agriculture and forestry account for more than 60 percent of national land use, and agriculture provides more than 50 percent of employment (Food and Agriculture Organization of the United Nations [FAO] 1998). But at the same time, less than 1 percent of landowners hold 75 percent of the best agricultural land, 90 percent of rural inhabitants live in poverty, and more than 500,000 campesino families live below the level of subsistence (Misión de Verificación de las Naciones Unidas en Guatemala [MINUGUA] 2000b).[2]

The historical expropriation of indigenous lands has had serious consequences for sustainable land use, for smallholder self-sufficiency, and for food security and health.[3] In some areas, population pressures on the land no longer allow for traditional practices of shifting cultivation, and intensive cultivation practices on marginal lands have led to severe soil erosion, lower yields, and dependence on seasonal and permanent migration for remittances to support family income needs.[4] In addition to problems related to distributional inequity, Guatemala's unequal land regime also leads to dispropor-

TABLE 1.1 Land distribution in Guatemala, 1950, 1964, 1979

Size	Percentage of Farms			Percentage of Total Farm Area		
	1950	1964	1979	1950	1964	1979
Less than 0.7 ha	21.30	20.39	31.36	0.77	0.95	1.33
0.7 to 1.4 ha	26.26	23.64	22.83	2.54	2.77	2.75
1.4 to 3.5 ha	28.62	30.94	24.19	5.70	7.85	6.40
3.5 to 7 ha	12.17	12.47	9.74	5.32	7.04	5.74
7 to 22.4 ha	7.72	8.87	7.6	8.36	12.95	11.91
22.4 to 44.8 ha	1.76	1.59	1.72	5.10	5.90	6.77
44.8 to 450 ha	1.86	1.88	2.31	21.86	26.53	30.66
450 to 900 ha	.16	.13	.17	9.52	10.03	12.81
900 to 2,250 ha	.10	.07	.07	13.32	11.22	12.00
2,250 to 4,500 ha	.03	.01	.01	8.81	4.92	5.43
4,500 to 9,000 ha	—	—	—	5.28	5.17	2.12
More than 9,000 ha	—	—	—	13.43	4.67	2.05
	Number of Farms			Number of Hectares		
TOTALS	358,687	417,344	531,636	3,720,831	3,448,737	4,180,246

Source: Hough et al. 1982; Sandoval 1987.

tionate channeling of government credit and other resources to the agro-export center and urban areas, in what Palma Murga (1997) refers to as "chronic underinvestment in the countryside."

The most widely accepted statistics on land distribution in Guatemala are based on data collected from the 1979 agricultural census (see table 1.1). The average minimum landholding necessary for family subsistence in Guatemala (allowing for differences in land quality, climate, and altitude) is between 4.5 and 7 hectares (Hough et al. 1982; Stringer and Lambert 1989). In 1979, 88 percent of productive farm units were less than family subsistence size, holding 16 percent of arable land, while 2 percent of units held 65 percent of arable land (see table 1.1). Between 1964 and 1979 the number of farms of less than 3.5 hectares doubled; between 1950 and 1979, the average farm size among those with less than 7 hectares fell from 2.4 to 1.8 hectares. Stringer and Lambert (1989) attribute the increased concentration of land in Guatemala not only to population growth but to a monopolistic landownership structure, an unwieldy and expensive land registration system, and a lack of agricultural credit available to small farmers. While there have been few reliable studies on land distribution since 1979, the Guatemalan Ministry of Agriculture and Food (MAGA) estimates that in 1998 approximately 96 percent of farm units fell into the subsistence or below-subsistence categories, comprising 20 percent of agricultural land (Misión de Verificación de las Naciones Unidas en Guatemala [MINUGUA] 2000b, 6).

Agrarian History

With the arrival of the Spanish in the 1500s, Guatemala's indigenous communities were resettled in centralized villages that facilitated a system of social control, allowing European colonizers to manage threats of rebellion, to control labor, to exact tributary payments, and to force changes in cultural practices and religion (Brockett 1998, 119). After Guatemala's independence in 1821, land tenure remained highly unequal, with the new government quickly passing resolutions to transfer large extensions of community held land to private ownership, under the premise that "the small number of private landowners is one of the causes for the backwardness of agriculture" (McCreery 1994, 54). Although this legislation specifically allowed for *Ladino*[5] occupation of indigenous communal lands, some village communities were able to maintain a parallel structure of indigenous authority alongside the laws advocating private ownership, and maintain in practice extensions of communally managed lands and forests (Barrios 1996; Hernández Alarcón 2001). After a peasant and indigenous revolt led by Rafael Carrera in the early 1830s, the merchant class engaged in a policy of "benevolent neglect" toward further land privatization. They were willing to forego seizure of additional community and indigenous lands as long as these lands continued to provide the main source of cochineal, at that time one of Guatemala's most important agricultural exports (Handy 1994).

The Liberal Reforms, 1871–1944

The displacement and disruption of indigenous communities from traditional communal land areas was renewed later in the nineteenth century. Under liberal reforms beginning in 1871, the administrations of Miguel Garcia Granados (1871–1873) and Liberal General Justo Rufino Barrios (1873–1885) encouraged the build-up of a national agro-export–based economy by expropriating communal indigenous lands in the fertile lowlands, subsidizing domestic and foreign operators, and running an advertising campaign in Europe to attract "modern farmers with capital" for the development of coffee as Guatemala's principal export crop. To foster a land market, public land on the southern coast was sold and massive landholdings of the Catholic Church were privatized.

In 1894, the first agrarian law of the reform period promoted increased settlement in the more remote areas of the western highlands and continued to privatize state and indigenous landholdings (Davis 1997). According to McCreery (1994), indigenous Guatemalans found themselves "priced out of the market for land they had always imagined was theirs" (183), and Ladinos continued to settle in areas previously controlled by indigenous communities.

Between 1896 and 1921, a total of 3,600 large landholders acquired 16 percent of national territory, both in the lowlands as well as in potentially profitable areas in lower altitudes of the highlands, where coffee, banana, sugar, and cotton plantations were established throughout the nineteenth and early twentieth centuries (McCreery 1990). Highland residents, cut off from the lowland areas they had formerly used seasonally for maize production, began to depend on seasonal wage earnings to replace the lost production areas. A second strategy to secure a constant source of seasonal labor was enacted through a series of coercive laws that ranged from outright draft, in 1876, to a 1934 vagrancy law that required individuals with less than 2.8 hectares of titled land (most of the indigenous population) to work 100–150 days each year as wage laborers (Lovell 1988). Designed to channel indigenous labor into agro-export plantations, these laws instituted a system of forced seasonal migration between highland *minifundios* (smallholder farms) and lowland *latifundios*[6] that has continued to the present day.

During the same period, many communal land areas were classified as *baldía*, or empty, despite their historical use for maize cultivation by indigenous populations. These areas were ordered to be subdivided among community inhabitants, and then privately titled. For example, between 1871 and 1879, 155 parcels of *terrenos baldíos*, measuring almost 75,000 hectares, were awarded to private coffee entrepreneurs (Davis 1997, 10). As Ladino and Creole Guatemalans used their legal and economic power to take over additional acreage for coffee plantations, indigenous communities are estimated to have lost about half the lands originally held during the colonial period (McCreery 1990; Palma Murga 1997; Smith 1984).

By the last decade of the nineteenth century, Guatemala had become the world's fourth largest coffee producer, with coffee comprising 96 percent of exports; between 1890 and 1900 alone the volume of international trade increased twentyfold (Handy 1994; Thiesenhusen 1995). In 1901, the United Fruit Company (UFC), known today as Chiquita, began operations in the country, and by 1924, the Guatemalan government had ceded to the company a total of 188,339 hectares in the fertile Pacific lowlands, in twenty-five- to ninety-nine-year leases (Thiesenhusen 1995). United Fruit quickly became Guatemala's largest employer, landowner, and exporter.

In 1931, the dictatorship of General Jorge Ubico began, initially with full support from the US. Over the next fourteen years, Ubico cultivated relations with the United Fruit Company, offering exemption from taxation and guarantees of low wages (Schlesinger and Kinzer 1999). At one point, Ubico enacted a land distribution policy designed to fill Guatemala's less populated lowland areas, but rescinded the offer when faced with protests from highland coffee plantation owners who feared the loss of their cheap labor (Handy 1994, 79).

The October Revolution and the Arbenz Reform

In 1944, in what came to be known as the October Revolution, the US began to support Juan Jose Arévalo, Ubico's nationalistic opponent. Also popular with the urban middle class, Arévalo was elected president in 1945 and called for a new constitution as part of his efforts to instill political democracy. The constitutional assembly of 1945 established the idea that land must fulfill a social function, and the resulting constitution included several articles that continued to protect private property, while also allowing for the expropriation of uncultivated *latifundio*. Article 96 of the new constitution also protected *ejido* (municipal) and communal lands, stating they were "inalienable, inprescriptable, inexpropriable, and indivisible." A titling law (*Ley de Titulación Suplementaria*) passed by the Arévalo administration awarded title to squatters who farmed land for ten years, but this law also served to legalize the holdings of larger landholders who had continued to encroach onto indigenous lands (Thiesenhusen 1995, 75).

While the political reforms of the Arévalo administration did little to alter rural social relations or to reduce the power of landlords and military, they laid the foundation for the agrarian reform program proposed by former defense minister Jacobo Arbenz, elected president in 1951. With the support of worker and campesino organizations that had gained strength since 1944, Arbenz vowed to "convert Guatemala into a modern capitalist nation through industrialization and land reform" (Hough et al. 1982). In 1950, two-thirds of the Guatemalan population depended on agriculture for their livelihoods, while 72 percent of agricultural land was controlled by just 2 percent of farms. The twenty-two biggest *latifundios* held more land than 249,169 peasant families, and according to a 1947 land tenure survey carried out by the Guatemalan government, only 12 percent of privately held land was cultivated (Handy 1994, 102).

On June 17, 1952, the Guatemalan Congress approved Decree 900, a relatively mild agrarian reform law that called for the elimination of large estates, the redistribution of uncultivated land, and the provision of land, credit, and technical assistance to the landless and land poor. Only uncultivated holdings larger than 90 hectares were available for expropriation; farms between 90 and 270 hectares with at least two-thirds of the farmland cultivated were exempt, as were farms engaged in cash-crop cultivation.[7] Land expropriated from private owners was allocated to beneficiaries who had to give up 5 percent of the value of crops harvested to the government; beneficiaries of state land received land with lifetime usufruct rights and paid a rental fee of 3 percent of production. State repayments for expropriated land were based on the value self-declared for tax purposes as of May 1952 (Christodoulou 1990; Hough et al. 1982; Thiesenhusen 1995).[8]

By 1953, President Arbenz declared in an address to Congress that agrarian reform had caused an "earthquake in the consciousness" of Guatemalans (Handy 1994, 112). Between 1953 and 1954, approximately 1002 decrees of expropriation were issued, affecting 603,615 hectares of land, in addition to the redistribution of 280,000 hectares of state land. Between 33 and 40 percent of rural households and 31 to 40 percent of the landless labor force received at least some land from the Arbenz reform, in parcels ranging from 3.5 to 17.5 hectares. Of the 232,682 hectares controlled by the United Fruit Company in 1953, only 10 percent was in cultivation. The Guatemalan government expropriated 146,000 hectares with just under $US1.2 million in compensation (Deere and León 1999; Thiesenhusen 1995).

Opposition to the Arbenz administration and the implementation of agrarian reform were swift and decisive. The Arbenz agrarian reform program was opposed by landed elites, the Catholic Church, the middle-class business sector, and foreign plantation owners, in addition to expropriated landowners. These actors protested the rapidity of the reform, the price paid by the government to landholders (indemnification), the lack of landowner participation in the agrarian committees, and a provision of Decree 900 that stipulated the total expropriation without indemnification of land owned by those who used violent or subversive means to oppose the reform (Hough et al. 1982, 43–5).[9]

Pressure from the US government to "ward off the Communist threat" and protect the interests of US companies (i.e., United Fruit), facilitated a military coup backed by the CIA and a complete reversal of the agrarian transformation attempted by the Arbenz regime. On June 18, 1954, Colonel Carlos Castillo Armas led a US-backed invasion force into Guatemala from Honduras, resulting in the resignation of Arbenz on June 27. Castillo Armas, supported by the US ambassador, was installed as president on July 8, 1954.

In the first six months following the coup, the majority of land expropriations were annulled. Of the 535,000 hectares of land awarded through Arbenz's modest land reform project, only 5 percent of families were able to keep this land; the rest was returned to former large landholders, including the United Fruit Company (Hernández Alarcón 2000).[10]

Three Decades of Dictatorship

The 1952 reform had threatened the hegemony of the agro-export elite, who proceeded to regain and preserve their rule through violence and repression throughout the next forty years. The support of the United States and of international institutions promoting Guatemala's focus on agricultural exports for the world market also served to cement the political lesson of 1954 as a warning against further discussion of land redistribution. The 1952 reform can be viewed as a short-lived experimental moment within a historical context of the consolidation of power of the landed few vis-à-vis the state and the potential beneficiaries.

While land expropriations were effectively eliminated with the repeal of Decree 900, the Ydígoras Fuentes government passed Decree 1551, the Law of Agrarian Transformation, in 1962. Passing an agrarian reform law was a requirement to receive funds from the US-sponsored Alliance for Progress, funds that were desperately needed to address the government's growing fiscal crisis (Berger 1992).[11] Decree 1551 institutionalized the post-Arbenz counter-reform measures, advocating administration and redistribution of state farms and the colonization of public lands by landless farmers.[12] Although Decree 1551 recognized constitutional provisions for expropriation of idle land, and while USAID estimates that 1.77 million hectares of idle land in the private sector were already accessible and had some infrastructure, more than two-thirds of land distributed between 1955 and 1982 was in frontier colonization areas. Of the remaining distribution of state farmlands expropriated after World War II, only 12 percent was located in the prime southern lowland areas (Hough et al.

TABLE 1.2 Effect of Decree 1551 on the landless

1964	262,750 landless (between 1955 and 1964, 8.9 percent of landless received land)
1973	267,058 landless (between 1965 and 1973, 3.5 percent of target landless received land)
1980	309,119 landless (between 1974 and 1980, 5.7 percent of target landless received land)

Source: Hough et al. 1982.

1982, 55). Instead, thirty-nine national farms were distributed to private owners as political awards, averaging over 3,000 hectares each, while others were divided among "deserving members of the military" (Brockett 1998, 107).

With its emphasis on colonization of frontier lands rather than expropriation, Decree 1551 was designed to demobilize demand for action on land reform by relocating the rural poor to remote (and ecologically fragile) areas, including the northern Petén and Northern Transversal Strip. Although a 1970 USAID evaluation concluded that the impact of these colonization projects on the land tenure structure in Guatemala had been negligible, and acknowledged that "land grabs by the elite" had denied distribution benefits to many intended landless beneficiaries, USAID still provided over US$5.6 million in the late 1970s for resettlement projects (Brockett 1998, 107).

In subsequent decades, factionalism within the state, continued pressure from the landed elite supported by the military, and an increasing transfer of funds from agrarian policies to counterinsurgency efforts effectively blocked the implementation of Decree 1551 (Berger 1992). As shown in table 1.2, progress of Decree 1551 quickly waned. Thiesenhusen concludes that the reforms of the 1960s in Guatemala "took away by stealth what it had given with a flourish" (1995, xi).

At the same time, displacement of indigenous and campesino populations increased rapidly due to civil unrest, and discussion of land reform became even more taboo throughout the period of the thirty-six-year civil war that began in 1960. During the 1960s and 1970s, a progressively more militarized and violent Guatemala followed an import-substitution model of economic development to build national industry and reduce economic dependence on food and technological imports. The western highlands, for example, were targeted as a priority wheat-producing area, and government programs provided high-yielding technology (hybrid seeds, fertilizers, herbicides), extension services, and, to a certain extent among the larger farmers, mechanization. This commodity production strategy was supported by public sector agricultural institutions and by the National Union of Wheat Growers, which played an important role in the territorial expansion of wheat production and in the increase in yield. Production was destined for regional flour mills, and the expansion of local flour production contributed to regional and national food security and rural employment, and it revitalized the small mercantile production of wheat and flour products for the national market. During this period seasonal migration to coastal plantations diminished, a practice that had supported the export-led model of development that had reigned from the end of eighteenth century to the middle of the twentieth century (Asociacíon para el Avance de las Ciencias Sociales 2001, 26–28). However, subsequent economic restructuring processes, including market liberalization, eliminated tariffs on wheat imports, and the displacement caused by state terror and repression in the highlands in the 1970s and 1980s placed small producers in the western highlands at a serious disadvantage, in relation to subsidized and mechanized imports. Wheat, as one of the area's primary cash crops, was decimated as high volumes of imported wheat from the United States caused prices to plummet for local production, forcing renewed dependence on seasonal migration to lowland coffee plantations for subsistence (Lovell 1988; Ordóñez 1998).

Leading Up to the Peace Accords: The Call for Agrarian Reform

After Guatemala's return to civilian government in 1986, a march of 16,000 landless workers to the National Palace in Guatemala City set the stage for the return of agrarian issues to the Guatemalan political agenda (Perera 1993). Facing extreme repression, peasant movements showed that land concentration had increased more than in any other Central American country between the 1950s and 1970s, while export booms had disproportionately benefited large commercial farms and displaced small farms. As Thiesenhusen points out, "in the 1960s and 1970s, it was considered subversive to even speak of land reform, but in the economically depressed 1980s, as civil war deepened and violence escalated, there came renewed public calls for structural agrarian changes" (1995, 85).

The National Coordination of Indigenous Peoples and Campesinos (CONIC) calculated that as of the mid-1980s, only 2.8 million of the 10.8 million hectares of land in Guatemala had been cultivated, representing about 40 percent of potential cropland. Another 2.4 million hectares of arable land were idle or misused (Peace Brigades 1996; Stringer and Lambert 1989). The most skewed land distribution countrywide continues to be in the relatively more productive coastal lands, where fertile lowlands are often left unused or are devoted to cattle grazing. For example, Gini-coefficients of land inequality in the coastal departments of Sacquitepequez and Escuintla are as high as 0.94 and 0.92 (1.0 signifies total land concentration), and farms of 450 hectares or more hold 53 and 59 percent of agricultural land, respectively (World Bank 1996). Another 40 percent of all farm units in Guatemala are located in the western highlands, where a typical *minifundio* ranges in size from 0.4 to 2 hectares, supporting five to fifteen family members. Almost half of western highland units are smaller than 0.7 hectares (Katz 2000). In general, "departments of high out-migration have low availability of arable land per capita" (Hough et al. 1982, 24–25), and the highland regions indeed have lost significant portions of their indigenous populations to out-migration. Estimates of landlessness in Guatemala generally vary at 26.6 percent or more of rural families, and Brockett cites figures estimating that by 1975, over 60 percent of the economically active rural population of the highlands had to migrate to find work during some part of the year, making this the "most migratory labor force in the world" (1998, 112).

The productivity rationale for a land reform that would successfully reduce the percentage of Guatemala's agricultural holdings in large plantations is supported by current production data. While agro-export plantations on the southern coast have, for centuries, produced bananas, cotton, sugar, and cattle for export, the relative importance of these products for Guatemala's export earnings has dropped from 58 percent in 1987 to 43 percent of total exports in 1997 (World Bank 1997a), as world market prices continue to drop for these commodities. In contrast, while a 1987 study showed that 75 percent of highland farmers grew only basic grains (Stringer and Lambert 1989, 4), a sharp increase in recent years in small-scale vegetable and coffee production has increased the economic importance of small producers in the agricultural economy of the 1990s.

The enormity of the landless and sub-subsistence sector presents a problem of scale when looking at the potential for land reform. According to calculations by Sandoval (1987), based on the 1979 agricultural census, over 5,400,000 hectares of land (more than half of Guatemalan territory and more land than was currently registered in farms) would need to be acquired and redistributed in order to provide all landless workers and rural farmers with the 7 hectares required for subsistence.

Although there were more strikes, protests, and land occupations in the first three years of civilian government than in the previous thirty years, President Vinicio Cerezo (1986–1990) refused to propose a new land reform policy (Brockett 1998).[14] The National Campesino Association (ANC) grew to 115,000 by 1988, but, based on its commitment to "nonviolence and the market economy," it only called on the government to purchase available farms and turn them over to peasant cooperatives. Beginning in 1995, the CUC (Committee of Campesino Unity) and CONIC increased political activity and began a program of land occupations to dramatize the land issue and to force official response to their demands. Brocket (1998) credits this increased social mobilization for putting land reform back on the agenda of the 1996 peace accords.

The 1996 Peace Accords

As part of the 1996 peace accords, the language of the Agreement on Socioeconomic and Agrarian Issues (ASESA) was the product of lengthy negotiations between the various constituent groups including the National Coordination of Campesino Organizations (CNOC), the guerilla forces, and the government. CNOC's demands included guarantees of landownership for the poor, fulfillment of human rights agreements including the demilitarization of the countryside, technical and financial support reflecting a Mayan worldview, and reform of state institutions and the constitution. CNOC also reintroduced the idea of "social property," used to advocate the recovery and protection of communal and other indigenous and former campesino lands acquired by large landholders since 1955. The evocation of "social property," which endorses state expropriation of idle lands held by large, private land holders, challenged the 1955 and 1985 constitutional definitions of private property upheld by every government since 1954.[15]

Campesino and human rights organizations argue that the attempts to create an agreement that would effect structural changes in current land tenure arrangements were diluted by pressure from the Coordinating Committee of Agricultural, Commercial, Industrial, and Financial Associations (CACIF), who actively opposed the idea of social property. Instead, CACIF advocated the privatization of communal and municipal lands and a "more rational and efficient use of the land to reflect Guatemala's comparative advantage in the new global economy" (Palma Murga 1997). Ultimately, the Coordination of

BOX 1.1 Objectives of the 1996 Agreement on socioeconomic and agrarian issues

- Strengthen local and national agricultural councils to increase participation and enhance decision-making role of rural organizations.
- Reestablish a land fund to improve access to landownership through market-based land reform.
- Promote the revision and update of legislation on idle lands, including incentives and sanctions to regulate land use for efficiency and ecological sustainability.
- Recover lands distributed in the past through corrupt means and distribute public lands.
- Create legal reform to simplify land registration procedures and to protect and regulate community-owned land.
- Develop legal land title registry through land surveys and a GIS system.
- Establish a land tax on underused and undeveloped lands.
- Establish conflict-resolution mechanisms to settle land conflicts.
- Implement agricultural development and rural investment programs that facilitate a more equal distribution of credit, technology, training, and information.

Sources: Palma Murga 1997; Guatemala 1996.

Organizations of Mayan Peoples (COPMAGUA) formed the sharpest critique of the failure to address issues of expropriation and redistribution in the agrarian agreement, stating that "this agenda breathes fresh life into structures inherited from the colonial period, and fails to challenge the overriding interests of large landowners" (Palma Murga 1997). The key government objectives outlined in the agreement are described in box 1.1.

The 1996 Agreement specifies four primary objectives:

1. The proposed revision of constitutional provisions for the expropriation of idle or underutilized land
2. The reaffirmed idea of redistribution of public land and state farms
3. The enforcement of tax provisions
4. The creation of a land fund to promote a market-based solution to the problem of distributional equity

The wording and program specifications of the 1996 Agreement regarding necessary changes to Guatemala's agrarian structure are remarkably similar to previous land administration and reform policies which have had little effect on Guatemala's inequitable land distribution. First, the agreement calls for a revised policy on expropriation of idle and underutilized land, and also mandates the recovery of lands taken illegally by large landholders, military officials, and professionals during the colonization programs of the 1960s and 1970s. But one of the major legacies of the failed Arbenz reform has been continued resistance by government actors to expropriate highly concentrated, privately held land. A new land registry law passed in 2005 was opposed by campesino organizations that had been involved in consultations since 1998, as it made no advances in terms of changing or enforcing existing legislation covering idle or underutilized lands. As has been historically the case, the process for determining what land is "idle" is still complex, laborious, and based on declarations of current owners, and property owners threatened with expropriation have been given ample time to put idle land into production (Sandoval 1987; Berger 1992; Stringer and Lambert 1989).

The 1996 measures regarding the allocation of state farm lands are also remarkably similar to the provisions of Decree 1551 of the 1960s, in which members of the military managed to gain control over lands intended for poor and landless beneficiaries. The Food and Agriculture Organization of the United Nations (FAO) (1998) asserts that a top-down redistributive land reform involving expropriation requires exclusive control of political power by the government, and the transfer or elimination of the power of the existing rural, land-based elite in order to succeed; neither of these conditions have existed in Guatemala in the twentieth century.

The tax reform provisions of the 1996 Agreement call for the establishment of an "easily collected" land tax from which small properties will be exempt, and a new tax schedule for significantly higher taxation of privately owned idle or underutilized land. Guatemala mandated taxation and management of land markets as early as 1936, when the tax law for *latifundios* established a 2 to 4 percent tax on farms larger than 500 hectares. But as history has shown, the Arbenz and the subsequent military regimes failed to enforce existing legislation to extract tax revenue from the owners of unutilized land. Decree 1551 also created a legal framework that made it possible to collect rents from the rural poor participating in colonization projects, while also making it even more difficult to collect the "idle land tax" from the rural landed elite, who often simply refused to submit to a system of land taxation (Thiesenhusen 1995, 13; Hough et al. 1982, 60).[16] In 1988 the National Institute for Agrarian Transformation (INTA) introduced legislation that would have increased taxes

BOX 1.2 Purported advantages of market-assisted
         land reform model

- The willing buyer–willing seller principle is more feasible when the possibility of expropriation is not politically viable.
- The selection process of beneficiaries seeks to identify those campesinos who are both most needy and most capable of paying back loans.
- Subsidies compensate for the lack of capital held by beneficiaries.
- Distributed land and subsidies are assigned according to specific needs, not in arbitrary average quantities.
- Supposedly, negotiated land reforms are less costly, less conflictive, and more effective than government-assisted land reforms.

Source: Molina 2001.

on privately held idle land, and it mentioned the possibility of expropriation in certain cases. However, the bill was never acted on by the Guatemalan Congress (Berger 1992).

To understand the fourth objective of the 1996 Agreement, "to enact market-based land reform programs," we can look at the historical failures of market-led land reform to address land distribution inequities in Guatemala. Negotiated and market-led land reform programs are now heavily promoted by international aid institutions like the World Bank, which assume that when markets work properly, they are the best arbiter of supply and demand (The Food and Agriculture Organization of the United Nations 1998, 89). For these programs, success is measured by whether small rural producers are able to compete in national land tenure institutions like the market, land registry, and mortgage systems as full economic and political participants (see box 1.2).

The 1996 Agreement on Socioeconomic and Agrarian Issues (ASESA) includes the provision of a land fund to promote the establishment of a transparent land market, thus enabling the poor who either do not have land or have insufficient land to acquire property through long-term transactions at commercial or favorable interest rates with little or no down payment. In particular, the agreement promotes the issuance of mortgage-backed securities guaranteed by the state, the yield of which is attractive to private investors, especially financial institutions (Section B[e]).

Market-driven reforms were recommended in Guatemala as early as 1980 by USAID, which noted that pressure for land access in Guatemala was higher than in other Central American countries. Opening up land markets and facilitating land transfers appeared to be a more viable, politically palatable, and nonviolent means of changing land distribution problems in contemporary Guatemala, and a cheaper option than further investment in colonization programs (Hough et al. 1982; Stringer and Lambert 1989).[17] Between 1984 and 1990, USAID funded the Fundación del Centavo (Penny Foundation) program that purchased twenty-eight farms and divided them into 1,400 parcels under collective title, with strict guidelines on production and marketing of farm products. In 1986, the Institute for Agrarian Transformation began to focus less on frontier colonization programs in favor of purchasing bankrupt plantations and reselling them at low interest rates to landless families. Between 1986 and 1988, however, only eighteen farms were purchased by INTA; these were subsequently divided among 16,000 households in sub-sub-sistence parcels averaging 0.61 hectares each (Berger 1992).

Guatemala in the New Century

The proposals offered by the 1996 peace accords on agrarian issues follow a legislative trajectory that appears to ignore the historical results of agrarian legislation in Guatemala and to offer few new solutions for improvements in equity and efficiency of land distribution. Unlike an adaptive land reform that learns from the failed projects of the past, the land-related proposals of the 1996 accords do not offer a strategic, long-term plan for resolving rural development problems and the inequitable system of land concentration in Guatemala. Instead, the programs of market-based (FONTIERRAS) and tax-based land reform and promises of conflict resolution are tools used to pacify political opposition by the rural poor, while fulfilling the agendas of modernization via the further power consolidation of the international agro-export sector. The failure of the FONTIERRAS land bank system to distribute significant areas of land is a clear example of this.[18]

In Guatemala today, however, increased grassroots organization and political activity is gaining strength from global indigenous and landless rights movements. Mobilizations for indigenous and campesino rights in Guatemala have increased rapidly in the last five years, with land occupations and protests both in the countryside and in Guatemala City. In January 2004 President Oscar Berger symbolically relaunched the provisions of the 1996 peace accords, and social movements continue to press for necessary legislative reforms related to land distribution and rural development programs.

The FAO sees a "new fire under land reform" worldwide, and notes that increasing support for agrarian reform among urban populations in Guatemala (many of whom are recent arrivals from rural areas) has fueled movements for rights already guaranteed in law (Food and Agriculture Organization of the United Nations 1998). Forster (1998) also argues that in Guatemala, national laws (or revolution from above) have achieved results only when supported by organizations of those at the grassroots. It is here, then, where we might look for the future transformation of the agrarian situation in Guatemala: in the combination of a struggling civilian government, a growing number of grassroots organizations that are recovering political power after forty years of repression, and the international social movements for landless and campesino rights. While considered inadequate in the current historical context, the land-related components of the 1996 peace accords are first steps toward more fully employable measures of agrarian reform in the future.

CHAPTER 2

An Introduction to Land and Agrarian Reform in Zimbabwe

Tom Lebert

Over the past decade, land has stormed onto the southern African regional agenda, thanks largely to developments in Zimbabwean land reform. The media in particular (regionally, as well as internationally) have latched onto these developments, overwhelmingly with a negative sentiment. This negative publicity has largely clouded the real situation and obscured important and valid grievances—primarily, the unresolved land issue that underpins much of the structural inequality characteristic of the country, and, in fact, the broader region.

This short chapter sets out to provide a broad sketch of the land question in Zimbabwe. It starts with a short introduction to the history of colonization, before focusing in greater detail on processes of land reform during the post-independence period (i.e., post-1980). It then outlines and describes approaches to land reform undertaken since independence, with some analysis and consideration of the problems associated with market-assisted reforms that have been implemented over the past two decades. The chapter does not enter into a discussion of whether the politicization of the land issue by the Zimbabwe African National Union–Patriotic Front (ZANU-PF) is being carried out altruistically, or is simply being done in the pursuit of self-preservation. Finally, this chapter is by no means exhaustive, and it contains many omissions and gaps as it only scratches the surface of this very complex issue. Nonetheless, the discussion will highlight the key aspects of land and agrarian reform in Zimbabwe.

Background to the Land Question in Zimbabwe

Colonization: The British South Africa Company

Although there are many similarities between the history of the land question in South Africa and in Zimbabwe, the underlying conditions are different. Unlike in South Africa, colonization in Zimbabwe began only in the 1890s, when the "pioneer column" of John Cecil Rhodes crossed north over the Limpopo. This movement north of European settlers was spurred by massive gold discoveries on the Rand (now Johannesburg) in South Africa in the 1870s. Gold hunger led mining capital to explore for further rich gold fields. These explorations penetrated as far inland as the Zimbabwe highlands, where gold was indeed discovered.

The British South Africa Company (BSA), a commercial venture, had obtained concessions from the British Crown to further the exploitation of minerals in the region. The company sponsored the settlement of Europeans at what was then Fort Salisbury (now Harare), where land was parceled out as farms. It should be noted that the BSA did not set out to govern or rule the territory; its sole objective was to seek and generate profit from the natural resources discovered there. Unfortunately, profits were not to be had there, since the gold discovered in Zimbabwe was not concentrated in reefs (as in South Africa), but rather was scattered and almost impossible to extract profitably. In fact, after three decades the company had still not generated any profit.

Unable to profit from gold exploitation, the BSA encouraged white settlement for farming purposes. This was seen as an alternative means of generating income for the company. This policy, however, necessitated the further dispossession of indigenous peoples of more of their land, and it coercively forced them into labor on settler farms.

Within the first decade of European settlement in Zimbabwe, African people rebelled against the forced alienation of their lands. The first Chimurenga[1] erupted in 1896 as locals attempted, through armed struggle, to drive the settlers out and to reclaim their territory. This rebellion lasted until 1897, ultimately failing, as the Africans were defeated by European weaponry.

Much like the highlands in South Africa, the Zimbabwean highlands are not particularly fertile. Farming, therefore, was not an easy or profitable enterprise, and white settler farmers struggled continuously through the early decades of the twentieth century.

Settler Consolidation: The Emergence of a British Colony Proper

By 1923 the BSA company wanted to leave the territory, profits having remained elusive throughout its tenure. An election/referendum was held, for white settlers only, to determine the future of the territory. Settlers were required to vote for one of three choices: to become a part of the Union of South Africa; to become a full British colony; or to choose self-governance (an autonomous British colony). The settlers opted for self-governance.

A few years after the election/referendum the Morris-Carter Commission of 1925 was established to lay out a framework for ensuring the emergence of Rhodesia—the colonial incarnation of what later became Zimbabwe—as a self-sustaining British (white) colony. The commission proposed landholding patterns to put the settler economy on a sound footing. The subsequent Land Appointment Act of 1930 separated land along racial lines, both qualitatively and quantitatively. This land structure has largely carried through into the post-independence period.

Under the Act, race groups (i.e., blacks and whites) were not allowed to acquire land in areas designated for other races. The Act reserved 50.8 percent of the land for white settlers, with the bulk of it in the arable central highlands. The indigenous African population (the majority of the population) was allocated 30 percent of the land, largely on the plateau sloping down into the Zambezi Valley and in the mountainous escarpment regions. This land was designated as African Reserve Areas (now known as communal areas). The remaining 20 percent of the land was owned either by commercial companies or the colonial government (Crown land), or it was reserved as conservation areas. A further, very small area (0.05 percent), called the Native Purchase Areas, was set aside for the acquisition of land, through freehold or leasehold, by richer Africans or by small groups of African people.

Between 1930 and 1980, the amount of land available to indigenous Africans was expanded. By Zimbabwean independence in 1980, the racial split in landownership and/or land access was approximately 40 percent for each group (i.e., white holdings had been reduced from 51 to 40 percent, between 1930 and 1980, and African land expanded from 30 to 40 percent). Population densities in white and African areas, however, were vastly different, with far greater numbers of people living on African land, a situation that still prevails. Further, not only did white settlers have the pick of land in the best agroecological regions of the country, they were also supported by massive state intervention in the development of the farming economy. Thus, the colonial state provided extensive communication and marketing infrastructure in commercial farming areas and made subsidies and loans available to white farmers.

Up through independence, differing levels of capital development in southern Africa created a wage hierarchy in the subregion. Wages for migrant laborers were highest in South Africa, followed by Zimbabwe and Malawi. Labor migration in the subregion, therefore, had a southward tendency. This posed problems in terms of labor supply for the emerging white colony in Zimbabwe, where, as the white economy grew, the need to "keep" local African labor became more urgent. Various measures were put in place and a labor supply commission was formed; access to Zimbabwean workers by South African recruitment companies was limited, as was the use of migrant labor from Malawi; and a limit was set on the number of Zimbabweans allowed to leave the colony.

Increasing population densities in the communal areas, and social and economic dislocation associated with labor migration from these areas, resulted in substantial environmental degradation and a growing production crisis by the post–World War II period. The situation was compounded by a massive eviction of African labor off white farms due to the increased mechanization of commercial agriculture. In 1951 the Native Land Husbandry Act was passed in an effort to address these problems. Central to this legislation (and in common with the actions of many other British colonies in Africa at the time) was the limiting of livestock numbers and the introduction of soil and water conservation methods and technology (terracing, for example). Improvement schemes undertaken in South Africa's reserves from the 1930s onward were implemented in response to a similar environmental and production crisis.

It is therefore not surprising to find that the iniquities and inequalities of land allocation that began prior to Zimbabwean independence, and the associated state support to white agriculture, were ongoing areas of conflict and contention; as was noted earlier, the first rebellion by indigenous peoples was fueled by these very grievances. In the mid-1960s, a second Chimurenga began, led by ZANU and the Zimbabwe African People's Union (ZAPU). Both of these liberation movements were committed to implementing radical land reform once in power. The dispossession of Africans was still very much a living memory for many of the elders in Zimbabwe who had lived through the first uprising. Though not officially in power, the ZANU/ZAPU Patriotic Front posed a significant challenge to any minority-led government that did not invoke policies in the interest of the indigenous African population. In this way, ZANU and ZAPU elicited much peasant support for the second

Chimurenga. Trade unions and civil organizations were not involved the second time; rather, it was guerrilla fighters and peasants who battled against a modern army of the white regime, largely in rural areas. It was a struggle for land on the land.

This civil war lasted for nearly two decades, before negotiations for a settlement were initiated in the late 1970s. The inequalities in Zimbabwe at that time were very stark. Population densities in the communal areas were three times that of the commercial farming areas. Most importantly, there was still a highly visible racial division of land, with 6,000 white farmers owning approximately 42 percent of the country.

Independence: The Lancaster House Agreement

In terms of seeking a resolution to the crisis in Zimbabwe at the time, the land reform experience of Kenya was influential. Kenya had had a comparable land problem, and guerrilla war fueled by land grievances made a clear case for intervention in pre-independence Zimbabwe. In Kenya the British sought to defuse the situation by buying out white farmers and making UK£500 million available for land acquisition and settlement support. A similar solution was now sought for Zimbabwe. Thus, during secret negotiations in the mid-1970s, an Anglo-American development fund for Zimbabwe was promoted. This fund, to which the British agreed to contribute UK£75 million, would be used to buy out white-owned farms. The endowment received broad support, including backing from what was then the ZANU/ZAPU Patriotic Front. At the time, the United States hinted it would contribute an extra US$200 million to the fund. However, as we will see in the following pages, this fund failed to materialize.

The Lancaster House negotiations began in 1979. The Lancaster House Agreement, named for the mansion in London at which it was negotiated, was the truce that paved the way for an independent, and majority-ruled (black), Zimbabwe. Colonial Rhodesia had unilaterally declared independence from the United Kingdom in 1964 and was governed by white minority rule. The Lancaster Agreement brought, together with a ceasefire agreement from the armed wings of ZANU and ZAPU, a means for "orderly transition" from white-minority to black-majority rule. By the time these negotiations got underway, a change in government had taken place in the United Kingdom. The development fund, which had been mooted in previous discussions during Lancaster, was used as "bait" to bring the liberation movements to an agreement with Rhodesian authorities; in the end however, the offer of the fund was withdrawn, and, instead, the UK government offered a compromise solution: In exchange for guaranteeing existing property rights in the new Zimbabwe, the United Kingdom would underwrite half of the cost of resettlement. The Zimbabwe government would have to match that funding to make up the full cost of the program. In 1980, the United Kingdom pledged an initial amount of UK£20 million.

Land would thus change hands through a willing buyer–willing seller mechanism; white farmers who wanted to continue farming would be free to do so. There would be no mass expropriation of land by the new postcolonial state. The state did retain the right to expropriate land for public and resettlement purposes, but in such cases compensation would have to be paid out in foreign currency. In the end, following pressure from the neighboring states and from the United Kingdom, ZANU/ZAPU conceded and accepted the settlement. The Lancaster House agreement was to remain in place for ten years, and its restrictions remained a constant theme in Zimbabwean land reform in the decades following independence.

This "crucial capitulation" (Palmer 1990, 166) by the newly independent Zimbabwean government effectively tied its hands in relation to agrarian transformation, and any significant redistribution of land was ruled out. Compounding these restrictions was the fact that following the war there was an urgent need for reconstruction and for measures to address mass displacement and the collapse of peasant production. Moreover, as a result of the collapse of peasant agriculture, 90 percent of the country's marketed food requirements was produced by white farmers. Ironically, this placed white farmers in a strong position, both economically and politically, at the end of the war.

Land and Agrarian Reform in Zimbabwe

The Zimbabwean government's Land Reform and Resettlement Program (LRRP) can be seen as comprising two phases: the first from 1980 to 1996; and the second, commencing with a public listing of 1,471 farms for compulsory acquisition, in 1997. The purpose of land reform in postindependence Zimbabwe was to redress past land alienation by creating equal access to land for the majority of the population. The LRRP's goals were to create political stability and an acceptable property rights regime; to promote economic growth through wider equity and efficiency gains from land redistribution; and to foster national food security, self-sufficiency, and agricultural development through labor-intensive small-farm production, optimal land productivity, and returns to invested capital. The land reform program particularly targeted four groups: the landless, war veterans, the poor, and commercial farm workers.

The number of households to be resettled on land acquired by the state changed a number of times in the first two years of independence. In 1980 the stated goal was 18,000 households over a five-year period. This figure was increased, in 1981, to 54,000 households; in 1982, it was fixed at 162,000 households, to be resettled by 1984 if possible. This final figure has remained unchanged since then and has proved to be a millstone around the government's neck.

Land acquisition was aimed at reducing by approximately 50 percent the 16 million hectares of agricultural land held by white farmers at independence. The target set for land acquisition and transfer to black small landholders was thus approximately 8 million hectares. The remaining white commercial farming areas would also be desegregated through the promotion of black entry into this sector.

State-Centered Market-Based Land Reform, 1980 to 1996

The dominant approach to land acquisition in the 1981–1996 period can be characterized as a state-centered market-based approach to land redistribution. Land was purchased by the state from willing sellers (as per Lancaster) and redistributed to beneficiaries. The private sector influenced the identification of land and controlled the supply available for resettlement, while the government played the role of buyer. The government, in turn, made land available to people selected mainly by its district officials under the direct supervision of central government officials. Consequently, land reform in Zimbabwe during the 1980s and 1990s was unable to redistribute land on any significant scale. Instead, reform has been confined to the planned and orderly settlement of beneficiaries (families and cooperatives) on land acquired by the state.

Acquisition of land through the willing buyer–willing seller setup moved forward with little resistance during the 1981 to 1983 period, drawing on a substantial supply of farms abandoned during the war and farms coming on to the market as white settlers left the country after independence. However, this supply of land eventually dried up. This turn of events may well have been the motivation behind the Land Acquisition Act of 1986, which provided the state with first option to purchase farms coming onto the market. The act also provided for compulsory acquisition of land deemed underutilized or derelict, although this approach was never successfully pursued during the first phase of land reform in Zimbabwe.

The settlement of beneficiaries on land took place through one of four models, although the bulk of reform made use of only one of these. The models were as follows:

1. *Intensive Settlement on an Individual Family Basis (Model A)* In this model, which was used to facilitate more than 80 percent of the land reform in the 1980s and 1990s, beneficiaries receive cropping land (10 to 65 hectares) as well as access to communal grazing land (55 hectares or the equivalent, depending on the agroecological region). Land was acquired by the state (usually in the form of large commercial estates), and then divided in to smaller plots that were then redistributed to beneficiaries. Tenure (on the part of beneficiaries) was in the form of three annual permits—one for settlement, one for cultivation, and one for grazing. A final contingency of this model was that black settlers (beneficiaries) who received land had to give up their rights to land in the communal areas they came from.

2. *Village Settlement with Cooperative Farming (Model B)* Model B was designed to take over existing large commercial farms and cooperatively organize farm production, in which decision making would occur through committee. Credit would be accessed by the cooperative, and income allocated either to individual families or allocated for farm development. Approximately fifty such cooperative schemes were set up, although many subsequently folded.

3. *State Farms with Out-Growers (Model C)* This model, which was not extensively implemented, involved the intensive resettlement of beneficiaries around a core estate. The estate provided settlers with certain services, and settlers, in turn, provided labor for the estate. Cropping land within this scheme was allocated on an individual basis, with settlers also gaining access to grazing land, which is managed communally. A professional farm manager managed the core estate.

4. *Commercial Grazing for Communal Areas (Model D)* Under Model D, which was implemented in the arid south of Zimbabwe, commercial ranches were purchased next to communal land. Livestock was then purchased for these neighboring lands and allowed to fatten on the ranch before being sold. The idea was that this would enable communal farmers to reduce grazing pressure on communal lands. This model, as well, was not extensively implemented.

On the whole, land allocations through the LRRP program were quite generous, compared with those of other African countries, such as Kenya. This was partly due to the fact that the program was modeled on the extensive land-use patterns characteristic of the (white) commercial sector. The downside of this approach to allocation was that fewer people were able to benefit from land redistribution (i.e., the number of potential beneficiaries is reduced). By June 1989, approximately 52,000 households (416,000 people) had been resettled, on approximately 2.8 million hectares of land acquired by the state for resettlement. This represented approximately 16 percent of the commercial farmland at independence. By 2000, the amount of redistributed land had increased to approximately 3.5 million hectares, and the number of beneficiaries to approximately 75,000 households. A further 400,000 hectares of state land had been leased out to 400 African commercial farmers, and 350 more farms had been purchased by Africans on the open market. The acquisition of land was, however, not evenly spread out over time. The process was extremely uneven, as is illustrated in table 2.1.

From the data, it is clear that, in addition to uneven progress, a general slowdown in the progress of the LRRP has occurred over time as well. A number of factors have contributed to the imbalance observed in the program and in the general slowdown over time in land redistribution:

1. Between 1980 and 1983 there was a massive spurt of redistribution made up largely of farms abandoned either during the war or shortly before or after independence.

2. After 1983, few farms in their entirety came onto the market, which made advance planning on the part of the government difficult. Moreover, farmers held onto their core productive land and sold off marginal holdings. This was especially the case as land prices began to rise due largely to postwar political stability.

3. White farmers wanting to sell land were legally obliged to offer it to the state first. If the state did not want the land, it would issue a "no present interest" certificate (valid for one year), which then enabled the seller to dispose of the land on the private market. According to Palmer (1990), throughout the 1980s at least there was a consistent oversupply of land available to the state. Many of the new black elite and senior members of the government were able to acquire farms through taking advantage of the state's "no present interest." Again according to Palmer (1990), farmland totaling over a million hectares transferred hands in this way.

4. The role of the Commercial Farmers Union (CFU) cannot be overlooked in examining the pace of land reform. The CFU has been a prominent player

TABLE 2.1 Land purchased by the state for resettlement, 1980–1989

Financial year	Land (hectares)	Financial year	Land (hectares)
1980/1981	223,196	1985/1986	85,167
1981/1982	900,196	1986/1987	133,515
1982/1983	939,925	1987/1988	20,319
1983/1984	159,866	total 1988	2,538,262
1984/1985	75,058	total 1989	2,713,725

Source: Palmer, 1990. Modified by author.

in relation to the land issue in Zimbabwe and has consistently argued that rapid land reform would undermine white confidence and threaten export earnings and employment. The inclusion of at least ten government ministers and over five hundred black members in 1989 (Palmer 1990) no doubt bolstered their position. The union was largely responsible for ensuring that the position of commercial farmers remained secure (at least up to the 1990s), through courting the government over a range of issues. Having the ear of the Ministry of Land and Agriculture (as well as influence in the seven other ministries involved in resettlement) the CFU was able to successfully slow the pace of resettlement.

5. Already by 1983, the domestic budget of Zimbabwe was strained. The Zimbabwean government came under increasing pressure from the World Bank and the International Monetary Fund (IMF), as well as from Western donor governments, to undertake belt-tightening. The government complied by cutting back on resettlement (but continued funding newly established schools and clinics).

6. In the mid-1980s, severe drought in the subregion hit Zimbabwe particularly hard. Some new settlers returned to communal areas in search of better conditions, and the government of Zimbabwe used extensive resources on relief efforts.

People-Driven Land Reform

Although land reform during the period of 1980–1996 was characterized as state centered and market based, people-driven acquisitions (what Moyo [2001, 24] refers to as a "community land occupation approach") occurred as well. This was especially so during the first four years of this period, in which action by the people was closely linked to the government program, in the form of the "accelerated resettlement program." In this approach, in which communities initiated land identification through the occupation of abandoned and underutilized lands, prompting the government to respond by purchasing the occupied land at market price. Most of the land acquired in this manner was in the liberation war zone of the eastern highlands. By 1986, however, the government had moved to end this practice. Such occupations were deemed illegal, and both police and farmers evicted occupiers. Occupations, and land redistribution in general, slowed dramatically after 1986, although occupations never disappeared entirely, and they would remerge strongly again around 1996.

The experience of market-based land acquisition over the 1980s and 1990s highlights three key trends that have become synonymous with World Bank–driven land reform models:

1. The amount, quality, location, and cost of land are driven by landholders (and their own interests).

2. By moving only select parcels of privately held land into the market, neither the government nor beneficiaries drive the process of distributing land with regard to need and the access to natural resources for subsistence.

3. The state as the key buyer of land distorts the land market by setting the parameters in terms of pricing and location, as determined by the government's broader settlement planning framework.

As a consequence of this poorly designed strategy for land redistribution, over 70 percent of land acquired for resettlement through the market has been agroecologically marginal and located mainly in the drier, more climatically erratic, southern regions of the country. The bulk of prime land in the three Mashonaland provinces (covering the central highlands) has largely been untouched. The land offered to the state has been geographically scattered, causing settlers to move in small groups from communal areas to isolated farms in disparate areas. This process has been both expensive and logistically inefficient.

The Role of Multilateral Agencies and International Donors

As noted earlier, the conditionalities imposed by Lancaster have been a central issue of contention in Zimbabwe, and have been especially significant in shaping the relationship between Zimbabwe and the United Kingdom. This section explores this issue in more detail by examining the role of multilateral agencies in shaping the scope and of the Lancaster Act and the subsequent LRRP.

During the 1980s, conflict between the governments of Zimbabwe and the United Kingdom were rooted in the conditionalities imposed by the United Kingdom (and, later, by other multilateral agencies) on its financial support of Zimbabwe's land reform program. The United Kingdom had laid down strict conditions about the Zimbabwe program, including requirements for detailed planning and surveying of land before settlement (in addition to the broader constraints of the willing buyer–willing seller approach). These restrictions were imposed in a particularly severe manner in relation to the Model B cooperative-ownership schemes.

The Zimbabwean government was not happy with this situation. Under the conditions set, the land being acquired was of a marginal quality and of a high price, which diminished the returns on the matching funding provided by the Zimbabwean state. In addition, by the late 1980s, as its fiscal deficits expanded the Zimbabwean government was at times unable to make matching contributions to UK government funds, a fact the UK government seized upon. Finally, Zimbabwe did not have the human capacity and other resources to meet the conditions regarding planning and surveying. As well, the overall costs of the program were also rising due to the increase in land prices since independence.

The United Kingdom, for its part, alleged that farms being acquired were not being willingly sold due to the land occupations. It was also alleged that certain monies were being used, not for land reform, but for state farming instead (state farms such as these were later handed over to black elites). The United Kingdom also consistently argued that the Zimbabwean government was always slow to match the finances provided by the United Kingdom.

In the midst of these disagreements in 1988, the United Kingdom's Office of Development Assistance (ODA) released its evaluation of Model A schemes. Although the evaluators at the outset had never viewed redistribution in itself as a means of development, they concluded that the scale of the resettlement was an impressive achievement. The program had made great progress in achieving its key objective, and in that sense the ODA saw the enterprise as successful. Most settlers had benefited from increased income generation and access to schools and clinics, and overall returns on government and donor investments were an impressive 21 percent. The resettlement program was found to be a worthwhile investment in terms of contributing toward the broader national economy as well. Later evaluations (for a good example see Kinsey 2000) support these findings.

Despite the positive assessment of the ODA, the relationship between the United Kingdom and Zimbabwe has continued to deteriorate. The key issue remains the overall market-based framework imposed by the United Kingdom.

Expiration of the Lancaster House Agreement

From 1989 to 1992, the growing disagreement between the Zimbabwean and UK governments focused, in particular, on the funding of land acquisition and securing of appropriate land through market mechanisms—the market had proved biased toward scattered, low-quality land. These differences came to a head when the Zimbabwean government introduced its policy of compulsory land acquisition (with compensation) in 1990.

During the negotiations, it had seemed that the UK government had wanted to perpetuate the Lancaster framework beyond 1990. From the point of view of Zimbabwe, however, this was not tenable. The situation in the country had altered considerably since the early 1980s, and the government felt there was sufficient stability to introduce other land acquisition mechanisms alongside the willing buyer–willing seller arrangement. The government wanted to buy specific blocks of land in favorable agroecological regions by means of compulsory acquisition, if sales could not be negotiated, and it put forward 10 million Zimbabwean dollars (Z$) to this end. It was hoped the United Kingdom would in turn put forward a further Z$15 million.

The United Kingdom, however, insisted that its continued cofinancing of the program depended on the use of the willing buyer–willing seller framework. Moreover, following intensive lobbying by the CFU, the United Kingdom wanted to largely restrict resettlement to less arable agroecological regions, and areas adjacent to existing communal areas.

Palmer's observation is pertinent in this regard: "As for the British government, which has taken such an intimate interest in the land question and whose financial support for the resettlement program is crucial . . . it appears determined that, by perpetuating the spirit of Lancaster House, it will ensure that the feeble flame of socialism still flickering in Zimbabwe in 1990 will be snuffed out. So it seems likely that peasants will wait much longer for land reform. South Africa is next on the agenda" (1990, 181).

The Impasse Continues

As the impasse between Zimbabwe and the United Kingdom over the market approach worsened up through the 1990s and into 2000, three additional key points of disagreement became apparent: (1) the extent to which redistribution should include small and medium black capitalist farmers to the exclusion of poor and landless peasants; (2) the United Kingdom's insistence that land redistribution be gradual, releasing 50,000 hectares per year to fewer than 3,000 households; and (3) the conditionality of UK support on demand-driven acquisition, and on decentralized and civil society–engaged institutional approaches, which, from the Zimbabwean perspective, limit the role of the central government.

A further factor in the dispute was the change of government in the United Kingdom in 1997 (with Labour replacing the Conservative Party). The new Labour government stated from the outset that it had no historical responsibility for Zimbabwean land expropriation, based on the ludicrous grounds that the Labour Party was not of landowning or settler stock.

It was, however, not only with the United Kingdom where relations were strained; relationships with other donors have been equally problematic. In the 1980s, for example, the World Bank also insisted on a market-based land reform in Zimbabwe, yet during the Economic Structural Adjustment Program (ESAP) period from 1991 to 1995, the Bank failed to mobilize the resources necessary to support this approach. The ESAP period thus failed to integrate land reform into the other economic reforms that took place, thereby aggravating market failures in land acquisition, and compounding existing land conflicts and generating new ones. For example, structural adjustment of the agricultural and finance sectors had the effect of entrenching colonial landholding patterns since most commercial farmers benefited from the new export orientation. This created an increased demand for land and fueled conflicts between black and white agricultural elites who were competing for the same scarce resources—while obviously also marginalizing the poor. ESAP also served to internationalize interests in Zimbabwe's land, as reflected in shareholder landownership arrangements, introducing further conflict.

Compulsory State-Led Land Acquisition, 1996 to the Present

A state-led approach to land acquisition has been in place since 1980 and has changed in scope and pace since that time (see table 2.2), in response to failures of the land market to make adequate and appropriate land available. Initial thinking was particularly concerned with the quality and location of land available to the state through the market. The key objective on the part of the state was to target blocks of suitably located land for resettlement (table 2.1 provides a quick snapshot of those efforts). In proposals of that time, land

TABLE 2.2 State-centered market-based land acquisition, 1980–2000

Period	Land acquired (Ha)	Annual average
Constitutional Constraints		
1980–1984	2,147,855	429,571
Land Acquisition Act 1985		
1985–1990	447,791	74,632
Land Acquisition Act 1992		
1992–1997	789,645	157,929
1998–2000	228,839	76,279
TOTAL (20 years)	3,614,130	190,217

Source: Moyo 2001.

acquired compulsorily by the state would still be fully compensated. However, in the face of both internal and external resistance to alternatives to the willing buyer–willing seller approach, the position of the Zimbabwean government began to harden. From the mid-1990s onward the state began to adopt a more radical posture in relation to land acquisition; full-market compensation began to fall away at this time, and, as well, an obligation for historical redress was placed on the United Kingdom. Developments since the mid-1990s suggest a growing alliance between the state and certain local social forces against the longstanding international conditionalities imposed on land redistribution in defense of narrow racial interests. The following section of the paper will briefly review the emergence and implementation of compulsory land acquisition in Zimbabwe.

Scale and Pattern of Compulsory Acquisition

The scale and pace of compulsory acquisition (either with market-based compensation for land and improvements, or compensation for improvements only) has been mixed. Attempts at compulsory acquisition by the state, however, were fairly widespread throughout the 1990s. In the 1993–1995 period, only twenty-six farms had been acquired in this way, amounting to 43,622 hectares of land. In these cases the state paid market-related compensation for both land and improvements. In 1997, 1,471 farms were designated for acquisition; of those, 109 were offered for purchase and were acquired by the state. The remaining farms were delisted following successful legal appeals. After the 2000 constitutional amendment, a further 2,159 farms were announced

TABLE 2.3 Compulsory land acquisition, 1993–1997

Period	Farms identified	Acquisition orders served	Farms acquired
1993	30	10	10
1995	100	100	16
1997	1,471	841	109
TOTAL	1,601	951	135

Source: Moyo 2001. Recalculated by author.

for acquisition. The success of these attempts was, however, minimal and often met by legal maneuverings and litigation on the part of large landholders (see table 2.3).

Since 1992–1993, approximately 7,000 hectares per year have been acquired in this way, as opposed to the approximately 100,000 hectares annually through the willing buyer–willing seller model during the 1990s.

Conclusion

Given that land reform has the potential to strike at the heart of societal structures, which often perpetuate colonial-class formations, it is not surprising that such reform processes are so strongly contested. By the late 1990s, as land distribution in Zimbabwe effectively ground to a halt (and as government failed to institutionalize its compulsory acquisition model), there was a strong resurgence of people's action. In August of 1997, land occupations started to take place across the country. These occupations came in waves, with just a few in 1997, but escalating until they reached well over a thousand by 2000. The explicit aim of these actions was to redistribute land from white farmers to the landless black population. Contestation of these acts were undertaken by local, white settler farmers as well as by the international community (including donors and bilateral agencies). On the whole, this push back was successful, and land reform in Zimbabwe has, as a result, been hamstrung. This end was accomplished first by the negotiated settlement as encompassed in the

Lancaster agreement and later by the postindependent government's dependency on foreign funding.

Zimbabwe represents a land reform experiment in which, for almost two decades, the market has been used as the sole mechanism for land redistribution. The situation in Zimbabwe can be contrasted with those in other parts of the world where market-assisted reforms have been attempted (see part II this volume). The recent shift in Zimbabwe toward a more compulsory land acquisition framework is in response to the failures and weaknesses of the market mechanism.

A great deal of the conflict between the Zimbabwean state and local and international stakeholders has been in relation to the state attempting to address these restrictions, and the stakeholders resisting such change (to ensure the preservation of their own interests, i.e., the *status quo*). The turning point in this conflict, however, occurred only with the emergence of a clearer alliance between the state and local rural social formations; the degree to which the state actively pursued such an alliance, or was forced into it, is, of course, debatable. Whether this alliance can succeed in implementing radical reform, and whether these reforms can be sustained and successfully create and support rural livelihoods, is still to be seen, as is the cost to the Zimbabwean state (and society) of the resulting increase in international isolation.

CHAPTER 3

Land and Agrarian Reform in South Africa

Wellington Didibhuku Thwala

In South Africa, land is presently not only one of the most defining political and development issues, but also perhaps the most intractable. The continuing racially unequal distribution of land will either be resolved through a fundamental restructuring of the government's land reform program, or it will be resolved by a fundamental restructuring of property relations by the people themselves. Which direction the country follows depends to a large degree on the urgent and immediate responsiveness of the government to the needs and demands of the country's nineteen million mostly poor, black, and landless rural people.

The past few years have given some disturbing indications of the government's intentions in this regard, from the narrowing of the redistribution program—the main vehicle for reversing the racially skewed landscape inherited from apartheid—to the targeted creation of a small African commercial farmer elite, which overlooks the large population of poor landless Africans, and the laissez-faire attitude toward the growing demands of landless people and their civil society allies for a land summit to address the country's land crisis.

Land reform is critical not only in terms of providing historical redress for centuries of colonial settler dispossession, but also in terms of resolving the national democratic revolution in South Africa. This is the case because it is through land reform that social and economic relations—embodied in property relations—in rural areas are to be transformed. This is a central aspect of the national democratic struggle to transform the colonial class formation in South Africa that has combined capitalist development with national oppression.

Historical Basis for Land Reform in South Africa

Relocation and segregation of blacks from whites started as early as 1658, when the Khoi people were informed that they could no longer dwell to the west of the Salt and Liesbeck rivers, and in the 1800s, when the first reserves were proclaimed by the British and the Boer governments (Pearce 1997).

The Native Land Act was passed in 1913. This act restricted the area of land for lawful African occupation, stripped African cash tenants and sharecroppers of their land, and, consequently, replaced sharecropping and rent-tenant contracts with labor tenancy. The act resulted in only 10 percent of the land being reserved for blacks. In 1923, a principle of separate residential areas in urban locations was established, and this principle was extended by the Group Areas Act of 1950. In an attempt to deal with problems of forcing more people to live on small areas of land, betterment planning was introduced, which included cattle-culling, the fencing off of fields and grazing land from residential areas, and the movement of people into villages set away from farming areas.

In 1936, the Development Trust and Land Act allocated already promised land to the reserves. In addition, squatting was made illegal. In 1937, the Natives Laws Amendment Act prohibited Africans from buying land in urban areas. Further, the Group Areas Act, promulgated in 1950, racially segregated areas with respect to residence and business and controlled interracial property actions. Continuing this trend of ensuring separate and unequal development, the Bantu Authorities Act was passed in 1951, allowing the establishment of tribal, regional, and territorial authorities. To affirm the complete illegality of squatting, the Prevention of Illegal Squatting Act was passed in 1951 as well. This act allowed the government to establish resettlement camps for the surplus of people being evicted from white farms.

More racial legislation followed. The Blacks Resettlement Act of 1954 gave the state the authority to remove Africans from any area in the magisterial district of Johannesburg and adjacent areas. In 1959, the Promotion of Bantu Self-Government Act was enacted to establish the Bantustans and to make the reserves the political homeland of black South Africans.[1] In the early 1960s, the first relocation camps were established. This was an attempt to remove and contain displaced labor tenants, unwanted farm workers, and unemployed urban people. In 1964, the Black Laws Amendment Act was enacted. Along with the Native Trust Act, it was used to finally abolish labor tenancy and squatting on farms.

The land acts and other related land laws, settlement planning, forced re-movals, and the Bantustan system contributed to overcrowding in the former homelands. It is estimated that more than 3.5 million Africans were forcibly removed and relocated to the homelands and black townships between 1960 and 1980 (Pearce 1997). The population in black areas consequently increased. For, example, the population in QwaQwa grew between 1970 and 1983 from 25,334 to 500,000 people (SALDRU 1995). Whereas the population density for the homelands averaged 151 people per square kilometer, the population den-sity for the rest of South Africa was 19 people per square kilometer. In QwaQwa, population density was as high as 500 people per square kilometer.

Furthermore, 88 percent of all whites, compared with 39 percent of black South Africans, lived in urban areas in the 1980s. Estimates have also shown that in 1985, whites had a housing surplus of 37,000 units, while black South Africans in urban areas and homelands had a deficit of at least 342,000 units and 281,269 units respectively (Pearce 1997).

This historical summary indicates the extent of inequality in resource allo-cation in South Africa. However, by the late 1970s, the state began to acknowledge that black people should have permanent land rights in urban areas and thus introduced the ninety-nine-year leasehold system in 1978 and, in 1986, the government officially abolished the Influx Control Act (South Africa Department of Land Affairs 1997a). These measures, however, did not affect land rights in rural areas, where the *status quo* prevailed. There is, there-fore, no doubt of the need for redistribution of resources and, hence, of wealth.

Race, Population, and Land Distribution

The historical dispossessions and segregation in South Africa contributed to a serious neglect of human rights, dignity, and acute inequalities already exist-ing in the country. It further led to differentiated social strata within the coun-try. The uneven distribution of land and resources has resulted in the uneven social and economic conditions that now prevail in different parts of South Africa. The land dispossession of the black population in South Africa was driven by the need to reduce competition among white farmers and to create a pool of cheap labor to work on the farms and mines and, later, industry. The pattern of landownership and control also fundamentally structured the social mechanism of control—wage labor—over black workers and the population surplus to the needs of the capitalist economy. As such, the highly unequal access to land was, and remains, an integral component of the political economy of South Africa as a whole. It must be emphasized that any post-apartheid land reform would be dependent on the extent and character of economic reconstruction.

Still further, the number of South Africans living within the nation has grown at a rapid pace, and land-use decisions have not escaped these mounting pressures. The estimated South African population for 1995 was between 41.9 million and 44.7 million.[2] It is estimated that the South African population grew by 2.32 percent between 1990 and 1995 (South African Institute of Race Relations 1996). However, the preliminary estimates for 1996 by the Central Statistical Services (CSS) indicate a decline in total population to about 38 million.[3] The Centre for Population Studies at University of Pretoria states that the country's population is expected to increase to 57.5 million and 70.08 million by 2010 and 2025, respectively (South African Institute of Race Relations 1996). CSS estimates also indicate that approximately 54 percent of all South Africans reside in Kwazulu-Natal, Gauteng, and Eastern Cape. Kwazulu-Natal alone constitutes 21.1 percent of the total population. Only 1.8 percent of the population resides in the Northern Cape (CSS 1995).

Population Density

Increases in population imply strain on the available land. The population density for South Africa almost doubled between 1970 and 1995, from almost nineteen people per square kilometer in 1970 to thirty-four people per square kilometer in 1995. Population density also varies considerably among provinces. Estimates by CSS indicate that in 1995, five provinces (Eastern Cape, Mpumalanga, Northern Province, Kwazulu-Natal, and Gauteng) had population densities above the national average. The population density of Kwazulu-Natal (94.5 people per square kilometer) was almost three times the national average, whereas that of Gauteng (374.7 people per square kilometer) was about eleven times the national average. Northern Cape had the lowest population density of two people per square kilometer. The reason for this is that, although Northern Cape constitutes about 30 percent of the total land area in South Africa (the largest in area), it accounts for only 1.8 percent of the population.

Population by Race

Of the 41 million people in South Africa in 1995, over 31 million were black (CSS 1995). This figure represents about 76 percent of the population in that year. White South Africans, therefore, constituted only 13 percent of the population. About 57 percent of all black Africans then lived in Kwazulu-Natal, Eastern Cape, and Northern Province. Kwazulu-Natal alone accounted for almost 23 percent of the black population, with Gauteng accounting for 41 percent of white South Africans.

As with population density, the distribution of population by race also differs among provinces. In 1995, 97 percent of the people in Northern Province were black. With the exception of Western Cape, black South Africans were in the majority in all the provinces. The 1995 CSS population estimates indicate that Western Cape was the only province where there were more whites than blacks; whites made up almost 24 percent of the population there, as opposed to blacks, who made up only 18 percent.

Rural versus Urban Population

In 1995, the Centre for Development Enterprise (CDE) estimated that 48 percent of South Africans lived in rural areas. Preliminary estimates for 1996 by the CSS, however, indicated that only 44.6 percent of the population was rural. These figures indicate a slight decline from the 1993 and 1994 estimates, when the rural population accounted for 51.7 percent of the total population in each year.[4] According to CDE estimates, the proportion of the population residing in rural areas and small towns will actually increase to 46.6 percent in 2011, whereas the proportion of the population in the urban and metropolitan areas will increase to 53.4 percent by 2011 (South African Institute of Race Relations 1996).

According to the Development Bank of South Africa (DBSA) estimates, Kwazulu-Natal had the highest rural population of 5.6 million people in 1995. Eastern Cape and Northern Province also had relatively large rural populations, of 4.9 million and 4.8 million respectively. About 83.6 percent of the people in the Northern Province lived in rural areas in 1995.[5] In North-West, Eastern Cape, Kwazulu-Natal, and Mpumalanga, 60 percent or more of the population lived in rural areas in 1995, while in Gauteng, which had the highest metropolitan population of 7.3 million people, only 3.1 percent of the population was considered rural. Most of the people in the Western Cape (83.5 percent) also resided in metropolitan areas. Still further, by 1995 there were no metropolitan areas in Free State, North-West, Northern Cape, and the Northern Province (now called Limpopo) (South African Institute of Race Relations 1996; CSS 1995). The 40 percent of nonrural dwellers in those provinces lived in small towns scattered throughout each.

Social Indicators

South Africa has one of the worse records in terms of social indicators of well-being (e.g., lifespan, education levels, household income) among comparable middle-income developing countries. In 1995, nearly 95 percent of South Africa's poor were black Africans (SALDRU 1995). Black South Africans have been shown to have the highest unemployment rate in the country. In 1995, the unemployment rate for black South Africans was 37 percent, nearly seven times the unemployment rate for whites, at 5.5 percent (CSS 1995). Black Africans have the worst unemployment rate compared to all races in South Africa. Poverty is also strongly linked to rural areas, accounting for approximately 75 percent of South Africa's poor. Most of the poor have been concentrated in the former homelands and states of Transkei, Bophuthatswana, Venda, and Ciskei (TBVC).[6] In 1995,nearly 63 percent of South Africa's poor resided in the Eastern Cape, Kwazulu-Natal, and Northern Province (SALDRU 1995).

Between 1995 and 1997, unemployment varied from province to province. Eastern Cape and Northern Province had the highest unemployment rate in the country, both with rates as high as 41 percent. During the same peiriod, KwaZulu-Natal and Mpumalanga had unemployment rates of 33 percent each, and Northern Cape an unemployment rate of 30 percent. Western Cape has the lowest unemployment rate of 8 percent (South Africa Department of Land Affairs 1997a).

The 1994 population estimates by CSS indicated that women constituted 50.5 percent of the South African population. In Eastern Cape, Northern Province, and Kwazulu-Natal, more than 50 percent of the population was female, at 54.1 percent, 53.8 percent, and 52.1 percent, respectively. In the other six provinces, Gauteng, Free Sate, Mpumalanga, North-West, Northern Cape, and Western Cape there were more men than women in 1993.

Poverty throughout the region has shown a strong relationship to gender and age. The poverty rate of female-headed households is, on average, 50 percent higher than male-headed households. In addition the unemployment rate among men has been shown to be 25 percent, while the rate for women was 35 percent (SALDRU 1995).

Inequality in income distribution has also become quite apparent. In 1995 the average total monthly wage per household varied, from 281 South African Rands (R) a month among the poorest black Africans, to R5,055 a month among the whites (SALDRU 1995). In 1993, the per capita income for black

South Africans and whites were R2,717 and R32,076, respectively (South African Institute of Race Relations 1996). These data imply a disparity ratio of 11.8 between blacks and whites. Income also varied among provinces.

Income inequality in South Africa is even more striking when the Gini-coefficient is considered.[7] The Gini-coefficient of 0.61 is one of the highest among middle-income countries (SALDRU 1995). Another inequality measure is household consumption. The lowest 40 percent of households, representing 53 percent of the population, have been shown to account for less than 10 percent of consumption, whereas the top 10 percent of households, accounting for between only 5 to 8 percent of the population, have accounted for over 40 percent of consumption (SALDRU 1995). These social differences form a strong basis for redistributing wealth among South Africans.

The historical dispossessions and the socioeconomic profile discussed above indicate serious inequalities in incomes and standards of living in South Africa. The most vulnerable are the rural people and women. In rural areas, land is considered a major asset and input in the agrarian system. One cannot begin farming without land. The ability to provide shelter also requires land. Agriculture continues to be the main source of income for many agrarian economies and, consequently, rural communities in many parts of the world. A reformation of regional rural economies to improve standards of living, therefore, has a strong relationship to agrarian reform. Land redistribution is a very important component of agrarian reform, as it involves the redistribution of wealth in rural areas. In South Africa, agriculture currently forms a small share of the total incomes of rural Africans. However, agricultural incomes have been shown to be higher for those Africans with access to land than for the entire rural African population (LAPC 1997). The redistribution of income and improvement of living standards in rural areas requires access to land.

Furthermore, the high population growth rates in rural areas have led to a movement of people from rural areas to informal settlements on the outskirts of cities. As indicated above, the rural population accounted for 51.7 percent of the total population in 1994. However, this is expected to decline to 46.6 percent by the year 2011. This shift will have severe socioeconomic implications for the country, with respect to overcrowding in urban areas and the associated socioeconomic ills that have accompanied this process across the globe.

Land reform may therefore mean much to rural incomes, and it therefore seems to be the rational starting point in the effort to address the huge imbalances and inequalities that have existed for many years. Land reform that can lead to some equality in land access and use is also critical in ensuring economic growth in rural areas in particular, and in preventing severe social and political instability in the country.

The Negotiated Roots of South Africa Land Reform

As early as 1993 the World Bank, arguably the institution most dedicated to the protection of private property rights in the world, warned that if post-apartheid South Africa did not undertake "a major restructuring of the rural economy centered on significant land transfers and smaller scale agricultural production units," the country faced the danger of rural violence and, possibly, even civil war (World Bank 1993). It was against this backdrop—and amid growing concerns about the need to inspire the confidence of foreign investors in a rapidly globalizing world economy—that South Africa's multiparty constitutional negotiators approached the thorny question of whether and how to reverse the centuries-old racially unequal distribution of the country's 122 million hectares of land.

The challenge was tremendous: On the one hand, the African National Congress government-in-waiting needed to fulfill its 1955 Freedom Charter promise to reverse the apartheid landscape that had put 87 percent of land in the hands of the state and 60,000 white farmers, while millions of black people eked out a living in overcrowded conditions on the remaining 13 percent. On the other hand, transforming the rural landscape—and the racially separated urban settlement patterns—while ensuring continued food self-sufficiency, and creating an investor-friendly environment, promoting economic growth, and fostering national racial reconciliation, presented multiple and interlinked challenges. The balance of forces at the time of the negotiations nevertheless ensured that the fledging South African constitution of 1996 that emerged from the multiparty talks contained a series of exacting state commitments to the country's landless. These included three fundamental rights clauses on land reform, as follows:

- Section 25(5): "The state must take reasonable legislative and other measures, within its available resources, to foster conditions which enable citizens to gain access to land on an equitable basis";
- Section 25(6): "A person or community whose tenure of land is legally insecure as a result of past racially discriminatory laws or practices is entitled, to the extent provided by an Act of Parliament, either to tenure which is legally secure or to comparable redress"; and

- Section 25(7): "A person or community dispossessed of property after 19 June 1913 as result of past racially discriminatory laws or practices is entitled, to the extent provided by an Act of Parliament, either to restitution of that property or to equitable redress." (Constitution of Republic of South Africa, Chapter 2, Section 25.)

While the enforceability of Section 25(5) on land redistribution would be open to challenges on the basis of an "available resources" determination, Sections 25 (6 and 7) granted secure legal entitlements to the intended beneficiaries of the remaining two legs of the government's land reform program, namely land restitution and land tenure reform.

Later policy documents and statutory laws drafted by the new government, including the 1994 Reconstruction and Development Program and the 1997 White Paper on South African Land Policy, further committed the government to redistribute 30 percent of agricultural land and complete the adjudication process on land restitution claims in the first five years of South Africa's democracy (1994–1999), and to undertake a land reform program that would address "the injustices of racially based land dispossession of the past; the need for land reform to reduce poverty and contribute to economic growth; security of tenure for all; and a system of land management which will support sustainable land use patterns and rapid land release for development," respectively (South Africa Department of Land Affairs 1997b).

While welcoming these commitments as an important step forward, the National Land Committee (NLC) and other progressive land sector stakeholders warned that other underlying commitments—to market-led, willing buyer–willing seller, demand-driven land reform—would hamstring delivery by making land reform too costly for the state, while also failing to effectively identify the poorly articulated demands of rural people. The colonial and apartheid states had played a central role in the creation of the existing grid of white-owned private property and black property exclusion; for this reason the NLC and other critics argued that the postapartheid state must intervene to change this pattern.

South Africa's Land Reform Program in Broad Outline

The postapartheid government regarded land reform as a key initiative to redress unequal patterns of resource distribution. Land redistribution was characterized as poverty policy for rural South Africa (Zimmerman 2000). Driven by the Department of Land Affairs (DLA), the new government planned and legislated and began implementing a complex package of land reform measures. Broadly, this land policy has three components, which are described below.

Land Restitution

Land restitution is designed to restore landownership or provide compensation to those who were dispossessed without adequate compensation by racially discriminatory practices after 1913 (South Africa Department of Land Affairs 1997b). The institutional machinery to implement the program includes provincially based restitution commissions and a land claims court that acts as final arbiter in restitution cases.

Land Redistribution Program

Land redistribution is aimed at providing the disadvantaged and the poor with access to land for residential and productive purposes (South Africa Department of Land Affairs 1997b). It is also designed to deal with the past injustices of land dispossession discussed above, to ensure equitable distribution of landownership, and to reduce poverty and contribute to economic growth. It makes it possible for the poor and the disadvantaged to purchase land with the help of a settlement land acquisition grant.

Land Tenure Reform

This land tenure reform is designed to provide security to all South Africans under diverse forms of locally appropriate tenure (South Africa Department of Land Affairs 1997b). It includes an initiative to provide legal recognition and to formalize communal land rights in rural areas; it also includes a recently legislated program to strengthen the rights of tenants on mainly white-owned farms.

Moving Forward: Approaches to Land Redistribution

The South African government has adopted a market-based approach to redistribute land. The market-based approach utilizes the forces of the market to redistribute land and is largely based on willing buyer–willing seller principles. There is, however, some state support. The government is committed to make land acquisition grants available, and is obliged to support and finance the required planning process. The government also assists individual households or communities to purchase and own land.

The Rationale for the Market-Based Approach

The market-based approach to land redistribution has been rationalized on the basis of efficiency. This rationale ensures that efficiency in the agricultural sector is maintained, so as to maintain or even improve the current production level of the country and ensure food self-sufficiency. It is also aimed at maintaining or improving investor confidence.

Land is a scarce resource, subject to competing uses, including agricultural production, residential development, urban development, public parks, and other amenities. The most important implication of economic analysis for policy making, however, is that, in a world of scarce resources, tradeoffs characterize any policy decision. The reallocation of scarce resources also implies a redistribution of income and wealth in society. The important problem facing policy makers is to choose among alternative consumption bundles and distributions that could result in different public policies.

Generally, five economic criteria are used to judge the efficacy of policies and decisions regarding resource allocation. Four of these criteria relate to the efficiency of the economic system, while the fifth regards equity considerations. Thus, land can be redistributed either for purposes of efficiency or equity. These two terms, "efficiency" and "equity," are opposing economic terms that are often confused in many writings. Both of these cannot always be achieved at the same time in any one redistribution.

Seven Years of Failure: Postapartheid Land Distribution

As of the end of 2001, less than 2 percent of the land had changed hands from white to black through the land reform program, and the long-awaited legislation to improve the tenure security of people living in the former Bantustans in terms of the state's Section 25(6) obligations had yet to be released. Of the 68,878 land restitution claims received, only 12,678 had been settled, benefiting less than 40,000 predominantly urban households more than 40 percent of which had received monetary compensation instead of land restoration. While monetary compensation is one form of redress, it is not land reform because it does not involve the transfer of land rights. The urban bias of restitution delivery also means this program had so far done little to transform rural property relations, with most rural restitution claims still outstanding.

Land redistribution transferred less than half a million (480,400) hectares to 45,454 households by March 31, 1999, falling far short of the estimated 25.5 million hectares of agricultural land that quantified the reconstruction and development program's 30 percent goal. Following the 1999 elections the entire redistribution program was put on hold, pending a lengthy period of internal policy development marked by a complete absence of public consultation. When the Land Redistribution for Agricultural Development Program (LRAD) was finally launched in August 2001, it clearly targeted "full-time farmers" and required beneficiaries to make a minimum R5,000 (US$500) contribution. The National Land Commitee (NLC) and other rural sector organizations have argued that this requirement will effectively exclude the poor rural majority, marking a reversal of the White Paper's pro-poor commitment.

The slow pace of land reform can be projected to continue, according to budgetary trends that consistently allocate about one-third of 1 percent of national expenditure to the Department of Land Affairs (DLA). Budget analysts predict that at current spending patterns, it will take 150 years to complete the restitution process, and 125 years to complete the redistribution of 30 percent of agricultural land to black people. While these projections clearly support the argument that market-based land reform will prove too expensive for the state, the consistent failure of the DLA to spend even its existing budget places it in constitutional jeopardy with regard to Section 25(5), which requires the state to effect land redistribution within its "available resources."

Beyond Rights: Why Land Reform in South Africa?

Despite the inclusion of fundamental rights to land reform in the South African Constitution, the state has exhibited a lack of political will to prioritize the fulfillment of these rights within its macroeconomic strategy. This suggests that there is a need to go beyond the current rights-based discourse surrounding land reform to demonstrate the socioeconomic importance of comprehensive land redistribution and rural development to growth and poverty reduction.

The South African government has committed itself to a conservative macroeconomic strategy, detailed in the 1996 Growth, Employment, and Redistribution (GEAR) strategy, which seeks to alleviate poverty in the long-term through a growth-oriented strategy designed to inspire export-oriented industrial expansion by creating the conditions for foreign direct investment. Implicit in GEAR and its associated development programs is an urban bias in development policy rooted in the belief that modernization brings urbanization, and that state resources should therefore concentrate on meeting the demands arising from this trend.

This strategy ignores the demographic profile of South Africa, which, while predominantly urban (55 percent) is still significantly rural (45 percent), with strong rural-urban linkages among households. With more than 70 percent of the nation's poorest concentrated in rural areas—many of these women, children, and the elderly—further growth along this path can only exacerbate rural-urban inequalities. Increased urbanization born of the desperation of rural poverty will further strain the already limited resources of urban metropolitan councils. The GEAR strategy also importantly ignores ample economic analysis, from the World Bank as well as some bilateral development agencies, that suggests that only certain kinds of growth can achieve poverty reduction, while others—particularly urban-biased, industrial-led growth in conditions of severe inequality—tend to increase both inequality and poverty while simultaneously slowing overall economic growth. Conversely, analysis of various developing country growth paths has demonstrated that agriculture-led growth—particularly following a redistribution of assets—can lead to higher overall economic growth, a reduction in inequality, and greater poverty reduction. The reason for this is that a more equitable growth in agricultural income—combined with the right development policies—can lead to the growth of a vibrant rural non-farm sector that lays the basis for further economic growth through industry.

The highly uneven distribution of rural incomes in South Africa is a direct consequence of landownership patterns. Some 60,000 large-scale, mostly white commercial farmers dominate the agricultural sector. As a result, access to the bulk of the nation's natural resources is denied to over thirteen million people living in more marginal areas of the country and to approximately seven million workers and tenants living on these farms. This imbalance in landholdings is reflected in gross income disparities between the two groups, greatly impeding growth in rural incomes for poorer households and effectively stalling rural non-farm sector growth and poverty reduction.

One reason for this link between equality in landownership and higher levels of economic growth in developing countries is the relative efficiency of farm production by large numbers of smaller farmers as opposed to small numbers of larger producers—the inverse relationship between farm size and productivity (see chapter 12 in this volume). Reducing land concentration is thus a more effective strategy against poverty than relying on agricultural growth alone. This is one important reason why the mere deracialization of commercial agriculture—while an important component of rural transformation—through the redistribution of land to a small number of emerging black commercial producers (as the Land Redistribution for Agricultural Development Program [LRAD] seeks to achieve) will not succeed in stimulating sustainable economic growth or substantial poverty reduction.

The Need for People-Centered Land Reform

These socioeconomic arguments, combined with the political imperatives that inspired South Africa's original rights-based provisions for land reform, clearly point out the way forward: an economic growth strategy based on comprehensive rural economic transformation, beginning with broad-based land and agrarian reform that targets the poor, as defined through popular participation and consultation.

The current policy focus of LRAD on redistribution limits development in several ways: it seeks to concentrate resources in the hands of a small number of black commercial producers who are unlikely to spend much of their disposable income in the rural economy, while it confines the poor majority to ongoing dependency on rural farm wages and paternalistic social relations; it limits the socially transformative impact of land reform to a small number of relative elites; and it delays the potential impact of asset redistribution on the ability of the poor to take economic risks and diversify their livelihood sources. In contrast, a genuinely participatory, pro-poor land reform policy would raise the incomes of the poor, whose marginal propensity to consume rural goods and services is high, while also transforming rural social relations and improving the prospects for the rural poor to engage in sustainable livelihoods.

People's participation (in particular, that of excluded groups such as women and youth) in development must be a transforming act. Participation combined with education transforms people's consciousness and leads to a process of self-actualization that enables oppressed people to take control of their lives. Such participation, however, must entail the achievement of power in terms of access to and control over the resources necessary to protect livelihoods.

Land is a primary means of subsistence and income generation in rural economies. Access to land allows rural families to put their labor to productive use in farming, while providing a supplementary source of livelihoods for rural workers and the urban poor. Land can be loaned, rented, or sold in times of extreme distress, thus providing a degree of financial security. Importantly, as a heritable resource, land is the basis of wealth and livelihood security for future rural generations. Rights in land and access in land are major determinants of a household's capacity to choose and determine their own level of farm capacity and use.

Access to land also strengthens the hand of the rural poor in their participation in the labor market, while contributing significantly to rural employment growth, both through multipliers—as people are able to reinvest the money—into agriculture and into the growth of a vibrant rural non-farm sector. Thus, broad-based land redistribution to the poor can reverse the pattern of rural asset extraction that has historically stymied developing countries' economic growth. Land reform can also promote more equitable patterns of growth that shift income and power to the poor.

Land redistribution is inevitably a highly politicized process. However, the persistence of poverty, poor economic performance, and growing inequality makes such reforms both necessary and urgent. Land reform has succeeded in combating poverty and promoting economic growth in many developing countries, particularly among many of the "Asian Tigers," such as South Korea and Taiwan. Key characteristics of effective land reform policies include explicit targeting of the poor; fixing ceilings on landownership; ensuring the existence of marketing opportunities for farm produce; providing agrarian support services as part of a broader rural development focus; establishing focused, coordinated programs that are sustained for a decade or more; including beneficiary participation in design and implementation of programs; and creating flexibly designed tenure reforms.

Achieving these results often requires a firm political commitment by governments to overcome the entrenched power of existing landowners. While this may present an uncomfortable challenge to a reconciliatory state concerned with stability, the failure to do so, and the resulting delays in asset redistribution, may weaken the political impetus of change, further entrenching extreme asset disparities and fueling increased tensions and potential for conflict. In short, for the sake of long-term political and economic stability, it is better for a country like South Africa, with the highest income disparity in the world, to face the pain of a radical redistribution of assets through land reform now than to face the long-term instability that would emanate from delaying the resolution of the land question.

Conclusion

While the birth of South Africa's democracy signaled the end of apartheid oppression, the period of transition since 1994 brought the birth of a neoliberal economic order that has continued to perpetuate the unequal economic relations of the past. This chapter has enumerated several problems that the current land reform program is facing in South Africa.

The South African state has committed itself both to land reform and to a macroeconomic strategy that presently appears to contradict its stated commitment to land reform. Nevertheless, the right to land reform is enshrined in three fundamental rights clauses of the constitution. These are further bolstered by the requirement (Section 7[2]) that "the state must respect, protect, promote, and fulfil the rights in the Bill of Rights," including those to land reform (South Africa 1996). A further fundamental right to just administrative action (Section 33), grants "the right to administrative action that is lawful, reasonable, and procedurally fair" and requires the adoption of legislation to promote an efficient administration. This implies both that rural people receive a fair share of national resources and that the state fulfill its obligations to the landless in a fair and efficient manner.

The state has not fulfilled this or any other of its obligations to landless people, and this failure has resulted in an escalation of the land crisis created by colonialism and apartheid. The fundamental choices made by the new regime serve to undermine the ability of the existing land reform program to create conditions for a "neoliberal" agrarian transition—this is particularly the case with regard to the property rights clause in the constitution and the opting for the markets as the mechanism for redistribution. These two choices on the part of the new regime automatically undermine the possibility for land reform to effect radical change in agrarian relations. Continued action along such lines will perpetuate the colonial class formations, which remain a definite reality.

The main objective of land reform in South Africa must be to bring a just and equitable transformation of land rights. This objective has a number of dimensions. First, land reform must address the gross inequality in landholding. Second, it must provide sustainable livelihoods in ways that contribute to the development of dynamic rural economies. Third, particular attention must be given to the needs of marginalized groups, especially women, in order to overcome past and present discrimination. Fourth, and finally, rural people themselves must participate fully in the design and implementation of land reform policies.

CHAPTER 4

Land Reform in India: Issues and Challenges

Manpreet Sethi

The Land Question in India: A Brief Historical Review

As the basis of all economic activity, land can either serve as an essential asset for a country to achieve economic growth and social equity, or it can be used as a tool in the hands of a few to hijack a country's economic independence and subvert its social processes. During the two centuries of British colonization, India experienced the latter reality. During colonialism, India's traditional land-use and landownership patterns were changed to ease the acquisition of land at low prices by British entrepreneurs for mines, plantations, and other enterprises. The introduction of the institution of private property delegitimized the community ownership systems of tribal societies. Moreover, with the introduction of the land tax under the Permanent Settlement Act 1793, the British popularized the zamindari system[1] at the cost of the jajmani relationship[2] that the landless shared with the landowning class. By no means a just system, the latter was an example of what has been described by Scott (1976) as a moral economy, and at the least it ensured the material security of those without land.

Owing to these developments in a changing social and economic landscape, India at independence inherited a semifeudal agrarian system. The ownership and control of land was highly concentrated in the hands of a small group of landlords and intermediaries, whose main intention was to extract maximum rent, either in cash or in kind, from tenants. Under this arrangement, the sharecropper or the tenant farmer had little economic motivation to develop farmland for increased production; with no security of tenure and a high rent, a tenant farmer was naturally less likely to invest in land improvements, or use high-yielding crop varieties or other expensive investments that might yield higher returns. At the same time, the landlord was not particularly concerned about improving the economic condition of the cultivators. Consequently, agricultural productivity suffered, and the oppression of tenants resulted in a progressive deterioration of their well-being.

In the years immediately following India's independence, a conscious process of nation building considered the problems of land with a pressing urgency. In fact, the national objective of poverty abolition envisaged simultaneous progress on two fronts: high productivity and equitable distribution. Accordingly, land reforms were visualized as an important pillar of a strong and prosperous country. India's first several five-year plans allocated substantial budgetary amounts for the implementation of land reforms. A degree of success was even registered in certain regions and states, especially with regard to issues such as the abolition of intermediaries, protection to tenants, rationalization of different tenure systems, and the imposition of ceilings on landholdings. Fifty-four years down the line, however, a number of problems remain far from resolved.

Most studies indicate that inequalities have increased, rather than decreased. The number of landless laborers has risen, while the wealthiest 10 percent of the population monopolizes more land now than in 1951. Moreover, the discussion of land reforms since World War II and up through the most recent decade either faded from the public mind or was deliberately glossed over by both the national government of India and a majority of international development agencies. Vested interests of the landed elite and their powerful connection with the political-bureaucratic system have blocked meaningful land reforms and/or their earnest implementation. The oppressed have either been co-opted with some benefits, or further subjugated as the new focus on liberalization, privatization, and globalization (LPG) has altered government priorities and public perceptions. As a result, we are today at a juncture where land—mostly for the urban, educated elite, who are also the powerful decision makers—has become more a matter of housing, investment, and infrastructure building; land as a basis of livelihood—for subsistence, survival, social justice, and human dignity—has largely been lost.

International Financial Institutions (IFIs) and Issues Related to Land in India

Any reform is as difficult an economic exercise as it is a political undertaking, since it involves a realignment of economic and political power. Those who are likely to experience losses under reform naturally resist reallocation of power, property, and status. The landholding class, therefore, is unlikely to willingly vote itself out of possession, nor should it be expected that they would be uniformly inflamed by altruistic passions to voluntarily undertake the exercise. Hence, one cannot underestimate the complexity of the task at hand. However, the political will of the landowning class is as much a challenge to the redistributive process as are the existing legal and structural dimensions of the current landholding regime. A brief review of the legal history that has accompanied India's land struggles is therefore a necessary detour for continuing this discussion in all its complexity.

Loopholes in land tenure legislation have facilitated the evasion of some of the provisions in land ceiling reforms by those large landholders who have wanted to maintain the *status quo*. At the same time, tardy implementation at the bureaucratic level and a political hijacking of the land reform agenda, by both the state and private interests, have traditionally posed impediments in the path of effective land reforms. Even in regional states throughout India that have attempted reforms, the process has often halted midway with the co-optation of the beneficiaries by those working to resist any further reforms. For instance, with the abolition of intermediary interests, some middle-income farmers have gained economic leverage through the expansion of agricultural export. The most affluent of these tenants have acquired a higher social status as the rise in agricultural productivity, land values, and incomes from cultivation have added to their economic strength. These classes have since become opposed to any erosion in their newly acquired financial or social status.

Land-related problems such as tenancy rights and access to land for subsistence farming continue to challenge India. The importance of the land issue may be inferred from the fact that, notwithstanding the decline in the share of agriculture in the GDP, more than half of India's population (nearly 58 percent) is dependent on agriculture for livelihood. Yet more than half of this population (nearly 63 percent) own smallholdings of less than 1 hectare, with large parcels of 10 hectares of land or more in the hands of less than 2 percent. The absolute landless and the nearly landless (those owning up to 0.2 hectares of land) account for as much as 43 percent of total peasant households (Mearns 1999).

The reality represented by these statistics, however, did not seem to worry the governments of the late 1970s and 1980s. It was only in the 1990s, with the initiation of the economic restructuring process, that the issue of land reform resurfaced, albeit in a different garb and with a different objective and motivation. Whereas the government-led land reforms had been imbued with some effort to attain equity, social justice, and dignity, the new land reform agenda is solely market driven, and aimed at increasing GDP regardless of any externalities or costs associated with the process. Promoted and guided by various international financial institutions (IFIs) such as the World Bank and the International Monetary Fund (IMF), government emphasis on land reform since the 1990s reflects and seeks to fulfill the macroeconomic objectives of these multilateral economic institutions.

While the return of land reform to the government's list of priorities is a welcome development, the manner in which it is being undertaken—its objectives, and, consequently, its impact on people, especially those already marginalized and now being further deprived of a stake in the system—raises a number of questions and prompts one to look for alternatives. The remainder of this chapter, therefore, will devote its energies to identifying and monitoring the implementation of certain specific IFI-sponsored programs in particular states with a view to examining their short-term and long-term impact on the lives and livelihoods of local residents. It is hoped this shall enable an informed critique of the IFI-led land reform programs and serve as a lesson for peoples elsewhere in India and in other regions of the globe.

Market-Led Land Reform: The Current Emphasis on Land Administration, Titling, and Registration

In their analyses of India's land reform program, most international financial institutions have highlighted the basic problems that rural poor people face is accessing land and security of tenure, and they advocate redress of this situation through the structural reform of property rights, to create land markets as part of a broader strategy of fostering economic growth and reducing rural poverty (Mearns 1999). A large emphasis has, therefore, been placed on the need to establish the basic legal and institutional framework that would facilitate a market takeoff in land and resource exchange. The goals of the new legal framework include efforts to improve property rights as a means to protect environmental and cultural resources, facilitate productivity-enhancing exchanges of land in rental and sales markets, link land to financial markets, use land to generate revenue for local governments, and improve land access for the poor and traditionally disenfranchised.

The neoliberal package endorsed by the IFIs includes a number of reforms that will transform the current system of land tenure into a market-oriented system of exchange. This tranformation includes a number of incremental steps that begin with titling and cadastral surveys (mapping). The latter are then formally tied to the establishment of state land registries, the creation of new landholding legislation, the concomitant establishment of a land administration department within the state, and finally the removal of restrictions on land leasing (see figure 1 in the introduction to part II of this volume). A similar plan had already been put forward as early as 1975, when a land reform policy paper published by the World Bank described land registration and titling as the main instruments for increasing an individual's tenure security and linked titling and registration to the establishment of flourishing land markets. The process of land tenure formalization provided the major tools—land titles and cadastral mapping—that were to enable the use of land as collateral for credit.

While none can argue against the need for straightening land records and providing secure land titles and registration, the motivation for the exercise must delve deeper than the mere creation of land markets for private profit. The belief that land markets alone would take off and address the historical inequality that was their foundation has been challenged by the reality of India's ongoing crisis in food security. The shift in agriculture that has taken place since the first period of World Bank–endorsed privatization schemes in the 1970s points to an important historical and economic trend that has complicated the more recent attempts at marketization and poverty reduction in the twenty-first century. Industrialization, and the limits placed on national development programs to that end, exacerbate already existing inequalities in land distribution. The shift in Indian agricultural policy toward export and the increased embrace of neoliberal economic model casts much doubt on the purported benefits of the current World Bank land reform agenda in India.

The Commercialization/Industrialization of Agriculture

The influence of industrialization on national and international economic systems has reshaped the manner in which agriculture is conducted and for what purpose. From a family, or, at the most, a community affair, agriculture has been "professionalized" into an industry in which a farmer produces for the global market. Indeed, modern farming methods and techniques[3] have transformed agriculture into a science of food production and a system of commodity distribution.

This shift in agricultural production goals has been promoted most fervently since the 1980s, by policy makers and politicians, who conceptualize agriculture more as an industry that must be conducted to maximize profits, and less as a way of life with social and ecological ramifications. The trend has been justified by the substantial increases in agricultural output, which, it is argued, has substantially eased India's national food-security concerns. Undoubtedly, Indian granaries are overflowing. And yet, the individual in the typical Indian village is starving to death, and a "failed" farmer resorts to suicide. Surely, the disparity between these two realities calls for a closer examination of the issues involved.

Commercialization of agriculture first gained a foothold in India in the 1960s, with the green revolution in Punjab, when the World Bank, along with the US Agency for International Development (USAID), promoted agricultural productivity through importation of fertilizers, seeds, pesticides, and farm machinery.[4] The Bank provided the credit necessary to replace the low-cost, low-input agriculture in existence with an agricultural system that was both capital- and chemical-intensive. The Indian government decided that the potential of the new technology far outweighed the risks and, accordingly, devalued the Indian rupee for the five-year plan period (1966–1971) to generate the purchase of approximately US$2.8 billion in green revolution–related technology, a jump of more than six times the total amount allocated to agriculture by the state during the preceding plan period (Shiva 1991). Most of the foreign exchange was spent on imports of fertilizer, seeds, pesticides, and farm machinery.

While subsidizing these imports, the World Bank also exerted pressure on the Indian government to obtain favorable conditions for foreign investment in India's fertilizer industry, for import liberalization, and for the elimination of most domestic controls on prices for basic agricultural products, e.g., grains and milk. The Bank advocated the replacement of diverse varieties of food crops with monocultures grown from imported varieties of seeds. In 1969, the Terai Seed Corporation (TSC) was started with a US$13 million World Bank loan. This was followed by two National Seeds Project (NSP) loans. This program led to the homogenization and corporatization of India's agricultural system. The Bank provided the NSP US$41 million between 1974 and 1978. The projects were intended to develop state institutions and to create a new infrastructure for increasing the production of green revolution seed varieties. In 1988, the World Bank gave India's seed sector a fourth loan to make it more "market responsive." The US$150 million loan aimed to privatize the seed industry and open India to multinational seed corporations. After the loan, India announced a New Seed Policy that allowed multinational corporations to penetrate fully a market that previously had not been directly accessible; Sandoz, Continental, Monsanto, Cargill, Pioneer, Hoechst, and Ciba Geigy now are among the multinational corporations with major investments in India's seed sector.

While the revolution did ease India's grain situation and transformed the country from a food importer to an exporter, it also enabled the rich farming community to politicize subsidies, facilitate concentration of inputs, and increase dependence on greater use of capital inputs such as credit, technology, seeds, and fertilizers. Moreover, the green revolution had increased Indian food production by only 5.4 percent, while the new agricultural practices resulted in the loss of nearly 8.5 million hectares, or 6 percent, of the crop base to waterlogging, salinity, or excess alkalinity (World Resources Institute 1994). Furthermore, although the amount of wheat production doubled over a period of twenty years, and rice production increased by 50 percent, greater emphasis has been placed on production of commercial crops such as sugarcane and cotton at the expense of crops like chickpeas and millet, traditionally grown by the poor for themselves. These changes in practice have steadily eroded the self-sufficiency of the small farmer in food grains.

Yet in the face of such statistics successive Indian governments remain stuck on the same model of agrarian reforms, and they are generously encouraged by the IFIs. Agriculture is the World Bank's largest portfolio in any country. One hundred and thirty agricultural projects have received US$10.2 billion in World Bank financing in India since the 1950s. These projects have generally taken the forms of providing support for the fertilizer industry, exploiting groundwater through electric or gas-generated pumps, introducing high-yield seed varieties, and setting up banking institutions to finance capitalist agriculture.

Water Sector Restructuring as Part of Agrarian Reform

Most supporters of land reform view the process as more than the mere redistribution of land to the landless. Rather, they place an equal importance on the availability of other inputs that can help turn the piece of land into a productive asset. In an agricultural country such as India, where two-thirds of the agricultural production is dependent on irrigation and irrigation accounts for 83 percent of consumptive water use (World Bank 1999a), irrigation schemes that can enhance agricultural productivity assume special importance. However, such projects launched by the government have often become entangled in a range of controversial issues. Questions have been raised about their actual merit, about cost versus benefit—especially in view of the numbers of people that may be displaced by such a project—about adequate rehabilitation schemes for people affected by the project, and so on. Big dams and other hydroelectric projects naturally bring with them the threats of submergence of hundreds of villages and the forced displacement of thousands of people. In the absence of people-friendly rehabilitation and resettlement packages, it remains questionable whether these development projects are truly worthwhile since they deprive one population of its livelihood to enhance that of another. In this context, land acquisition by the government in the name of public purpose can be seen to raise doubt about the efficacy of such infrastructure development in the name of agrarian reform. Such issues prompted the World Bank to withdraw all funding for the still-incomplete Sardar Sarovar Project.[5]

In an attempt to steer clear of national and local controversies, IFIs have begun to finance and promote water sector restructuring projects of another kind. Highlighting the need for a "total revolution in irrigated agriculture" (World Bank 1999a, xiii), the government of India and the World Bank have identified the following goals for national rural development:

- Modernization of irrigation agencies to make them more autonomous and accountable.
- Improvements in irrigation systems by organizing farmers to take up operation and management responsibilities. Formation of water-user associations at the minor and distributaries levels.
- Reforms in irrigation financing in order to make state irrigation departments financially self-sufficient, rationalizing water charges, and improving collection rates.
- Institution of a system of water rights.

In the past, irrigation schemes had led to more severe environmental problems such as a rise in soil saturation and salinity in irrigated areas, which in turn brought more severe soil degradation. Not surprisingly, the World Bank came forward with new aid programs to resolve these problems, and it is now well into a second phase of water project loan disbursements. In 2001, the Bank announced two water and irrigation projects in the states of Rajasthan and Uttar Pradesh (UP).[6] The US$140 million credit for Rajasthan and the US$149.2 million credit for Uttar Pradesh are both on standard IDA[7] terms, with a forty-year maturity and including a ten-year grace period.

Premised on the assumption that irrigated agriculture could be the engine of agricultural growth but has been constrained by a failing public irrigation and drainage system, these two projects aim to initiate fundamental reform in water resources management and irrigation as a means to improve the living standards of the poor. The projects claim that improving agricultural productivity will generate additional jobs in the rural sector. In Rajasthan, projected aims are to benefit an estimated 250,000 farm families and stimulate demand for labor estimated at approximately 29,000 jobs per year, while in UP, the project is expected to generate additional employment for 22,000 rural farm families per year, representing a 24 percent increase in rural farm employment.

In addition, it is claimed that the formation of community groups under some of the project components will empower the rural population, particularly women and other disadvantaged people. The project also supports environmental management capacity, which will benefit affected communities by reducing pollution, preventing water-related diseases and improving public health.

These projects, with their laudable objectives, have just been initiated, and it would be instructive to monitor their implementation and progress vis-à-vis the actual impact on people in the regions affected. It must be kept in mind that the present IFI-led ventures in the sector of water are basically premised on the following two assumptions: First, in view of the impending water scarcity there is a need for water resources management in the form of large projects, for the storage and transfer of river waters. This requires huge investments that are beyond the capabilities of the government, and hence require liberal participation of the private sector. Second, in order to ensure water conservation and its proper distribution, there is a need to establish stable water markets and fair pricing. The emphasis, therefore, is on the creation of water markets, which will impinge on important issues of equity, social justice, and sustainability.

At the same time, the language being used in the water sector restructuring projects is reminiscent of the Joint Forest Management (JFM) and its emphasis on participatory management. Under the new World Bank projects, the irrigation sector, too, is being couched in the same rhetoric of community management, though now in a less pervasive and publicized manner. In the management of tanks and lift irrigation (so-called minor irrigation) and even in the management of canal irrigation, phrases such as "participatory irrigation management" (PIM), or the more explicit "irrigation management turnover" (IMT), are the new catch phrases. Consequently, all sectoral reform programs or development projects speak of "joint management," "co-management," or "shared management."

Forestry Projects: The Relationship Between Land Reform and Environmental Sustainability

The land within a forest area relates in a unique fashion to issues of land reform. It is important to have an ecological balance among the proportions of land designated for forestry, agriculture, and nonagricultural purposes, and, ironically, land reform can help to maintain and sustain this balance. Several studies have linked the problems of reduction in area under forest cover with the historical patterns of development that result in skewed land distribution. Hence, land reform that can ensure more equitable landownership can go a long way in relieving pressure on forests, even more than dedicated forest development programs that look on forests as a narrow environmental issue, devoid of a human dimension. The human element in forests, however, is very important, especially in several states of India where groups of populations have depended on forests for their livelihood for generations.

The concept of social forestry was originally conceived by the government of India as a response to the accelerating deforestation in India. Its objectives included assisting rural communities and landless people in meeting their needs for fodder, fuel wood, small timber, and minor produce through community planned and managed tree plantations and nurseries. However, the social forestry projects came under criticism for failing to adequately involve local communities and rural poor, supposedly the main beneficiaries of the projects. Instead, the projects catered to urban and commercial interests through the widespread promotion of fast-growing tree species for pulp and paper manufacture, rayon production, urban fuel-wood supply, and other commercial uses. Such plantations were even encouraged on private farmlands, community lands, and wastelands.

The net result of this activity was to further reduce the access of the poor to fodder, fuel wood, and other forest products. Meanwhile, monoculture plantation of tree species, and in some cases the widespread plantation of water-consuming trees like eucalyptus, a pulpwood species and the Bank's favorite monoculture—for use in the very profitable paper and pulp sector—resulted in the degradation of soils and a falling water table. Further, these trees were not able to meet the fodder and fuel-wood need of the local forest dwellers/dependents.

Given the failure of this first round of social forestry projects, and in the face of the ongoing deterioration of the country's forest resources, the Indian gov-

ernment introduced a new forest policy (NFP) in 1988, which called for sub-
stantive change in the management of that sector. The NFP altered the aims
of forest management, shifting them from a more commercial and industrial
focus toward those that stressed the functions of environmental preservation
and the preservation of basic needs for people living in or near forests. The
NFP required that forests be managed first as an ecological necessity, second
as a source of goods for local populations, and, finally, as a source of wood for
industries and other nonlocal consumers. This policy was pioneering to the
extent that it recognized the people living in and around the forest as an essential factor in the governance of forests, considering them to be in partnership
with the forestry department and giving primacy to their needs with regard to
use of forest produce.

In 1990 the government directed all states to develop a participatory
approach, similar to that of the NFP, in their efforts to restore the nation's
degraded forests. Within seven years of this directive, seventeen states had
issued orders enabling what is now known as JFM. Several states had used
bilateral/multilateral funding to initiate forest sector projects, each with JFM
as the guiding principle and value. By 1998, the vast majority of the states had
introduced JFM programs and policies, most often with financial and technical support from the World Bank.

One such project was initiated in the state of Madhya Pradesh in 1995. Its
goals included increasing the productivity and quality of forests, protecting the
environment, alleviating poverty, and strengthening and streamlining the policies of the forestry sector that the project hoped to achieve through the adoption of better practices and new technologies to increase forest productivity, the
promotion of private sector participation in forestry sector development, the
maintenance and improvement of biodiversity, and the strengthening of
institutions involved in forest sector management.

This project was deemed to be successfully completed in December 1999,
and the World Bank subsequently proposed a second phase, to be implemented
beginning in 2002. It would be worthwhile to assess whether the earlier project did, in fact, meet the needs of the rural poor and indigenous peoples. By its
own admission, the Bank now holds that the JFM project in Madhya Pradesh
fell short of delivering the full measure of control and access required to alleviate the poverty of forest-dependent communities; what it now suggests is a
new strategy of community forest management that envisages additional rights
and responsibilities for local groups.

Returning Land Reform to the National Agenda

The present economic trends in India are negatively affecting land use and distribution in a variety of ways, some of which have been described above. Attempts to either reverse these trends or propose alternative approaches to development present a significant challenge to the landless in India. As the neoliberalization of the Indian state decreases the opportunity to resist the top-down World Bank models, there is an increased awareness of the problem with land use and distribution both within the Bank itself and among international nongovernmental organizations more generally (see introduction to part I of this volume). However, the need to sensitize people to these realities cannot be underestimated. Increasing the prominence of land reform challenges through public discourse and Indian politics is particularly important since more comprehensive agrarian reform has virtually disappeared from the popular, political, and elite radar screen throughout the country.

The growing size of the urban-based population in India presents another challenge to establishing a national, comprehensive land reform policy. Most urban dwellers perceive land in a compartmentalized and detached way, and are unable to identify with the problems of the small or marginal farmers or fathom the larger linkages of land use to the functioning of the macroeconomy. For instance, the urban middle-class market demand for cheaper products pushes farmers toward agricultural systems that have a low-unit cost of production. This is only possible if the yield per acre is increased through the use of artificial fertilizers, pesticides that reduce crop losses, and, more recently, through genetically modified crops that claim to be more resistant to pests. All of these require access to and maintenance of capital for cash-poor farmers. Higher capital costs on the part of farmers drive the demand for borrowing from individual or credit institutions. As farmers' debts rise, along with the frequency of bankruptcy, they are forced to sell land to richer farmers or corporate houses and move into cities in search of other jobs. Equipped with few skills, these now landless people live in the slums. The environmental and social costs of cheap agricultural produce are huge; but this scenario is largely invisible to urbanites. Few acknowledge or appreciate the link between huge entertainment complexes or wildlife sanctuaries and the fate of the displaced, or between rising urban crime and increasing rural dislocation as a result of commercialized agriculture, bankrupted farmers, and environmental degradation.

Importance of Land Reform to India's Future

From an economic perspective, the question of land is linked to critical issues of agricultural productivity, agrarian relations, industrial uses, infrastructure development, employment opportunities, housing, and other related issues. Each one of these aspects is crucial for enhancing national security by ensuring consistent economic growth, food security, goods for export, and so on, which reinforce the country's economic strength, and therefore, its bargaining power in the international community.

A National Food Security Requirement

For a country the size and population[8] of India, food security is an especially crucial component of national security, and, until recently, it was on an upswing due to technological breakthroughs in rice and wheat production, a price policy ensuring minimum support prices, agricultural subsidies providing cheaper modern inputs, and a closed market. However, with economic liberalization has come the entry of cheaper foreign agricultural goods into the country and the removal of agricultural subsidies for Indian farmers, which will threaten food security in the future. With a reduction in the role of the state to ensure food security and the eventual takeover by market forces, there is sure to be a decrease in the access to food for the poorest Indian citizens.

Apart from its economic function, land ownership has a more profound social function, in that the distribution of land impacts the quality of the social fabric in a community and the dynamic of gender relations within that community. If the patterns of land ownership are perceived as fair and just, this, in turn, enhances an ethic of justice and equity within a community. By contrast, skewed land distribution patterns, alienation, or poverty eventually lead to social discontentment, widespread unrest, and violent venting of frustration and anger,[9] which could further increase volatility within a multiethnic, multireligious country such as India. Such unhappiness could also provide a fertile base for extranational powers to foment disharmony and encourage separatist tendencies in a bid to fragment the country; movements for greater autonomy or even independence from the Indian Union already place strain on Indian national security apparatus in the Northeast, Jharkhand, Punjab, and elsewhere.

It becomes imperative, therefore, to strike a balance between the economic and social functions of land. A model of development that excludes one in favor of the other loses out on the very basic meaning and purpose of development. In order to envisage viable land-use patterns that ensure high agricultural production along with social justice and environmental sustainability, land must be conceived within an equity-based development strategy that is economically viable, ecologically sound, socially acceptable, and politically feasible through the creation of an institutional framework. This, of course, is easier said than done. This chapter will now turn to addressing a few of the complex issues involved in developing such a strategy for land and agrarian reform in India.

Challenge 1: Shifting Economic Imperatives

National economic development should ideally bring about an enhancement in the quality of life for all citizens within a given nation. But the question remains, are these parameters met by the present model of development? It seems, instead, that "development has become a big business, preoccupied more with its own growth and imperatives than with the people it was originally created to serve" (Dorner 1992, 72–75). The present economic model is premised on the centrality of markets. But the market forces themselves are a function of economic power and control. In cases in which economic resources and opportunities are widely distributed, economic activity may best be left to individual, private initiative, and market forces, but in societies with a skewed distribution of natural resources and opportunities, a free play of market forces could marginalize an increasing proportion of people, without state intervention through reforms. In these circumstances, land reform holds a key to the removal of current socioeconomic abuses and serves as a means to break the age-old bondages of exploitation and poverty, to foster greater equity and justice.

Increasing people's access to land and creating a more equitable redistribution of land assets are important for India, particularly in view of its high and ever-increasing person-to-land ratio. Increased emphasis on industrialization should not result in an abandonment of the rural sector. For an economy that has little capital but a surplus of labor, optimal land utilization is an important component of land sustainability, and should be based on a consideration of land's labor-absorption capacity—to avoiding crowding and soil degradation—in a bid to achieve higher output per unit of land. Policies aimed at liberalizing markets and privatizing natural resources fail to address the problem of land and labor in the rural sector of India.

Challenge 2: Maintaining Ecological Balance

Forests. The case has been made above for an ecological balance between the proportion of land designated for forestry, agriculture, and nonagricultural purposes. There is a need to explore the linkages among rural poverty, landlessness, and skewed land tenure systems with particular attention to the problems of deforestation. The reduction of forests inevitably disturbs the ecological balance. Cyclical patterns of droughts followed by floods have been clearly linked to this. At the same time, there is no guarantee that the already existing skewed distribution of land outside the forests will not be replicated. Unless the government engages in the exercise with a blueprint for land reforms in mind, fertile lands cleared by the government are most likely to be taken over by rich farmers, private companies, and state enterprises, or held by speculators as a hedge against inflation.

Traditionally, impoverished farmers moving into forests have been identified as the principal, direct agents of forest loss. Hence, land reform that can ensure more equitable landownership may well do more to relieve pressure on forests rather than any other policy of forest resource development. In this context, and as suggested above it would be helpful to explore the efficacy of social forestry programs already undertaken in states such as Andhra Pradesh.

Land Degradation. Patterns of land use also have an impact on soil erosion and land degradation. For instance, agricultural practices designed to suit market conditions presuppose a permissive use of agrochemicals to maximize productivity. When land is perceived as a commodity or investment that must be made good upon, it is rigorously exploited to generate immediate, short-term profit, often at the expense of a long-term impact in the form of severe land degradation. In arid and semiarid regions, the introduction of perennial irrigation in order to increase yield causes salinization of the land. Irrigation on poorly drained land has waterlogged the soil, causing salts in the groundwater to rise and accumulate on the surface, turning farmland into a salt-encrusted desert. Artificial fertilizers and chemical sprays undermine the natural fertility of soils and increase its vulnerability to erosion. Of a total land expanse in India of 329 million hectares, nearly 141 million hectares (43 percent) of the land is subject to water and soil erosion. Other types of land degradation such as waterlogging, alkaline and arid soils, salinity, ravines, and gullies affect another 34 million hectares (Vyas 1999, 18).

Given the fragile nature of the ecosystem and land quality that has resulted from such a dependency on chemical inputs, care must be exercised in determining land-use patterns in the future. Agriculture is expanding to wastelands that are not suited for cultivation, hence pushing India's small farmers into a less fertile land base. Additionally, the rising demand for irrigated agriculture has led to massive overexploitation of groundwater. And, with the demand for more water, local wells often dry up, leaving small and marginal farmers to either pay for expensive state-provided water or abandon the unproductive farm. In response to the same crisis in water access, wealthier farmers, corporations, and the state resort to expensive technology-dependent extraction of groundwater, which exacerbates the overall problem of groundwater depletion. The ecological consequences of the current dominant model of development are serious and need to be addressed.

Challenge 3: Preserving Human Diversity

Tribal Displacement and Deprivation. The concept of land as a commodity comes into conflict with traditional concepts of common property and with societies, such as those of many tribal peoples throughout India, who generally do not have a documented system of land rights. The issue of land use arises in this context because many tribal groups, 7 percent of the total Indian population, live in resource-rich regions. Consequently, both the government and the private sector have a keen interest in gaining access and control over the land or its mineral wealth. In the process, depriving tribal groups of land has become the norm, as they are routinely displaced, and, in most cases, not even able to claim compensation since they have no legal proof of ownership.

It is estimated that over 20 million people have been displaced by large projects (e.g., dams, railroads) since independence, and a majority of these people have been tribal groups. This has happened despite the fact that special legal provisions exist to protect the land and other assets of tribal people. Driven away from their homes and with little or no resettlement assistance, they join the ranks of the landless. One attempt at correcting this ongoing marginalization was the official endorsement of five principles that valued the preservation of tribal land use patterns and land distribution practices.

The *Panchsheela*, or five principles of tribal development, state the following:

1. Tribal people have the right to develop according to their own culture and join the mainstream as equals, while maintaining their identity.

2. Tribal rights on tribal lands and forest will be safeguarded.

3. A team built from among tribals will develop their land.

4. State administration in tribal areas will work through traditional tribal structures.

5. Achievements in tribal areas will be judged according to human growth rather than productivity.

The *Panchsheela* principles have been most difficult to achieve, and in many ways they lack sufficient definition for use in policy making. The resource-rich regions of the tribal peoples in India have been drawn into the plans for national development, with its emphasis on industrialization and ever-higher productivity. Already, industries and irrigation schemes built on large dams have displaced many tribal people and transformed them into landless migrant labor. The Indian government has presented tribal development schemes as a principal tool for poverty alleviation. However, these schemes have not taken into account the total dependence of the tribal population on land and their lack of other productive assets. It is critical that the unique existence and subsistence patterns of tribal people be empathetically understood so that economic development can be harmonized with social change. Without such understanding, India may well have to face more indigenous struggles for national identity, as it has already in Nagaland, Jharkhand, and many other regions.

Women and Land. With farms linked to the wider market economy, the condition of women's participation in farming has also undergone a change, and not for the better. Traditionally, rural women have been responsible for half of the world's food production. They remain the main producers of the world's staple crops—rice, wheat, and maize—which provide up to 90 percent of the rural poor's food intake. Their contribution to secondary-crop production, such as that of legumes and vegetables, is even greater. Grown mainly in home gardens, these crops provide essential nutrients and are often the only food available during lean seasons or when the main harvest fails. Women's specialized knowledge of genetic resources for food and agriculture makes them essential custodians of agrobiodiversity. In the livestock sector, women feed and milk the larger animals, while raising poultry and small animals such as sheep, goats, rabbits, and guinea pigs. Additionally, once the harvest is in, rural women provide most of the labor for postharvest activities, taking responsibility for storage, handling, stocking, processing, and marketing.

However, in the market-driven agriculture, a conceptual division of labor

between what are considered the productive tasks of farming and the unproductive tasks of household and reproduction recasts the women's role as "mere
'supporters' of the 'producers'" (Clunies-Ross and Hildyard 1992). This view,
however, tends to overlook the effects of the realities of the rural-urban migration of men in search of paid employment and rising mortalities attributed to
health problems such as alcoholism and HIV/AIDS, which have led to a rise
in the numbers of female-headed households in the developing world. This
"feminization of agriculture" places a considerable burden on a woman's
capacity to participate in agriculture, in view of the difficulty in their ability to
gain access, control, and recognition with regard to ownership of valuable
resources such as land, credit and agricultural inputs, technology, extension,
training, and services.

Certain communities in India (especially in the northeast and the south)
have practiced the tradition of customarily recognizing women's property
rights. In these areas inheritance laws and marriage practices have been so tai-
lored as to provide and protect these rights; many studies have been devoted
to examining these practices. Several matrilineal and bilateral systems of land
inheritance have also given women advantages in many respects, especially in
granting them economic and social security, and considerable autonomy and
equality in marital relations. These systems, however, have eroded over time.
Interventions by both colonial and postcolonial government policies, particularly in the legal and economic spheres, as well as the complex processes of
social and cultural change (which the former set in motion), have degraded
customary practices. Large joint family estates have fallen into disuse; formerly
egalitarian tribal societies have grown economically differentiated; there has
been an increasing penetration into the culture of market forces and notable
shifts in the techniques of production, the social division of labor, and land
relations; sexual mores have altered; and patriarchal ideologies have spread
their influence. Women, in particular, have been profoundly affected by these
changes, and their customary exclusion from major authority in public bodies has meant that they are not the ones directing the change or are even in a
position to effectively protect their interests. The task is a complicated one, and
government intervention in the form of honest land reform could go a long
way in ensuring social justice and equity for women.

Challenge 4: Complexities of Common Property Regimes

Resources, both natural and manmade, controlled and managed as common
property present another challenge in the context of land-related issues.

Besides private property or property owned and controlled by the state, common property such as forests, grazing lands, water, and fisheries can also be held and managed through a community resource management system. These are different from open-access land and natural resources, e.g., forest areas and lakes, where there are no rules regulating individual use rights. The system of common property operates through a "complex system of norms and conventions for regulating individual rights to use a variety of natural resources" (Runge 1992, 17). Specifying rights of joint use, common-property regimes envisage tacit cooperation among individuals.

Traditionally, common-property regimes have contributed substantially to village economies by providing a source for fodder, fuel wood, small timber, and employment in local products derived from raw material. At the same time, they have also proved to be a stable form of resource management. However, the combination of population growth, technological change, and political forces has in many cases destabilized existing common-property regimes, while the institution of common property itself has often been blamed for these problems and accused of resource mismanagement. The imposition of private property rights has been instituted as a remedial measure. But enforcement of private property rights from outside the group or village is not a sufficient condition for optimal resource utilization and may lead to the adoption of land use patterns that are incompatible with local needs or place land use in the hands of those, such as absentee owners, with fewer incentives for efficient, equitable local management.

The scenario described above may become especially worrisome if lands are subjected to a new zoning system, in which grazing land may be redesignated as commercial land and local forests turned to conservation forests with concessions for tourism companies. In either of these cases, the access of those who have traditionally depended upon the communal land is curtailed. The worst affected are the women whose daily lives have been severely strained by the additional load of daily livelihood activities of food, fodder, fuel wood, and water collection. Alienation and involuntary migration are, again, the inevitable outcomes, as is erosion in the long-term capacity of such land development.

On the counts of efficiency and equity, common-property regimes have traditionally existed as a viable proposition for more equitable national development. This has been especially true for a developing economy in which poverty and natural resource dependency have arisen out of a skewed distribution of resources. Common-property regimes have provided a hedge against uncertainties, in times of poor crop harvests and harsh growing conditions. When facing such challenges, the pooling of resources—land in this case— ensures that at minimum larger numbers of farm families will maintain a level of subsistence. In fact, the implications of such systems of resource management are immense since the poorest members of society, e.g., the indigent and the elderly, can obtain a share of their sustenance from the public domain while remaining connected to members of their rural communties. In these ways, common-property regimes enhance the general welfare of rural dwellers and increase the sustainability of equitable resource distribution practices.

Conclusion

The framework of analysis provided above describes the increasing importance of land reform to the national and global agenda from national food security, economic, ecological, and social perspectives. The direction of land politics and land reform in India will continue to be one of struggle and hope. It will be important to widen the scope of land reforms beyond the mere activity of redistribution of land or revisions of ceiling limits. In order to be effective, land reform must be seen as part of a wider agenda of systemic restructuring that undertakes simultaneous reforms in the sectors of energy and water. Deeper structural reforms will ensure that the exercise of land redistribution actually becomes meaningful, enabling small farmers to turn their plots into productive assets. The case of expropriation in Brazil (see chapter 15 in this volume) offers one such example of the necessary structural reforms that could help facilitate a solution to some of the challenges posed here.

PART TWO

Land Reform:
Critical Debates and Perspectives

Critical Themes in Agrarian Reform

Raj Patel

The end of the Cold War was accompanied, in the words of Francis Fukuyama, by "the end of history." This is more accurate than Fukuyama knows. It turns out that "the end of history" describes not the era of the Washington Consensus but its goal: the erasure of history through the market. In this section we look at how post–Cold War land policy, authored by the World Bank and tweaked by local and international consultants to suit local conditions, has worked out in a range of countries. The countries chosen for examination here are those most often cited as examples of World Bank–led success (Deininger 2001; Deininger and Binswanger 2001). Under closer scrutiny by scholars and activists familiar with both the history of reform and the history of alternatives, the veneer of success is rather quickly peeled away.

This section opens with Saturnino Borras's overview of market-led agrarian reform. Borras outlines the promarket critique of Cold War land policies, detailing its catalog of errors and omissions, with evidence from the Philippines, Brazil, and South Africa—countries in which the World Bank has most vigorously piloted its market-based land policies. Borras argues that the Bank's policies have failed in their own terms and that the state-led agrarian reforms to which they are supposedly superior have, in fact, been much better than market-led policies in creating the conditions for just and sustainable rural economies and societies.

Subsequent chapters then consider the effects of the World Bank's land policies in different contexts. Market-led agrarian reform is a single, homogenous series of policies that form a sequence (as shown schematically in figure 1). The policies begin with mapping and surveying the land and then move to

FIGURE 1. Sequence of typical World Bank reforms

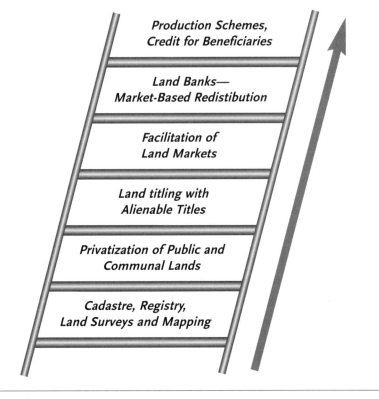

Production Schemes,
Credit for Beneficiaries

Land Banks—
Market-Based Redistibution

Facilitation of
Land Markets

Land titling with
Alienable Titles

Privatization of Public and
Communal Lands

Cadastre, Registry,
Land Surveys and Mapping

Source: After Rosset 2002, 2004

create private property rights for the land: privatizing communal and public lands where possible and creating land titling regimes, markets to facilitate the transfer of these titles, and credit facilities to fund these transfers; and, finally, providing production schemes to fund the productive activities of beneficiaries of these land transfers. The countries affected are at different points on this policy ladder—some, such as India, already have achieved full land titling, while others, such as Thailand, are still in the process of creating a titling regime. The final goal of the process is, however, the same: complete private ownership of land, and "functioning land markets" in which land—that essential asset of rural life—is bought, sold, and rented like any other commodity.

In Thailand, Rebeca Leonard and Kingkorn Narintarakul Na Ayutthaya follow the twists and turns of the land titling program there. Thailand's is one of the first attempts to begin a system of titling, with its origins in the 1980s. The results have systematically benefited landlords, who have used the opportunity to engage in land speculation, retaining land that previously had been protected for community use. The titling regime has, however, been largely unsuited to the needs of the poorest members of the community, who have found their traditional homes titled away from underneath them. Even those not facing direct eviction have found themselves unable to afford the rising price of land. This theme is echoed in Ana De Ita's essay, in which she investigates the processes of land concentration in Mexico after the intervention of the neoliberal social policy called PROCEDE. De Ita's work serves as an important reminder that land policies do not exist in a vacuum but are part of a broader constellation of neoliberal policies that have invariably left the poor in a more precarious situation, forced, to all intents and purposes, into survival strategies that have the effect of disenfranchising them from the land.

In some cases, disenfranchisement from land occurs in a context of violence, and nowhere is this clearer than in Colombia. Héctor Mondragón details agrarian reform processes there, showing that while there has indeed been agrarian reform in Colombia, it has been somewhat schizophrenic. At one level, the process of land redistribution to the poor has been in decline, with fewer resources being devoted to it, and with a growing backlog of land redistribution cases that the government seems unwilling to address. Pilot projects with this kind of land reform have spawned their own failures, while being praised outside the country. Yet, as Mondragón points out, agrarian reform is more than just land reform—it involves a spectrum of trade, extension, and investment policies, all of which have been handed over to the private sector and which, as a consequence, have resulted in an agrarian reform process that impoverishes the majority at the same time as it reforms the macroeconomy, making land concentration and exploitation easier for those with access to substantial sums of capital. Thus, the crawling pace of reform for the majority coexists with a vigorous agrarian reform for the few.

Conscious of its failings in other programs but attributing those to "endogenous" institutional arrangements, the World Bank has invested in creating land reform programs from whole cloth. While Borras touches on these, Sérgio Sauer analyzes the highly publicized *cédula da terra* program, the most controversial of all of the land projects backed by the Bank. The *cédula* program is a land bank in which "beneficiaries" receive loans to buy land on the market. It is fraught with problems, ranging from a profound lack of transparency to the precarious financial status of the indebted beneficiaries.

Perhaps the single unifying critique in all the country case studies is the stubborn refusal of market-led land reform policies to acknowledge the existence of differences in power between those who control land and those who do not. Markets compound and consolidate these power relations. The epitome of these differences in power is that between the sexes. In her paper, Sofía Monsalve Suárez describes the processes through which gender inequities have been addressed not by the market but despite it, through social movement struggles and engagement. She outlines the processes through which specific social organizations are engaged in the on-the-ground creation and development of both "a politics of recognition and a politics of redistribution," at the heart of which is a transformative project on gender.

Another important component of these differences in power stems from colonial history. Colonialism has been successful in exterminating or effectively disabling indigenous populations in large parts of the world, and that process continues under neoliberalism. This contemporary colonial project has, like its predecessors, encountered staunch resistance. Rodolfo Stavenhagen offers a compact overview of the modes of these struggles, focusing on institutional forms. Just as a gendered critique forces us to reconsider relations of power when thinking about what constitutes "work" on the land, indigenous land claims force us to reconsider the basic category of "land" when looking at modern agrarian struggles. This, in turn, should prompt us to rethink what a just and socially equitable agrarian policy might look like if we abandon that category in favor of more historically and socially bound ideas of "territory."

Together, these chapters deconstruct and build a contemporary terrain of struggle for agrarian policy and, ultimately, for food sovereignty, for peoples' right to choose their own food politics though democratic processes of contention and intervention.

CHAPTER 5

The Underlying Assumptions, Theory, and Practice of Neoliberal Land Policies

Saturnino M. Borras Jr.

In the early 1990s, neoliberal land policies emerged within, and became an important aspect of, mainstream thinking and development policy agendas. These policies have increased in prevalence since their inception at the end of the Cold War. They deal with both public and private lands, and have manifested in four broad policy types: (1) privatization and individualization of public/communal lands, (2) privatization and individualization of property rights in state and collective farms in (ex-)socialist and capitalist settings, (3) promotion of land rental markets, and (4) land sales. These policies have been formulated by broadly promarket scholars and policy makers, and have been aggressively promoted by the World Bank and other international development institutions as the solution to persistent landlessness and poverty in the countryside of most developing countries.

Neoliberal land policies emerge from a promarket critique of conventional (generally state-directed) land policies. To understand better the land reform debate today, we need to understand this critique because it provides the theoretical foundation of neoliberal land policies. Supported by accounts from different countries, it is argued here that the promarket critique of conventional land reforms is theoretically flawed and is unsupported by empirical evidence, and that initial outcomes of promarket land policies show that they do not significantly reform preexisting agrarian structures in favor of the rural poor. While general reference is made to mainstream policies pertaining to public/communal lands and state/collective farms, the bulk of the discussion in this chapter will be on policies concerning private lands. This chapter is organized as follows: it provides an overview of the changing global context for land reform; it presents the promarket critique of conventional land policies, which is followed by a critical examination of the promarket critique and policy models, both conceptually and empirically; and it provides short concluding remarks.

Changing Global Context for Land Reform

Redistributive land reform was highly popular in official development agendas during the past century, beginning with the 1910 Mexican revolution and ending with the fall of the Berlin Wall. Economically, it was generally accepted that large landed estates were economically inefficient because the land is underused. Two broad paths in land reform emerged out of the common perception that inefficient large farms should be restructured. One course is the advocacy for small family farms. Given the fact that in most developing countries rural labor is abundant amid relatively scarce land resources, it was thought that the creation of small family farms should maximize land use by applying abundant labor to it. This brand of land reform has usually been advocated and implemented in capitalist settings.[1] Other approaches involve either the formation of state farms or the creation of farm collectives. While the former course has been generally advocated and carried out in socialist context, the latter has been implemented in both socialist and capitalist settings. It is the assumption here that restructured large farms can be more efficient and productive than small family farms because they allow for the mechanization of farm technologies, as well as for the attainment of economies of scale in the farm input-output market, and they allow for more integration of development processes between rural and urban environments as well as between agricultural and industrial sectors.[2] Thus, given these bases, only economically inefficient and underproductive farms are subject to land reform.

Politically, the bases for land reform have been diverse. The decolonization processes occurring after World War II played a critical role in the emergence and implementation of land reform policies as part of the development and political agendas of nationalist governments.[3] The Cold War, as well, provided a crucial context for land reform from the 1950s to the early 1980s. The capitalist bloc led by the United States tried to compete with popular socialist land reforms by carrying out preemptive capitalist-oriented land redistribution campaigns, such as those promoted through the Alliance for Progress in Latin America[4] or the sweeping land reforms after the end of World War II in Japan and South Korea. In addition, land reform was used as a strategy to legitimize the rule of one political group that assumed state power either through party electoral victories by the left (for example, in Kerala and West Bengal, in India, or in Chile), or through military takeover (for example, in Peru).[5] Furthermore, land reform was an important item on the political agendas of victorious peasant-based revolutions, such as the ones in Mexico and Bolivia.[6] Finally, land reform has always been an important component in the continuing state-building processes of nation states: standardized cadastral records, systematization of tax base, and so on. In every case, the motivation for land reform has always been due to some combination of these reasons.

By the 1990s, the global context for land reform had transformed from that which had informed the large-scale state interventions after the Second World War. Economically, the question of large versus small farms has remained relevant, yet two further issues emerged. One was the perceived problem of the inefficiency and underproductivity of state/collective farms in socialist settings, such as in Eastern Europe, Vietnam, and China (Deininger 1995, 2002). The second issue concerned the same problem but in the form of farm collectives/cooperatives in capitalist contexts, such as in Mexico and Peru (World Bank 2003). Moreover, the imperative to create private and individual property rights in public lands to entice investments into the rural economy had become even more urgent for mainstream development circles.[7]

Despite the dominance of economic-related discourse in the neoliberal land policies, the changes in the political context have also significantly influenced the contemporary land policy debate. A number of important political imperatives that helped popularize land reform in official development agendas in the past have, to varying degrees, disappeared in the current context. The struggles for decolonization that underpinned many of the nationalist land reforms in the past are no longer perceived as urgent, on the global stage, despite the persistence of decolonization-related processes and politics in many countries today, such as Zimbabwe. Moreover, most peasant-based national liberation movements were weakened and dissipated by the late 1980s, removing a central source for political pressure for governments to pursue redistributive land reforms. Finally, the end of the Cold War has also taken away one of the most important contexts for past land reform (Herring 2003). Capitalist countries no longer feel threatened by socialist alternatives, and, thus, the past pressure on capitalist countries, which had resulted in their efforts to promote preemptive capitalist-oriented land reform, no longer exists. Meanwhile, other political reasons for land reform have remained, for example, the continuing imperatives to modernize cadastral records, as part of the continuing state-building process.

While old forces have dissipated, new forces, and issues, have emerged. One of these issues is the distinct rights of indigenous peoples;[8] another is gender land rights.[9] Moreover, greater concern about the environment is also part of the context of land reform today (see Richards 2002). Meanwhile, post-conflict democratic reconstruction and consolidation, such as in postapartheid South Africa and post–civil war El Salvador,[10] as well as the persistence and resurgence of violence,[11] have also provided significant bases, and imperatives, for land reform in these settings. The end of many centralized authoritarian dictatorships and the subsequent regime transitions have also added to the context of land reform in several countries.[12] Finally, the emergence of (human) rights-based approaches to development and the proliferation of civil society organizations during the past few decades have also broadened the discourse. Many old imperatives coexist with these new issues; a summary of these can be found in table 5.1[13] (see pages 104–105). It is within this context that the broadly promarket camp has systematized and advanced its critique of conventional approaches to land reform, a critique that has become the basis for today's neoliberal land policies.

The Promarket Critique of Conventional Land Policies

The promarket critique of conventional land policies relating to public/communal lands and state/collective farms can be summarized in two broad points. On the one hand, the rural poor remain poor either because most of them live and work on lands that do not have clear property rights, or because these poor households do not have sufficiently secure private property claims over these lands. From a purely fiscal standpoint these conditions are considered insecure, and they discourage banks and other financial institutions from investing in the rural economy. On the other hand, there is a perceived widespread economic inefficiency in many state and collective farms, both in socialist and capitalist settings, supposedly because (private/individual) property rights are unclear, which, once again, discourages both domestic and international investment.

The fundamental promarket critique points to the issue of economic underuse of land resources. The main policy reform called for by mainstream thinkers and policy practitioners is the privatization and individualization of property rights in the remaining public/communal lands, and in state and collective farms. In some cases, where mainstream development policy practitioners allow the existence of (formal) communal/community property rights, the basic approach is to privatize and individualize some bundles of property rights within these communal/community lands (for example, creating private individual land use rights), which can be traded in the open land market.

Meanwhile, the promarket critique of conventional land reform policies is founded on the assumption that state-led agrarian reform (SLAR) has failed to redistribute land to the landless poor. Deininger and Binswanger conclude that "most land reforms have relied on expropriation and have been more successful in creating bureaucratic behemoths and in colonizing frontiers than in redistributing land from large to small farmers" (1999, 267). The promarket critique then proceeds to explain the reasons for such failure.

The promarket critique is particularly hostile to the state-led approach's concept of a "land-size ceiling" that limits landownership to a specific maximum farm size. Deininger and Binswanger argue that "ceiling laws have been expensive to enforce, have imposed costs on landowners who took measures to avoid them, and have generated corruption, tenure insecurity, and red tape" (1999, 263). The same scholars explain that the usual payment to landlords, which is often below the market price and is made through staggered part-cash payments and part-government bonds, allows time to erode the real value of the landowners' money. It is this reason that landlords resist reform (Binswanger and Deininger 1996, 71). In turn, this conservative reaction has led landlords to subvert the policy, evade coverage by subdividing their farms, or retain the best parts of the land. Protracted legal battles launched by landlords have slowed, if not prevented, reform implementation.

Moreover, according to this critique, the state-led approach has been "supply-driven": it starts either by first identifying lands for expropriation and then looks for possible peasant beneficiaries, or by first identifying potential peasant beneficiaries and then seeking lands to be expropriated. This leads to heightened economic inefficiency, when (1) productive farms are expropriated and subdivided into smaller, less productive farm units, or when environmentally fragile (usually public) lands are distributed by the state; or (2) when peasant households considered unfit to become beneficiaries are given lands to farm (World Bank, n.d., 2). The critique continues, arguing that the state-led approach relies heavily on the central state and its huge bureaucracy for implementation through top-down methods that fail to capture the diversity between and within local communities and are unable to respond quickly to the actual needs at the local villages (Gordillo 1997, 12). Binswanger (1996,

TABLE 5.1. Economic and sociopolitical bases of and imperatives for land reform

Pre-1980s period	1990s onward
ECONOMIC	
Existing large landed estates are economically inefficient; must be restructured via land reform	Continuing relevance/currency
Creation of privatized & individualized landed property rights to boost investments in rural economy	Continuing—and has seen greater expansion in coverage
	Issues related to inefficiency (& accountability) in (former) socialist state farms and cooperatives, e.g., Eastern Europe, central Asia, Vietnam, China
	Issues related to efficiency in farm collectives brought about by past land reforms, e.g., Mexico and Peru
SOCIOPOLITICAL	
Decolonization	While to a large extent it is not a burning issue with the same intensity as decades ago, decolonization process-related issues have persisted in many countries, such as Zimbabwe
Cold War	Not anymore
Central state's "management" of rural unrest usually instigated by liberation movements for revolutionary societal/state transformation	Diminished substantially as liberation movements waned. But rural unrest persisted usually not in the context of armed groups wanting to seize state power but to push for radical reforms, e.g., Chiapas

As a strategy to legitimize and/or consolidate one elite faction's hold on to state power against another, e.g., Left electoral victories, military coup d'etat.

Continuing, e.g., Zimbabwe, tenancy reform by the Left Front in West Bengal

As an integral component of the central state's "modernization", i.e., standardized cadastral maps, etc. for taxation purposes, etc.

Continuing, and has seen unprecedented degree of technological sophistication (e.g., satellite/digital mapping, computerized data-banking)

a. Post-conflict democratic construction and consolidation, e.g., postapartheid South Africa, post-civil war El Salvador (Pearce 1998; Foley 1997), Colombia (Ross 2003)

b. Advancement of knowledge about the distinct rights of indigenous peoples (e.g., Yashar 1999; Korovkin 2000)

c. Advancement of knowledge about gender-land rights issues (see, e.g., Razavi 2003b; Agarwal 1994; Kabeer 1995; Deere 1985; and Deere and León 2001)

d. Greater concern about the environment (see, e.g., Herring 2002)

e. Persistence and resurgence of violence related to drugs and ethnic issues (see, e.g., Pons-Vignon and Lecomte 2004)

f. Emerging "[human] rights-based approaches" to development

g. The phenomenal rise of NGOs as important actor in development question at the local, national, and international levels

Source: Borras, Kay, and Akram Lodhi 2005, 17.

141–42) explains that "public sector bureaucracies develop their own set of interests that are in conflict with the rapid redistribution of land [. . . and] expropriation at below market prices requires that the state purchase the land rather than the beneficiaries. While not inevitable, this is likely to lead to the emergence of a land reform agency whose personnel will eventually engage in rent-seeking behavior of its own."

A further disadvantage of SLAR is the distortion of the land market. This distortion prevents more efficient producers from acquiring or accumulating lands and forestalls the exit of inefficient farmers. According to Deininger and Binswanger (1999, 262–63), most developing countries are plagued with distorted land markets, primarily due to prohibitions on land sales and rentals by land reform beneficiaries or to land being already marked for expropriation by landlords (see de Janvry et al. 2001). Such action is thought to have prevented more efficient producers from acquiring or accumulating lands, blocked the entry of potential external investors, and prevented inefficient and bankrupt beneficiaries from quitting production (de Janvry, Sadoulet, and Wolford 2001). Further, these prohibitions have led to informal land market transactions that, in turn, breed corruption within state agencies and drive land prices upward, bringing further distortion of land markets.[15] Furthermore, the promarket critique laments that SLAR has been implemented usually without prior or accompanying progressive land taxation and without a systematic land titling program, the absence of which contributes to land price increases beyond their "proper" levels, encourages landlords toward "land banking" or speculation, and leads to complex competing claims over land that, again, result in land market distortions (Bryant 1996).

The promarket critique complains that the implementation sequence within state-led agrarian reforms, i.e., "land redistribution *before* farm development projects," has led to an essentially "land redistribution–centered" program because in most cases the state has failed to deliver support services to beneficiaries (Deininger 1999). On most occasions, support services are delivered mainly via production and trade subsidies that are universal in nature; in reality, the politically influential sector of large farmers and landlords benefited more than the small farmers. In addition, Deininger and Binswanger conclude that, "[c]entralized government bureaucracies—charged with providing technical assistance and other support services to beneficiaries—proved to be corrupt, expensive, and ineffective in responding to beneficiary demands" (1999, 266–67). Post–land redistribution development has therefore been uncertain and less than dynamic, without important efficiency gains, and has "resulted in widespread default (in repayments) and non-recoverable loans" to beneficiaries (ibid., 267). Furthermore, it is argued that the state-led approach has driven away credit sources because expropriation pushes landlords (a traditional source of capital) away from farming, while formal credit institutions do not honor land-award certificates from beneficiaries due to land sales and rental prohibitions (Deininger 1999). For the same reasons, potential external investors are discouraged from entering the agricultural sector (Gordillo 1997, 13).

Finally, according to the promarket critique, the fiscal requirement of the state-led approach is too costly to the state. Landlords are paid whether or not the beneficiaries pay anything for the land. This is the same concept of "sovereign guarantee" that has been applied in government-sponsored credit programs that have failed in general. Moreover, the production- and trade-related "universal" subsidies are too costly and wasteful, while the huge land reform bureaucracy eats up much of the program budget (Binswanger and Deininger 1997).

The promarket critique is the most unsympathetic but, arguably, the most systematic critique of state-led approaches to agrarian reform from a strictly economic perspective. The neoliberal land policies, including the market-led agrarian reform (MLAR) model for private lands, have been constructed out of this promarket critique of SLAR. Deininger (1999, 651) explains that the new land policies are a "mechanism to provide an efficiency- and equity-enhancing redistribution of assets." Deininger and Binswanger (1999, 249) explain that these new land policies can help overcome longstanding problems of asset distribution and social exclusion. Based on the promarket critique, the MLAR model has developed strategies that are exactly the opposite of those of the state-led approach. Table 5.2 summarizes the promarket view of these different approaches.

The neoliberal land policies on public/communal lands and state and collective farms (in both socialist and capitalist settings) have been carried out through different land policy instruments, resulting in variegated and uneven outcomes among and within countries over time—not always in favor of the poor. For mainstream perspectives, see Deininger (1995, 2002), Deininger and Binswanger (1999), and the World Bank (2003). A more critical examination, however, exists outside the knowledge funded by the World Bank itself—see Spoor (1997, 2003); Spoor and Visser (2004); Akram Lodhi (2004, 2005); and Borras, Kay, and Akram Lodhi (2005).

The MLAR model has, to varying extents, been implemented on private

TABLE 5.2 Key features of state- and market-led approaches based on the pro-market explanations of how to carry out land reform in private lands

Issues	State-Led	Market-Led
	GETTING ACCESS TO LAND	
Acquisition method	Coercive; cash-bonds payments at below market price, and so is opposed by landlords leading to policy "failures"	Voluntary; 100% cash payment based on 100% market value of land, and so will not be opposed by landlords thereby increasing chances of policy success
Beneficiaries	Supply-driven; beneficiaries state-selected therefore "unfit" beneficiaries have usually been included	Demand-driven; self-selected, therefore only "fit" beneficiaries will be included in the program
Implementation method	Statist-centralized; transparency and accountability = low degree	Privatized-decentralized; transparency & accountability = high degree
Pace & nature	Protracted; politically & legally contentious	Quick; politically & legally noncontentious
Land prices	Higher	Lower
Land markets	Land reform: cause of/aggravates land market distortions; progressive land tax & land titling program not required—all resulting in the inefficient allocation and use of land resources	Land reform: cause & effect of land market stimulation; progressive land tax & titling program required, and so will result in the efficient allocation and use of land

Program sequence; pace of development & extension service	Farm development plans *after* land redistribution: protracted, uncertain & anemic post-land transfer development; extension service state-centralized = inefficient	Farm development plans *before* redistribution: quick, certain, & dynamic post-land transfer development. extension service privatized-decentralized = efficient
Credit & investments	Low credit supply & low investments, resulting in economic stagnation and poverty	Increased credit & investments, and will result in economic growth & therefore poverty eradication
Exit options	None	Ample
FINANCING		
Mechanism	State "universal" subsidies; sovereign guarantee; beneficiaries pay subsidized land price; "dole-out" mentality among beneficiaries = resulting in the waste of public funds and persistence of inefficient land users/producers	Flexible loan-grant mechanism; co-sharing of risks; beneficiaries shoulder full cost of land; farm development cost given via grant, and so will result in greater economic/fiscal efficiency
Cost of reform	High	Low

Source: Borras 2003a.

lands in Brazil from 1998 to 2001 through the *Projeto Cédula da Terra* (PCT) (Sauer 2003), which has been renewed and expanded during the Lula administration (Deere and Medeiros 2005); in Colombia from 1995 to 2003 through the Agrarian Law 160 of 1994 (Mondragón 2003); and in South Africa since 1995 through the Reconstruction and Development Program (RDP). A small pilot project was also carried out in the Philippines, although a much larger MLAR-like voluntary land transfer (VLT) scheme has also been implemented there (Borras 2005). While MLAR proponents have claimed impressive successes in these countries (Deininger 1999; Buainain et al. 1999; World Bank 2003), such claims are now seriously questioned by a range of scholars.[16] Most civil society organizations oppose these land policies and have launched coordinated local, national, and international campaigns to stop them. Such an initiative is currently being coordinated internationally by La Via Campesina, the FoodFirst Information and Action Network (FIAN), and the Land Research and Action Network (LRAN).[17]

Problems with the Promarket Critique and Mainstream Policy Model

A critical examination of the promarket critique of conventional land policies can be made from two interlinked areas, namely, public and private lands. Although in reality these types of property rights regimes are interlinked, it is useful to approach the question as separate analytic categories.

Public/State Lands

By public/state lands, it is meant here the remaining public and communal lands in most developing countries today, as well as state and collective farms both in (ex-) socialist and capitalist settings. The main promarket critique holds that due to conventional land policies, many of the public/state lands have remained economically underused. The key of promarket thinking and advocacy is the promotion of privatized and individualized property rights in these lands.

It is, however, crucial to underscore what Anna Tsing (2002) has argued in the context of her analysis of Indonesian landed property rights and agrarian relations. Tsing states that property rights are not things; they are social relationships. It is these social relationships that land reform in its conventional sense is supposed to reform. Moreover, land-based social relationships have multiple dimensions and expressions. Social relationships are not confined to economic relationships; social and political relationships between different classes and groups in society are inherently part of the agrarian structure. Therefore, any land policies that concern public/state lands under different forms of production organization (collective or individual farms) in different development and political regimes (capitalist, socialist, or transition economies) should reform the preexisting multidimensional social relationships in an explicitly "pro-poor" manner, meaning that the transfer of wealth and power must flow from the landed classes (or from the state) to the landless or near-landless groups in society.

Based on the brief explanation above, the fundamental problem with mainstream thinking about land policy concerning public/state lands and collective farms lies in its purely economic consideration of relationships. The social relationships underlying the process and outcome of such private property rights generation are accorded secondary relevance, if not completely ignored. Gone too are questions of equity or justice. It is not surprising, therefore, that the processes and outcomes of privatization and individualization of property rights in transitional economies has resulted in the emergence of new monopolies in landownership and control, as well as in other land-related resources, and in the rising inequality among rural households.[18] Preliminary evidence suggests that the campaign for massive privatization of public lands has also undermined the land claims of landless and near-landless households in the Philippines.[19] Finally, the prediction that the privatization of farm collectives would result in vibrant (pro-poor) land markets favoring the poor seem also not to have been realized.[20]

Private Lands

The promarket claim that SLAR has failed in terms of redistributing land has little empirical basis. The land reform literature, both traditional and promarket, has employed a rather crude, dichotomous framework in assessing outcomes of land redistribution. Either land reforms succeed under this rubric, or they do not. This is analytically problematic. Most, if not all, land reform policies that have been implemented in most countries, regardless of their orientation (revolutionary, conservative, or liberal), have resulted in varying degrees of success or failure. Land redistribution outcome is always a matter of degree.[21] Indeed, many SLARs have been able to achieve varying degrees of success in redistributing lands to millions of landless peasant households—and many of these cases involved the redistribution of privately controlled lands.[22] Table 5.3 shows the land redistribution outcomes in a number of countries.

In some countries, higher degrees of land redistribution through SLAR has been achieved, but subsequent market-friendly or market-inspired policies reversed some reform accomplishments to some extent. Such are the cases of Chile after Pinochet forcibly took power in 1973 (Kay and Silva 1992), Nicaragua after the Sandinistas were voted out of power in the early 1990s (Thiesenhusen 1995), and Guatemala (Handy 1994). In instances in which a significant portion of productive farmlands have been excluded from land reform, it has been due to promarket considerations and the failure of the state to carry out SLAR, and not due to any inherent characteristic of SLAR per se. This has been the case with the exclusion of the following: productive lands in Brazil (Hall 1990, 221), commercial plantations in Kerala (Herring 1990, 199), and white commercial farms in Zimbabwe from 1980 until the second half of the 1990s.[23]

The reported and claimed land redistribution accomplishments by MLAR (in Brazil, a few thousand households [see Sauer 2003; Deere and Medeiros 2005]; Colombia, a few hundred households in five *municipios* [see Forero 1999]; South Africa, a few hundred thousand households [see Lahiff 2003; South Africa Department of Land Affairs 2000; Greenberg 2004]; and the MLAR pilot in the Philippines, not more than a thousand households [Borras, Reyes, and Carranza 2005]) is miniscule in comparison to SLAR achievements over time. In contrast to the overwhelming track record of success of SLAR, the jury is, at best, still out over MLAR accomplishments (Borras 2003b, 2005).

Arguments for MLAR look better when the case for SLAR is weak. Yet the assertion that SLAR has failed to effect rural development and poverty eradication is analytically and empirically problematic. On the one hand, most, if not all, advocates of SLAR, past and present, have explicitly maintained no illusion that land redistribution is a magic panacea to rural poverty and underdevelopment. What has been asserted has been the notion that land redistribution is a necessary but insufficient condition of rural development and poverty eradication.[24] To assess SLAR using a metric of unequivocal, positive transformation, despite the insistence by its advocates that it is no guarantee of anything of the kind, is to deliberately muddle the terms and mislead the direction of the debate. Empirical evidence shows that countries (or subnational regions therein) that have carried out a higher degree of land redistribution in the past have tended to have achieve a better level of national devel-

TABLE 5.3 Land redistribution outcomes in selected countries

Country	Period	Total lands redistributed[a]	Total number of beneficiaries[b]
Cuba (1)	since 1959	80	75
Bolivia (2)	1952–77	74.5	83.4
South Korea (13)	since 1945	65	77
Chile (3)	1964–73	nearly 50	20
Taiwan (11)	1949–53	48	48
Peru (4)	1963–76	42.4	32
Mexico (5)	1970 data	42.9	43.4
Philippines (14)	1972/1988–2004	half	two-fifths
Japan (12)	1945–	one-third	70
Syria (12)	—	one-third	—
Ecuador (6)	1964–85	34.2	no data
El Salvador (7)	From 1980 thru 1990s	20	12
Venezuela (8)	Up to 1979	19.3	24.4
Egypt (12)	1952–61	10	9
Costa Rica (9)	1961–1979	7.1	13.5
South Africa (10)	1995–2000	1.65	2.0

Sources: (1) Kay 1998; (2) Thiesenhusen 1989: 10–11; (3) Kay 1998; (4) de Janvry 1981: 206; (5) Thiesenhusen 1989: 10–11; (6) Zevallos 1989: 52; (7) Paige 1996: 136; (8) Paige 1996: 136, Dorner 1992: 48; (9) Paige 1996: 136; (10) South Africa Department of Land Affairs 2000; (11) Griffin, Kahn, and Ickowitz 2002: 304–305; (12) King 1977 (Taiwan, 192; Egypt, 329; Syria, 390); (13) El-Ghonemy 1990: 283; (14) Borras 2004a.

[a]Percentage of total agricultural land

[b]Percentage of agricultural HHs

opment, or have at least performed better in poverty eradication, than those countries (or subnational regions) that have had a lower or negligible degree of land redistribution. This is demonstrated, for example, in the cases of Japan, South Korea, and China, where national development achievements have been phenomenal after land reforms (Stiglitz 2002, 81; Griffin, Kahn, and Ickowitz 2002); Kerala and Cuba, where the degree of poverty eradication and broad-based human development has been exceptionally high (Herring 1983; Deere 2000); and Chile, where the contemporary vibrant fruit-exporting sector traces it foundations, in part, to earlier land reforms (Kay 2002a).

Finally, most of the relatively successful national agricultural and rural development initiatives that have been undertaken post-land reform have tended to be ones that were carried out within inward-looking, state-led development policies, especially during the import-substitution industrialization era. Japan, South Korea, Taiwan, China, Kerala, Vietnam, and Cuba are a few examples (Kay 2002b).[25] Yet, despite these cases, the MLAR critique continues to attract attention and to command the heart of the debate. It is therefore worth looking specifically at the MLAR claims against SLAR, in order to question the integrity of these claims. The following section will discuss in depth ten MLAR objections to SLAR.

1. One of the main causes of SLAR failure is its land acquisition method: it is expropriative and coercive. Given this, compensation to landlords via cash and bonds payments for land expropriated at below market price level is a veneer for confiscation that provokes and promotes landlord opposition to reform.

It is true that most SLARs have, to varying degrees, been coercive and have usually paid landlords below-market rates for their land. These policy features have direct influence on the chances of success or failure of a land redistribution campaign, but not in the way the promarket critique would suggest. Most land reform policies have had varying degrees of expropriative powers, but even revolutionary policies have made selective compromises, for example, in Nicaragua in the 1980s. Conservative policies have themselves possessed some elements of expropriation, even when selective and limited; the Marcos land reform in the Philippines in the 1970s is one such example (see Kerkvliet 1979; Wurfel 1988).

This conceptual clarification is crucial in understanding the flaw of the promarket argument: empirical evidence in many countries shows that land reform policies with fewer expropriative and coercive powers have delivered lower degrees of land redistribution outcomes. In other words, administrations that have opted for more expropriative powers have tended to accomplish greater degree of land redistribution than administrations that have opted to minimize use of state coercion.

This equation can be seen in the varying land redistribution outcomes among and within countries. There is, for example, a lower degree of land redistribution in contemporary South Africa (Lahiff 2003) than in contemporary Brazil (Guanzirole 2000); a lower degree in contemporary Brazil than in the current Philippine experience (Borras 2001, 2004a,); a lower degree in revolutionary Nicaragua (Thiesenhusen 1995) than in revolutionary China (Griffin, Khan, and Ickowitz 2002); a higher degree during the 1930s in

Mexico under Lazaro Cardenas than accomplished under subsequent administrations since the 1940s (Sanderson 1984); a lower degree during the Frei era than in the Allende period in Chile (Kay and Silva 1992; Thome 1989, 159); and a lower degree during the Macapagal-Arroyo presidency (2000–2004) than during the Ramos administration (1992–1998) in the Philippines (Franco and Borras 2005).

The presence of evasive and subversive actions of landlords against a land reform policy is a good indicator of the degree of real redistributive reform character of the policy. Redistributive reforms "change the relative shares between groups" (Fox 1993, 10). As Diskin, speaking of El Salvador, explained: ". . . it would be naive to assume that those who monopolize power and land will simply step aside and divest themselves of their wealth and social position. The Salvadoran rural oligarchy regularly advocates a 'trickle-down' argument while lobbying for less 'statism,' that is, less reform" (1989, 431). Thus, landlord resistance is not unexpected. The cases of SLAR with higher degrees of success have demonstrated that the key challenge is not to look for reform models that will be unopposed by landlords—but rather to find ways to defeat landlord opposition.

The promarket model assumes that a land acquisition method that is voluntary and that provides a 100 percent cash payment to landlords for 100 percent market value of their land will lead to successful land reform. But when understood as power redistribution, "land redistribution" and "voluntary policy" become inherently contradictory terms. Landlords are unlikely to voluntarily cede power in favor of traditionally powerless peasants, despite attractive monetary valuation of their estate. Continued control of their farms not only means material wealth for landlords, it also provides political power, captive votes during elections, access to broader political networks, and social prestige, among other benefits. In the Philippines, cases of "voluntary" land transfer (VLT) transactions have demonstrated faked land redistribution involving "on-paper sales," "on-paper beneficiaries," and peasants who were coerced to "voluntarily" agree to a landlord's evasive scheme (Borras 2005; Franco 2005). In fact, the biggest landlords in that country are now using VLT as a way to effectively evade the land reform law in a larger scale.[26]

Pro-MLAR scholars may argue that the problem with the Philippine VLT lies with the ongoing, parallel state-led expropriation and not with VLT itself. Yet elsewhere antireform maneuvers made by landlords through market-based land transfer schemes have occurred both in settings with ongoing, parallel state-led expropriation programs, for example, in Brazil; and where there are none, for example, in Colombia and South Africa. Landlords in Brazil, Colombia, and South Africa have warmly received MLAR (Navarro 1998; Deininger 1999), just as VLT was welcomed by Philippine landlords. In Brazil, Colombia, and South Africa, the main antireform maneuver employed by landlords within the context of market-led approach was to overprice excess marginal lands and sell them to the program.[27]

2. SLAR's so-called supply-driven approach is responsible for bringing in unsuitable beneficiaries and land into the reform, leading to greater inefficiency in land use and a "dole-out" mentality among beneficiaries.

This assertion is theoretically problematic and empirically unsound. It is analytically in conflict with the political-economic and "social justice" conception of redistributive land reform as the redistribution of land from landowning to landless and near-landless people. A policy does not constitute real redistributive reform when the change in ownership and control over land resources occurs within elite classes (landowning or not). Meanwhile, the notion of demand, or articulated or effective demand, among landless peasants has to be perceived as problematic. Effective articulation of demand for land by landless peasants is mediated by a range of factors within the rural political economy (see Fox 1994, 1995; Platteau 1995). It is certainly shaped by existing power relations between different classes in the countryside. On many occasions, landless peasants are coerced, repressed, or tricked by the landowning classes into not articulating their demand for land.[28] Historically, articulated demands for land have either been made by autonomous peasants and peasant movements and their allies (political parties, working classes, middle classes, the church), or, in a different context, by landlords and their co-opted peasants and peasant groups to stage-manage partial or even fake reforms (Borras 2005).

The promarket notion of taking in only the fittest beneficiaries—i.e., the most economically efficient and financially competitive peasants—is diametrically opposed to the fundamental notion of redistributive land reform, which has been conceptualized precisely because of the need to create a class of efficient and competitive peasants (and/or rural proletariat), one requirement of which is the control over land resources by the actual tillers and workers, facilitated through land reform (see Lipton 1974; Byres 1974). But landless and near-landless rural poor are, compared with their richer, better resourced, and more experienced counterparts, inefficient and uncompetitive precisely because they have no control over land. Such property-based deprivation breeds greater disadvantages, such as social exclusion, political disempowerment, and a lack of formal education, all of which contribute to and perpetuate economic inefficiency and financial noncompetitiveness.

Consider, for example, the South African context: how can the black landless rural poor be more economically efficient and competitive than the white commercial farmers when the former, reduced to the status of destitute (semi-) proletarians, have been denied, by decades of apartheid and centuries of colonialism, the right to farm their own land with proper support services? (See Bernstein 1998; Levin and Weiner 1997.) Or, to take another example, how can the landless semi-proletariat Muslims in the island of Basilan (Philippines) be more efficient and competitive in running rubber plantations than the settler-Christian farmworkers, when the former have generally never worked in such plantations, and have been evicted from their homelands by agribusiness corporations to clear the area for plantation development?[29] In short, the idea of "fittest beneficiaries who are economically efficient and competitive" in the promarket critique exposes the latter's non-redistributive character.

On the issue of unfit lands being redistributed, two interrelated points need clarification. First, numerous SLARs have redistributed productive farmlands under the control of big landlords precisely because it is in these big estates where injustice and exploitation—notions that mainstream economists tend to downplay—were prevalent. Redistribution of these big landholdings to landless peasants has not always resulted in economic inefficiency; in fact, on many occasions, quite the contrary has been the case.[30] Second, many SLARs have redistributed unproductive and environmentally fragile lands such as those, on some occasions, in Brazil and Colombia (Thiesenhusen 1989, 1995; Feder 1970). When these did occur, it was precisely and usually in settings where redistribution of privately controlled productive lands was not being carried out by the state, making the chances of land claims by landless people on ecologically fragile public lands more likely to succeed, and prompting governments to formalize such peasant land claims in some cases (see Dorner 1992, 2001). In short, it is the failure of states to implement SLAR of productive farmlands in some countries, and not SLAR per se, that has caused ecologically fragile lands to be redistributed to poor peasants.

The promarket model assumes that demand-driven self-selection will ensure proper "beneficiary" targeting. This self-selection principle fits well with that of the voluntary land transfer (VLT) scheme in the Philippines; that is, total acceptability of the set of beneficiaries by the landlords who are supposedly volunteering their land for land reform. The net result produces types of beneficiaries such as those described earlier: fake beneficiaries or peasants coerced to become beneficiaries in landlord schemes to evade land reform (Borras 2005). Thus, on many occasions, it is possible that demand from the side of the rural poor is staged, instigated, distorted, coerced, or concocted by antireform actors.

In many agrarian societies, the effective articulation of demands by poor, landless peasants is constrained or facilitated by contending class forces in perpetual political conflict (see Fox 1994). Moreover, some demands articulated by autonomous peasant groups might be hidden or excluded from the mainstream policy discourse. This happened in the case of permanent and seasonal farmworkers on big plantations in the Philippines, where farmworkers who asserted their right to autonomous organization were purged by the landlord or company from the land reform scheme (Borras and Franco 2005; Franco 2005). Such problems have likewise plagued the MLAR program in Colombia, as admitted by Deininger (1999).[31] This occurred to a significant extent in Brazil (Navarro 1998) and South Africa (Deininger and May 2000).

3. SLAR has been state-centralized, and so has been slow, if not totally flawed, in implementation.

To a large extent, it is true that many of the SLARs that have actually existed have been state-centralized—but with a contrary outcome: land reform campaigns that have had higher degree of land redistribution have tended to be the ones in which the central state played an active role in vastly centralized manner (Barraclough 2001; El-Ghonemy 2001), cognizant of the fact that to decentralize responsibility for land reform would be to put the land reform agenda into the hands of those who are most opposed to it, as landlords tend to dominate the local state apparatus.[32] This recognition is not the monopoly of socialist regimes. Many of the most enduringly successful land reforms have been state centered, for example, those in Japan, South Korea, Taiwan (Tai 1974; Griffin, Khan, and Ickowitz 2002; King 1977); in Peru in late 1960s and early 1970s (Kay 1983); and in Egypt in the 1950s and early 1960s (Migdal 1988). In contrast, SLARs with a lower degree of success in land redistribution have been ones in which the state has had a low degree of political autonomy and a smaller capacity to carry out a truly sweeping redistributive land reform.

Many SLAR policies when implemented have taken a more dynamic view of state-society interaction. These interactions have been relatively less state-centered and centralized, and more dynamic and polycentric—as the pro-reform forces within the state and in society asserted and assumed greater roles in actually interpreting and implementing the land reform law (Houtzager and Franco 2003; Franco 2005). Some examples of this are Mexico during the Cardenas period,[33] Niger (Lund 1998), and contemporary Philippines between 1992 and 2000 (Borras 2001). Even those regimes generally perceived to be highly centralized have in fact depended upon their coalition with pro-reform societal forces, such as in revolutionary China (Shillinglaw 1974).

It is the assumption of the neoliberal land policy model that a privatized-decentralized implementation approach to land reform will lead to a greater degree of accountability and transparency in policy implementation. While this may be correct at the most abstract level, the idea ignores empirical and political realities. Evidence in the Philippines, for example, shows that some local government officials have indeed provided information for the land reform process, but in favor of landlords and other elite players rather than the poor, landless peasants. In some cases local officials have either coached landlords on ways to use the voluntary land transfer (VLT) scheme to evade expropriation, or have assisted in forging partnerships, between landowners and multinational companies, that involved market-friendly land transfer schemes that have essentially undermined land reform. In return, these officials have gained favor, either becoming listed as beneficiaries in the land transfer fraud or collecting finder's fees from companies, or both.

Moreover, the voluntary land transfer scheme has been carried out most extensively by government officials in provinces where the presence of autonomous NGOs and peasant organizations is thin and weak. As such, corrupt practices are unlikely to be closely checked (Borras 2005). In Brazil and Colombia, local government officials have also taken control of various aspects of MLAR programs in ways not always beneficial to poor peasants, from information manipulation and the selection of buyers, to land pricing (Navarro 1998; Buainain et al., 1999). These outcomes run counter to MLAR's theoretical predictions.

4. SLAR implementation has been protracted and legally contentious.

SLAR is concerned with redistributing property rights and political power in society, and, therefore, it changes the relative shares between groups (Fox 1993, 10). It is to be expected that this process will be legally and politically contentious. Land reform policies that have not been not legally and politically contentious have tended to be nonredistributive, conservative, or less redistributive. SLAR has not, however, necessarily been protracted in its implementation. In fact, the more successful land reforms have been done swiftly (Prosterman and Riedinger 1987), as in Japan, South Korea, and Taiwan

(Griffin, Khan, and Ickowitz 2002), Kerala (Herring 1983), and China (Shillinglaw 1974). Putzel (2002) and Bernstein (2002) remind us, however, that such land redistribution campaigns must be viewed from a perspective of "episodes" within a more strategic, longer continuum of policy implementation. This is partly illustrated in Mexico during the sweeping implementation in the 1930s under the Cardenas period, and again in the 1960s in the northern part of Mexico (Sanderson 1984; but see Harvey 1998, 131).

Furthermore, SLARs that have been slower and narrower in implementation are ones that have provided significant roles to nonstate market mechanisms. An example of this is the commercial reselling of "friar lands" in the early twentieth century Philippines (Corpuz 1997, 266–70; also Kerkvliet 1977, 198–99), and even in the contemporary Philippines, where built-in market-friendly mechanisms such as the voluntary land transfer and stock distribution schemes have opened up highways through which landlords have launched antireform maneuvers (Putzel 1992; Borras, Reyes, and Carranza, 2005). This is also true of the Alessandri and Frei periods in the 1960s Chile (Thome 1989); in Zimbabwe between 1980 and the early 1990s (Moyo 2000, Bratton 1990; see Worby 2001); of the coffee sector in the El Salvadoran land reform (Paige 1996); and in Chiapas, through the agrarian rehabilitation program (PRA) that was started in the early 1980s (Harvey 1998, 153–54; see also Bobrow-Strain 2004).

5. Prices of land redistributed under SLAR are high and are more expensive than if transacted in the open market.

This argument contradicts the first promarket critique about expropriation and and is a "thin veil" for confiscation. Some land reforms have confiscated lands and redistributed them for free to peasants, although most have paid the landlords a below-market price. In general, SLAR that has actually existed has underpaid landlords for the lands.[34] Certainly, there have been some cases of overpricing, and these are of two broad types: One is the work of corrupt government officials (see, for example, Putzel [1992, 363], for the cases in the Philippines), but this is not an inherent or dominant feature of SLAR, as shown by most other positive country cases. The other is what has proved to be more expensive and pervasive: the lands covered under market-friendly mechanisms that have allowed landlords to overprice lands. There are several examples of this: market-friendly schemes under the Alessandri and Frei administrations in Chile in the 1960s (Thome 1989); lands by the monarchy confiscated after the 1789 revolution in France but then resold at full cost, totally unaffordable to poor peasants (Tuma 1965; Moore 1967; Jones 1991);

the 1903 case of friar lands in the Philippines (Corpuz 1997, 266–70; and Kerkvliet 1977, 198–99). Nevertheless—and arguably—the notion of over-pricing is inherently "economistic" and is fundamentally at odds with the con-cept of land having multidimensional character. That is, if a land's value has political, social, economic, and cultural dimensions, then the notion of over-pricing cannot and must not be reduced to the narrow "economistic" per-spective (Borras 2004a).

Evidence shows that, under certain circumstances, land prices in fact depend not on some "politically neutral" technical mechanisms in land valu-ation and payment schemes, but more on landlords' political-economic inter-est and power to perpetuate ownership of and/or control over land. Hence, the issue is not one of pricing, in solely monetary terms, and is not so much about free markets but very much about power and power relations, confirming the multidimensional function of land. In the Philippines, some big landlords have supposedly sold their lands through the voluntary land transfer scheme at prices that are many times lower than the court-declared prices; some have even given their lands for "free." Thus, on some occasions, monetary prices are inconsequential to the voluntary land transfer scheme precisely because the scheme itself is an ersatz land reform process. Still, it is convenient for landlords to declare reasonable price levels, so as not to attract critical atten-tion to the fraud. Without such attention, the evasion process can be con-summated at once through a cash-based transaction (Borras 2004a). In Brazil and Colombia, the MLAR mode of land valuation and payment to landlords has led to highly overpriced marginal lands. In Brazil, some lands sold through MLAR programs have been 30 to 50 percent more expensive than lands (with comparable features) sold through the state-led land reform (Groppo et al. 1998); overpricing was worse in Colombia (see Deininger 1999; Forero 1999).

6. SLAR undermines the land market.

Land markets in most developing countries are (already) distorted in one way or another, and these distortions are principally caused by preexisting land monopolies. The secondary (and temporary) cause of land market distortion stems from existing land sales and rental prohibitions within land reform laws. Perfect land markets—the heart of the MLAR theoretical model, supposedly toward achieving land reform—cannot emerge and function without real prior redistribution that would effect a more egalitarian distribution of property rights over land resources.[35] Already-distorted land markets have been exac-erbated not by SLAR but by market-friendly mechanisms. Such cases of

MLAR implementation can be found in northeast Brazil (Groppo et al. 1998; Sauer 2003), South Africa, Colombia (Borras 2003c; Mondragón 2003), or in the implementation of the voluntary land transfer scheme within the current Philippine land reform program (see Putzel 2002; Franco 2005). But again, there is an inherent tension between the concept of land as having multi-dimensional character and the economistic notion of land market. In fact, "distortion" is a relative concept: for economistic, promarket scholars, distortion occurs due to state regulations; for the advocates of the concept of land as having multidimensional character, distortion occurs due to an unregulated monopolistic land market that is controlled and manipulated by the landowning classes.

7. SLAR's sequence of farm plans and development after land redistribution has caused the failure of agrarian reform in particular and the agriculture sector in general; supply-driven, state-centralized extension services have been inefficient — contributing further to SLAR's failure.

Most SLAR has been implemented in the order of land redistribution first, with farm plans following after. To claim that this is the cause of failure in farm and agricultural development, however, is to lead the debate astray. While land redistribution is a necessary factor for rural development, it is never the sole one. There are many more factors at play.[36] SLAR that has carried out such a sequential approach has produced mixed results: a higher but varying degree of agricultural and national development, such as those in Japan, South Korea, Taiwan, China, and Kerala (Griffin, Khan, and Ickowitz 2002; Kay 2002b); or lower but varying degrees of agricultural development, such as the case in contemporary Philippines.[37] There is no empirical evidence that this sequential approach is the culprit in the lackluster performance in post–land transfer agricultural development in some countries.

The notion that farm plans must come before land redistribution is used by antireform landlords. Where this rhetoric has been successful in influencing government policy, land reform and agricultural development have tended to slow down, such as in the Philippines since the late 1990s (Borras, Reyes, and Carranza 2005) and postapartheid South Africa (see Lahiff 2003; Lahiff and Cousins 2001). Finally, there is no empirical basis for the promarket claim that the supply-driven and state-centralized character of most extension services has contributed to SLAR's failure (when and where failure did occur) to effect rural development. The debate in this regard goes far beyond the issue of agrarian reform into the broader issues of micro- and macroeconomic and industrialization policies (Lehmann 1974) — and the empirical evidence does not always support promarket arguments and claims (see, for example, Spoor 2002; Kay 2002b; Saith 1990).

8. SLAR has drained credit from the rural economy and driven investors away.

The claim that investors are driven away by SLAR is not supported by empirical evidence from most of the countries that have undergone a significant degree of land redistribution, such as Japan, Taiwan, South Korea, Kerala, Chile, and contemporary Philippines. The logic of capital dictates that credit and capital will go where it can make profit—it can be in either the (land) reform or nonreform sector. The same logic governs investment dynamics. In fact, empirical evidence shows that public and private investments have come to land reform areas—and that new investments have come not only from traditional elites or government, but, more importantly, from peasant beneficiaries (see, for example, Franco 1999, for recent Philippine cases).

It is true, as predicted by MLAR, that voluntary land transfers do not drive away landlord-based investments and credit; they even attract fresh inflows. The critical question is, who actually benefits from the maintenance and fresh inflow of investments and credit? This same question is posed regarding the issue of privatized-decentralized extension services. In the cases presented here, the investors and landlords have benefited much more than the poor beneficiaries. In cases in Brazil, Colombia, and South Africa, evidence shows that because lands sold under programs there were marginal and located in remote places, credit and investments were unlikely to be forthcoming.[38] It has since become clear that, as in the Philippines, in the few cases in which external investors did come in on redistributed farms in South Africa, beneficiaries needed urgent protection against antireform manipulation by the investors (see Deininger and May 2000). The broader literature on the "contract growing scheme" has already pointed out the onerous terms of these contracts in different settings (see, for example, Watts 1994; White 1997).

9. SLAR's funding mechanism in the form of "universal subsidy" is wasteful and cultivates a "dole-out" mentality among peasant beneficiaries.

From among the spectrum of public investments, subsidizing poor peasants' ability to secure property rights over land resources and corollary extension services by way of funding land reform has perhaps been one of the most useful, not wasteful, kinds of investment (see, for example, Herring 1990, 73). A more egalitarian distribution of control over land resources and access to extension services have been crucial ingredients to several agricultural and national development campaigns. This is true in countries without a history of a significant degree of land monopoly before their national development, such as the United States (except its southern portion [see Byres 1996]), and Argentina, or in countries with significant degree of land redistribution before accomplishing national development such as Japan, South Korea, Taiwan immediately after World War II, Vietnam since 1975 (Griffin, Khan, and Ickowitz 2002), and Cuba (Deere 2000). The investments made by states in these countries in the form of universal subsidies to poor peasants have been extremely useful and productive (Kay 2002b).

There is no consensus in the literature as to whether so-called repayment default by peasants on their loan obligations from land redistribution programs or extension services constitutes a phenomenon of dole-out mentality. This may be an issue that needs deeper empirical investigation aimed at moving the analysis beyond mere assertions (by the promarket critique). As it happens, MLAR in Brazil and Colombia has been plagued by the same phenomenon (see Sauer 2003). Finally, targeted public spending via market-friendly land redistribution mechanisms based on commercial land sales turns out, in fact, to subsidize landlords and penalize poor peasants and the public. In other words, it is a way of promoting a dole-out mentality among landlords. This is seen in many cases of commercial land sales that have been passed off as land reforms, either through the MLAR programs, or through MLAR-like mechanisms such as the Philippine VLT.

10. SLAR's financial cost is high and unaffordable.

It is true that land reform programs require significant public spending, especially when these involve the expropriation of highly productive farms. When viewed from the perspective of strategic public investment, however, such spending can be reasonable and affordable (Herring 1990, 73). It must also be noted that, historically, the more expropriative the land reform policy, the less expensive it has become. Conversely, the more market friendly it was, the more expensive it has turned out to be. This can be seen partly by comparing cases within nations, such as the cases of the Frei and Allende land reforms in Chile in the 1960s and 1970s, respectively (Thome 1989), or the state-led national land reform versus the market-based PCT project in Brazil;[39] as well, this can be seen in a comparison of countries, such as China and the Philippines.[40]

Major state-led land reform campaigns proved financially affordable even in circumstances marked by fiscal difficulty, such as in revolutionary China (Shillinglaw 1974), Nicaragua (Collins, Lappé, and Allen 1982), Chile (Thome

1989), and Kerala (Herring 1983). In contrast, even less dramatic market-friendly land reform initiatives proved financially unaffordable, such as in contemporary South Africa and Colombia (Borras 2003b).

The MLAR's underlying motivation of reducing public spending appears to be more urgent than its interest in having government to carry out redistributive reform. For example, using the same MLAR argument, the Macapagal-Arroyo administration in the Philippines announced in early 2002 its adoption of the voluntary land transfer scheme as the main strategy for land reform.[41] The administration has been candid enough to admit that the choice for this type of scheme was driven by the desire to cut down government spending. And, while President Arroyo admitted that she never asked congress for any money for land reform, she and her key cabinet officials were particularly excited about the voluntary schemes (Borras 2005). Moreover, beginning in 2004, the Philippine congress has been deliberating on the passage of a new law that would dilute the land reform policy by removing the land sales and rental prohibitions, making land titles tradable legal instruments (allowing, for example, the immediate use of an agrarian reform land title as collateral for commercial bank loans). Therefore, for governments pressed by international financial institutions to cut back public spending, MLAR and its variants seem an attractive option and a convenient means to effectively drop redistributive land reform from the policy agenda.

The choice by the ANC government of South Africa to take on the World Bank–proposed land reform policy was made amid pressures from international financial institutions to minimize state expenditures, among other considerations (see Levin and Weiner 1997). The same pressures more or less pushed the Brazilian and Colombian governments to agree to pilot test the World Bank's policy model, and caused the subsequent program expansion during the Lula administration (Deere and Medeiros 2005). The financial consideration, not the aspiration for redistributive reform, has become the starting point of MLAR, as shown in the Philippines, Brazil, Colombia, and South Africa.

The ten-point discussion above has addressed the crucial issues of the pro-market critique of SLAR. But the promarket critique of SLAR misses valuable insights that motivated SLAR in its original context, and conflates SLAR failures with other political problems. We can group these omissions and distortions into three categories. First, the promarket critique ignores SLAR's basis in broad theoretical, policy, and political frameworks:

- In general, SLAR has been conceived based on a political-economic perspective of agrarian structure, where power and power relations between different social classes within the state and in society are at the center of the push toward, or the pull away from, a more egalitarian distribution of property rights over land resources. Instead of confronting SLAR within the political-economic framework, the promarket critique limits its analysis to a purely economic perspective, neglecting the questions of power relations between inherently antagonistic social classes.

- SLAR has always been developed within a domestic historical perspective, with the view of attempting to correct historical injustice committed against landless peasants. Instead of addressing SLAR within such social justice context, the promarket critique centers its analysis on a generally ahistorical view of the problem of landlessness and limits its concerns to the issue of economic efficiency today. For MLAR, history has ended, despite all evidence to the contrary.

- SLAR has always treated land as having a multidimensional character (socioeconomic, political, and cultural); the promarket critique ignores such a view about land, and instead puts forward a critique of SLAR that is based solely on the assumption that land is merely a factor of economic production.[42]

Second, while the promarket critique does not include in its analysis several significant aspects of SLAR, it does include several analytic issues that are not, strictly speaking, inherent components of SLAR. For example, the promarket critique repeatedly hammers SLAR on the basis that the latter has failed to effect rural development and poverty eradication, despite the fact that past and present proponents of SLAR have repeatedly clarified that while SLAR is a necessary requirement in the development process, it cannot by itself solve all rural problems; SLAR is not a panacea to rural socioeconomic ills. This earlier clarification is captured in Keith Griffin's explanation: "A land reform, in isolation, is not sufficient to remove rural poverty, but it is a *conditio sine qua non* in many countries. Unfortunately, it is a necessary step that is difficult to implement; there are no easy or painless solutions to the problems of poverty and underdevelopment, and it would be disingenuous to pretend otherwise." Griffin concludes: "On the other hand, to refrain from making the effort on grounds of political impossibility would be defeatist as well as historically inaccurate" (1976, 10).

Third, the promarket critique presents and analyzes SLAR as if reform were a singular, homogeneous theoretical construct and policy model: MLAR is indeed homogenous, depending precisely on a single set of standard policies and insights. But SLAR is not homogenous: it has multiple theoretical-ideological conceptions, policy designs, and actual practices—broadly categorized in its ideal typical types, namely, revolutionary, conservative, and liberal, and socialist- or capitalist-oriented.[43] Moreover, most SLARs have varying degrees of market-oriented mechanisms within them. A simplistic, undifferentiated view of SLAR is thus not useful.[44]

Conclusion

Redistribution of wealth and power from the landed elite to landless and near-landless people is the essence of land reform. For private lands, the MLAR land transfer scheme requires 100 percent spot cash payment to the landlord for 100 percent value of the land, and requires 100 percent of this cost (plus the transaction cost) to be shouldered fully by the buyer. MLAR proponents claim a bias in favor of the poor, but the theoretical and operational assumptions of the policy model tend to contradict this. Thus, arguably, even within its strictly economistic perspective about land, redistribution of wealth is absent in MLAR. "Exchange" of goods in the market between sellers and buyers is not the same as, nor does it necessarily constitute, redistribution of wealth and power.

Furthermore, evidence from the Philippines has contradicted most MLAR predictions. The policy outcomes in that country are broadly similar to the MLAR experiences in Brazil, Colombia, and South Africa. In Brazil and Colombia, MLAR was found to have facilitated land transfers that have not been redistributive, thus undermining potentially redistributive state-led land reform. In South Africa, MLAR has blocked the chances of a more radical exispropriative redistributive land reform being enacted into law. Meanwhile, privatization and individualization of landed property rights in public/communal lands and state/collective farms have resulted in variegated outcomes, but they are almost always unfavorable with regard to the rural poor. This is true in both (ex-)socialist and capitalist settings.

In closing, this chapter has demonstrated that the promarket critique of state-led agrarian reform, and the subsequent promarket land policies promoted to repeal the conventional policies, are theoretically and empirically problematic. In the context of the ongoing debate, the most crucial promarket assumption is the so-called failure of SLAR to redistribute lands and effect rural development and poverty alleviation; this assumption is not supported by empirical evidence. Meanwhile, predicted pro-poor outcomes of neoliberal land policies have, to a large extent, failed to materialize. This is not to claim that conventional land policies have been flawless. The conventional land policies have major problems in theory and practice, and many of these issues have been correctly raised in nuanced analyses put forward by critical thinkers.[45] Yet these failures ought not to be allowed to overshadow successes, or to sanction a mode of land reform that seeks to achieve legitimacy through the rewriting of history, despite its own disastrous outcomes.

CHAPTER 6

Thailand's Land Titling Program: Securing Land for the Poor?

Rebeca Leonard and Kingkorn Narintarakul Na Ayutthaya

The World Bank's land titling program in Thailand was one of the largest land titling programs in the world. The Bank has praised itself in several of its own reports[1] for what it sees as the success of the program, which has subsequently served as model for Bank programs in other countries in the region (for example, in Indonesia, Lao PDR, and the Philippines) and around the world. We will examine the scope of this program's success, with emphasis on its impact on poverty in northern Thailand.

Access to Land for the Poorest Rural Communities

Access to land is fundamental to the livelihoods of poor communities in rural areas. Land continues to be a means of providing subsistence needs as well as income generation. Holding land enables family labor to be put to productive use and provides a safety net for family members who work in temporary or insecure employment elsewhere. This scenario was particularly evident in Thailand during an economic collapse in 1997, when the sudden threefold rise in urban unemployment was mitigated by the absorption of labor by rural areas. Agriculture is still an important sector of the Thai economy employing approximately 54 percent of the workforce (out of a total workforce of 33.4 million people).[2] The poorest sectors of Thai society are households in rural areas without land or with very meager land assets (that is, with limited areas and poor-quality soils). Thailand's Office of Agricultural Economics estimated in 1995 that the income of the population working in agriculture was approximately fifteen times lower than the income of the population outside the

TABLE 6.1 Distribution of landholding in Thailand

	Farming households				
Region	Without land	Less than 0.8 hectares	0.8–1.6 hectares	Over 1.6 hectares	Total
North	181,125	290,695	275,248	866,602	1,613,670
Northeast	107,556	116,910	202,089	1,821,566	2,255,124
Central	168,992	74,694	79,295	780,537	1,073,518
South	27,146	83,497	91,428	439,436	641,507
TOTAL	454,819	565,799	658,060	3,908,141	5,586,819

agricultural sector. It was also found that the national average household income in 1999 was 12,729 Baht (US$318) per month, whereas the average income for farming households was no higher than 1,000 Baht (US$24) per month (Office of Agricultural Economics 1999 in Bamford 2000). Land also continues to provide important social functions such as identification with family roots and cultural and community identity.

The Land Institute Foundation, an independent Thai research organization, has estimated that over 30 percent of the 5.5 million households in the agricultural sector have insufficient land from which to derive a livelihood. In the northern region, this is considered to be less than 10 râi (6.25 râi = 1 hectare) or about 1.6 hectares (see table 6.1). The number of people without land has increased in recent decades, not only due to population increase but to a range of other factors. These include the somewhat artificial classification, in the 1960s, of 50 percent of the country as national state forest, an estimate that included areas that had been used for agriculture prior to classification. Large areas of agricultural land have also been bought up or kept out of production. This was particularly evident during the high economic growth years of the late 1980s and early 1990s, when investors began to acquire land on a massive scale, speculating on rising land prices. The Land Institute Foundation has estimated that the annual economic cost of underutilized land (including that in urban areas) to the country is approximately 127.4 million Baht (approximately US$3 billion) (Land Institute Foundation 2000).

Much of this land was used by landlords as collateral to borrow huge sums that were never repaid. Figures from the Bank of Thailand reveal that the total value of nonperforming loans (NPLs) could be as high as 2.92 trillion Baht (approximately US$68 billion) over the period 1997–2000. The majority of these loans were in the real estate sector (Land Institute Foundation 2000, 6–31). As a reaction to the unfolding economic crisis in 1997, the Thai government was compelled to bail out creditors holding bad debt (especially that owed in foreign currency) under the conditions of emergency IMF loans. Thus the costs of imprudent private lending were transferred onto taxpayers throughout the country.

The World Bank's Land Titling Program in Thailand

The land titling program originated in the early 1980s, in discussions between the Thai government and the agricultural sector of the World Bank about a structural adjustment loan. The program was divided into four aims or phases: (1) "to accelerate the issuance of title deeds to eligible landholders"; (2) "to improve the effectiveness of land administration, both in Bangkok and in the provinces"; (3) "to produce base maps and cadastral maps in both urban and rural areas on one homogeneous mapping system, and showing all land parcels"; and (4) "to improve the efficiency of the Central Valuation Authority." Authorized by the government on September 22, 1994, the objectives of phase three were adjusted to "provide secure land tenure to eligible landowners," "develop long term sustainability of the Department of Lands' (DoL) institutional capacity," "improve land administration service delivery," and "develop an effective national property valuation function." Phase four of the program is yet to begin implementation.[3]

Overall, US$183.1 million was loaned by the World Bank to cover the three initial phases of the project. To date, 8.7 million land titles have been issued. This is a substantial number, despite being less than the number of titles targeted by the program. However, as will be demonstrated, this figure can be misleading and should not be taken as evidence that 8.7 million farmers have benefited. Notably, the program did not set targets for the number of beneficiaries.

Essentially, the program was aimed at the acceleration of the land titling process. Thailand's land code of 1954 required individuals to present at the very least an occupancy certificate (*Bai Yeub Yam*) to acquire a land title deed. The land titling program amended the land code to remove this requirement and quicken the official process to approve land title deeds. "The DoL was hard pressed to meet the demand for land records in the form of land use certificates, title deeds and property maps. . . . [At] the rate in which title deeds had been produced since DoL was established in 1901, and with current resources, the DoL would take 200 years to complete the registration of rights in land throughout Thailand. Even with a proposal to expedite the surveying and mapping in support of land registration, the time estimate was still 85 years." (Rattanabirabongse et al. 1998).

As the titling process was not simply a matter of clarification of land rights, but a platform for the establishment of a land market, it was regarded as important that a uniform register providing complete coverage be established. "The purpose of a land registry is to provide an authoritative record of the status of landownership. It is therefore essential that this institution be complete and define unambiguously the status of individual parcels. The ensuing desire to establish a unified framework that covers both rural and urban areas has been a main reason for most of the Bank's land administration projects to adopt programmatic approaches that would accomplish the overall objective in phases." (World Bank, n.d., 11). Given the perceived urgency to achieve complete coverage, changes were made to the national code in order to make the titling process easier. Thus, the land code was modified to allow the NS3K (*Nor Sor Saam Kor*) certificates of use to be upgraded to full title deed NS4 (*Nor Sor Sii*) on request, without a field survey. The land code also allows full land title to be issued when there are no documents of occupancy or land claim reservation certificates.

While applicants should have had possession of the land prior to the time the code came into force, minimal proof to support such a claim is required by local Department of Lands officials. Most official project documents highlight the safeguards designed into the survey and titling process, such as thirty-day prior and subsequent notice posted at the house of the village head, as well as at various relevant land offices. Another change to the law involved the replacement of the provincial governor as the authorizing officer on title deeds with the provincial land officer or branch office head. According to an internal review of the program, this change in the law was a "bold step perhaps, but necessary to complete the project in twenty years" (Rattanabirabongse et al. 1998). However, by allowing for faster processing of land titling applications, the authorities provided an ideal opportunity for investors and state officials to abuse the system, particularly during the high economic growth period.

Important Omissions in the Land Titling Program

While aimed at increasing land tenure security for existing landholders, the land titling program did not attempt to address two critical issues of importance to low-income farming groups in Thailand. The first was the issue of forest tenure. The Thai land titling program dealt exclusively with "nonforest lands." This is because all lands designated as forest are considered to be state property, whether or not communities have been living and farming in those areas for several generations. The state was ostensibly reluctant to offer secure rights for fear of legalizing forest destruction. Consequently, some of the poorest farming groups in the country, including Thai farmers and ethnic minority groups who occupy forests, especially in the highland areas, have been left in a precarious legal position.[4] They continue to be threatened with eviction or forced restriction of their agricultural practices, and are harassed by officials. This prolongs the opportunity for politicians to cast ethnic minorities as scapegoats for all manner of national problems. The land titling program did not seize the chance to regularize the land rights of this large group of people, many of whom have occupied their village lands for hundreds of years.

A second important omission was that no provision was made in the planning or preparation of the project for the recognition or registration of rights to village commons, or common property resources. The land titling program was aimed at the registration of existing land rights in order to give them validity under the national legal framework. However, the only registration option available was that of individual rights. While, in theory, local tenure systems that recognize common rights to community resources could continue to exist extralegally as before, the legalization of individual rights alone allows for the possibility that common rights lose their legitimacy, leading to the breakup of community-based resource management systems. It was foreseeable that some, if not all, common lands would be appropriated under individual claims. Without protection from misappropriation, this possibility was acted on by both powerful insiders and outsiders to the community. As the case studies from Lamphun province in the following section illustrate, many false claims of individual ownership of commonly held land were made with minimal notice to local communities and with little bureaucratic difficulty.

Impacts of the Land Titling Program

The evaluations of the World Bank program summarize the positive impact of the program as follows. There has been a substantial increase in the price of land (127 percent), vastly increased access to institutional credit (132 percent), increased use of purchased farm inputs (117 percent), increased yields in newly titled areas, and an increase in the areas used for farming, when compared with such activity in areas that had not yet been titled under the program. High fiscal benefits for the Department of Lands were also considered significant. The experiences of farmers in Baan Hong district, Lamphun province, in Northern Thailand provide a different perspective, however.

Background of the Land Issue in the Baan Hong District

In the Baan Hong district, seven villages and adjoining farmland were established at the boundaries of an area of 15,000 râi (2,400 hectares) of common land. Access to these community lands had been governed under local tenure arrangements until the introduction in the 1960s of a land allocation program, which attempted to distribute certificates to parcels of land on the basis of a grid map, irrespective of any existing use of this area, of the suitability of each parcel for agriculture, or of the proximity of the parcels to a beneficiary's other lands. The plots were identified only by numbers on a map, so few families were absolutely sure where they were allowed to farm. Sometimes, villagers were allocated land that was not suitable for farming, so they moved elsewhere. In practice, available land was put to use by the farmers, but often not in accordance with the papers that were issued to them.

As a result of the confusion, the creation of competing official claims to land, and the impracticality of access, few farmers could actually use the land officially allocated to them though they retained the *bai jong* (certificate). In the 1970s, the Department of Lands, in an attempt to resolve the disputes, created another map, which confused the matter even further. Recognizing the procedural mistakes made earlier, the government, in one administrative stroke in the mid-1980s, revoked all certificates issued during the allocation program, with the intention of reregistering the land rights at a later stage. As a result, in the 1980s, few formal claims to this land were recognized, and there was a need for clarification of land rights in the area. Unfortunately, however, the land titling program did not present the local farmers with the opportunity to secure title to these lands, as the disenfranchised local farmers were not involved when the project officers came to issue title.

Misappropriation of Land in Baan Hong District

As the economy grew in the late 1980s and early 1990s, financiers began looking for secure long-term investments for their accumulating capital and found that buying up rural land areas was an ideal investment. Such land could be acquired cheaply and issued with title, with the likelihood, in the prevailing economic climate, that it would swiftly rise in value. In Lamphun province, titles for extensive areas of land were issued during the height of the economic growth period of 1990–1993 without the knowledge of local communities, which became aware of the alienation of their community lands only when fences started appearing in the fields. The entire 15,000 râi in Baan Hong district, described above, land that had previously been held in common by local communities and that was supposed to be allocated to local people, had been sold; it is now titled under the names of nonresident companies and wealthy individuals from outside the community.

Local farmers have vigorously challenged the legality of the title deeds. Villagers state that no notice was given, either posted in the village or announced over the village loudspeaker, of the intention to survey the area and issue title. Research into the title deeds shows that many were issued on the basis of incomplete survey information, sometimes under false names, and from nonexistent or long-dead sellers (in at least one case, the space for the name and address of the seller was blank). In this manner, villagers in Baan Hong have been prohibited from using their community land, around which fences were constructed in approximately 1990.

Seeing such fences and boundary markers appearing in the lands they had traditionally claimed for village use, people from Sritia village rose up in protest at the illegal transfer of this land to outsiders. A youth leader involved in the protests was shot and killed by unknown gunmen. Continued protests by farmers eventually led to the establishment of a joint government and community representative investigation committee in 1997, to look into the acquisition of land in state land areas around the country.[5] Despite findings that such transfers were illegal, official action has yet to be taken to revoke the deeds. The majority of plots in the Baan Hong area were left abandoned, possibly kept fallow to allow for quick sales when the time and price was right, or perhaps simply because it was not a priority for the titleholders. By 1997, the entire area had been mortgaged and, during the financial crisis at that time, duly became nonperforming loans. Local communities, themselves facing hardship during the economic depression, continued to be excluded from the land.

Land Reform by Communities

Understandably perhaps, villagers have not been very impressed by the various processes which were intended to secure their land rights over the past decades. It has taken a substantial amount of research on the part of non-

TABLE 6.2 Participation in land occupation, Lamphun province

Year	Village, District	Area (râi)	No of Families
1975	Wlang-Laopongseu, Wlangnonglong	800	136
1997	Paetal, Wlangnonglong	600	99
1997	Taluk, Wlangnonglong	700	160
1997	Tachang-nonglong, Wlangnonglong	100	50
1997	Nongklad, Baan Hong	1,700	81
1996	Sritia, Baan Hong	3,000	560
2000	Takoamuang, Baan Hong	1,000	111
2000	Nongsoon, Baan Hong	1,300	215
2000	Lalkeaw, Baan Hong	120	58
2000	Raldong, Baan Hong	426	282
2002	Dongkiek, Pasang	1,000	160
2002	Sanpahak, Pasang	55	64
2002	Pongroo, Pasang	303	150
2002	Nakornchedl, Pasang	204	143
2002	Sanhangseu, Pasang	330	275
2002	Ralkoaka, Pasang	170	98
2002	Prabat, Pasang	300	247
TOTAL		12,108	2,889

governmental groups and lawyers to identify the current official owners of specific plots of land. Many deeds had passed through several hands in the early 1990s, increasing in value upon every transfer. In some cases, it has seemed that the transfers have been deliberately obscured, with properties returning to their original owners after seven or eight transactions (though now registered in the name of a company rather than an individual). In frustration at the lack of action by local officials to recover the land, local people began to organize themselves and take the matter into their own hands. In 1997, villagers in WlangNongLong and Baan Hong districts took the decision to occupy lands that had been left abandoned for several years. Neighboring communities, similarly desperate for land for subsistence, followed suit, and cases of land occupation increased throughout the province and elsewhere. As of 2002, a total of 3,798 families had joined the land occupation movement, putting over 14,305 rai (about 2,150 hectares) of abandoned land to agricultural use in twenty-three areas of Lamphun, Chiang Mai, and Chiang Rai provinces (see table 6.2 for indicative data for Lamphun province).

Until that year, local authorities had, by and large, tolerated the land occupations in areas throughout Lamphun province, taking no action against the farmers who had by now established fruit orchards, prepared and cultivated the fields, and set up huts and shelters and access tracks among the fields. However, in January 2002, police authorities began issuing arrest warrants for farmers on charges of encroachment onto titled land. On April 23, 2002, a resolution by the Council of Ministers effectively gave the police the green light to begin arresting occupation leaders—often deploying hundreds of officers to arrest one or two people in a village. Many of the arrested farmers were initially denied bail and underwent prolonged imprisonment prior to being brought to court. Due to the way in which the police had filed the charges, sums for bail at first exceeded several million Baht for each farmer. After appeal to the courts, bail was set at more reasonable sums, which were secured by the personal guarantees of sympathetic senators and others. An agreement was finally reached between the farmers' groups and the state to desist from imprisoning any more farmers. Seventy-four farmers and one NGO worker were subject for trial.

Land Concentration under the Land Titling Program

The cases highlighted above point to the resistance in northern Thailand by community groups to the transfer of lands outside their community, and the keenly felt imperative to put abandoned land to use where there is widespread indebtedness and poverty in the neighboring areas. In both cases, the land was transferred illegally. The revocation of the titles that were illegally issued in Lamphun province and elsewhere around the country would allow the restoration of lands to their rightful owners, relieve the tensions between farmers and the government, and go a long way toward remedying significant problems brought about during the implementation of the World Bank's land titling program. However, corruption is not the only way in which villagers may lose their land. The land titling program was established to set in place a framework for a "free market in land" to begin functioning optimally. Within this framework, land is deliberately decoupled from local histories, social norms, responsibilities, and other noneconomic factors so that individuals throughout the country might acquire land at an open market price. Accordingly, if incomers are unconcerned with the local community, so be it. From the point of view of policy, this cost is balanced by the benefit that price competition should ensure an incentive to make the most profitable use of the land.

As was seen in the cases in Lamphun province, however, the most profitable use is not necessary the most productive. In the right conditions, high profits can be made by simply biding time and speculating on rising prices, without a single crop being produced, building being built, or business being managed on the premises. In practice, the greater access to information and extra bargaining power of wealthier and politically more influential people favors the accumulation and concentration of land by large landholders. While the land code appears to favor small landholding by placing a basic limit of landholding at 50 râi (8 hectares) per title deed (exceptions to this limit are allowed at the provincial governor's discretion), there is no legal restriction on the number of title deeds a landowner can hold. Initial studies into the accumulation of land in Lamphun province show that in NongPlaSawai subdistrict just seven companies or individuals have acquired a total of 4,786 râi (765 hectares).

Investigating the existing data on land concentration is a very time-consuming task in Thailand, and it is made even more difficult when officials prohibit access to information by the public, as discovered by the community land reform movement in Lamphun province. A detailed study by the Land Institute Foundation in one district in a northeastern province of the country managed to examine data on the sixty-nine largest landholders in the district, whose holdings, taken altogether, totaled 31,290 râi (about 5,000 hectares). As shown in table 6.3, most landowners in the top twenty did in fact hold less than the nominal limit of 50 râi (about 7 hectares) per deed, but they were also in possession of dozens or hundreds of deeds, allowing their overall landholding to substantially exceed the accepted limit. The authors of the study point out that the full extent of large landholdings has not yet been revealed due to incomplete access to the record. The Department of Lands does not keep data on land concentration, despite the importance of such information as an indicator of how many households ultimately benefit from its titling program.

The World Bank recognizes that land markets often exist autonomously, without a national land register and without the need for formal title. This is evidenced in Sritia, Raidong, and other villages taking part in Thailand's community land reform movement, where land has been traded even without formal land deeds, relying on community authorization, trust, and social network

TABLE 6.3 Concentration of land in Dankunbot district, Nakhon Ratchasima province, Northeastern Thailand

Ranking of landowner	Râi	Number of deeds held by single owner	Average size of landholding per deed
1	2,786.78	83	33.57
2	2055.16	159	12.93
3	1,931.08	45	42.91
4	1,884.73	86	21.92
5	1,116.80	63	17.73
6	1,107.26	60	18.45
7	877.55	42	20.89
8	823.03	105	7.84
9	767.51	257	2.99
10	697.71	45	15.50
11	644.95	35	18.43
12	530.90	52	10.21
13	520.86	1	520.86
14	499.64	22	22.71
15	481.23	67	7.18
16	401.82	4	100.46
17	400.00	8	50.00
18	394.95	35	11.28
19	381.67	17	22.45
20	374.74	20	18.73

Source: Land Institute Foundation 2000.

responsibilities. Transactions involving tenure certification other than title may be considered economically less efficient than transfers based on formal title and open market values. Such nontitle transfers, however, traditionally have been more successful in maintaining land in the hands of a large group of smallholders within the local community than has a free market mechanism.

Escalation of Land Prices

One important benefit claimed by the government from the land titling program is the rise in land prices conferred by issuing formal land titles.

Providing title confers "a considerable implicit wealth transfer" that should benefit existing landholders, including poor farmers, once a land market is set up and properly functioning (World Bank n.d., 3). In the evaluation of the third phase of the land titling program, it was found that "legal title is the main factor in explaining differences in land prices . . . titled land was between 75 percent and 197 percent more valuable than land without any documents" (Rattanabirabongse et al. 1998, 11). However, it is difficult to see in practice how increased land prices have benefited the poor and the landless. For one thing, high prices increase the barriers to land access for the landless, including new generations of farmers. The acquisition of land itself becomes a major long-term debt for new landowners, which diverts a substantial proportion of future income into mortgage repayments. Where prices rise sharply out of line with local incomes, the exclusion of poor purchasers is inevitable. A more fundamental problem relates to the commodification of land, the process of transforming it into a freely tradable asset. This process encourages the purchase of land by wealthier groups. As stated above, the very existence of title can vastly increase the value of land. This in itself creates a significant incentive for rich entrepreneurs to buy up untitled land, pay their registration dues, and make a very quick profit. In Thailand, only 12 percent of agricultural land was held under title deeds prior to 1982 (Brits, Grant, and Burns 2002). To go from minimal coverage to total coverage in a relatively short period opens up a lucrative opportunity for those with the resources and information to exploit the titling system.

The process of titling generates interest in the purchase and sale of land. It is rarely the poor who benefit from such property speculation and rising land prices. The experience in nothern Thailand shows that land is taken away from local people and becomes concentrated in the hands of a limited number of wealthy landowners. Stiglitz states that Thailand provides a case in point that speculative real estate lending is a major source of economic instability. "Before liberalization, Thailand had severe limitations on the extent to which banks could lend for speculative real estate. It had imposed these limits because it was a poor country that wanted to grow, and it believed that investing the country's scarce capital in manufacturing would both create jobs and enhance growth. . . . The pattern is familiar: . . . as real estate prices rise, banks feel they can lend more on the basis of the collateral; as investors see prices going up, they want to get in on the game before its too late—and the bankers give them the money to do it. Real estate developers see quick profits by putting up new buildings, until excess capacity results. The developers can't rent their space, they default on their loans, and the bubble bursts." (Stiglitz 2002, 101).

Certainly, assuming they actually acquire title, poor land users may benefit from the "implicit transfer of wealth" of titling by being legally entitled to sell their land and dispose of the proceeds. Assigning a market value to land gives people an objective means of assessing the value of their assets overall. The World Bank's theory predicts that free market valuations should allow people to make rational decisions about the best way to trade their assets and maximize their earning potential. But poor people are unlikely to sell their primary means of livelihood unless under pressure to do so. Of all income groups, they are perhaps most likely to be limited in alternative choices of lifestyle or workplace. Farmers may have no interest, for example, in selling land that is important to social identity or that is a major part of the family heritage as well as their main source of food and regular income. Wealthy landowners, on the other hand, are in a position to take advantage of the vulnerability of poorer farmers to environmental hazards, product price fluctuations, or family hardship by buying up their land while local demand and market values are depressed.

In a situation in which land prices are rising fast or consistently, wealthy land users have an incentive to buy up land, even if to leave it empty or undeveloped, as was the case of the land buying frenzy in Lamphun province in the early 1990s. At height of the boom, people were buying and selling within a day, making 100 percent profits. In the context of rising prices, once poor people sell their land, it is difficult for them to buy it back (Deininger and Feder 1999). Thus in times of hardship, which can affect many members of the community at one time, the poor are divested of their rights to land in order to pay off their debts, and they have little choice but to rent land or find whatever wage labor they can elsewhere.

Institutional Credit, Institutionalized Debt

One of the main rationales for the introduction of title is to stimulate credit. The importance of securing farmers' rights to land through title for the stimulation of credit was particularly supported by the extensive studies carried out by Feder et al. (1988) in the mid-1980s. A midterm evaluation of the land titling program found that access to institutional credit increased by 27 percent and that interest rates were cheaper with the more formal lending sources (Rattanabirabongse et al. 1998, 11). Agricultural credit is promoted as an instrument to stimulate the adoption of new technology to increase yields and therefore raise farmers' income from the sale of greater quantities of higher-quality produce. Higher land valuation will enable greater access to credit. However, the equation between the provision of credit and high incomes is complex. While it is true that access to credit can provide the leverage for productive investment that might be impossible to achieve on an operating budget of family resources alone, without the appropriate support or caution, credit can often result in serious indebtedness of poorer farmers (see box 6.1).

Long-term indebtedness is a major problem for smallholder farmers throughout the country, and, rather than promoting productivity, accumulated debt can pose a serious constraint. Macroeconomic statistics show a decline in the average net income from agriculture in Thailand, even before the economic crisis of 1997. The average net income from agriculture per household decreased by 6 percent between 1992 and 1997. However, over the period 1991 to 1999, the average debt increased at a rate of 40 to 60 percent a year. The Office of Agricultural Economics expressed a warning that if this trend continues, the agricultural sector will face insolvency as have businesses in other sectors (Bamford 2000).

According to research carried out by the Northern Peasants' Federation (NPF), a farmer's organization in northern Thailand, in fifty villages in five provinces of the upper north of Thailand, including Lamphun, each farming household, on average, owed as much as 70,000 Baht (US$1,600) to various banks and village money lenders. Approximately 90 percent of the households in the surveyed villages were in debt (Northern Peasants' Federation 2001). Sums are often borrowed for investments that do not generate the expected return for a variety of reasons. Where income is diverted into loan repayments, less disposable income is available in the following season, and, particularly among low-income groups, an increase in borrowing is then required to make ends meet in the subsequent farming season. Commonly in this situation, subsequent loans are not entirely used for productive investments but to pay for household goods, fulfill family obligations, or other important long-term expenses such as their children's education.

The operational policies of the government's Bank for Agriculture and Cooperatives (BAAC) do not appear to support the villagers in maximizing their chances of repaying loans. The case of one villager in Raidong who was seriously in debt to the BAAC appears typical. He became unable to repay his loan in the first couple of years, due to the collapse in longan prices. He was told that he should borrow money from informal moneylenders to make the

BOX 6.1 "Being in debt is a natural thing; you can get out of it when you die."*

A farmer in Sritia village in Lamphun province described how he took out a loan of 5,000 Baht (approximately US$200) ten years ago to start raising pigs. Due to high family expenses, however, he was unable to pay back the original loan from his own resources. A combination of taking out short-term loans from various local dealers at high interest rates and the fluctuating income from longan (similar to lychee) fruit farming led to the rapid escalation of his debt over ten years.

Four to five years ago, this farmer thought of selling his land (then valued at 170,000 Baht, or US$4,250) in order to pay back the debt. However, officers from Thailand's Bank for Agriculture and Cooperatives (BAAC) advised him not to sell and encouraged him to take out further loans to develop the land instead. The BAAC officers promoted hormones to stimulate the growth of the longan fruits, potassium chlorate for fertilizer, vaccines for his livestock, and the purchasing of an electric water pump. The BAAC also offered further unsolicited loans, a couple of years later. However, these farm inputs were very expensive, while the market price for his primary crop kept declining. The farmer's debt has now reached 150,000 Baht (approximately US$3,750), and there is little likelihood of his ever earning enough profit from his investments to repay this amount. He says he is now hoping to win in the lottery.

* Response from a local official with Thailand's Bank for Agriculture and Cooperatives (BAAC), when asked whether he thought there was a chance that farmers could get out of debt (see Bamford 2000).

repayments to the bank. At first, he borrowed from a friend to pay off his bank loan, but he subsequently had to borrow more to pay off his friend. Then the crops failed, so no one in the village had any spare money to lend any more. Borrowing from high-interest moneylenders became the only option. As all BAAC debtors must pay into a district welfare association (or "funeral fund"), the bank is guaranteed to recover its loans in the case of death, and this reduces the incentives of bank officers to make sure the loans are issued for productive investments. While these problems are not directly attributable to the land titling program, the program is based on the premise that titling is an important priority to facilitate increased access to financial resources, which will ultimately benefit the poor. This premise appears flawed on the existing evidence, as it is based on the assumption that credit is not facilitated without title documentation, and that there is a direct relationship between increased access to credit and increased agricultural profit margins of the poor.

There is no shortage of credit supply in poor communities. In Thailand, borrowing from agricultural cooperatives and the Bank for Agriculture and Cooperatives is possible on the strength of a certificate of use (NS3K), pre-emptive claims certificates (NS1), other land-use licenses, or with personal or group guarantees. Informal lending is also widely available. Credit is now being offered in rural areas through a variety of government schemes, includ-ing a program to loan one million Baht to every village in the country. Part of the problem of increasing the supply of official credit is that while initial loans may be obtained from official lending institutions, if they cannot be paid back on time, loans are then obtained from informal moneylenders with higher interest rates. Following the economic crisis, the proportion of informal sec-tor debt rose to 17 percent of the total debt. In a context of increasing input costs, declining product prices, and adverse climate conditions, the cycle of borrowing has become virtually impossible for many farmers to escape.

Macroeconomic data from Thailand point to increasing indebtedness, rather than a net increase in disposable income among lower income groups. A 2000 research report by the Thailand's Bank for Agriculture and Cooperatives states that the total debt of the agricultural sector (comprising 5.6 million families or 28 million people) was about 411 billion Baht (US$9 bil-lion). Rather than finding new mechanisms to make available further supplies of credit, farmers often need support in reducing their existing debt. In other words, it is simply not possible for promoters of the land titling program to claim that the program makes a contribution to the alleviation of poverty, on the mere basis of increasing access to credit. In fact, very little evidence has been put forward by the Department of Lands or in World Bank documents to support the existence of this beneficial relationship for the poorest groups.

Conclusions

Land is not simply an economic commodity with physical dimensions that can be plotted on a grid, registered on a computer, and traded in exchange for other economic assets whenever that would make most economic sense. Little attempt was made in the planning stages of the land titling program to understand, adapt to, or incorporate rural land tenure systems, particularly in areas with strong local contexts and customs. To consider land in its social con-text requires an understanding of local community livelihoods that adapts to a wide range of land uses, including individual farmlands, village commons, and community forests.

There is nothing inherently wrong with clarifying land rights or issuing legal documents to existing land users.[6] However, the implementation of the land titling program in Thailand has gone beyond clarification and formalization. As a result of the program, land has been transferred from small landholders in local communities to large landholders from the cities, and rights have been transformed from commonly held informal rights to individually held formal rights, and in some cases from complex layers of rights over one piece of agricultural land to a simple layer of ownership rights. Researchers into local land tenure systems around the world have documented the effectiveness of numerous other tenure regimes within local contexts (for example, Toulmin and Quan 2000). While individually held title deeds may be appropriate for landholders who place greatest importance on the transferability of their assets, it is not necessarily the best option for farming and rural community groups that place relatively high importance on maintaining their landholdings for future generations.

Ensuring the security of access to land, particularly for the poor, was the starting point of the World Bank's intervention in land policy in Thailand. However, an internal evaluation of the program from the Bank's own Operations Evaluation Department (1999b) confirms that land tenure in Thailand was "secure."[7] Those who held the most precarious land rights, including the very poorest groups in the state forest areas, were left out of consideration of the project. No assessment was made of existing rural tenure regimes outside state forests. In order to promote an efficient market, only a title deed could suffice. Most of the emphasis of the program has been placed on improving the administrative mechanisms for bestowing formal rights and enabling their efficient transfer. The experience in Lamphun suggests that success of this aspect of the program has benefited urban-based affluent groups.

While investors can gain benefits from the rapid sales of land, farmers rarely seek to trade land for capital gain. Further, although technological developments such as sophisticated mapping techniques and computerization may enhance efficiency in future transfers, they are not a first priority for farming communities that aim to hold land for a medium to long term. Little attention was paid to farmers' interests in formalizing land rights, such as assisting local farmers to retain their rights, and thus the program was insensitive to the risks farmers faced regarding the alienation of these rights against their will.

In fact, the impact of the program on poverty alleviation has not been a direct avenue of inquiry of the various evaluation teams. The Bank itself seems to be in some doubt about how the effectiveness of such a program could be measured. A Bank concept paper acknowledges that "despite the significant resources being invested by the donor community for modernizing land administration infrastructure, there is little systematic discussion of the key elements of such a system, and of what constitutes effectiveness within particular socioeconomic, cultural and temporal contexts" (Brits, Grant, and Burns 2002, 1).[8] No data has been kept at the Department of Lands that would enable an evaluation team to monitor the number of beneficiaries of the titling process.

A plan for alleviating poverty needs to begin with an analysis of the problems facing the poor. In rural areas of Thailand, these problems include the lack of agricultural extension services and research into low-input sustainable farming practices, the continuous decline in product prices to levels below the cost of production, and the increasing trend toward the alienation of land from the poor. Even if the clarification of land rights were a priority in areas where uncertainty exists, the mechanisms adopted by the program were insufficiently safeguarded, leading to loss of security for local landholders, as in the case of the farmers in Lamphun province.

The land titling program has had a significant impact on Thailand's economy as a whole. The transfer of wealth through the provision of title was a significant factor in fueling land speculation as well as increasing land concentration in the economic growth years until 1997. The program made it possible for generally urban-based and already wealthy financiers to acquire land as a tradable commodity. The rapid increases in the value of land, held up by the Bank as evidence of the benefits conferred by the land titling program, have benefited a new band of entrepreneurs who sought to make quick profits rather than maintain productive use of the land. This had a serious impact on the national economy, as the inflated land values were used to borrow money for unproductive investments, eventually causing massive defaults on private debts contributing to the economic crisis in 1997.

Monitoring and evaluating the impacts on the poor are an essential part in the process of poverty alleviation. In the case study presented above, the very people who were supposed to benefit from World Bank program have become worse off. Yet the program is often presented as an example of best practice, as well as evidence of the virtues of establishing land markets rapidly. If the World Bank still dreams of a world free of poverty, it might do well to consider participatory approaches that assist the poorest sections of society to gain and maintain access to land. In this approach, land would be understood not simply as a tradable commodity with an economic value but as an important part of the livelihood assets of the rural poor, containing social, cultural, and environmental value.

CHAPTER 7

Land Concentration in Mexico after PROCEDE

Ana de Ita

Profound agrarian reform in twentieth-century Mexico began with the revolution of 1910 and ended with the World Bank. In 1992, neoliberal planners under Bank guidance began to drive a series of counterreforms to the agrarian legislation established in Article 27 of the Mexican Constitution, with the objective of making land tenancy more secure in terms of private property. The Program for Certification of Ejidal Rights (PROCEDE) was set in motion in 1993, as the instrument that would give juridical stability to land tenancy, regularize agrarian rights, and grant individual property certificates to *ejidatarios* (people who live on *ejidos*, land owned and supported by the government). The most fervent reformers wanted to push the plan to privatize the social sector's area in just two years (1993–1994); their critics assumed that the program would be rejected by a popular groundswell, which would cement opposition to the reforms. After ten years of PROCEDE's operation, neither has occurred. Mexico's arable land area has still not been entirely certified, yet neither has there been a massive rejection of PROCEDE. This chapter is a first attempt to estimate the impact of PROCEDE on agrarian conflicts and on the concentration of land in Mexico.[1]

Historical Background: Agrarian Structure and the 1910 Revolution

At the beginning of the twentieth century, the agrarian question represented one of Mexico's major problems. Fewer than 11,000 haciendas controlled 57 percent of the national territory, while 15 million peasants—95 percent of rural families—lacked land. By 1910 the degree of land concentration in Mexico was greater than in any other Latin American country. During the dictatorship of Porfirio Diaz (1876–1911), the climax of the liberal period, indigenous communities had lost 90 percent of their lands (Klooster 1997, cited in Merino 2001).

The Mexican Revolution of 1910–1920 had an essentially agrarian character. Thousands of communities demanded the restitution of their lands and the reinstatement of the traditional rights that they had lost during the colonial period, especially during the porfiriato (Tannenbaum 1997). Consequently, the Mexican Constitution of 1917 was substantively radical. Article 27, in force until 1992, allowed the expropriation of large landholdings in order to create small individual or communal properties, and it prohibited Church institutions from possessing any land unrelated to Church functions. Further, it established the state's ownership of lands and waters and its right to transfer their control to particular entities, and it created three distinct categories of property: small private property, communal property, and ejidal property. Private property holdings were limited to one hundred irrigated hectares or their equivalent in rain-fed land. Land was given to members of an ejido for their use and usufruct. Known as "communities," communal property basically amounted to indigenous lands either granted by the Spanish Crown or through restitution thereafter, while ejidos were collective landholdings created by land distribution. At the center of the ejido is an administrative unit, known as a "nucleus," which provides for the operation, administration, and control of the ejido. The rights of the ejidatarios and communal landholders over agrarian properties were historically inalienable, imprescriptible, not subject to embargo, and nontransferable.

Over the course of the following eighty years, this agrarian reform distributed 103 million hectares (52 percent of the 196 million hectares that make up the Mexican territory, or 56 percent of its agrarian land and 70 percent of its forests) to 3.5 million ejidatarios and communal landholders, collected into 30,322 ejidos and communities that constitute the social sector.[2] The patterns of ownership are outlined in table 7.1.

Of the social area, 7 out of every 10 hectares are lands held for communal use. More than two-thirds of forested areas under use belong to ejidatarios. On the other end of the spectrum, 1.7 million private proprietors own 77 million hectares (39 percent of the surface area of the national territory). National lands comprise 6.5 million hectares (3.3 percent), and urban lands, roads, and bodies of water on the remaining 11.3 million hectares. More than half of the ejidatarios, 78 percent of communal landholders, and 62 percent of private

TABLE 7.1 Current Mexican agrarian structure

Type of property	Agrarian nuclei*	Properties (number)	Surface (hectares)	Percent	Beneficiaries
Ejidos*	27,941	0	84,686,536	43,19	3,271,916
Communities†	2,157	0	16,838,790	8.59	617,660
Agricultural and livestock colonies	650	61,184	3,639,140	1.86	0
Private properties		1,637,981	73,216,097	37.34	0
National territories		144,317	6,600,975	3.37	0
Others‡		35,313	11,072,947	5.65	0
TOTAL	30,748	1,878,795	196,054,475	100	3,889,576

Source: Registro Agrario Nacional. July 29, 2002.

* Does not account for the surface corresponding to insular territory. Source: INEGI.

† Includes only land actually redistributed through presidential resolution

‡ Includes bodies of water, federal zones, national parks, ecological reserves, urban and vacant properties, and others.

proprietors are *minifundistas* (small landholders), since their plots are smaller than 5 hectares.

The Market Agrarian Reform of the 1990s

Security of land tenancy was at the heart of the so-called market-based agrarian reform. Promoted by the World Bank as a new agrarian reform, various countries have set it in motion, ostensibly to give land access to peasants who lack it, or to guarantee the private ownership over land they already possess, as was the case of Mexico.

In February 1990 the World Bank drafted an agricultural policy document (Heath 1990). Its recommendations—allegedly based on the existing social and political structures—were oriented toward eliminating the differences between private and ejidal property, with an emphasis on the security of land tenancy, and the individualization of the collective functions of the ejido and its destruction as a unit of production and organization. A 1969 study (Dovring) had shown that the ejidal sector and small agricultural private properties of under five hectares—jointly amounting to half of Mexico's arable land—then employed more than 70 percent of the vast rural labor force's

resources, while using only 38 percent of the agricultural investment and producing approximately half of the agricultural product. Yet the Bank blamed the
ejidal system for rural and indigenous poverty and the scarcely functioning
land market, which accounted for the reduction of plots and the low productivity of their crops. In his study for the World Bank, Heath (1990) determined
that the size of the property is a more important factor in terms of productivity than whether a given unit is an ejido or a private business.

As part of a program for the neoliberal modernization of the countryside,
the Mexican government in November 1991 reformed the agrarian law with
the purpose of allowing and even promoting the privatization of the previously
inalienable ejidal land. This action was closely followed by the reform of Article
27 and by the new agrarian law of 1992, which aimed to increase incentives
for investment and improve the functioning of land and labor markets in rural
areas. In their first phase, these "new agrarian reform" policies emphasized
the security of property rights and the granting of full rights to the holders of
lands through a process of privatization. The guiding idea of these reforms was
to create an active land market that would promote the efficient allocation of
resources and improve agricultural investment (Appendini 2001). Among the
principal changes were the following:

- The government was no longer obliged to redistribute lands in favor of
  peasants who demanded it.
- Ejidatarios could obtain individual title deeds or certificates over their
  parcels if the ejido accepted participation in PROCEDE.
- Ejidatarios who demarcated and certified the limits of their parcels had
  the legal right to rent them, sell them, hire a work force, or use their land
  as loan collateral. The decision to authorize the sale of lands of the ejido
  to external persons would be approved by two-thirds of the general
  assembly's vote.[3]
- Common lands used by ejidatarios collectively as pastureland or forest
  resources could also be sold for commercial development if the majority
  of ejidatarios decided to do so.
- Ejidatarios were not obligated to work their plots personally.
- To prevent the excessive concentration or privatization of ejidal lands, the
  government would continue to reinforce the maximum legal limits of the
  size of the properties. Individual private property would be limited to 100
  irrigated hectares, or its equivalent in lands of lesser quality. No individual ejidatario may acquire more than 5 percent of the land of an ejido or

community. Title deeds for commercial corporations are limited to 2,500 irrigated hectares per company. Commercial corporations created for the purpose of acquiring privatized ejidal land must have at least twenty-five individual members. Joint ventures between ejidos and private firms could possess more land than the limit permitted for each one of its individual members.

- Ejidatarios who did not opt for the rental or sale of their land may enter into joint ventures with external investors (individuals or companies), or they may form associations among themselves in order to increase the size of the productive unit and maximize economies of scale. They could also sign long-term production contracts with external agents (Cornelius and Mhyre 1998).

The reform of Article 27 opened up the ejidal sector to foreign direct investment. It eliminated the prohibition to form associations between foreign investors and ejidatarios, though it limited the participation of foreign investment to 49 percent. For its planners the reform of Article 27 was necessary to guarantee well-defined property rights protected by the judicial system, given that the lack of security in the tenancy of land had obstructed agricultural investment (Tellez 1994). They intended for agrarian reform to promote the functioning of land markets—completely liberalizing rental and permitting sale among members of an ejido—to increase investment incentives and to improve governance and regulation in the countryside. From the point of view of its critics, reform was unnecessary and potentially harmful. It focused on erroneous themes, and it could lead to the disappearance of the ejido, causing irreparable damage to the social structure of the countryside. It would further polarize the Mexican countryside, where a bimodal agricultural system would then coexist, one business-oriented, modern, and competitive in the international market; and another peasant and indigenous, and subsistence-oriented.

The reform initiated by the passage of Article 27 was followed by the PROCEDE. The program permitted the regularization of land tenancy and defined clear property rights in the ejidos and agrarian communities for millions of peasants, in addition to endowing them with title deeds over those rights. PROCEDE created new conflicts and reignited a series of old disputes that acquired renewed force, since certification would define the territorial limits of the communities and ejidos and the rights of each ejidatario or commoner within the agrarian nucleus—rights that often put communities and individuals into direct conflict with one another.

PROCEDE after Ten Years in Operation

PROCEDE allows ejidatarios to choose a property regime, delimit the contiguousness of the ejidos, measure individual plots, and eventually issue certificates for individually owned parcels and for individual parcels of common lands. PROCEDE intended to conclude the certification of rights at the end of 1994; initially, however, various ejidos, communities, and peasant organizations rejected the program, so as to make their rejection of the overall reforms patent. During his administration (1995–2000) President Zedillo committed himself to concluding the agrarian certification by the end of his term, which, in 2005, had still not been achieved.

PROCEDE was introduced as a voluntary program. However, because local or regional authorities often (illegally) demanded PROCEDE certificates for various transactions, such as receiving subsidies and soliciting credit, between 1993 and 31 October 2003, approximately 79.9 percent of all ejidos and communities—24,384 agrarian nuclei—concluded the regularization of their rights, to the "benefit" of 3,431,752 peasants, to whom 66,787 million hectares were certified (see table 7.2). Although 79.9 percent of the agrarian nuclei and 84.5 percent of the subjects (ejidatarios or communal landholders) have adopted PROCEDE, the certified surface area represents only 65.7 percent of the surface area of the social sector. Further, the surface area actually titled represents just 0.27 percent of all of the surface area endowed to ejidatarios and communal landholders. The limited scale of this success was attributed to PROCEDE, for initially harvesting "low-hanging fruit"—by first certifying ejidos with fewer conflicts due to voluntary acceptance. Over the years, the difficulty of incorporating the remaining ejidos and communities into the program increased. According to the World Bank, "the ejidos that still have not been certified are larger, more conflictive, poorer, more difficult to access, and, with less human capital than the average, will have implications in the completion of the program" (Deininger et al. 2001). The remaining ejidos either reject the program or are in dispute over limits and inequity in access to land.

Of the nearly 66.8 million certified hectares, 69 percent have been certified as lands of common use, and 30.6 percent were certified as parcels. In this ten-year period 7,587,801 certificates and title deeds have been expedited of which 4,193,824 were parcel certificates (55.3 percent); 1,528,351 were common-use certificates (20.1 percent), and the remainder were 1,865,626 plot certificates (24.6 percent).

TABLE 7.2 Historical progress of PROCEDE, in hectares, 1993 to (October 31) 2003

	PROCEDE total	National total	Percent
Nuclei	24,384	30,513	79.90
Beneficiaries*	3,431,752	4,060,580	84.50
Certified parceled	20,430,583.50		20.11
Common use	46,080,602.70		45.36
Titled	275,993		0.27
TOTAL	66,787,179.20	101,591,095	65.74

Sources: CECCAM with SRA data, third internal work report, 2003; and RAN, PROCEDE, internal progress report 2003.

*According to PROCEDE, beneficiaries surpass the number of total beneficiaries when new subjects with resident and owner rights are incorporated.

On a national average, ejidatarios possess 8.8 hectares each, although in twelve states the average surface area is much smaller. The size of the property of half of the ejidatarios is below 5 hectares; jointly, the ejidatarios in these areas possess 15.6 percent of the surface area, with an average property size of 2.7 hectares. Another 26.8 percent of the ejidatarios possess properties of over 5 and up to 10 hectares. They have usufruct for 25.6 percent of the land, and the size of their properties averages 8.4 hectares; 10.3 percent of the ejidatarios have more than 10 and up to 15 hectares, and they own 15.3 percent of their ejidos' surface area, with an average property size of 13 hectares. Of the ejidatarios whose properties exceed 25 hectares, 3.6 percent have an average of 53.4 hectares and possess 22.2 percent of the parceled ejidal surface area.

Difficulties in the Adoption of PROCEDE

One of the tasks PROCEDE has set itself is to certify the limits or perimeter of a community. In some agrarian communities lands are collective, including the parcels that are cultivated every year by the same family. Individual certification is therefore irrelevant since *usos y costumbres* (customary law and practices) recognize the right of usage of each parcel. What is relevant for these communities is the obtaining of a list of communal landholders who are recognized and therefore have rights in the community. For the list to be legally acceptable, it must be updated periodically. This has rarely happened, and the resulting conflicts have complicated the certification process (Appendini 2001).

In the 1992 law, communities preserve their legal status as landed communities under the communal regime, and land cannot be sold, rented, or mortgaged. However, the law permits them to adopt the ejidal regime (which would allow them to privatize the land) or to enter into association with external agents and provide the land for commercial corporation investments. The law also recognizes in agrarian communities the existence of private parcels and the cession of rights to a successor or resident, but it does not permit sale, nor does it recognize formal inheritance or the registration of a successor, as in the case of the ejido.

Oaxaca is the state with the least adoption of PROCEDE, with only 20.5 percent of the social sector surface area being certified. Chiapas follows with 27.6 percent, Guerrero with 35.7 percent, and Nayarit with 38.4 percent. Oaxaca is characterized by the importance it gives to communal property. It absorbs 34 percent of Mexico's communal lands, and 62 percent its surface area is communal property. Two-thirds of the land registered in PROCEDE is certified as common-use land. Less than 0.2 percent of the social sector surface area reached the entitlement process. The low rate of adoption of PROCEDE in Oaxaca must be related to the high proportion of communal property. Before considering their individual right to obtain a document respecting possessed land, communal landholders sought to conserve the collective interest (Gómez 2001).

In Chiapas, the second state with the least adoption of PROCEDE, the agrarian counterreforms of 1992 constituted a touchstone because they cancelled the state's obligation to land redistribution, and with it the possibility for a vast majority of peasants with no land to obtain it. The cancellation of distribution was one of the factors that led to the Zapatista rebellion of 1994. In contrast with Oaxaca, 47 percent of the surface area in Chiapas is ejidal, and only 11 percent belongs to the communities. Two-thirds of the surface area was certified as individual parcels, one-third as common-use lands, and only 0.25 percent of the land has been titled.

Currently, 58.2 percent of forest land and farmland in Chiapas is in the hands of ejidatarios and communal landholders, many of them indigenous. By 1994 there were 40,000 petitioners for land. At the beginning of 1994, 340 occupied properties were registered, representing a total of 50,000 hectares, with an average extension of 100 hectares or less per parcel, which is to say that these properties did not surpass the small-property limit. The Zapatista uprising functioned as a catalyst for the occupations that, throughout that year, reached unprecedented numbers.

The demand of lands to be acquired through purchase in Chiapas was of 588,713 hectares; of these, 438,294 were bought, for 109,306 peasants, equivalent to 75 percent of the initial demand and to 10 percent of the surface area of the state's social sector. Once these lands were distributed among them, the peasants demanded the creation of ejidos and did not accept the transformation of land into small private properties, against the grain of the Article 27 reforms and its underlying intention, the privatization of social property (Reyes 1998). In the framework of the dialogues between the federal government and the Zapatista Army for National Liberation (EZLN), one of the demands of the San Andrés Sacamch'en accords was the installment of an agrarian board, to justly solve the conflicts over land (Reyes 1998).

Guerrero is the third state with the least incorporation of lands into PROCEDE. Only 35.7 percent of its surface area has been certified, though it integrates 71 percent of the agrarian nuclei and 65 percent of the ejidatarios and communal landholders. Approximately 16 percent of the certified land has been certified as individual parcels and 19 percent as lands for common use.

PROCEDE made the least advances in Oaxaca, Chiapas, and Guerrero, states with a very high indigenous presence. Unable to understand why this is the case, the World Bank has formed a conclusion that employs a combination of denial and racialized dogma: "There is very little difference, if any, between certified ejidos found in communities with a high indigenous presence and ejidos found in nonindigenous municipalities. . . . The slow adoption of PROCEDE in indigenous communities is due to the existence of conflicts, inequity in the access to land and resources, and the lack of human capital and economic potential, more than to the specifically indigenous character of the ejido" (Deininger et al. 2001).

Common-Use Lands and Forest Property

Common-use lands function as reserves and social security nets, even in cases in which their value is low, by offering mechanisms to ejidatarios to diversify their sources of income, or to protect against unexpected events. The most important complementary activities (cattle husbandry and food gathering) that ejidatarios develop in common-use lands are directed toward local consumption, as a source of complementary income, and they play an important social role. Occasionally, common-use lands constitute a reserve to compensate ejidatarios with a few areas of parceled lands, or to be distributed among new ejidatarios.

The principal activity developed in common-use lands is the exploitation of forestry and natural resources. By 1992, communal forest production provided 40 percent of the national production of raw material and 15 percent of lumber (Merino 2001). Despite these data, a study by the World Bank and the *Procuraduría Agraria* (Special Attorney's Office for Agrarian Issues) reports that 40 percent of ejidatarios do not use common resources, 44 percent scarcely use them, and 16 percent consider them important (Robles and Deininger 2000).

Reforms of the agrarian legal framework pave the way, though not directly, for the parceling of common-use lands, thus posing a threat to their existence and to their participation in the production and reproduction of ejidal or communal life. In the case of forest ejidos and communities, "although the modifications to constitutional article 27 and the agrarian statutes created the possibility of privatizing the agricultural land of the ejidos, they establish the impossibility of parceling or privatizing common-use lands, like forests. Nevertheless, the agrarian law allows forest ejidos to associate with private capital, ceding the use of their lands for periods of up to 30 years for the establishment of forest plantations. In this way the planters can get to control extensions of up to 20,000 hectares" (Merino 2001). From the perspective of the neoliberal planners of the agrarian and forestry policies, the main achievements of the agrarian reforms were the creation of the small forest property and the opening of the path to long-term investment in commercial plantations, to which, as of 1996, the forestry law grants subsidies.

Possible Reasons for the Continued Adoption of PROCEDE

The great majority of agrarian nuclei (79.9 percent) have accepted PROCEDE, and 84.5 percent of the country's ejidatarios and communal landholders have participated in the process of certification of their agrarian properties, although only 65.7 percent of the social sector's surface area has been certified. In general, PROCEDE was simply induced—it was not voluntary. One of the possible causes for the relatively generalized acceptance of PRO-CEDE—besides the fact that governmental institutions increasingly require it for gaining access to other programs—is that it legalizes and grants control over land and natural resources to ejidatarios and communal landholders that are very interested in maintaining and guaranteeing their rights over their resources.

While the majority of the agrarian nuclei have accepted some level of PRO-CEDE, it is worth remembering that the process of actual titling has taken place for 0.27 percent of the surface area. According to the Agrarian Reform Secretariat, only 0.94 percent of the social sector's surface area and 0.43 percent of the ejidos have adopted full ownership; most of these are situated in peripherally urban areas, and thus are interested in selling their lands at a higher price.

The World Bank attempts to explain the ejidatarios' lack of interest in titling their properties by arguing that private property is subject to taxes (Lavadenz and Deininger 2001). The lack of interest in titling, however, can be related to cultural and historical criteria, and not only to commercial ones. Ejidatarios fought to obtain land, which for them is not merely a commercial resource but rather the space in which their identity is formed and re-created. They are therefore not interested in debilitating the social bonds that integrate the ejido, but rather in maintaining and strengthening them. This hypothesis is reinforced by the fact that social property certification has advanced in a relatively higher proportion in the form of common-use lands, and by the increase in the rental of lands, which has not been accompanied by either titling or sales.

PROCEDE: Resolution or Cause of Agrarian Conflict?

The World Bank considers PROCEDE to have had a positive impact on equity, by recognizing as agrarian subjects approximately one million possessors and residents who previously had very limited rights and a precarious security of tenancy based on the occupation of land (Deininger et al. 2001). One of PROCEDE's effects has been an increase in the number of ejidatarios by 20 percent, on average, and by as much as 60 percent in some cases.[4] The recognition of residents and possessors can provoke new conflicts in the ejidos:

TABLE 7.3 Nuclei with agrarian conflicts registered
by PROCEDE, to 2003

Total agrarian nuclei	30,513
Total nuclei with problems	4,735
Conflicts over limits (not under judicial review)	941
Internal conflicts	498
Inconclusive agrarian actions that suppress rights	106
Rejection of PROCEDE	1,164
Conditional participation in PROCEDE	186
Invasion of lands not under judicial review	196
Agrarian nuclei under judicial review	317
Without possibility of judicial review	580
Displaced ejidatarios	188

Source: RAN internal progress report, October 15, 2003

"The extreme minifundizacion [sic] of the land takes those lands out of competition, thus affecting the whole of the market by devaluing properly commercial operations" (Concheiro and Diego 2001), creating the grounds for conflict. This contradicts the World Bank. Based on a sample of 1,291 ejidatarios (de Janvry, Gordillo, and Sadoulet 1997), the World Bank concludes that PROCEDE has *reduced* conflicts and increased the social unity within the ejido (Deininger et al. 2001). However, between 1992 and 2002, agrarian tribunals charged with resolving conflicts have received 116,404 cases, the majority of them of ordinary jurisdiction, an indication that the new agrarian organization has resulted in a high rate of conflict. The suggestion is that the possible saturation of unresolved cases might be due to the great number of conflicts related to inheritance. One of the results of the changes in the agrarian law is that land parcels have ceased to be family patrimony. The new law allows an ejidatario to appoint any person as rightful successor, whereas formerly, successors would have been a farmer's spouse and children. One out of five ejidatarios is a woman, and the question of inheritance is an important gender issue, but the rights of women have been weakened by the new law (Appendini 2001). Current legislation recognizes only the right to purchase by family members, who rarely can exercise this right, should the head of the family decide to sell, due to insufficient means. Thus, the ejidatario's family is disadvantaged by the changes to the agrarian law: the end of state-led agrarian distribution cancelled any avenue to land access other than inheritance or purchase and temporary rental. In the case of poor peasants this leaves only inheritance which, as we have seen, is precarious (Concheiro and Diego 2001).

PROCEDE cannot enter regions with severe agrarian conflicts, such as the Chimalapa mountains, the Huichol region, or Montes Azules. In areas where problems are less rampant, PROCEDE is divisive. By 2003, the National Agrarian Registry reported that 15.5 percent of the country's ejidos and communities had problems; among the most recurring were the rejection of PROCEDE in approximately 25 percent of the nuclei followed by problems related to limits in 19.9 percent of them (see table 7.3).

PROCEDE and the Land Market

Within the old framework, land was a social right and not a commodity. One of the main objectives guiding the agrarian counterreforms of 1992 was the drive to set land markets into motion. For the neoliberal planners of Mexico's agrarian policies, as well as for multilateral institutions like the World Bank, the lack of land market activity (which was due to the social nature of ejidal and communal property, according to which land was nontransferable, inalienable, and not subject to embargo) was considered one of the gravest problems of the rural sector, the cause of the poverty of the population as well as of the sector's low productivity and income-yield capacity. PROCEDE therefore encouraged the functioning of the land market.

Land Rental Markets

One of the principal changes effected by the reforms is that the rental of land, formerly prohibited, is now legal for all ejidatarios, and those who have adopted PROCEDE have an additional certificate that recognizes their rights to do so. According to the World Bank, the increase in the security of tenancy that results from titling should, in theory, result in an increased supply in the land market (Deininger et al. 2001). Part of this theory assumes a priori that "land markets function better for private agriculturists, less so for certified ejidos, and worse for noncertified ejidos." A further asumption is that "with constant profits according to scale, and a proper functioning of the markets of the production factors and credit, the amount of operated land should be independent of the quantity of land possessed, of the statute of tenancy, and of any other characteristic of the unit of exploitation. Operations will put land out for rental, or will rent land, according to the optimal land area for the type of operation" (Deininger et al. 2001). The theory, the Bank admits, runs into difficulty when faced with reality. The Bank admits that, "In the private sector and in the noncertified ejidos the quantity of operated land is highly dependent on the quantity possessed, and that the markets do not operate perfectly . . . Even more surprising, once the factors are controlled, land markets do not operate more efficiently in the private sector than in the ejidal sector" (Deininger et al. 2001).

The Bank's surprise might have been avoided with a little more knowledge of the places and contexts in which they were instituting policy. According to Concheiro and Diego (2001), even before reform, the rental of land was a common practice; between 50 and 70 percent of the lands of the ejidos in irrigated districts were rented. Rented parcels were primarily those dedicated to commercial and income production, where the opportunity cost of the land was high and where it was necessary to have a high cash flow or access to sources of credit. At the beginning of the 1990s the rental of land—though difficult to quantify because it was illegal—comprised more than 50 percent of the best agricultural, pastoral, and forestry lands belonging to ejidos and communities. The tendency, brought about by the reform, to the reconcentration of land gives rise to a *neolatifundismo* (neo–estate system) built around agrarian capitalists, transnational agro-industries, and big cattle breeders, that are no longer obstructed by legal limits (Concheiro and Diego 2001). The land rental markets have been affected more by the implementation of PROCEDE, then, than by the changes in the legal framework.

The World Bank considers PROCEDE as supporting the functioning of the land markets: "In noncertified ejidos the big producers rent out their lands to the small producers, while in certified ejidos the opposite happens" (Deininger et al. 2001). Empirical observation and case studies (Concheiro and Diego 2001) do not allow one to accept this bold statement. In Mexico, as a consequence of the agrarian counterreforms, we are witnessing the selective reconcentration of land, primarily of high productive potential, in the hands of big producers, agricultural capitalists, *caciques* (local political bosses), government officials, and others, and not the rental of land by the small producers who have little capital. Land is not rented for redistribution among small producers or peasants who lack it, but rather out of necessity, a profound disadvantage primarily for small producers, caused by their incapacity to make land productive due to lack of capital, inputs, credit, income-yield capacity, and market access. For peasants, entry into the land rental market implies the impossibility of making the land productive and obtaining higher profits.

Despite these observations the World Bank concludes that "there is very little evidence that the political reforms of 1992 and the implementation of PROCEDE favor the concentration of land. On the contrary, the certification of rights to land increases the demand to cultivate land and allows small producers entry to the market from the demand side" (Deininger et al. 2001). In fact, experience demonstrates that small producers generally enter the land market from the supply side. From the peasant viewpoint the increase of share-cropping and renting is generated by the need to survive, by the search for certain stability, or by a combination of other, external activities; nonetheless, the peasants show a clear will to continue being ejidatarios, and thus to conserve the possession of their land.

Markets for the Sale of Land

PROCEDE has not had as significant an impact on markets for the sale of land in comparison to its impact on markets for land rental (Deininger et al. 2001). According to the World Bank, the possession of land, or at least long-term rental, is necessary as an incentive for investment. The case studies of Concheiro and Diego (2001) show that the purchase and sale of land has increased substantially with the constitutional changes. The buyers who make the land market dynamic are local *caciques*, private hoarders that make up an elite of ejidatarios. In some cases, interest by external agents for renting community or ejido land foments the interest of the local elites in purchasing land in order to rent it out to such external agents, who are interested in establishing plantation crops.

In most cases, community lands are sold by communal landholders in order to confront emergency situations. In principle nobody wants to sell the land, and least of all to anyone from outside the community, so the least possible amount of land is sold. This explains why many ejidal lands are sold as fractionized lots, where part of the area is kept, despite the fact that this is prohibited by the law (Concheiro and Diego 2001).

Access to Credit

The hope that the certification of land would increase the access by ejidatarios to credit was one of the guiding ideas of the agrarian reforms. However, there has been no registered impact on the access to credit. On the contrary, there has been a general credit decline—not only among ejidatarios, but in the entire sector, due to the Mexican economic crisis—between 1992 and 2000.

Conclusions

According to the World Bank, PROCEDE is potentially important for other countries facing the task of shifting from a type of land tenancy that is based on tradition, toward a type of tenancy that is more individualized (Deininger et al. 2001). The World Bank views PROCEDE as reducing the incidence of conflicts in the countryside while facilitating the working of the land market; it counteracts the lack of opportunities, propitiates investment in the rural sphere, and stops the exodus of peasant labor. On the other hand, conclusions derived from seven case studies (Concheiro and Diego 2001) point to the following detractions:

1. A sense of territoriality in the communities is lost through the land market, whether the market is used for rent or for purchase and sale, caused by the loss of control of the physical space necessary for their social reproduction, with the consequential increase in the need to migrate among youths who have lost their access to the land.
2. The market program has instigated a process of dispossession of lands, whether through rent or sale, whereby local or external minorities are gaining control over the best ejidal and private lands of rural communities, while an increasing number of peasants are losing access to the land.
3. The decision to cede the usufruct or possession of the land is forced by the circumstances. Sales are made in order to resolve the emergencies of poor ejidatarios, and the buyers tend to be ejidatario elites, who take advantage of an emergency situation to buy at low rates.
4. Peasants do not participate in the market with the idea of making a profit, or of obtaining a benefit; on the contrary, those who rent out their

land assume the temporary or permanent impossibility of working it directly and that a greater benefit will be obtained through the sale of their products.

In Mexico land markets reflect a profound inequality and inefficient distribution of wealth, resources, and opportunities. Further movement along this trajectory is bound to undo the successes of the original, and far more just, Mexican agrarian revolution. It would seem as if the World Bank were setting up the conditions for a third agrarian reform.

CHAPTER 8

Colombia: Agrarian Reform— Fake and Genuine

Héctor Mondragón

During the last thirty years, the World Bank and the Colombian government have introduced a variety of initiatives under the guise of agrarian reform. In this chapter, we track the failures of the Colombian agrarian reform project, and show that these disappointments are yet more tragic than they first appear, given that genuine agrarian reform has the promise of addressing directly a range of ills that persist in Colombia today.

The issue of land reform remains pertinent. Although the rural population in Colombia has dropped in relative terms, it has continued to increase in absolute terms, from 6 million people in 1938 to 11.6 million in 1993. A similar dynamic has occurred with the economically active population in the farming sector, which grew from 1.9 million in 1938 to 2.7 million in 1993. Moreover, those who can be considered self-employed workers, medium-scale *campesinos*, went from 600,000 in 1938 to 700,000 in 1964 and to 800,000 in 1993. Campesinos no longer face only landowners as employers, but now must deal with a range of other forces as they compete directly as entrepreneurs in the global market. Such a market, and its "globalization" model, seeks to "clean" territories of "inefficient" people. While elsewhere this happens as a result of so-called Darwinian economic competition, in Colombia it is being attempted through war. Not only are people displaced because of war, there is war in order to displace people. The agrarian reform that has come as a consequence is geared not to addressing the causes of the war, but to legitimating its outcome. The Colombian case offers an extreme example of the use of contemporary agrarian reform as a means of entrenching, rather than addressing, inequality.

The Failure of Colombian–World Bank Agrarian Reform

The World Bank has been part of the Colombian agrarian context since it first began disbursing loans. In 1949 and 1954, the first World Bank credits for the Colombian farming sector were put in place. They were given for the purchase of farming machinery, with further credits of US$16 million following, in May 1966, to foster cattle ranching. The Bank supported the policy of modernization and of extending farming areas, although credits were never aimed at directly supporting the policy of land redistribution. Farming credit programs increasingly became the Bank's specialty, with a few large infrastructure projects thrown in.

In 1996, however, the Bank for the first time introduced loans directly aimed at land reform and its subsidized land market program, established by Law 160 in 1994. On June 30, 1996, the World Bank granted an induction credit of US$1.82 million to fund pilot projects and a technical unit, with the goal of preparing for a subsequent project entailing complete support for market-based agrarian reform.

The subsidized land market program was announced with bells and whistles, touted as a way to guarantee land access to campesinos that would eliminate bureaucratic interference and unnecessary state intervention. The program, called Incora, has been a failure: high interest rates, defaults in payments by beneficiaries, and the ongoing reductions to Incora's budget have resulted in a vast slow-down of beneficiary disbursement. We discuss each of these in turn.

Beneficiary Disbursement

Incora had only enough money to subsidize the purchase of 42,527 hectares (3.7 percent of the total made available). In 1997, of 38,451 applicant families, 3,113 were chosen. Despite early enthusiasm, from that time on, the program fell flat: beneficiary families were reduced to 1,767 in 1998, to 845 in 1999, and to approximately 650 per year in 2000 and 2001. Since its creation, therefore, the program has allocated subsidies for the purchase of land to a total of almost 13,000 families (see table 8.1).

It is clear that the program has grown considerably weaker after 1997, which may explain why the World Bank continues to describe the project as

TABLE 8.1 Number of beneficiary families
and amount of land purchased, 1995–2001

Year	Families	Hectares*
1995	1,308	17,479.3
1996	4,633	71,616.1
1997	3,113	42,527.0
1998	1,767	22,879.4
1999	845	10,454.0
2000	646	7,087.9
2001	662	8,167.3
TOTAL	12,974	180,211.0

Source: Incora, various years

*1.0 hectare = 2.4 acres

"in preparation." Of the 1,547,676 families that were interested in acquiring land in 1997, only 356,957 knew about the program, and of those, only 38,451 were registered. Of those applicants, only 8 percent were placed in 1997 and in 2000 less than 3 percent were placed.

There is a serious bottleneck here. The demand for land is much larger than the government's ability to provide it, and it would be even higher if more information were available. The selection of beneficiaries is difficult—most applicants need land and know how to cultivate it, and therefore cannot be discriminated against on these grounds. The supply of land is also greater than the government can afford to buy, and there is a proliferation of political and other pressures to sell a quantity of land, with the knowledge that less than 4 percent will be acquired under the scheme. These pressures are reflected in the selection of beneficiares in areas where landowners have more political influence or other ways of creating pressure.

Overall, the program has had a small impact on one segment of the market: in the supply of land made available by medium-scale landowners, with an average plot sale of 223 hectares until 1997, and 180 hectares between 1998 and 2001. Generally these were businessmen ruined by structural adjustment, and who had never been large-scale landowners. Due to the nonexistence of credit for the past three years, desperate small-scale landowners who are ruined and sell their land opt to take a 30 percent loss on its market value. It has become a market among poor people who trade within one segment of the market, outside the circle of better-located and better-quality land.

Default in Payments

In the subsidized land market program, campesinos have received 70 percent of the land price as a subsidy, and have had to commit to paying the remaining 30 percent, for which they have been advanced credit at commercial and variable interest rates, at a rate of increase of the consumer price index plus two points. This arrangement is slowly suffocating campesinos, due to the fact that interest rates are much higher than the actual income from working the land. Nearly all of the beneficiaries from 1998 have defaulted (Marulanda 1998, 11; Caja Agraria 1998), and the amount in arrears is almost ten thousand million pesos.

It is important to remember that, despite its failures, this is meant to be a pilot project, and such projects cannot escape a double isolationist approach. On the one hand they experiment in a costly laboratory that tries to remain separate from real life; on the other they formulate recommendations that, from the outset, leave the mainstay of the socioeconomic context intact, precisely because they were developed, trialed, and analyzed with the prevailing context as a given, rather than as something that contributed to the problem at hand.

For the same reasons, pilot projects create their own trouble; the subsidy covers the excess land price, but also helps to maintain it, making it hard to increase the project beyond a pilot stage. Furthermore, the subsidy does not cover money needed for housing and other non-land purchase investments. Only 259 families in the pilot projects aided by experts paid by the World Bank could benefit from the 732 million pesos for land improvements sent to the DRI fund and to municipalities, and they requested another 500 million pesos for investments apart from the land (Unidad de Gestión para la Reforma Agraria 1998).

Condemned to the status of a miniprogram, there have seemed to be only two alternative paths to continuing it. One would be to maintain the profile of the poor campesino as the beneficiary, offering not only subsidies to buy land, but also subsidies to pay the interest on the loan. This also involves legally establishing the possibility of expropriation through administrative means if a large-scale landowner refuses to negotiate or doesn't sell at prices suitable for profitability. Another alternative would be to transform the program by redefining the target population, and to subsidize land purchases only for people who have the capacity to invest and to contribute productive assets as well as administrative qualifications. Instead of a program to convert poor campesinos, rural salaried workers, small-scale landowners, and sharecroppers into small businessmen, the program would instead subsidize experienced businesspeople.

In fact, the proposal to subsidize producers with investment capabilities is nothing new. It was the country's previous model of rural development from 1922 to 1978, and between 1982 and 1990. Law 1483 of May 11, 1948, is illustrative of government subsidy for the expropriation of land through the market by the rich. It is the true precursor of the current World Bank program, not only because of its content, and of its failure, as a substitute for agrarian reform, but also because it coincided with a period of intense violence and massive displacement of campesinos in Colombia.

Shift in Agrarian Policy, 1980–2000

In Colombia in 1988, the proposal to divert land purchase subsidies to farmers with investment capabilities was just one small element within a larger move to return to large estates. At the center of this process were large investment projects in rural areas, and it was characterized first by the farming crisis, the bankruptcy of rural businessmen involved in transitory crops (medium- and small-scale businessmen), and finally by the displacement of hundreds of thousands of campesinos due to violence.

In 1998, the government of Andrés Pastrana sought to substitute the subsidized land market program with what the government called "strategic alliances" between large- and small-scale landowners and businessmen, and what the Bank called "associations for production," none of which sought to strengthen the campesino economy, but rather sought to subordinate campesinos and hand over their property to large farms.

The development plan of the Andrés Pastrana government assigned campesinos a completely subordinate role to large landowners. Its text, "Change in order to build peace," states:

> [F]arming and forestry production units are promoted, in which state support efforts are focused on rural development. This is defined as socioeconomic processes generated around a primary activity in which rural communities integrate with the business sector in strategic alliances within successful production projects that are already underway or that have a high probability of competitiveness . . . This strategy will also have access to resources from the private sector, public funds from the Peace Fund and international cooperation agencies.

In implementing the agrarian reform program, the trend will be towards an efficient and transparent model of voluntary negotiation and land purchases within concrete production projects carried out in a decentralized manner and with citizen oversight . . . and towards those in which, depending on their cost, not only land but also production assets can be partially or totally funded . . . (Cambio para construir la paz 1988, 260)

In short, the government proposed a rural reform that would be completely dependent on a large central investment, creating as satellites small-scale producers in the "alliance" system, a euphemism for their actual subordination. The new subsidy model made clear that there were two major, incompatible rural development alternatives in Colombia, and that these had been in conflict for decades. One approach was to achieve development by maintaining and consolidating large rural properties. The other was to foster development through the redistribution to campesinos of large-scale landholdings that are suitable for agriculture and are extremely underused. For example, some 5 million hectares are generally being used for extensive livestock ranches, which require minimal labor and involve the clearing off the land of its inhabitants. These landholdings, vast and underfarmed, are ripe for redistribution to landless and land poor campesinos (IGAC 1988; IGAC-Corpoica 2001; Fajardo and Mondragón 1997, 159).

Fans of the first alternative have spent twenty-five years accusing the second alternative of being obsolete or antiquated. What they don't seem to realize is that the development proposal based on large property holdings is equally old or older, and what is truly obsolete is the structure of rural property ownership, the large estate. These two alternative means of approaching the agrarian problem seem destined to continue to be in conflict; it remains for the Colombian government to find a path to real reform.

Preconditions for Genuine Social Transformation

When land prices are higher than their potential farming profitability, the policy of creating small-scale businessmen from among the campesino population is not actually viable, save with few exceptions. Conditions that impede small-scale businessmen from being successful would have to be addressed. There are six such conditions: (1) the concentration of landownership by large landowners; (2) land speculation and price; (3) the use of 5 million hectares of agriculturally suitable land for extensive cattle ranching and, as a counterpart, the cultivation of thousands of hectares of land that are not suitable for farm-ing; (4) high interest rates; (5) the absence of a strategy for food sovereignty; (6) the absence of a national foreign trade strategy.

The first three conditions can be corrected only through an agrarian reform that redistributes land among owners in accordance with adequate use of the land. The second condition also demands an adequate land tax system that contributes to the elimination of speculative accumulation of land.

The phenomenon of high interest rates is very complex, and has a variety of causes. Nevertheless, agrarian reform and the reorganization of land taxes would contribute to lowering interest rates in a decisive manner. Keynes (1958, 232) showed that some landowners have behaved as though they considered land to be a "liquid premium" because land, like money, is available in limited quantities. This premium, which produces a preference for accumulating land, fixes this kind of interest at a very high level that surpasses the yield of the land and stops growth. In Colombia those able to accumulate this land are often connected to the drug trade, and they hold their money in US currency, adding yet more downward pressure to the peso.

The regular economy must compete with the yields of drug trafficking, the high profitability of which raises interest rates. The success of drug trafficking in Colombia depends directly on thousands of tenant farmers who face a lack of land in the "agricultural frontier" and who move to the jungles, where they devote themselves to narco-crops, the only profitable crops in certain areas, and the only ones that landowners allow campesinos to grow, at least for the time being.

Agrarian reform would not only eliminate the premium of land accumu-lation, but would remove the labor force from drug trafficking, which would help to lower interest rates. It would reduce the space for businesses whose exaggerated, illegal, and atypical yields raise interest rates to extreme levels, and it would reduce the quantity of hoarded dollars, forcing those who have legal routes to reinvest them or to offer them on credit.

Campesinos who are already landowners operate without credit (only 7 per-cent of producers use credit). They flee from credit because they know that under the current conditions, if they lose their credit, they lose their land. Paradoxically, beneficiaries of the subsidy program for land purchase become losers: Forced to take credit they cannot repay, they subsequently lose the land, and, to add insult to injury, are entered into a database as being in arrears. Thus, in addition to no longer having land, which they did not have in the beginning, they now can no longer receive any kind of credit. Campesinos in this situation, as evidenced by in the requests for authorization to sell land that are continually presented to Incora's board, see no other way out than to sell their land. This result leads to a distortion of the objective of the subsidy, which itself ends up being distributed among a campesino who stops being a campesino, a landowner who is selling, and another buyer. As well, of course, this system lends itself to corruption.

To prevent such disasters, the World Bank's technocratic approach aims to give support to the beneficiary, first selecting them through "cream-skimming" criteria that exclude the majority of the less fortunate or endowment- and skill-poor campesinos; second, designing a financially sustainable production project; and third, guaranteeing a contract to market what is produced. These conditions, necessary for the success of the program, suggest that the cost and skills would be excessive.

The philosophy that fostered Law 160 has fallen by the wayside, as the pure market does not work. In light of the market's failure to resolve the agrarian problem, the reaction has been to return to plans to support large-scale land-owners, such as in the so-called strategic alliances and production associations.

The issue of land can be put forward in another way, in the context of a peace treaty, unlike that in Guatemala, in which neoliberal reform was a pre-condition of funding for the peace process. What is needed is a peace process that includes an agrarian reform program based on campesino needs, and not economic dogma, and provides for interest rates to be lowered and subsidized, together with a strategy that protects national food production in the name of food sovereignty. This would, in other words, reverse the conditions imposed by neoliberalism, which ruined national agriculture, adopting instead community planning and management. A real solution should also promote a special regime of landownership that protects campesinos and their communities in a way that truly enables them to manifest their goals.

Campesino Reserves: A Concrete Proposal for Land Reform, Redistribution and Sustainable Development

Agrarian reform isn't about markets. It's about transforming regions, and the lives within them. There is no reason to insist on a casuist, marginal, and mercantile model. If we plan to abide by the ecological and economic goals of reform, the first areas chosen should be those in which soils suitable for agriculture are currently being used for extensive cattle ranching. These lands should be expropriated and declared as campesino reserve areas. The buying and selling of plots should be limited to commerce among campesinos, property size should be given maximum and minimum limitations, and campesino land rights should be inalienable. If the land market is not limited, the effect of redistribution is consumed and ends up in a new cycle of concentration.

Other campesino reserve areas might be tenant farmer areas. At this time there is no enforcement of Law 160, according to which all tenant farmer areas become campesino reserves if they have not been declared for business development. Only five campesino reserves have been created in Pato-Balsillas. Only two of these and part of one other are included in the World Bank's pilot program: Pato-Balsillas, Calamar (part of the Guaviare reserve), and Cabrera (Cundinamarca). These reserves have suffered a great deal of violence since the peace negotiations broke down.

While the entire process to approve the Valle del río Cimitarra as a reserve has been completed, its approval has nevertheless been delayed, and violence against in that region has intensified. The World Bank and other international entities could voice their support for the development plan for Magdalena Medio with the Campesino Reserve of the Valle del río Cimitarra, but thus far, certain interests have blocked the resolution declaring the reserve. The procedure in the lower Ricaurte (Boyacá) has also been delayed, and there are requests in process for Arauca, Lozada-Guayabero (Meta), Montes de María (Bolívar-Sucre), and Tomachipán (Guaviare, the first area to request reserve status, has received no attention).

It seems clear that these requests would multiply if Incora had legal norms that allowed it to redistribute land to land-poor people through administrative expropriation and through an end to the domination of large amounts of property that are inadequately used. The weakness in the reform program, as it has been developed to this time, is in the redistribution of land; the law, as has been explained here, does not provide adequate instruments for its implementation. For example, only two estates have been redistributed to a campesino reserve (Pato-Balsillas).

We have seen in recent years the intensification of conflicts, the displaced, the black communities, the assassination of indigenous people, the marches by campesinos and indigenous, and campesino work stoppages in Colombia—yet the country seems deaf and blind to this situation, and commitments made are broken.

If there is no change of perspective regarding the budget allocated to campesinos, to indigenous peoples, to black communities, and to agrarian reform, the Colombian conflict will continue to intensify. Attempts to destroy rural life through a neoliberal model have run up not only against campesino resistance but also against complex rural communities from an economic and social point of view. Instead of trying to break this rural community dynamic, these communities should be treated as a huge economic and political force capable of fostering transformation from the very roots of society.

Conclusion

There is a need in Colombia today to recognize the role of the campesino economy and to consider it as a strategic sector, to recognize rural communities as subjects of development with a collective capacity for decision making. The viability of the campesino economy can be maintained by taking advantage of some of its characteristics:

- The capacity to devote itself to producing widely accepted products in the world market and to consolidate itself for long periods in their production
- Its knowledge of agroecological environments that require special management, primarily in the Andean region and in the Amazon, but also in other areas
- Its ability to produce more cheaply certain goods for consumers who do not have access to other markets
- Its key role in the reproduction of a labor force, given that Colombia's food comes from rural areas

Since 1993, Colombian campesino organizations have actively confronted the World Bank's subsidized land market project, especially the Bank's attempts to offer it as a substitute for agrarian reform. Campesinos carried out mobilizations in September, 1993, after which they reached a partial agreement with the government, the terms of which were ultimately not fulfilled because the congress did not approve administrative expropriation. This result emphatically underscored the reality that Colombia does not have agrarian reform through expropriation, a program that can be applied only after a long judicial process.

In October 1998, February and June of 1999, and September 2000, campesinos mobilized to make clear the complete failure of the program. In September 16, 2002, they mobilized again, in favor of real agrarian reform and against neoliberal policies and the FTAA.

Campesinos articulate the following points as forming a basis for an alternate reform plan:

- Devolve state-level responsibilities and power to communities directly, instead of giving decentralized power to local and departmental caciques
- Renegotiate international trade agreements for the Colombian farming sector that protect national production and guarantees access to local markets
- Carry out a massive agrarian reform that benefits 1 million families and puts 5 million hectares of land suitable for farming into use for production, lands that have been underused by large estate owners engaged in speculation
- Make campesino reserves a priority of agrarian reform programs as well as the reorganization of areas for the campesino economy
- Recognize campesino communities' right to land and create a constitutional norm affirming the inalienability of campesino reserves
- Establish real credit with special low interest rates for campesinos
- Create a cooperative or associative campesino program for marketing and agro-industrial processing of rural products
- Undertake assessment and planning for the production, reproduction, and conservation of renewable natural resources and respect for community ownership of genetic resources
- Contract with campesino, Afrocolombian, and indigenous communities for the management of areas of ecological importance
- Approve a law to protect national food production that would serve as the basis for a national strategy of international trade, and establish norms to control the use of mechanical, chemical, and biological technologies

Such a program would be expensive, but the question is whether it costs more than the current war that attempts to carry out a classic program of "cleaning," or clearing, the countryside for development. The discussion about the viability of the campesino sector coincides with the discussion about the viability of peace. Violent paths, such as the war in Colombia, represent one alternative. The other is to foster massive campesino participation, and not simply the marginal participation of a few campesinos favored by programs and politics that are compatible with, and part of, a policy of war.

Many people in government and the World Bank believe that the participation of campesino communities takes place through workshops and, particularly, through state-program committees. While these forums are important, the real problem has to do with power and the availability of economic means. As long as they have no power, committees will be abandoned by people who see that they are useless. As long as decentralization means strengthening local and departmental caciques, participation will be a lie. As long as campesinos and indigenous peoples cannot participate in decision making, including in shaping international agreements that affect their lives, participation will not be real.

The change required implies not a "conservation" or maintenance of miniprograms of political favoritism; it involves replacing the model of domination for one of participation, poverty for campesino development, and marginalization for respect as part of a new national life. Current affairs in Colombia tell us this, as do the numerous new agrarian struggles throughout Latin America, to the surprise of those who had declared the agrarian problem to be nonexistent.

At this crossroad, the path to choose should not be the route already taken, of subsidized land markets as part of a new project of privileges for large-scale landowners. It should be the path of agrarian reform as an in-depth solution to the problems of poverty, violence, and disempowerment in Colombia.

CHAPTER 9

The World Bank's Market-Based Land Reform in Brazil

Sérgio Sauer

Brazilian rural and people's movements (members of the National Forum on Agrarian Reform and Rural Justice) have raised serious criticisms of the World Bank's market-oriented land reform ever since the first loan was first announced. The criticisms have ranged from questions about the market's ability to deconcentrate land to doubts about the real objectives of this kind of financial mechanism (political interests and real beneficiaries) in countries like Brazil, South Africa, and the Philippines.

Five years after the creation of the *Cédula da Terra* (literally, "land bill," as in a dollar bill) project, through the first pilot project of the three successive versions of market-oriented land reform in Brazil, these organizations began research to appraise the situation of families participating in the project. The data from that study corroborate many of the criticisms regarding the objectives and the effectiveness of the World Bank's market land reform program.[1]

Brazilian Agriculture and the Present Government's Land Tenure Policies

Brazil's 8,547 square kilometers of land, including its 415.5 million hectares of tillable farmland, make it nearly a continent in itself. It reaps 90 million tons of grain per year. A 1996 agriculture census by the Brazilian Institute of Geography and Statistics (IBGE) revealed that there are 25 million hectares of "fallow" land (unplanted for up to four years), accounting for nearly 60 percent of all land suitable for annual or perennial crops.

The country has one of the world's most perverse and highly concentrated landholding structures, with a Gini-coefficient near 0.9—nearly total concentration of ownership in few hands—as a result of a its *latifundio*-style (large estate–based) agriculture and land tenure system, exacerbated since the 1960s and 1970s by the introduction of the policies of the green revolution.

According to the 1996 census data, there are a total of 4.8 million farms in the country, covering 353.6 million hectares. Of the total number of farms, 89.1 percent are *minifundia* (smaller than one fiscal module, the minimum deemed necessary to support a family) and farms under 100 hectares, yet these account for only 20 percent of the land area. At the other extreme of the landholding structure, large holdings (over 1,000 hectares) account for 1 percent of the total number of farms and 45 percent of the farmland area. These large landholdings make up a sector that includes over 35,000 farms classified as unproductive *latifundia*, covering a total land area of 166 million hectares.

Other land tenure figures reveal that, in 1970, farms smaller than 100 hectares accounted for 90.8 percent of total farms, covering 23.5 percent of the area. In the 1996 census, the share of the number of small farms had dropped to 89.3 percent, and their area to 20 percent of the total. On the other hand, only 0.7 percent of landholdings in 1970 were over 1,000 hectares in size, covering 39.5 percent of the total area. By 1996, these latter figures had evolved to 1 percent of total farms, and 45 percent of the area.

An estimate produced by the federal government's own Applied Economics Research Institute (IPEA) places the number of potential beneficiaries of a land reform program in Brazil (landowners, renters, sharecroppers, squatters, and wage earners) at approximately 4.5 million families.[2]

Under Brazil's constitution, land reform must take place through the expropriation of large landholdings (areas over 15 fiscal modules) that do not fulfill a social function or are considered unproductive. Unproductive farms are those classified as not achieving 80 percent of the use of tillable land, or whose yields are below 100 percent of the average per-hectare productivity rates. The expropriation process includes long-term payment of compensation (through twenty-year bonds) for the value of the land, and cash payments for improvements. This process and the settlement of landless farmers (the execution of the land reform policy) are the responsibility of the National Settlement and Agrarian Reform Institute (INCRA), currently a branch of the Ministry of Agrarian Development (MDA).

Early in its second term in 1998, the former government of Fernando Henrique Cardoso (FHC) launched a new agrarian policy, labeled the New

Rural World.[3] The policy focused on three key issues that embody a break with the discourse and practice of the FHC government during its first term.

The first thrust was to reduce agrarian policy to a compensatory or social welfare–type of policy. In the thinking of international agencies, particularly the World Bank, land reform has become a tool to alleviate or to fight rural poverty, rather to develop the economy. Democratization of land access is nothing more than a means to ease social pressures in rural areas, especially through poverty alleviation. Democratization of landholding is not seen as a way to distribute assets or to allow for any innovation in the development model (even though extreme poverty is, in fact, considered an obstacle to current concepts of development).

The second novel aspect in Brazil's present agrarian policies was the decentralization of all landholding actions. This is a strategic issue for the implementation of agrarian policies as a process of defederalization that delegates responsibilities heretofore reserved to the federal government. All programs, projects, and policy proposals for agrarian policy making are now made with reference to the drive to decentralize actions, therefore interlinking decentralization, democratization, and efficiency.

Yet decentralization does not in fact mean democratization or greater participation by the most directly affected people and families. It is a delegation of power to state and municipal authorities, which are more intimately related with and susceptible to the political influence of the local power structures made up of the landed oligarchy, which still carries political weight in broad sectors of the state. Rather than a solution (through greater efficiency and agility), therefore, decentralization can actually make land reform actions unfeasible. Programs and projects like the Cédula, the Land Bank (Banco da Terra), and Land Credit (Crédito Fundiário) are mechanisms that help consolidate this defederalization or decentralization by depleting and then destroying land reform. These programs pass the buck, not to states or municipalities, but to the market, where they come into the hands of landowners. The INCRA's loss of power then justifies budget cutbacks and cost containment, as part of the movement to downsize the state and privatize its responsibilities.

The third part of this New Rural World policy is the commodification of landless farmworkers' historic demands. Commodification takes on several guises, but the launching of the so-called market-oriented land reform is the most explicit of them.

These features of present-day agrarian policies in Brazil are aligned with guidelines and policies set out by the World Bank for poverty-alleviation programs. The government's agrarian policy follows the World Bank recipe book, which goes beyond market-oriented land reform to propose a number of changes (including decentralization) as a recipe for a country's economic development.

The Cédula da Terra project

On November 30, 2000, the board of directors of the World Bank approved the request for a second loan of approximately US$200 million to expand Brazil's market-oriented land reform. World Bank documents show that these funds would ensure continuity of the Cédula da Terra pilot project, expanding the land-purchase mechanism from five to fifteen Brazilian states.[4] The initial proposal was to earmark the funds for the creation of the Land Bank (Jungmann 1999, 4). In response to outright opposition from all organizations and movements in the National Agrarian Reform and Rural Justice Forum, the World Bank decided to redirect this loan to finance the establishment of the Land Credit Program for Fighting Rural Poverty (also included in the law that created the Land Bank), as a continuation of the Cédula da Terra "experience."

The Cédula da Terra program (its official name is the Land Reform and Poverty Alleviation Pilot Project) arose from a partnership between the federal government and the World Bank that was written into Loan Agreement 4147-BR. Originally conceived as a pilot project, the Cédula was officially announced in 1996 and implemented beginning in 1997 in five states (Ceará, Maranhão, Pernambuco, Bahia, and northern Minas Gerais). The selection of those states was justified by the tremendous concentration of poverty in Brazil's northeast.

The Cédula da Terra project basically involved creating a credit line for landless farmworkers and *minifundistas* to buy land. Beneficiaries would organize in legally constituted associations responsible for directly negotiating the purchase of land from owners. Associations would then choose the farms to be purchased with bank funds, which—once the project was approved by the state technical unit—would go directly to the owner. Although the Cédula began as a pilot project, by 1999 (before any kind of evaluation) the Brazilian government had created the Land Bank (Banco da Terra), modeled on the Cédula. Despite promises to support this project, the World Bank ended up funding the creation of the Land Credit project (Crédito Fundiário, created in 2001), essentially an attempt to rename these efforts to evade pressures and questions raised by Brazilian and international people's movements and NGOs. The Land Credit project actually has the same features and objectives as the Cédula and the Land Bank, amounting to a mere change of names to maintain the World Bank's money and purposes in Brazil.

The Cédula's target participants was made up of landless wage earners, renters, and sharecroppers, as well as *minifundistas*, poor farmers without enough land for subsistence. The goal was to settle 15,000 families in three years (this was later extended to four years). The total cost was estimated at US$150 million, with US$45 million coming from the federal government to purchase land. The World Bank's US$90 million loan was to be used to fund complementary community investments.[5] The remaining amount was committed by state governments (US$6 million) and a community counterpart (US$9 million), mainly in the form of labor.

Both the purchase of land and the loans (grants) for community investments were done through the beneficiaries' associations. Initially, the project was to make loans for the purchase of land to be paid back in ten years, including a three-year grace period. The families' debts would be indexed to the long-range interest rate (TJLP, in Portuguese), somewhere around 15 percent per year in 1997, well above the annual inflation rate. In response to criticism from social movements, the federal government changed the conditions (when it created the Land Bank, in 1999) to extend the payment term to twenty years, still maintaining the three-year grace period. Servicing and interest on the loans would cost 4 percent per year, well below the TJLP and closer to inflation rates.

At first there were no restrictions on the land to be purchased with the loans, even for areas that could be expropriated under the constitution. This allowed the Cédula to be used to pay for unproductive *latifundias*, paying in cash for areas that could be expropriated by issuing bonds. Questioning and pressure from rural social movements forced changes to these loan conditions, forbidding the purchase of areas larger than 15 fiscal modules, which could be expropriated for agrarian reform purposes. According to the preliminary evaluation report contracted by the World Bank, the general objective of the Cédula da Terra was to reduce poverty in the northeast by increasing the income of approximately 15,000 poor rural families, who would gain access to land and would also participate in complementary subprojects that respond to the communities' own demands. Another major objective was to test this pilot land reform project, in which beneficiaries are funded for the purpose of buying land through direct negotiations between rural communities and landowners (Buainain et al.). One specific objective of the Cédula was to have the government monitor the project's efficiency so as to build the government's capacity to accelerate its own land reform program by lowering the cost of land. The project was also justified by the creation of more agile and effective mechanisms than those state-centered ones considered "burdensome" (in the World Bank's own language) expropriations for agrarian reform. These were market mechanisms.

The Ministry of Agrarian Development has justified the creation of the Cédula project based on three objectives: cheaper and faster market-facilitated settlements; pacification of the countryside, as the landless negotiate land acquisitions themselves; and the ministry's contribution to fiscal adjustment through cost reductions as part of IMF-mandated structural adjustments. A peaceful, debureaucratized land reform that is more compatible with new times of economic stabilization is the official language government officials use to justify their adherence to the World Bank's market-based land-reform policy. The common thread running through all such justifications (explicit in the official discourse) is the idea that market mechanisms will provide access to land without confrontations or disputes and therefore reduce social problems and federal expenses at the same time.

From the point of view of critical organizations and people's social movements, however, the Cédula had other objectives and principles in mind. First of all, it aimed to take "ideology and politics" out of land reform in Brazil. Buying and selling would remove confrontation from the struggle for land and isolate rural movements and organizations that had struggled for decades for a broad-based agrarian reform. In the official discourse, the Cédula project would bring peace to the countryside. Instead of confrontation (land takeovers and demands for agrarian reform), families would peacefully and directly negotiate the purchase of land from *latifundia* owners. The interest of the latter would be assured because they would be paid in cash (rather than twenty-year bonds) for their unproductive land.

To date, Cédula money has been a very effective tool in undermining grassroots support for rural organizations and people's movements fighting for land. The availability of money to buy land—coupled with talk of peaceful land reform, no more takeovers, etc.—helps to demobilize anyone wanting a piece of land to work, because it raises the false expectation that one can get land without political struggle. This pattern has continued with the creation of the Land Bank and Land Credit project, also funded by World Bank money.

The Reality of the Cédula Project: Research Results

In 2002, a study (sponsored by several Brazilian land reform organizations and on which this paper is based) was commissioned to evaluate whether this kind of program achieved its minimal objectives of providing better living conditions for Cédula beneficiaries. There was wide agreement that it is incapable of democratizing Brazil's concentrated landholding structure or of promoting any kind of agrarian reform. Even so, the study sought to assess whether there had been improvements such as political emancipation, access to land at lower prices, or access to infrastructure (water, power, basic sanitation, etc.) for families buying land through the Cédula. The information came from interviews with families living in sixteen different Cédula areas, interviews with technical officials responsible for the project, and analysis of official documents in the five states involved in the project. Despite difficulties in acquiring access to official data (the general official attitude is that agencies should not provide documents or data on the project), the study corroborates many of the criticisms and questions from people's movements and NGOs.

Living Conditions of Beneficiary Families

The overriding goal of the World Bank's market-oriented land reform (and others aimed at rural development) is to alleviate poverty. Since the phrase shows up in every single World Bank document, the study set out to discover whether there has actually been any improvement in living conditions for families on land bought through the Cédula.

Overall, the beneficiaries' generally gave a positive evaluation of their living conditions as a result of using the Cédula da Terra to fulfill their desire to own land. People reported that the most significant change was that they were now "owners" of land and were thus working, as well as administering their own labor (the "peasant project" of free labor). They also stated that now they had a place to live, although they were aware that they had to pay for it and that they could be expelled if they did not pay the loan they had signed.

In accordance with the Cédula project's general rules, aimed as it is at poor people, interviewees had been in a precarious situation and lived in extreme poverty before buying land. The overwhelming majority had temporary jobs and were underemployed, with low income and wages and very bad living conditions. This previous situation of precariousness and extreme poverty led to an evaluation that living conditions had improved with landownership. This kind of situation makes the Cédula a lifesaver, especially since, in addition to the land, during the first months beneficiaries receive what is called a salary.

Even seeing the Cédula as the only option, however, many interviewees voiced negative opinions regarding their situation on the new land in several areas. Many even stated that they now face greater hardships than they had in the past. Unkept promises, particularly when funds are not released for production or for infrastructure, were among the most common reasons for this generalized discontent.

Dissatisfaction was recurrent in the various areas surveyed, for a variety of reasons and motives, but the holding back of funds for infrastructure (World Bank funds) and for production (public funds) topped the list of complaints. The shortage of funds—along with the lack of technical assistance—has created many problems that have resulted in precarious living conditions in the areas. Drought, for example, is a serious problem in the entire region where the Cédula has been implemented. Without money, people cannot afford to confront the problem. There are several areas with no supply of drinking water because the funds were not released. To varying degrees, all sixteen projects visited for this research reported problems regarding access to water (lack of water, no water pipes, and—above all—delays in funding for irrigation projects), as well as difficulties with transportation, schools, basic sanitation, and health. Electric power was also a public service not available to most projects (and for others not affordable).

Even when "having a place to live" was seen in a positive light, there were cases in which, three to four years after a project was launched, not all the houses had yet been built because funds had not arrived or were insufficient. Many schools were not built and children had no transportation to go to schools in the closest towns. In contrast to these problems and delays in getting enough funds released, interviewees did not report major difficulties in the release of money to pay for the land once their loans were approved. The payment was made directly by the bank to the landowner.

One important indicator of the hardships and precarious living conditions faced is the high rate of families who have abandoned the land. It was hard to obtain such general data on the Cédula, but in the areas visited there were high dropout rates, with up to 60 percent of the families having given up in some cases. Reasons for this were directly related to the difficulty of surviving off the land due to lack of production, income, and other related factors.

Negotiation Process and Knowledge of Project Rules

The Cédula da Terra was conceived according to and is executed following market-based rules, especially regarding the purchase of land. This means, in the first place, that a project can buy only farms that are for sale. Land markets are still incipient in Brazil, and the lack of funds obliges people to buy cheaper, low-quality land. The market price of land doesn't fall in the negotiating process (considering the buyers' bargaining power). Rather, the short supply and lack of funds force buyers to purchase cheaper farms that are far from markets and have poor soil. The limit on funds to buy land (US$11,000 per family, including the price of the land and the cost of infrastructure) is a further problem in the purchase process. This limit pushes projects into less dynamic regions on less valuable land with poorer soil and severe limitations on production, which has a direct impact on farmers' ability to produce or to meet obligations and makes it hard to pay for the land in the first place.

Second, the survey confirmed that families have had little or no influence over decisions, such as choice of farms, or in the negotiating process, such as setting the price of land. Most of the negotiations are done by the government officials in charge—a clear challenge to market-based logic—who ultimately set the course of any deal, based on their knowledge of the funding limits (and, at times, their personal relations with the seller). There have been reports of cases in which bargaining did actually lower the final price, but in no case has the negotiating been done directly by the interested families themselves. The survey revealed that all the individuals interviewed—including association presidents—in all five states stated that they had not participated directly either in the choice or in the purchase of the farm and that these decisions were made by the local agency responsible for the Cédula. Official agencies that should play supporting roles end up taking the lead. The power to choose is wielded by government officials, blocking any participatory or educational process.

Obstacles to participation are aggravated by the families' own situation and their lack of information. Their hardships and this chance to move up in life make families anxious to purchase their land. They are often predisposed to pay any price and deal with the affordability problem later (their immediate demand is to get the land). This short-sightedness on the part of beneficiaries is heightened by the competition for funds, as families know that there is little money in the program for the many who want to participate, and a delay in the negotiation process may mean exclusion from the project.

Another real obstacle to participation is that people have not known the rules of the game. Interviewees revealed they have had no information about the project's basic elements. This became clear when they were asked about loan payment conditions. Except for the grace period and final payment term (although some still thought it was ten years), not a single interviewee knew what the interest rate would be or even the amount to be paid in the first installment (which was about to come due at the time), much less the alternatives available if they were unable to pay. This situation implies a tremendous imbalance between the two negotiating parties and explains the dominant presence of public officials in the land-buying process. The same imbalance was also identified in the preliminary evaluation, which found that "in all the situations listed, negotiations are on an unequal basis. The parties meet divided by unequal rights vis-à-vis the land market, and what is supposed to be full information is a fiction."

Interviewees also stated that only landowners sit down to negotiate with the government (the responsible public official), making any participatory process impossible. Their willingness to sell depends on the guarantee provided by an official presence (the program is the state's responsibility, which should be assurance enough of a good price for the land). The major role and intervention of the state denies any chance for true market logic to operate, thus revealing this program's underlying faults.

Associations, Participation, and Building Citizenship

One of the World Bank's basic guidelines for funding social programs is to foster the participation of the people and social groups directly involved in the projects. At the same time, to gain access to Cédula da Terra funds, landless families must be organized in a legally registered community association. Interested families must organize an association (which a priori is a forum for participation and decision making) through which they can then apply for funding.

The preliminary evaluation had already observed a number of problems related to the formation of and decisions made by these associations, including the influence and participation of local politicians and landowners in their organization and creation. Such problems became apparent in the interviews. While confirming the importance of their associations, the majority of interviewees said they had little participation in them, and they reported fre-

quent cases of deviation of funds, imposition of leaders (even by local authorities), and decisions taken from outside the association regarding matters such
as kinds of investments and forms of organization, and imposed on the group.

In addition to these problems with associations, there were also reports of
impositions regarding decisions on collective investments. Public agencies
responsible for organizing the Cédula da Terra in the states decided that each
area should create collective plantations (under the association's responsibility).[6] The basic objective of the collective areas is to produce cash crops to
assure payment for the purchase of the land. In addition to, or perhaps as a
result of, the imposition of collective investments, community or collective
plantations operate by paying day wages. Funds from the infrastructure sub-
project (SIC) are earmarked for these kinds of payments, making community
or collective labor a way to pay for the funds allocated to the families' initial
maintenance in the areas. Each project organizes the work as it sees fit, but
generally every person works two or three days per week in the community
investment. This labor is paid on a daily basis (interviewees said it ranges
between five and seven Brazilian reals per day), thus reproducing the logic of
exploitation of rural wage laborers.

The practice of paying those who work in collective initiatives through daily
wages turns people into "wage-earners" or "employees" of their own association or community. First, these people do not control or appropriate the
process because they are being paid to provide a service, just as in any wage-
earning situation. Second, they do not appropriate their own investment
because it is not theirs but is seen rather as belonging to "the association" or
to "the responsible agency."

The entire process is authoritarian because it imposes certain practices and
values. The people should not be forced to carry out activities (collective initiatives) or adopt lifestyles to which they are not accustomed just because they
participate in a loan program.[7] This kind of imposition is diametrically
opposed to "free-market philosophy" and to social organization based on com-
petitiveness and efficiency, as espoused by the Cédula da Terra. It also runs
contrary to the logic of community empowerment touted by the World Bank
because it blocks social processes capable of fostering free and autonomous
citizens. The survey also revealed that most of these attempts to organize production have been failures. They have not paid enough for people to cover their
installments, and the imposition of "collective labor" has discouraged community help and cooperation initiatives, thus causing both social and economic losses for families included in the *Cédula* program.

Farm Production and the Ability to Repay Loans

Situations differed in the various areas surveyed, particularly in terms of soil quality (for example, fertility, depth, and gradient) and availability of other natural resources such as water. Despite this geographic diversity, the data revealed similarities, among many interviews, regarding problems and precarious situations in the areas, including a clearly generalized hardship to keep up with installments on the loan to purchase the land.

Perceptions of soil quality were diverse, ranging from "the land is good" to evaluations like "part is good and other parts are weak" and even statements that the "land is not good at all." In all the projects visited, most people reported difficulties in farming, especially on their individual lots (lack of technical assistance and funds for investment were the most frequent complaints).

Drought is a constant problem in the northeast, but there were serious problems related to the quality of the land purchases, such as soil fertility, the depth of the soil, its rockiness or unsuitability for many crops, or that the purchased areas were located in forests protected by environmental laws, and so on. As a result, farm production on the projects surveyed was basically for subsistence.

Interviewees stated that production on individual lots did not generate enough income even for survival, much less for capitalization or new investments in production. Families interviewed used a variety of survival strategies, such as working as day laborers or taking jobs away from the farm as domestic workers, or employees in stores. The most common strategy was to take an occasional day-labor job doing chores on other farms in the region.

Farm output has not allowed families to achieve the ambition of competitive insertion into markets. The Cédula da Terra project has not gotten people into the market by allowing for production and income generation in the countryside. Instead it has reproduced precarious situations that have driven family members into outside jobs to survive.

The same problem appeared in collective investments, which have taken a larger share of funds to build infrastructure (as in irrigation projects), purchase farm inputs, and pay for technical assistance. These investments were supposed to produce monoculture cash crops and generate income to pay back the loans, but this has not happened, due to a variety of obstacles to collective production. First, local agencies have put most infrastructure funds into making collective production viable, leaving individual lots to fall to second place in priority. Collective lots have then received the greatest amount of investments in technology (mainly for irrigation) and technical assistance. Such investments in the collective lots, however, mean even greater losses for families who for many reasons (including poor technical advice) cannot harvest enough to keep up on their Cédula loan installments. Of the sixteen areas surveyed, only two reported no problems with this kind of initiative. The problems observed varied from the imposition of this form of organization by local agencies and delays in release of investment funds to mistaken technical orientation, all of which have created serious barriers to the viability of such initiatives.

The survey has allowed us to conclude that very few families covered by the Cédula da Terra earn enough to eat and survive. Most don't harvest enough to feed their families, much less to save money or to make a reserve for their loan installments. While details have varied considerably from one project to another, there was near unanimity in stating that people have not been able to afford to cover the first installments on their loans.

While they denied the credibility of these denunciations and of the questioning of people's ability to pay, agencies had already been expecting delinquency regarding payment. During a visit to Maranhão (one of the states included in the program), INCRA's national superintendent in 1997, Milton Seligman, voiced serious doubts about the Cédula families' ability to pay. A local paper reported that Seligman ". . . recognized that the government has doubts about whether people settled by the Cédula da Terra can afford to pay their loans, which is why the program is being launched as an experiment" (*Estado do Maranhão*, September 16, 1997).

In the state of Bahia, our survey coincided with a process of "recompacting" contracts whose first installments were coming due. Unofficially, the renegotiations were to cover over forty-nine projects, extending the terms and modifying payment conditions. The negotiations were case-by-case and payments were being rescaled with lower payments during the first years, at values that, in the words of one official, now made them "something nearly symbolic, to give 'em a break." We had no access to these documents, but the term-extension process revealed the hardships faced by families in achieving the Cédula project's goals.

While willing to pay, interviewees were unanimous in stating that they would not be able to comply with their commitment to make the first installment. This inability to make any kind of payment was recurrent in all interviews, leaving no doubt as to the precarious situation in the areas surveyed.

The difficulty in earning enough income has not been caused only by the loan conditions (interest rates, service charges, terms, etc.), although these have been totally inappropriate for the project's reality and purposes. Problems have also arisen from a variety of factors, including production shortfalls, which have totally compromised the success of this kind of project. Production shortfalls, as we have seen, are caused by a combination of factors such as poor soil (buyers cannot afford to buy better land), lack of investments and technical advice (or bad advice), precarious natural resources (rainfall, water supply), and so on. Families included in the project not only have continued to be poor but have not been able to afford to pay back their loans. This situation was made very clear in all the interviews, and was most meaningfully put by one respondent to the 2002 study, interviewed at the Acary Farm Project in Matto Grosso, who said, "Before I had nothing and owed nothing. Now I have nothing and owe money. I have land, but a debt too."

Conclusion

Despite some recognition of improvements, living conditions in the Cédula areas surveyed have been shown to be very precarious. Families have been unable to produce enough to survive, forcing family members to take outside jobs. Many of the parcels bought were on poor-quality soils because better-quality areas were beyond the means provided by the Cédula. Spending more on better land would have meant less money for investments, making the funding ceiling an insoluble problem.

The hardships, however, have gone far beyond natural problems like soil quality and drought and have involved causes inherent to the project's own internal logic. The problems of people fighting to survive under serious limitations (lack of education and skills, poor health, etc.) will not be solved merely by gaining a piece of land (although this is the underlying dream of families included). High-quality, long-term technical assistance needs, which were not included in the project design, will never be met through market mechanisms.

Problems are further aggravated when the release of funds is delayed or denied, both for infrastructure projects (World Bank funds) and for production (public funds for agricultural credit). In all the projects surveyed these delays occurred, seriously compromising the families' capacity for production. The difficulties highlighted a precarious situation for the settlements (no production, inadequate basic infrastructure, etc.) and revealed why interviewees were unanimous in stating that they would not be able to pay their debts (not even their first installment).

In conclusion, this dramatic situation of poverty will not be overcome by any kind of market mechanism, much less through a credit line to buy a piece of land. It is crucial that the struggle for a broad agrarian reform be strengthened, to invert the political balance of forces and the dynamic of social exclusion, making true social development into a viable pathway.

CHAPTER 10

Gender and Land

Sofía Monsalve Suárez

The processes of women's self-organization and self-empowerment
that we are building are the new spring that will inspire our struggle
for agrarian reform.
—*Cochabamba Declaration*

One of the dangers of presenting an analysis of gender and land is that it can
too easily be compartmentalized and plucked away for examination from the
patriarchal mainstream of land politics. Decontextualized in this way, free-
floating ideas about gender and land lend themselves to policy interventions
that attempt to mainstream them once again. Yet gender politics in debates
about land are not supplementary analyses to be mainstreamed, nor are they
ahistorical complaints about power; they are actively constructed engage-
ments with existing institutional politics. To address this concern, this chapter begins with a short introduction to the institutional context and location of
the gender issue, specifically looking at gender issues within the international
peasant movement, *La Via Campesina,* and its Global Campaign for Agrarian
Reform (for which I work) before moving to consider the gendered land politics that have been addressed through these forums.[1]

Background

Structural adjustment programs and regional and global trade agreements in
play since the 1980s have had disastrous effects on the lives of rural communities, and have unleashed profound social and economic transformations in
the countryside. It is within this landscape that La Via Campesina formally constituted itself in 1993, with the avowed purpose of collectively confronting
threats from, and the perpetrators of, these policies, while articulating the
visions and demands of diverse rural groups.[2] La Via Campesina's creation
resulted from a series of encounters and exchanges primarily between peasant

organizations from the Americas and Europe. These organizations sought a common analysis and understanding of their position in current, increasingly globalized economic, social, and political relations; and of the principal changes affecting rural communities all over the world, such as increasing poverty and inequality, the accelerating disappearance of small- and medium-scale producers, the destruction of the social fabric in the countryside, and the continued devaluation of the peasant identity, and peasant forms of life and production as a result of this latest attack by agricultural modernization, among other pressures. This convergence was also motivated by the need to exchange experiences and strategies for organization and struggle in the face of such threats, and to explore possible forms of collective resistance and action.

In this analysis, the peasant organizations identified the international financial institutions (IFIs), particularly the World Bank and the International Monetary Fund (IMF), and the regional and global free-trade treaties that preceded and have since accompanied the World Trade Organization (WTO), as the main promoters of structural adjustment policies. The policies of fiscal austerity, reductions in social spending, and market liberalization had a severe effect on peasant and indigenous communities. Noteworthy among these policies are the processes of the deregulation of landownership and agrarian counterreform; the dismantling of rural public services and those that supported production and commercialization by small and medium producers; the fostering of highly capitalized, high-technology agricultural exportation; the push toward the liberalization of agricultural commerce and toward policies of food security that are based on international commerce. In this analysis, the peasant organizations also identified the fact that the institutional framework and the decision-making processes of agrarian and agricultural policies had shifted from the national to the larger subcontinental and international levels, and it was thus crucial that peasant organizations also articulate their efforts beyond national frameworks in order to effectively act and defend their rights and interests regionally and internationally.

The food sovereignty framework was thus developed as an alternative proposal to the neoliberal orthodoxy (Rosset 2003). La Via Campesina has become a leading global social movement, radically opposed to neoliberalism, seeking to strengthen the processes of self-organization and autonomy of the peasant movement. It also seeks to strengthen alliances with other sectors in order to develop policies and institutional frameworks alternative to the current ones, so as to achieve a more just world. It is within this framework, and within the constitution of La Via Campesina, that the concrete demand emerged for "The recognition of the rights of peasant women who play an essential role in agricultural and food production."

Rural women have actively participated in the debate and the political construction of this movement, and La Via Campesina is seriously committed to the struggle for gender equality. It was women who, for example, demanded that "the right to produce our own food in our own territory" be placed at the very heart of the notion of food sovereignty (Desmarais 2003a, 2003b; La Via Campesina 2003). Furthermore, women introduced the issue of health into the critique of an agriculture that is highly dependent on chemicals, and they articulated the need for a sustainable agriculture that protects the environment. It should be emphasized that the International Coordinating Commission of La Via Campesina comprises equal gender representation; every region must elect a male and a female representative. The fact that La Via Campesina has attached such importance to the topic of gender has forced the issue onto the agendas of member regions and organizations, and it has opened up important opportunities and forums for peasant and indigenous women at the national and international levels.

One of the institutional instruments assisting this cooperation has been the collaboration between La Via Campesina and the FoodFirst Information and Action Network (FIAN). FIAN is an international human rights organization that lobbies for the right to adequate food and places a particular emphasis on the right to feed oneself. The organization was founded in Germany in 1986, and it has sections and offices in twenty-one countries and individual members in over sixty countries. The network was founded by human rights activists who noticed that civil rights violations were usually preceded by a great number of economic and social rights violations. Because of its focus, FIAN has not outlined a vision of food sovereignty but rather has worked to define the legal content of the right to food and the obligations that states and the communities of states have with respect to this right.[3] At the same time FIAN has worked to develop strong mechanisms for the articulation of complaints by people whose rights have been violated, monitoring of these rights, and ultimately their defense in the face of violation by states and international organizations.

In 1996, at the World Food Summit, La Via Campesina and FIAN came together from their different but complementary approaches to agree to a joint effort sharing a common perspective: to work to identify and confront chronic injustice in the distribution of lands and in the growing destruction of property and family agriculture, and to promote new redistributive, integral, and broad-scale agrarian reforms; these efforts are fundamental and a prerequisite to the transformation of the prevailing agricultural model, and to the full observance of the human rights of rural communities. It was in this context that the Global Campaign for Agrarian Reform (GCAR),[4] which La Via Campesina and FIAN have been promoting since 1999, emerged.[5]

The subject of gender was not raised until 2002 within the GCAR: the organization's operating capacity was limited due to a shortage of resources and to lack of better coordination between the GCAR and the gender commission of La Via Campesina. The GCAR's first activity regarding gender was to organize, at the invitation of the Federación Nacional de Mujeres Campesinas de Bolivia "Bartolina Sisa," an international fact-finding mission on gender to Bolivia in November 2002 (FoodFirst Information and Action Network and La Via Campesina 2002).

International research missions are an instrument of human rights work; this one was adapted by the GCAR for its purposes. The objective of GCAR missions is to verify reports of specific cases in which the human right to food seems to be threatened or violated for the following reasons: nonimplementation of agrarian reform, failures in the implementation of agrarian reform, processes of agrarian counterreform, or repression of agrarian reform activists and their organizations. These reports are documented and disseminated, at both the national and international levels, as a way of supporting the struggles of those social movements and bringing pressure to bear on nation-states to fulfill their obligations to uphold human rights.

Under the GCAR rubric, an international delegation made up of women and men from Paraguay, Chile, Brazil, Nicaragua, Austria, and Germany traveled to Bolivia in 2002 with the aim of learning about the specific conditions and principal problems faced by Bolivian peasant and indigenous women, with respect to access to and control over land. The delegation was to document concrete cases of violations of the right of these women to food and to address the issue of gender relations within peasant organizations that struggle for land.

This mission was significant from several points of view: First, it mobilized international support for and solidarity with Bolivian women by stressing the legitimacy of their demands at a moment when they faced the repression of the government. Second, it was an opportunity to intensify the exchange of experiences and learning regarding gender and agrarian reform between Bolivian women and the women and men of the various countries who made up the international delegation. Third, the mission served as the beginning of the development of a specific working methodology in the GCAR that guarantees a comprehensive focus on gender and makes possible a process of women's self-organization and training within La Via Campesina.

As a result of the exchange of information and the awareness raised about the subject through the Bolivian mission, the GCAR began to use other forms of action to address the gender issue. For example, in February 2003 the GCAR's Emergency Network[6] launched an international letter-writing campaign in support of the demands of a group of landless women principally affiliated with the peasant organization CNTC, who had occupied idle lands belonging to the Honduran government, in order to pressure the authorities into parceling out those lands and thereby implement legislation on agrarian reform that had been passed in their favor. In March of the same year the Emergency Network also launched an international letter-writing campaign in support of a national mobilization of rural Brazilian women who were demanding that the government prioritize a wide-ranging agrarian reform policy that included the following features: expropriation of land and *latifundios* (large estates) that do not fulfill their social function; rendering obligatory a joint adjudication of lands, so that title deeds in the various agrarian reform programs are listed not only under the names of male heads of household but also female; the creation of subsidized credit lines specifically for female rural workers; the affirmation of the victories and retirement rights obtained by rural working women in the current reform; and information and literacy campaigns for women at a national level.

All such struggles and movements take time to make advances. The case of Honduran landless women continues unresolved, and as part of its contribution to the campaign, FIAN continues to closely follow the women's struggle and assists them in obtaining sound legal assistance and support for further development of productive projects on occupied land. In 2004, on October 16—the date on which FIAN celebrates Global Action Day for the Right to Feed Oneself—FIAN made a call to its entire network, requesting that all members mobilize and address Honduran embassies in their respective countries, to demand that the lands be turned over to the women and their rights observed.

While it did not succeed in broadening the agrarian reform process, the mobilization of rural women in Brazil was successful in making joint adjudication of land obligatory and in creating specific lines of credit for rural women. Winning new, inclusive rights is an important step, while the implementation of those rights can become a new barrier; the results of a recent GCAR fact-finding mission to Brazil identified problems with the implementation of these hard-won measures (FoodFirst Information and Action

Network and La Via Campesina 2004). The PRONAF women's credit program has not been able to overcome discriminatory practices against rural working women seeking access to credit. Women applying for loans under the program must first demonstrate that the projects for which they are applying are "complementary" to those of their husbands. As a result, women have severely restricted access to loans because the family comes, ultimately, to mean the male head of household. Furthermore, many women do not have identification documents and do not have title deeds in their names, which could serve as collateral for credit.

The Agrarian Reform and Gender Seminar

The GCAR's most important activity in the area of gender, so far, has been the international seminar entitled "Agrarian Reform and Gender," which took place in Cochabamba, Bolivia, in June 2003. Delegates from peasant, indigenous, and human rights movements from twenty-four different countries came together in Cochabamba to exchange their experiences of struggle for land and for gender equity, and to generate accords and common work strategies that would systematically integrate the focus on gender into all aspects of the work of the GCAR. Due to insufficient funding, participation by Asians and Africans in the seminar was, unfortunately, limited but despite this, the seminar marked the first time within Via Campesina and FIAN that the subject of the discrimination against women in past agrarian reform processes was discussed in depth and in detail. Moreover, specific current challenges regarding women were addressed and strategies for handling these offered and considered. The seminar included the participation of two internationally recognized experts in this area, Carmen Diana Deere and Shamim Meer, whose contributions to the work carried out there were invaluable. The following section presents some of the themes and debates that emerged in the seminar, particularly emphasizing those aspects that, in the view of the meeting, had been missing in the international debate on gender and land, and which require more reflection and development.

Cochabamba Reflections: Women's Rights to Land; a Trojan Horse of Neoliberalism?

Legal reforms that guarantee the equal right of rural women to possess and inherit land, and to be beneficiaries of agrarian reform, have constituted the principal axis of the debate about gender and land. Legal discrimination and the lack of recognition and effective protection of women's right to land are still not completely overcome and continue to seriously affect rural women in many countries. Furthermore, although women have *de jure* won the equal right to land in numerous countries, and important advances have taken place in all regions, there continue de facto to be multiple problems (administrative, institutional, cultural, for example) that impede the effective enjoyment of women's right to land. An important part of the current debate focuses on analyzing these factors and determining how reforms could be effectively implemented (Agarwal 1994, 2003; Deere and León 2002; Deininger and the World Bank 2003; Food and Agriculture Organization of the United Nations 2001; FoodFirst Information and Action Network and La Via Campesina 2003a; Razavi 2003).

In Cochabamba, a particular aspect of this topic emerged in the discussion: many of the constitutional and legal reforms that strengthened the principles of equality and nondiscrimination and, concomitantly, the rights of women to land in Africa and Latin America, coincided with the introduction of structural adjustment policies. In some countries, these issues ran parallel to other constitutional reforms that made viable the deregulation and privatization of land and the liberalization of the economy. Consideration of this phenomenon led some women in Cochabamba to point out that the reforms that recognized and strengthened women's right to land in these circumstances did so within the neoliberal framework of protecting and strengthening individual property rights, and to that extent, such reforms represented a doubtful or, at least, ambiguous advance. To place the issue squarely in context: how secure can individual entitlement to lands for peasant women be when established in a context of privatization and economic liberalization policies that have already brought about the dispossession and loss of lands of many families and communities?[7] As noted by Deere and León (2001a) in their research, although legal reforms have substantially increased the proportion of female beneficiaries with respect to the total in access-to-land programs, what good is this development if the processes of land redistribution in Latin America have practically ceased or are reduced to a minimal expression?[8]

The linkage between advances in women's right to land with those of women's individual right to private property continues to be an implicit one, and is a predominant idea in a great many public policies and in the debate over gender and land. The identification of women's right to land with that of their individual titling of land has been intensely questioned and debated in sub-Saharan Africa, perhaps more than in other regions, because some have seen in the issue the intention of changing customary systems of land tenancy to the market and to foreign investment; it also calls into question customary law and practice and interferes with the customary law of local governments, also guaranteed and protected by constitutional reforms (see FoodFirst Information and Action Netword and La Via Campesina 2003b; Tsikata 2003; Walker 2002; Whitehead and Tsikata 2003).

In Latin America the contradictions of women's rights to land and property constituted as individual rights have been called into question primarily by indigenous peoples. Deere and León record an Ecuadorian indigenous woman who, in the early 1990s, said: "[T]he whole issue of gender and rights to land is irrelevant, since indigenous peoples have not put forward the individual demand to land; it has always been collective from the community's perspective" (Deere and León 2002, 305). The tension between the rights of women and the rights of indigenous peoples to preserve their traditional customary law and practices is still there, even though several steps have been taken toward reconciling the feminist vision with the indigenous vision. Indigenous women have started to question the construction of customary normative systems and the decision-making structures of their towns and communities, pointing out that they are excluded from those processes (Deere and León 2002, 323).

This sphere of the debate was reflected in Cochabamba, where the hosting organizations, while presenting their experiences of defending indigenous and communal lands, as well as some of their legal victories toward the recognition of indigenous territories, made the following two observations:

- Communal property, in its diverse modalities considered in the law, could become an important tool in stopping neoliberal purposes. If it is intelligently taken advantage of by peasant and indigenous organizations, it can be an instrument for counteracting the expansion of the new *latifundio* and, more broadly, the land market.
- Communal norms, which are necessary for keeping collective property intact, defy individualism and its economics. In many cases it will not be enough to base a case solely on customary law and practices, so communities will also need to adapt norms, reconstruct them, or even create them, in order to respond to contemporary demands, on top of the sometimes enormous existing differences between communities and peoples. In the latter sense, this body of norms for administrating and conserving

communal or collective property will have the opportunity to incorporate measures that tend toward gender equity. One such opportunity has arisen in Bolivia. According to Bolivian law, land management and land use are regulated by community norms. The current cultural context is very fluid in the sense that landless families from the Andes region are migrating to the lower Amazonas region, meeting and mixing with other indigenous peoples and traditions. The construction of "new traditional norms" offers precisely such a chance to integrate gender concerns into new communal norms. It remains to be seen, however, whether this opportunity is seized (Almaraz 2002, 90).

This defense of communal lands and territories, as important alternatives to neoliberal models not only for indigenous peoples but also for peasant communities and organizations, is an idea that has been gaining ground in Latin America. Following the example of indigenous peoples, an increasing number of peasant communities in Latin America are reclaiming their cultural identity as peasants, for whom land is not merely a commodity or capital, but the basis for the very existence of their communities and the integrating axis of all of their fundamental rights.[9]

The participants in the Cochabamba seminar advocated communal forms of land tenancy, and it remained clear that this did not exclude also advocating women's individual right to land, as a personal right and under conditions equal with men. The question now, therefore, is how to strengthen women's rights to land in different systems of land tenancy, and not only as individual private property.[10] The discussion of how to develop concrete proposals for protecting both women's right to land and alternative systems of land tenancy and production that guarantee effective protection to peasant and indigenous communities, and which adjust to the specificities of different contexts and situations, was left pending and will surely be a field of work for the coming years. The drafting of proposals will have to take into account that, from the perspective of gender equality, proposals of alternative systems of land tenancy and production must be linked to the demand for land redistribution, at least in countries with a high concentration of land property.

Bina Agarwal recently studied the problems of women's individual access to land markets, and she presented the experiences of purchase, rental, and collective work on the land by groups of women in Andra Pradhesh, India, as a possible solution (Agarwal 2003). Although Agarwal does not address the broader context of neoliberal agrarian and agricultural policies in which land markets function today—which it is imperative to do—the study is interesting for its exploration of alternative ways in which landless women gain access to land not only by way of the market, but also through processes of land redistribution conducted by the state. Her study points to the range of policy possibilities that exist at the moment, and the importance of forging new policies based on experience and analysis from mixed-gender and women's organizations. In this process it would be vital to intensify the exchange of experiences among Latin American, African, and Asian movements, and to deepen the understanding of the impacts of agrarian, agricultural, commercial, macroeconomic, and international policies on the matter of gender and agrarian reform, so as to find effective ways to confront them (Patnaik 2003).

The New Rurality

Another issue discussed in Cochabamba, and one that can be said to characterize La Via Campesina, is the revalorization of peasant identity, as a general group, and of peasant and indigenous women in particular. Many of the declarations made by La Via Campesina address this issue, but here I will cite only the preamble to the declaration of the Fourth International Conference in 2004, in which it is expressed in a clear and concise manner: "We meet to reaffirm our determination to defend our cultures and our right to continue existing as peasants and peoples with our own identity." The women of La Via Campesina have made clear that their struggle is not only economic and class-based, but that it also concerns the revalorization of their cultures and their traditional wisdom regarding the production of food, the selection and management of seeds, the breeding of animals, and the care of the earth and nature.

Anyone who has had the opportunity to participate in La Via Campesina events knows the central importance that the *mística* (a moment of symbolic expression of peasant and indigenous values and ideals) has for developing and illuminating all of their work, for strengthening ties of solidarity, for identifying themselves, and for nourishing a spirit of struggle. It is worth noting that the preparation of the *mística* is principally the task of women.

The *mística* of La Via Campesina has been criticized from various points of view. For social actors who are secularized and close to Western rational thought, the term "mystic" is a cause of irritation because of its intense, almost irrational spiritual sense; as such, it seems out of place in contemporary public forums. By contrast, for some indigenous people, the *mística* seems to be a fabricated ritual taken out of the context that gives it meaning. Following Iris

Marion Young's analysis of social groups (1990), the *mística* of La Via Campesina would be the most tangible expression of peasant men and women's demand to define themselves, more as a creation and construction than as a given essence, to give positive meaning to that group difference, and to demand effective recognition and representation in the public space that, until now, has oppressed and marginalized them.

La Via Campesina can thus be understood as a class movement that struggles against poverty, exploitation, and oppression, and to that extent, struggles also for the redistribution of productive resources and economic autonomy. At the same time, it can be a movement that struggles against the predominant cultural standard, which considers urban values to be superior to rural ones; against the paternalism of other social actors toward peasants (NGOs, academics, development agencies, governments); and, finally, a movement that struggles for the recognition of peasant identities and cultures, and the right to continue developing them autonomously.[11]

I emphasize the twofold character of La Via Campesina's struggle for redistribution and for recognition, to use Nancy Fraser's categories of social justice (Fraser and Honneth 2003), because it seems to me that the latter aspect is one that tends to be ignored in studies of land and agrarian reform and in public policies, with disastrous consequences. For example, it is a well-known fact that the making of decisions concerning the countryside and rural development is a province dominated by masculine urban groups for whom urbanization is practically natural law. Accordingly, agrarian reform, if it is even considered an option, appears as a mere transitory social policy for mitigating unemployment and the lack of income sources of the rural population until it can move to the cities in search of better life opportunities.

Brazilian rural sociology has done much work in recent years on the rural-urban dichotomy that has relegated the rural to oblivion or to a position antithetical to the urban and the modern (Sauer 2002). In Brazil there has been a resurgence in the theoretical analysis of rural issues in contemporary society's current moment and in the context of globalization, a resurgence sparked, without a doubt, by the actions of strong social movements that are reconceiving or re-creating the countryside through the struggle for land. In addition to improving material living conditions, the struggle for land in Brazil encompasses cultural and symbolic transformations that engender new values and social representations, and that democratize society's structures of political power (Heredia et al. 2004). In that sense, the struggle for land does not signify backwardness or a return to archaic forms of life condemned to disappear, but rather the contrary: it is gestating a new rurality that redefines urban-rural relations and therefore has an impact, through this reinvention, on the society as a whole.

Environmental problems and ecological movements, illnesses produced by a food system that is heavily dependent on farm chemicals, social problems and the deterioration of the quality of life in the world's great urban centers, atomization, consumerism, the lack of solidarity and meaning that are perceived in contemporary societies—all of these factors have also converged in the resurgence and revalorization of the rural, not only in the Global South but also in the industrialized northern societies. It therefore seems pertinent to expand the debate about gender and agrarian reform to incorporate these terms as well.

Women's Right to Land from the Human Rights Perspective

From the beginning of the 1990s the women's movement has called attention to the fact that the international human rights system has not paid sufficient attention to the promotion and protection of women's human rights. Even though the standards and procedures of international law on human rights are perceived as neutral from the gender perspective, that neutrality, in practice, amounted to ignoring violations of the human rights of women (Tomaševski 1999).

Feminist movements have questioned not only the international system of human rights in practice, but also central notions of human rights such as *universality* and *equality*. Indigenous peoples throughout the world have done the same by refuting the notion of universality (from the standpoint of cultural relativism), the notion of individuality, and, as well, the disavowal of collective rights. Rights are social conquests and, as such, all of these criticisms and debates have enriched and improved the standards and procedures of human rights. Although important steps have been taken toward integrating these diverse perspectives, much work remains to be done. A comprehensive approach to human rights, especially of economic, social, and cultural rights, is very much still in construction; our challenge at the moment is to see, through the lens of gender, how existing human rights instruments can be put to the service of the struggle for land.

The human rights approach introduces a new nuance to the justification and legitimization of women's rights to land.[12] Human rights are those rights possessed under equal conditions by all people by virtue of their humanity and for no other reason. To conceptualize rural women's access to land in terms of human rights means to acknowledge that right for women solely on the basis of their humanity and not as a function of their specific social role as producers and providers of food, or to increase the efficiency of agricultural production, or to improve the welfare of their daughters and sons. The human rights approach does not render these arguments less important, nor are they incompatible with it, but, in some circumstances, it has a broader reach: What would happen, for example, if studies were to demonstrate that women are not efficient agriculturists? Would they lose their right to land? What consideration do childless women receive? Do they have no right to land? In Cochabamba, a Brazilian woman brought up for discussion a case they had had in a settlement. It concerned a woman who had abandoned her family and gone with another man. The community wanted to take from this woman the land that belonged to her, until someone asked: "What would happen if this woman were a man? Would we take his land? If a man does not lose his right to land for leaving his family, why should a woman have to?" The focus on human rights is then closer to, and in some cases intersects with, the justifications that are treated in the literature under the rubric of achieving gender equality and women's empowerment.

In many cases the lack of access to and control over land by women constitutes a human rights violation. Qualifying these situations in this way grants them a relevance that would not be attained if we described them solely as unjust or disadvantageous. The reason for this relevance lies in the terms on which human rights are based. To speak in terms of human rights is to speak about the obligations of states, or nations, to their citizens. In that sense, action or lack thereof with regard to gender and agrarian reform is not a question of the state's goodwill, but rather a binding juridical obligation. Legal obligations also make possible the demand of rights before courts of law, and open up the possibility of maintaining vigilance over the state's performance and submitting it to public scrutiny.[13]

Furthermore, the indivisibility and interdependence of human rights— that is, that in exercising a right another right cannot be impaired, and that the enjoyment of a right depends on the exercise of other rights—allow for an integral approach to the question of gender and land. The rights to recognition as a person before the law, with regard to property, education, and freedom of association and expression, are fundamental to women's struggle for their own means of living. Similarly, the right to an adequate standard of living is fundamental to the exercise of the right to participate in cultural life and enjoy one's own culture, and to participate in the direction of public affairs.

The challenges to effectively applying this approach in reality are enormous, starting with education and training in economic and social rights with a focus on gender, to the documentation of the violations of rural women's human rights—so as to denounce these violations and make them visible—and going through to the litigation of these cases in the courts. Without going into the complexity posed by the defense of rural women's human rights in systems of customary law, as analyzed by Tsikata (2003) in the case of Tanzania, the defense of the economic rights of rural women confronts FIAN with new challenges. I will illustrate this with a practical example. In an international conference on agrarian reform, an agriculture minister listened to a number of denunciations made regarding discrimination that peasant and indigenous women suffer in his country. Among many different forms of discrimination, the discrimination against women in peasant associations and organizations was mentioned, to which the minister responded: "Freedom of association is also a human right. How can you ask the government to intervene in associations to guarantee the equality of women?" Without a doubt, such interference could prove fatal. Nevertheless, neither is it right that the state simply wash its hands of the issue. In the case of domestic violence, for example, the state also used to say, at first, that it could not intervene in the private affairs of a couple, although more states accept that domestic violence is an urgent and justiciable problem. In addition to confronting the state and other parties (employers, businesses, institutions) for their direct violations of the rights of women, we should also explore ways in which the state could support rural women in their struggle against discrimination occurring within the private sphere of their families, communities, and mixed associations, which impede the full enjoyment of and control over their own means of living.

Some critics of human rights work point out that they see no real sense in waiting for the state to guarantee the rights of women, given that the state itself is the main agent of neoliberal policies and, therefore, the violator *par excellence* of rural communities' human rights. The Marxist critique that the state is simply an instrument of domination of the bourgeoisie, and that formulating a social demand in terms of the bourgeois state amounts to playing by the rules of the system, somehow resounds in this criticism.

It is beyond a doubt that states and legal codes are dominated today by national and transnational oligarchic interests, which have not only been dismantling the economic and social rights guaranteed by communist states, but also the welfare state, the fruit of worker victories, and the pact between capital and work that came about in Western capitalist countries and in some countries of the southern hemisphere. The state and the law are therefore a crystallization of the correlation of social forces, and, in that sense, they are contingent historical products. Struggles for rights—from the struggle against monarchicy and absolutism to the workers' struggles and struggles against racial and gender discrimination—have all been struggles to defend people from power, be it political or economic. In this sense, the struggle for economic and social human rights today is part of the different social efforts to radically democratize the economic sphere and the international order. This struggle implies, therefore, a profound transformation of political institutions such as states and the United Nations, and of the capitalist economy.[14]

Final Observations

I would like to end this chapter by making reference to the main challenges that lie ahead and the tasks that we have assumed for the future. The Cochabamba Declaration endorsed, as had the founding documents and periodic summit declarations, the demand by the women of La Via Campesina for gender equity in the decision making of their organizations, communities, and families, and in representation in all organizations and events. At the World Forum on Agrarian Reform in Valencia, Spain, in December 2004, close to 45 percent of the more than 500 participants were women. Guaranteeing gender equity in the forum caused conflict within the organizing committee. Although parity was not achieved in actual participation or in the various panels, the intense discussions on the subject were positive in that they mobilized the women within the forum, and many of their positions and viewpoints were gathered in the final Valencia declaration (World Forum on Agrarian Reform 2004).

The Cochabamba Declaration also contains a commitment to work toward changing the norms of customary law and practices that discriminate against women in communities and organizations. It also calls for developing mechanisms within organizations that allow them to denounce violations of the rights of peasant and indigenous women at a national and international level. Discussions about how to do this, however, have not yet occurred.

Also highlighted in the Cochabamba plan of action is the commitment to continue research on gender in the rural sphere, in collaboration with researchers committed to the gendered struggle for agrarian reform, in order to spread this knowledge, exchange experiences, and enrich reflection within the organizations. Similarly, the importance of developing mechanisms for grassroots training was emphasized. Currently, the women of La Via Campesina and the Land Research Action Network (LRAN) are discussing a joint work proposal that would encompass three axes: documentation of the struggles and organizational processes of the women of La Via Campesina; research on topics of gender and agrarian reform that the women of La Via Campesina identify as necessary; and the drafting of grassroots training material, based on their documentation and research work.

Separately, in November 2004, the itinerant First International School for Sociopolitical Training was opened and its first course carried out in Temuco, Chile, for the women responsible for the work on gender in the organizations that make up the Coordinadora Latinoamericana de Organizaciones del Campo (CLOC) and La Via Campesina. The central objective of the course was to strengthen the peasant leaders' capacity to analyze and comprehend social and political reality, as well as to make proposals for change in the construction of the society to which they and their organizations aspire. This first course was a complete success.

Additionally, the GCAR faces the challenges of guaranteeing that all of its actions focus on gender, of interacting with more rural women's organizations, and of strengthening their joint work with the La Via Campesina's gender commission. Another key challenge is to further integrate into these organizations the women's movements of Asia and Africa.

I will end this article with the words of Shamim Meer in Cochabamba: "The task is to build strong women's movements, and to build among activists— women and men—strategic skills that are based on an understanding of the history of the dispossessed, and of the current moment of globalization. An essential part of the construction of this movement has to include an end to the oppression of women and to gender inequality in the access to and control over resources, as well as in the exercise of authority" (Meer 2003). It appears that La Via Campesina and the GCAR are on this path. The forum for articulation and action that La Via Campesina represents for rural women across the world is a novel arena that is already contributing to the advancement of rural women's liberation struggle.

CHAPTER 11

Indigenous Peoples: Land, Territory, Autonomy, and Self-Determination

Rodolfo Stavenhagen

While most of the chapters in this book tend to treat land the way that farmers often see it—as a productive resource—indigenous peoples tend to see land as part of something greater, called *territory*. Territory includes the productive function of land but also encompasses the concepts of homeland, culture, religion, spiritual sites, ancestors, the natural environment, and other resources like water, forests, and belowground minerals. Agrarian reform directed at nonindigenous farmers in many cases may reasonably seek to redistribute "any and all" arable land to the landless, irrespective of where the landless come from. For example, the Landless Workers' Movement (MST) of Brazil demands and occupies land all over the country, and the members of their land reform settlements sometimes come from states far away from the land they occupy. In contrast, indigenous peoples' movements do not demand just any land but, rather, what they consider to be *their* land and territories. Thus, closely linked to the concept of territory are the demands by organizations and movements of indigenous people for autonomy and self-determination. This chapter lays out the key issues and controversies associated with these concepts.

Land and Territory

For most indigenous peoples, survival is the major challenge in a world that has systematically denied them the right to existence as such. Historically linked to the land as the source of their main livelihood, they have long struggled to gain and keep access to this precious resource that is also the essential element of their identity as distinct cultures and societies. Land rights are the major issue faced by native peoples around the world and are at the center of numerous conflicts involving indigenous communities, particularly as a result of globalization. The impact of new economic processes can be dramatic, as seen in agricultural modernization, for example. The widespread introduction of commercial crops for export, based on the intensive use of modern inputs (mechanization, improved grains, fertilizers, insecticides, and, more recently, genetically modified seeds) tends to displace traditional subsistence farming, on which most indigenous communities depend for their survival. Increasing production costs and the need for economies of scale favor the consolidation of larger productive units and integrated agribusiness, putting traditional farms at a disadvantage in highly competitive markets. Agricultural development policies, instead of helping small subsistence farmers overcome their handicaps, have in fact pushed the poorer peasants out of business and favored the concentration of larger agro-industrial enterprises, and they have forced the peasants to become increasingly dependent on, and therefore vulnerable to, the globalized agricultural economy. Current negotiations concerning agriculture within the framework of the World Trade Organization do not bode well for the continued existence of indigenous farming.

From time immemorial indigenous peoples have maintained a special relationship with the land, their source of livelihood and sustenance and the basis of their very existence as identifiable territorial communities. The right to own, occupy, and use land collectively is inherent to the self-conception of indigenous peoples, and, generally, this right is vested in the local community, the tribe, the indigenous nation, or group. For productive purposes land may be divided into plots and used individually or on a family basis, yet much of it is regularly restricted for community use only (forests, pastures, fisheries, etc.), and the social and moral ownership belongs to the community. While such rights are protected by legislation in some countries, powerful economic interests often succeed in turning communal possession into private property. From southern Chile and the Amazon basin to Canada's northern forests; from the tropical jungles of Southeast Asia to the bush of southern Africa, there is no longer any territory that is not coveted by some international corporation, either for its mineral wealth, its oil deposits, its pastures, tropical or hardwood forests, its medicinal plants or its suitability for commercial plantations, its hydraulic resources, or its tourist potential. Indigenous peoples are the most recent victims of globalized development, and if these tendencies continue unabated, indigenous peoples' chances of survival will become ever weaker, their very existence as distinct societies and cultures seriously endangered.

Closely linked to the land problem is the issue of territory. Indigenous peoples have historically been rooted in specific locations, their original homelands, which in some cases constitute well-defined geographical areas. Indigenous peoples' organizations now demand the recognition and demarcation of these territories as a necessary step to ensure their social, economic, and cultural survival. The territory of the San Blas Kuna is constitutionally protected in Panama; so is that of the Yanomami in northern Brazil. The Mapuche of southern Chile and the Miskitos of Nicaragua, among many others, have been in the forefront of these struggles in their countries. The Colombian constitution of 1991 recognizes the traditional homelands of a number of indigenous groups and assures them of legal protection. Philippine legislation recognizes indigenous ancestral domains. In some Canadian provinces aboriginal title to territory is legally recognized.

Convention 169 of the International Labour Organization, adopted in 1989, calls upon states to respect indigenous lands and territories, and proclaims the right of indigenous peoples to control their natural resources. This is a most important right, because many of the current conflicts over land and territory relate to the possession, control, exploitation, and use of natural resources. In a number of countries it is the state that keeps for itself the right to control such resources, and in numerous instances multinational corporations are asserting their economic interests, unleashing complicated conflicts over ownership and use-rights with indigenous communities. In Chile, for example, one law recognizes the rights of indigenous communities to their lands, but other laws allow any private party to claim possession of subsoil and water resources on them. Under these circumstances, indigenous communities are hard put to defend their ancestral claims.

Indigenous peoples in Southeast Asia face the loss of control over land and resources due to nonrecognition of customary land rights. In most southeast Asian states there are no legal rules granting indigenous peoples the right to their land, and many indigenous peoples are threatened by logging, mining, and other exploitative activities, or by infrastructure programs (such as dams and roads) pursued by national governments. In Resolution 55/95 on Cambodia, the UN General Assembly notes that illicit logging "has seriously threatened full enjoyment of economic, social, and cultural rights by many Cambodians, including indigenous people" (United Nations 2001). A major recent development in Cambodia is the 2001 land law, which states that ownership of land "is granted by the State to the indigenous communities as collective ownership. This collective ownership includes all of the rights and protections of ownership as are enjoyed by private owners."

While access to land for productive purposes (agriculture, forestry, herding, foraging) by individual members of indigenous communities is certainly of the greatest importance for indigenous people, there are other factors involved as well. Indigenous communities maintain historical and spiritual links with their homelands, geographical territories in which society and culture thrive and that therefore constitute the social space in which a culture can reproduce itself from generation to generation. Too often this necessary spiritual link between indigenous communities and their homelands is misunderstood by nonindigenous persons and is frequently ignored in existing land-related legislation.

Many argue that the recognition of indigenous territorial rights is necessary for the full protection of the rights and fundamental freedoms of indigenous peoples, whereas others seem to fear that such recognition might undermine the unity and integrity of existing states built up around them. Nevertheless, in a number of countries such rights have indeed been legislated, and experience suggests that national unity is not threatened by these developments.

In Mexico, the Zapatista uprising in 1994 put the issue of indigenous rights squarely on the national agenda, but a peace accord, signed in 1996, remained on paper. In 2001 the new government passed a constitutional reform on indigenous issues that deviated from the agreements and further stalled the peace process. Subsequently, in 2003, a number of indigenous municipalities, which earlier had declared their autonomy, created parallel government structures to promote their own vision of development as set out in the peace agreements.

At the local level, conflicts over land and resources often turn into acts of violence, and indigenous persons frequently become the victims of a corrupt and biased judiciary system. Indicators of social well-being are much lower in the indigenous rural communities than in nonindigenous urban areas, leading to massive migrations of Indians to other parts of Mexico and across the border to the United States. If carried out as announced, the Puebla Panama Plan of the governments of Mexico and Central America may further affect the potential of indigenous communities to survive as distinct cultural entities in a globalized world. Indigenous organizations demand not only respect for their culture and languages, but also for their rights to self-determination and autonomy and to full participation in the political and social process.

After a decades-long struggle for legal redress concerning ancient land rights and aboriginal title, the Inuit people of northern Canada, who had linked land claims to territorial autonomy, negotiated a political agreement with the federal government, whereby they achieved the creation, in 1999, of the self-governing territory of Nunavut. Rather than weaken national unity, this arrangement has strengthened the federal structure of Canada and met the claims and aspirations of the Inuit people.

In Panama seven indigenous peoples, the Ngöbe, Kuna, Emberá, Wounaan, Buglé, Naso, and Bri Bri, who together represent 8.3 percent of the national population, are mostly concentrated in five legally constituted territorial units (*comarcas*) that make up almost 20 percent of the country's total land area. These *comarcas* are semiautonomous regions governed by local councils and traditional governors (*caciques*).

In Guatemala, more than half of the national population is indigenous, mainly Maya, who are now officially recognized in the Peace Agreement on the Identity and Rights of Indigenous Peoples, signed in 1995 after more than thirty years of brutal civil war. Access to land and resources is nevertheless still the main problem faced by indigenous communities, which also continue to be the victims of discrimination and marginalization. Indigenous identity, extreme poverty, and poor access to educational and health services are all closely related. One of the areas in which discrimination against indigenous people is especially strong is in the administration of the justice system; despite a major effort made by the government in recent years, it is still cumbersome and inefficient. Social conflicts are often criminalized, creating dissatisfaction with the judiciary among the indigenous communities. Lynchings of suspected offenders have become commonplace in local communities where the reach of the law is absent. In many places local police forces are still controlled by members of the paramilitary groups that committed brutal atrocities during the war, and, despite the peace agreements and a supervisory mechanism set up by the United Nations, human rights violations are again on the increase.

How can and should existing states coexist with the notion of indigenous territories? Are these notions incompatible? To what extent is the idea of legally recognized indigenous homelands a necessary ingredient for the full enjoyment of the range of rights by indigenous peoples? How can constructive arrangements be found between the legitimate concerns of states regarding territorial integrity and national unity, and the equally legitimate concerns of indigenous peoples regarding their collective survival as peoples linked to the earth in myriad ways within an international system made up of sovereign states? These are still open and debated questions, and answers will vary by region and country. While there are a number of practical experiences that illustrate the problems involved, more research is needed to address the particular issues, which are frequently controversial in public discourse.

Social Organization, Local Government, Customary Law

Cultural identities are sustained not only by a discrete list of aspects that members of a cultural group carry along as they go through life. In fact, these elements may vary from individual to individual and they may, and frequently do, change over time. So it is not the contents of a culture that defines any group's identity. It is rather in the field of social organization that identities are wrought and sustained. To the extent that a system of social relations defines the identity of each individual member and that individual's link to the group as a whole, the social institutions and relationships characteristic of a given community are the necessary frame of reference for any thriving culture. Indigenous communities know this well because when they claim the right to maintain their social organization in the face of the pressures of the wider society, they are actually appealing for the preservation of their culture.

Too often the larger society has taken the stance that indigenous social institutions are contrary to the national interest or, worse, are morally reprehensible. This position was taken for a long time by the dominant institutions within colonial empires. The question is frequently debated whether adherence to indigenous communal institutions may lead under certain circumstances to the violation of individual human rights (for example, the rights of women and girls).

Local community organization is often upheld by adherence to a generally accepted system of customs and mores or customary law, which in numerous countries is not accorded any formal legal recognition and may in fact be considered as competing with the formal state legal system. Do community members who accept the norms of unwritten customary law stand in violation of a country's legal system? Does the application of customary law violate nationwide legal norms? Yet what about situations in which the application of positive law entails a violation of community norms and customs? Might that not constitute a violation of human rights as well?

These issues are dealt with in different ways by individual states (and by different scholars), and the various solutions run from some form of accepted legal pluralism to the absolute rejection by the official legal system of any kind of indigenous customary law, with a number of possibilities in between. Under what circumstances might the application of indigenous legal systems (customary law) threaten internationally accepted standards of individual human rights? And conversely, under what circumstances could the limitation or elimination of indigenous customary law violate the human rights of members of indigenous communities? These are complex issues about which there is much debate and little agreement, but which need to be addressed objectively and without bias.

Since time immemorial, local communities have evolved some form of local government within the structure of a wider polity into which they have been integrated as a result of historical events. Indigenous communities are no exception. Throughout history, local communities have struggled to defend their autonomy against outside encroachment, sometimes successfully, sometimes not. To the extent that indigenous people were incorporated into state structures not of their own choosing during times of colonization or the expansion of the modern nation-state, their local forms of government were modified or adapted to suit the interests and needs of the state, creating tensions that have often led to conflict and violence.

Indigenous organizations seek to preserve or regain the right to local (and sometimes regional) self-government; they consider this right to be part of the fundamental freedoms that international law accords to all peoples. Through negotiations and treaties, constitutional reform or special legislation, indigenous peoples have been able in numerous instances to establish agreements with states regarding this right to self-government. In other cases, however, this has not been possible, and national- or regional-level government units still take it upon themselves to administer the affairs of indigenous communities. Indigenous affairs ministries, departments, or bureaus often have specific mandates to that effect, and local indigenous governments must deal with these institutions rather than with those of the national political or administrative system in general. Indigenous organizations may consider this to be a form of discrimination, whereas governments argue that such arrangements are designed for the protection of indigenous people themselves, in keeping with their best interests (as defined by the state).

Recognizing these issues, the Draft Declaration on the Rights of Indigenous Peoples states in Article 33: "Indigenous peoples have the right to promote, develop and maintain their institutional structures and their distinctive juridical customs, traditions, procedures and practices, in accordance with internationally recognized human rights standards."

Poverty, Standards of Living, Sustainable Development

As already noted, indigenous people are very often found among the poorest strata in society, and their levels of living are considered to be substandard in many respects. Studies have shown high levels of infant mortality, lower than average nutritional levels, lack of public services, difficulty of access to social welfare institutions, lower than average delivery of the services provided by such institutions, inadequate housing and shelter, and other indicators associated in general with the idea of human development. While poverty and extreme poverty are widespread all over rural and urban Latin America, where development has been highly unequal and the benefits of economic growth concentrated at the upper end of the social and economic scale, the indigenous peoples are mainly concentrated at the lower income levels. The World Bank reported in the 1990s that "the living conditions of the indigenous people were abysmal, and that their poverty was persistent and severe, especially when compared to those of the non-indigenous population" (Psacharopoulos and Patrinos 1994, 206–7).

What has been done and what can be done? The International Labour Organization's Convention 169 states in Article 7.1: "The peoples concerned shall have the right to decide their own priorities for the process of development as it affects their lives, beliefs, institutions and spiritual well-being and the lands they occupy or otherwise use, and to exercise control, to the extent possible, over their own economic, social and cultural development." Unfortunately, for many reasons, this does not always occur. In September 2003 a Korean farmer killed himself in front of the posh convention center in Cancun, Mexico, where the World Trade Organization was deciding the fate of hundreds of millions of poor peasants—among them most of the world's indigenous peoples. The unrestricted tearing down of tariffs on agricultural and food products demanded by the leaders of the most powerful economies, together with continued high subsidies that rich countries pay their own farmers, has sentenced millions of poverty-stricken farmers in poor countries to a slow death. Unless the principles of Convention 169 are adhered to and implemented, the condition of poor indigenous farmers the world over will only deteriorate further.

Recent experience has shown that economic growth must go hand in hand with social concerns if the results are to be effective and make a difference in the lives of individuals and communities. A new approach seems to be taking hold in international discourse: human rights–centered sustainable development, meaning that unless development can be shown to improve the livelihoods of people within a framework of the respect for human rights (to be distinguished from the legal rights of a citizen of a country, since these do not currently address many rights issues), it will not produce the desired results. This approach may be of particular importance to indigenous peoples whose human rights have frequently been neglected when not actually impaired by traditional economic development approaches.

Political Representation, Autonomy, Self-Determination

Indigenous self-organization has made considerable progress over the years. From the local level to the regional, national, and international levels, indigenous peoples' associations have become social and political actors in their own right, as witnessed by their continuing participation in the yearly sessions of the Working Group on Indigenous Peoples (WGIP). They speak with many voices, but on the fundamental issues of their human rights, their objectives and their aspirations are usually in remarkable agreement. In some countries they are now recognized as legitimate partners and interlocutors of governments and other social sectors on the national scene. In other countries the going has been more difficult; their organizations may not be officially recognized, and their human right to free association may not be completely respected. To the extent that the rights of indigenous peoples themselves are sometimes neglected and ignored within existing power structures, their organizations and other human rights advocacy associations that take up their cause may also become victims of abuses and be denied adequate protection under the law. Numerous communications to this effect have been addressed over the years to the UN Office of the High Commissioner on Human Rights (UNHCHR), the ILO Committee of Experts, and, among others, the Inter-American Commission of Human Rights.

Beyond respect for their human rights, indigenous organizations also claim the right to political representation *qua* indigenous peoples at the national level, an issue that may or may not be compatible with existing political structures. More insistent has been the demand for some kind of autonomy, and in a number of countries this has been achieved, whereas in others it is not contemplated in current legal arrangements. A case in point is the constitution of the Philippines, which recognizes the right of Muslim and Cordillera peoples to self-determination in the form of autonomy, while the latter are still awaiting the creation of their autonomous region (Daoas 1995, 80, 97–107).

One of the more controversial topics surrounding the human rights and fundamental freedoms of indigenous peoples concerns the much-debated right of peoples to self-determination. In their statements to international forums, indigenous representatives demand the recognition of their right to self-determination as peoples. Equally insistently, some states argue that such a right should not extend to the indigenous. The concept of self-determination is closely linked to the use of the term "peoples." There does not appear to be a clear and unequivocal definition of this term in any of the multiple international legal instruments that have been adopted over the last half century nor, for that matter, in national legislation. Without a clear definition that may command a broad consensus, it is not obvious what the debate is really all about. In political science and legal literature the term is usually linked to all the citizens of an existing state, whereas in more sociological texts the notion of a people refers to certain commonalities, shared identities, and identifications.

The principle of the right of peoples to self-determination has been present in international debates for almost a century, and the current claims to this right by indigenous organizations is only the latest instance of its use in the expanding debate about human rights. Whereas some national constitutions do indeed refer to the right of self-determination of indigenous peoples (for example, Mexico's polemical reformed constitution of 2001), other legislations avoid it, and the controversy relates to the meaning given to the term in both international and national law. Chile's congress, for example, has voted against several initiatives that would constitutionally recognize the country's indigenous peoples as such. Africa provides another example of conceptual difficulties. In 1981 the Organization of African Unity approved the African Charter on Human and Peoples' Rights, and yet nowhere is the term "peoples" defined. Specialists continue to debate whether the term should apply only to all citizens of a given state or whether it has other applications as well (such as regarding indigenous peoples). It is this debate that is holding up the adoption of the Declaration on the Rights of Indigenous Peoples in the United Nations.

Obviously, then, when we speak of potential policies concerning indigenous peoples, land tenure, and territory, the issues of land versus territory, autonomy, and self-determination must necessarily receive priority.

PART THREE

Agrarian Reform:
Alternatives and Resistance

Alternatives: Between the State Above and the Movement Below

Peter Rosset

In part II of this volume we saw how the currently dominant market-based solutions to issues of access to land are unlikely to resolve longstanding problems of landlessness, excessive land concentration, poverty, and exclusion. Yet there are other contemporary approaches to the question of land and territory. These range from the state-led agrarian reforms currently underway in Cuba and Venezuela, to what is often called "land reform from below," in which grassroots movements use occupations or "reclamations" of land as both a mechanism to access land and a political lever with which to apply pressure on national governments to act on agrarian reform. In this section of the book we review some of these alternatives.

In chapter 12, a group of Cuban and foreign authors summarize what might be called "reform of land reform," or the second great agrarian reform of the Cuban revolution, entailing the breakup of large, unwieldy state farms and the implementation of a smaller farm model based on more sustainable farming practices. This chapter shows both what can achieved when a committed state carries out reforms, and how the nature of the agricultural practices used by the beneficiaries (i.e., green revolution–style, chemical- and capital-intensive farming, versus agroecological practices), can make a significant difference to the outcome of reforms.

Chapter 13 is devoted to a snapshot-in-time evaluation of the new agrarian reform being implemented by the government of President Hugo Chávez in Venezuela. This is a rapidly developing process that is filled with both obstacles and potential and that will have surely evolved further by the time readers have this volume in their hands. A key feature of the Venezuelan story is the need for, or the absence of, a well-organized peasant or landless movement that can exert effective pressure from below, even when the government is in the hands of a sympathetic president.

The majority of the countries in the world do not enjoy governments committed to state-led redistribution of lands based on expropriation, with or without compensation to former landowners. This is the fundamental cause behind the phenomenal rise in land occupations and reclamations being carried by a new generation of sophisticated social movements around the world. In Indonesia, some 1 million hectares of land have been occupied by landless peasants since the end of the Suharto dictatorship. Of this land, approximately 50 percent was land formerly in crop plantations (such as rubber or oil palm), 30 percent was in corporate timber plantations, and the remainder was a mixture of state-owned land and tourism development areas. About three-quarters of the occupations have been reclamations of land previously occupied by the same villagers before they were displaced, often violently, to make way for the plantations; the other one-quarter have been new occupations.[1]

In Zimbabwe, as many as 11 million hectares have been transferred in recent years, in large part due to land occupations. In Brazil, according to the Landless Workers' Movement (MST), by 2002 some 8 million hectares of land had been occupied and settled by some 1 million people newly engaged in farming.[2] Other countries with escalating land occupations include Paraguay, Bolivia, Nicaragua, Argentina, Honduras, Guatemala, Mexico, India, Thailand, South Africa, and others.

One of the central debates in the discussion of contemporary visions of land reform concerns the tactic of land occupation. Chapters 14 and 15 focus on Brazil, where the MST has set the standard for other landless movements both within Brazil and around the world. They are noted for both their success in occupying land (as measured by the amount of land occupied, the number of people settled, and a rate of abandonment of the settlements that remains well below 10 percent of new settlers), and for the sophisticated nature of their internal organization.

The MST uses a two-step method to move people from extreme poverty into landownership and farming (Stédile 1997; Movimento dos Trabalhadores Rurais Sem Terra [MST] 2001a, 2001b; Mançano Fernandes 2001, 2002; Rosset 2002a; Branford and Rocha 2002; Harnecker 2003; Wright and Wolford 2003). They begin by reaching out to the most excluded and impoverished segments of Brazilian society, such as landless rural day laborers, urban homeless people, people with substance abuse problems, unemployed rural slum dwellers, or peasant farmers who have lost their land. Organizers give talks in community centers, churches, and other public forums, and landless families are given the opportunity to sign up for a land occupation.

Step one sees these families move into rural "camps," where they live on the side of highways in shacks made from black plastic, until a suitable estate—typically land left unused by absentee landlords—is found. Families spend at least six months, and sometimes as long as five years, living under the harsh conditions of the camps, with little privacy, suffering heat in the summer and cold in the rainy season. As the MST discovered almost by accident, however, the camps are the key step in forging new people out of those with tremendous issues to overcome. Camp discipline, which is communally imposed by camp members, prohibits drug use, domestic violence, excessive drinking, and a host of other social ills. All families must help look after each other's children—who play together—and everyone must cooperate in communal duties. People learn to live cooperatively, and they receive intensive training in literacy, public health, farming, administration of co-ops, and other key skills that can make their future farm communities successful. When people used to occupy land directly, they usually failed to stay more than few months. But when they have first been through an MST camp, more than 90 percent of them stay on their land long term.

Step two is the actual land occupation. It usually takes place at dawn, when security guards and police are asleep, and it involves anywhere from dozens to thousands of families rapidly moving out of their camp onto the estate they will occupy. Crops are planted immediately, communal kitchens, schools, and a health clinic are set up, and defense teams trained in nonviolence secure the perimeter against the hired gunmen, thugs, and assorted police forces that the landlord usually calls down on them. The actual occupation leads to a negotiation with local authorities, the result of which may be the expropriation (with compensation) of the property, under the country's social use of land clause, or the negotiated exchange of the occupied parcel for a different one of equal value. In some cases security forces have managed to expel the occupiers, who typical return and occupy the parcel again and again until an accommodation is reached.

In chapter 14, Mônica Dias Martins examines collective struggle, empowerment, and the meaning of participation in the MST. It is precisely the formation of a highly trained cadre of militants and the personal and political growth that people undergo in the movement, that hold the key to its remarkable success, and she explains how these takes place.

Chapter 15 presents a landmark study of the impacts of agrarian reform settlements in Brazil, which have been created through the collective action of the MST and other movements, leading to the expropriation and redistribution of land by the state (this stands in contrast to the market-led model that also exists in Brazil, which was examined in chapter 11). The authors find that the members of these settlements have significantly improved living standards, and the presence of settlements has had a positive impact on local economic development.

The final chapter pulls together both of these categories of alternatives to neoliberal land policies, as well as historical lessons from earlier periods of agrarian reform. Placing agrarian reform in the context of national development and food sovereignty, the chapter concludes with a series of policy recommendations for the future.

CHAPTER 12

Surviving Crisis in Cuba: The Second Agrarian Reform and Sustainable Agriculture

Mavis Alvarez, Martin Bourque, Fernando Funes,
Lucy Martin, Armando Nova, and Peter Rosset

When trade relations with the Soviet Bloc crumbled in late 1989 and 1990, and the United States tightened the trade embargo, Cuba was plunged into economic crisis. In 1991 the government declared the Special Period in Peacetime, which basically put the country on a wartime economy-style austerity program. An immediate 53 percent reduction in oil imports not only affected fuel availability for the economy, but also reduced to zero the foreign exchange that Cuba had formerly obtained via the reexport of petroleum. Imports of wheat and other grains for human consumption dropped by more than 50 percent, while other foodstuffs declined even more. Cuban agriculture was faced with an initial drop of approximately 70 percent in the availability of fertilizers and pesticides, and a decrease of more than 50 percent in fuel and other energy sources produced by petroleum (Rosset and Benjamin 1994).

A country with an agricultural sector technologically similar to California's suddenly found itself almost without chemical inputs, and with sharply reduced access to fuel and irrigation and a collapse in food imports. In the early 1990s average daily caloric and protein intake by the Cuban population may have been as much as 30 percent below levels in the 1980s.

Fortunately, Cuba was not totally unprepared for the critical situation that arose after 1989. It had, over the years, emphasized the development of human resources, and therefore had a cadre of scientists and researchers who could come forward with innovative ideas to confront the crisis—while it

This chapter is composed of selections chosen and edited by Peter Rosset, from the introduction and chapters 1, 2, 4, and 5 of Funes et al. 2002.

makes up only 2 percent of the population of Latin America, Cuba has almost 11 percent of the region's scientists (Rosset and Benjamin 1994).

Because of the drastically reduced availability of chemical inputs, the state hurried to replace them with locally produced and, in most cases, biological substitutes such as biopesticides (microbial products) and natural enemies to combat insect pests, resistant plant varieties, crop rotations and microbial antagonists to combat plant pathogens, and better rotations and cover cropping to suppress weeds. Scarce synthetic fertilizers were supplemented by biofertilizers, earthworms, compost, other organic fertilizers, animal and green manures, and the integration of grazing animals. In place of tractors, for which fuel, tires, and spare parts were often unavailable, there was a sweeping return to animal traction (Rosset and Benjamin 1994).

When the crisis began, yields fell drastically throughout the country. But production levels for domestically consumed food crops began to rise shortly thereafter, especially on agricultural production cooperatives (CPAs) and on the farms of individual smallholders or *campesinos*. It really was not all that difficult for the small-farm sector to produce effectively with fewer inputs. After all, today's small farmers are most often descendants of generations of the same, with long family and community traditions of low-input production. They basically did two things: remembered the old techniques—like intercropping and manuring—that their parents and grandparents had used before the advent of modern chemicals, and they simultaneously incorporated new biopesticides and biofertilizers into their production practices (Rosset 1997a, 1997c).

The state sector, on the other hand, faced the incompatibility of large monocultural tracts with low-input technology. Scale effects are very different for conventional chemical management and for low external input alternatives. Under conventional systems, a single technician can manage several thousand hectares on a "recipe" basis by simply writing out instructions for a particular fertilizer formula or pesticide to be applied to the entire area by machinery. Not so for agroecological farming. Whoever manages the farm must be intimately familiar with the ecological heterogeneity of each individual patch of soil. The farmer must know, for example, where organic matter needs to be added, and where pest and natural enemy refuges and entry points are (Altieri 1996). This partially explains the difficulty of the state sector to raise yields with alternative inputs. A partial response was obtained through a program that had begun before the Special Period, called *Vinculando el Hombre con la Tierra*, which sought to more closely link state farm workers to particular pieces of land, but it wasn't enough (Enriquez 1994).

In September 1993 Cuba began radically reorganizing the state sector in order to create the small-scale management units that seemed most effective during the Special Period. The government issued a decree terminating the existence of the majority of state farms, turning them into basic units of cooperative production (UBPCs), a form of worker-owned enterprise or cooperative. Much of the 80 percent of all farmland that was once held by the state, including sugarcane plantations, was essentially turned over to the workers. The UBPCs allowed collectives of workers to lease state farmlands rent free, in perpetuity. Property rights would remain in the hands of the state, and the UBPCs would need to continue to meet production quotas for their key crops, but the collectives were the owners of what they produced. What food crops they produced in excess of their quotas could be freely sold at newly opened farmers markets. This last reform, made in 1994, offered a price incentive to farmers to make effective use of the new technologies (Rosset 1997b).

The pace of consolidation of the UBPCs varied greatly in their first years of life. With a variety of internal management schemes, in almost all cases the effective size of the management unit was drastically reduced. It was clear that the process of turning farm workers into farmers would take some time—it simply could not be accomplished overnight—and many UBPCs are still struggling, while others are very successful. On the average, small farmers and agricultural production cooperatives (CPAs) probably still obtain higher levels of productivity than do most UBPCs, and do so in ways that are more ecologically sound.

By the latter part of the 1990s the acute food shortage was a thing of the past, though sporadic shortages of specific items remained a problem, and food costs for the population had increased significantly. The shortage was largely overcome through domestic production increases that came primarily from small farms, and in the case of eggs and pork, from booming backyard production (Rosset 1998). The proliferation of urban farmers producing fresh produce also became extremely important to the Cuban food supply (GNAU 2000; Murphy 1999). The earlier food shortages and resultant increase in food prices suddenly turned urban agriculture into a very profitable activity for Cubans, and, once the government threw its full support behind a nascent urban gardening movement, it exploded to near epic proportions.

Formerly vacant lots and backyards in all Cuban cities now sport food crops and farm animals, and fresh produce is sold from stands throughout urban areas at prices substantially below those prevailing in the farmers' markets. There can be no doubt that urban farming, relying almost exclusively on organic techniques, has played a key role in ensuring the food security of Cuban families.

Historical Background: Revolution and Agrarian Reform

Cuba before 1959

Before 1959 Cuban agriculture was characterized by the ubiquitous presence of foreign capital, the fusion of the self-interest of foreign investors with that of local agricultural and financial oligarchies, and by an extreme concentration of landholdings in large sugarcane plantations and cattle ranches. Thirteen American sugar companies owned 117 million hectares of land; an estimated 25 percent of total arable land was under foreign control. Of the rest, just nine large Cuban sugarcane plantations covered more than 620,000 hectares, which together with the agricultural bourgeoisie controlled more than 21 percent of the land (1.8 million hectares). The rural middle class, lower-middle class, and campesinos that owned their own land, had approximately 2.5 million hectares. Overall, 9.4 percent of landowners had 73.3 percent of the land, a very inequitable distribution of the means of production (Acosta 1972).

Cuba had a distorted agricultural economy, essentially based on one crop and one export; that one crop was, of course, sugar, and it accounted for more than 75 percent of the total value of Cuban exports (see table 12.1, where sugar makes up virtually the entire category labeled "Processed foodstuffs"). One consequence

TABLE 12.1 Cuban exports, 1953–1957 (percent of total exports)

Type of export	1953	1954	1955	1956	1957
Durable goods	5.0	0.6	0.6	—	0.6
Nondurable goods	86.6	84.7	84.7	86.2	87.6
Fresh foodstuffs	0.8	1.5	1.9	4.5	2.7
Processed foodstuffs	78.6	74.9	74.3	74.3	78.2
Preserved foodstuffs	0.4	0.3	0.4	0.5	0.7
Beverages	0.2	0.2	0.3	0.2	0.2
Tobacco	6.5	7.6	7.3	6.6	5.9
Other	0.1	0.2	—	—	0.1
Fixed capital goods	0.2	0.2	0.3	0.3	0.4
Intermediate capital goods	12.7	14.5	14.9	12.8	11.4

Source: DGE 1957.

TABLE 12.2 Imports as a percentage
of total consumption, 1988

Item	Percent
Edible fats	88
Vegetables	33
Cereals	40
Meat products	63
Canned fruits	84

Source: Adapted from different sources in Cuba.

of this economic structure was poor living conditions, particularly among rural people. The maximum annual income of agricultural workers was less than 300 Cuban pesos, and they lived in subhuman living conditions—60 percent of them in palm huts with dirt floors. There were no sanitary installations, not even simple latrines or running water. Seventy-nine percent used kerosene for light, while the rest had no nighttime illumination at all. In terms of food, only 11 percent consumed milk, 4 percent meat, and 20 percent eggs, while the main staples of their diet were rice, beans, roots, and tubers. With regard to education, 43 percent were illiterate and 44 percent never attended school.

In the prerevolutionary period, agriculture was a mixture of semifeudal remnants combined with capitalist practices. The remnants of feudalism included payment with coupons for the company store and the use of the army for labor control. Among the capitalist features were salaries, new methods of organization, and use of modern implements and technology. While the prices that small farmers received for the crops were low, intermediaries and middlemen made large profits at their expense.

The long historical process of distorted development had, by the 1950s, converted Cuba into a supplier of raw materials, mainly sugar, and a buyer of all kinds of goods, especially from the United States—even though conditions might have been favorable for producing these goods within the country (see table 12.2). Above all this setup produced a great dependence on the American market.

Cuba After 1959

After the 1959 triumph of the revolution, Cuba implemented agrarian reforms. Under the first and second agrarian reform laws the Cuban state took control of more than 70 percent of the arable land and created the state sector in agriculture. The area nationalized reached 5.5 million hectares, of which 1.1 million were turned over to those working the land, leaving the state in control of approximately 71 percent of the total area.

The existence of the large state sector made a planned reorganization of land use possible (Vilariño and Domenech 1986). The strategy was always to diversify agriculture to reduce the dependence on one product, sugar, and increase the variety of foodstuffs exported; and to substitute national production for imports. When the United States cancelled Cuba's sugar quota—one of the first actions taken against the Cuban revolution—it was decided, given the diversification policy, to reduce the area devoted to sugarcane. Nevertheless, the ex-Soviet Union and the rest of the socialist countries in Eastern Europe decided to purchase Cuban sugar in bulk, thus creating a secure market, with long-term stable and preferential prices. This led to a decision to reconsider the reduction of area devoted to sugarcane, thus prolonging dependence on a one-product farming system.

A number of other factors also contributed to the revised direction of policy, including having ideal natural conditions for sugarcane production, and possessing both a vast knowledge and experience in sugarcane growing and sugar production and the huge, installed industrial capacity and investment already devoted to sugar processing.

The policy directions followed in the first years of the revolution regarding the use of nationalized land were clearly expressed by Fidel Castro at the closing session of the First Farm Workers Congress in February 1959: "To maintain consumption, to maintain abundance, to carry out agrarian reforms, the land cannot be distributed in one million small pieces . . . cooperatives must be established in the right places for each type of production, and the crops to be sown must be planned . . ." (Castro 1959).

The National Institute for Agrarian Reform (INRA) was created to be in charge of the application and enforcement of the agrarian reform law. Given the characteristics of the nationalized plantations and ranches, two systems were created to organize production: so-called people's farms on former cattle ranches and virgin lands, and cooperatives on the sugarcane plantations. After the 1960 harvest a large portion of the expropriated sugarcane areas was transformed into sugarcane cooperatives, in which the state still owned the land and other means of production, while the workers tilled the land in usufruct. Then in late 1962, policy makers decided that these cooperatives were not working out, and they were transformed into "people's state farms." When the agricultural enterprises were created in 1963 to organize state production, there were approximately 272 people's state farms, 613 sugarcane cooperatives, and 669 administrative farms (formed directly from expropriated plantations). By the end of 1964, 263 new enterprises had been established.

During the period from the first agrarian reform law until 1975, no important changes occurred in the collective organization of production among small landholders, except for the creation of credit and service cooperatives (CCSs) and agricultural communities. Then, at the Fifth Congress of the National Association of Small Farmers (ANAP), following up on decisions made at the First Congress of the Cuban Communist Party, the collectively run agricultural production cooperatives (CPAs) were created. By 1998 some 1,139 cooperatives of this type had been formed, covering some 710,000 hectares (an average of approximately 625 hectares per cooperative), and with more than 63,000 members. Development of the CCSs continued as well; they now cover some 980,000 hectares and have more than 168,000 members. Finally, there are approximately 250 farmers' associations (more loosely organized than CPAs or CCSs) with more than 9,400 members, covering an area of more than 26,000 hectares.

In transferring most of the expropriated lands to the state, the aim was to accelerate the adoption of advanced technologies and boost productivity, while maintaining a nonexploitative labor system. This would be the starting point for the establishment of large agricultural enterprises. The more just distribution of wealth and the new relations of production that were favorable to the development of the productive forces led to the beginning of sustained growth of agricultural production that would stretch over nearly three decades.

At the end of the 1980s, however, there was a generalized decrease in yields and in other indicators of efficiency in an important group of commodities. This came about in an intensive development model, based on high levels of external inputs and a high external dependence (mainly machinery, fuel, and agrochemicals), that was similar to the situation faced by other countries applying the same production model (Rosset 1997a, 1997b, 1997c). Furthermore, the quantities produced were not always sufficient to fully cover the demands of the population with any economic effectiveness. Meanwhile a very significant proportion of arable land was used for export production (see table 12.3), and many soils had begun to show signs of degradation (such as salinity, erosion, acidity, poor drainage). These factors already made it important to carry out economic, structural, technical, and organizational transformations in

TABLE 12.3 Arable land use, 1989

Use	Percent (of total)	Percent (state)	Percent (private)
Exports	53	54	48
Foodstuffs	44	43	48
Other	3	3	4
TOTAL	100	100	100

Source: Adapted from CEE 1989.

Cuban agriculture. As the unraveling of the Soviet Bloc began, the task only became more urgent.

The Crisis of the European Socialist Bloc: The Special Period in Cuba

In 1989 an acute crisis erupted in Cuba when the European socialist countries collapsed and the Soviet Union distintegrated, and, simultaneously, the United States tightened the economic blockade of Cuba. In 1992 the Torricelli bill was approved, barring shipments to Cuba of food and medical supplies by overseas subsidiaries of US companies, and, later, the Helms-Burton Act (1996) restricted foreign investment in Cuba. These laws have been strengthened by a variety of amendments, multiplying the effects of the blockade, which took on increasingly extreme characteristics.

Cuba is not blessed with abundant capital nor with sufficient domestic energy supplies. Prior to 1989 more than 85 percent of the country's trade was with socialist countries in Europe, and a little more than 10 percent with capitalist countries. Cuba imported from socialist countries two-thirds of its foodstuffs, almost all of its fuel, and 80 percent of its machinery and spare parts. With the crisis, Cuba's purchasing capacity was reduced to 40 percent, fuel importation to approximately 33 percent, fertilizers to 25 percent, pesticides to 40 percent, animal feed concentrates to 30 percent. All agricultural activities were seriously affected. Suddenly, US$8 billion a year disappeared from Cuban trade. Between 1989 and 1993, the Cuban GNP fell from US$19.3 to $10.0 billion. Imports were reduced by 75 percent, including most foodstuffs, spare parts, agrochemicals, and industrial equipment. Many industries were forced to close, and public transportation and electric plants worked at minimum capacity (Espinosa 1997). Unexpectedly, a modern and industrialized agricultural system had to face the challenge of increasing food production while maintaining production for export, all with a more than 50 percent drop in the availability of inputs.

The Cuban government put economic austerity measures and emergency changes into practice, such as a new domestic economic policy, an opening to foreign investment, the liberalization of the rules governing the possession of dollars by Cuban citizens, and the granting of licenses for private work in various sectors. Together with structural reorganization, new agricultural techniques developed in recent decades received their first extensive implementation, and a variety of measures were introduced, including:

- Decentralization of the state farm sector through new organizational forms and production structures
- Land distribution to encourage production of different crops in various regions of the country
- Reduction of specialization in agricultural production
- Production of biological pest controls and biofertilizers
- Renewed use of animal traction in place of machinery
- Promotion of urban, family, and community gardening movements
- Opening of farmers' markets under "supply and demand" conditions

The objective of agrarian policy during this Special Period was to move to a low external input form of agriculture, while at the same time boosting production. This required a greater level of organization of Cuban research and agricultural extension structures, a better flow of information, and a reduced emphasis on technologies requiring a lot of capital and/or energy.

Restructuring Land Tenure and Management: A New Agrarian Reform

Since the end of 1993 important modifications of land tenure have been made, and while they have not established new production relationships, they have provided the necessary conditions to boost economic effectiveness. These were the first major changes since 1977. Many of the state farms have been broken up into the smaller scale UBPCs, and the agricultural sector was opened to foreign investment in joint ventures with the state. Furthermore, unused lands

TABLE 12.4 New forms of agricultural organization

STATE SECTOR		State farms
		New-type state farms (GENT)
		Revolutionary Armed Forces (FAR) farms, including farms of the Young Workers' Army (EJT) and the Ministry of the Interior (MININT)
		Self-provisioning farms at workplaces and public institutions
NON-STATE SECTOR	Non-state sector collective production	Basic Units of Cooperative Production (UBPC)
		Agricultural Production Cooperatives (CPA)
	Individual production	Credit and Service Cooperatives (CCS)
		Individual farmers, in usufruct
		Individual farmers, private property
MIXED SECTOR		Joint ventures between the state and foreign capital

were distributed in usufruct to new farmers. These changes represent a broadening of the land-tenure matrix, generating a new mixed economy based primarily on individual farmers—with both private and usufruct tenure—private cooperatives, and collective farms with usufruct tenure (Figueroa 1996). Ten distinct forms of organization can be identified and grouped into three sectors (see table 12.4).

The State Sector

From the beginning of the revolution through the early 1990s, the state was the most important sector of production. In recent years, however, the state farms have been drastically downsized in terms of landholdings, number of workers, and equipment, reducing the economic importance of the state sector. Since 1993 holdings in the state sector have shrunk from more than 75 percent of the arable land to less than 33 percent in 1996. The remaining workers in the state farm system are concentrated in strategic fields such as animal breeding, large-scale pig and poultry production, and others that require heavy mechanization, qualified personnel, and emerging technologies. Thus most of the remaining state farm employees have little in common with traditional farm workers.

The state sector also includes farms belonging to the Ministry of Interior (MININT), the Revolutionary Armed Forces (FAR), and the Young Workers' Army (EJT), which is a subdivision of the FAR. The primary purpose of these production units is to provide for their respective organizations, though they also sell considerable quantities of surplus food through state-owned wholesalers. The EJT has its own commercial arrangements and is one of the most efficient producers within the state agricultural sector.

Self-provisioning areas are also considered part of the state sector. During the 1990s many factories and workplaces and public institutions like hospitals, schools, and office buildings were given unused lands to produce food for their own cafeterias and to sell to their employees at reduced prices. Today subsidized lunches and discount produce represent an important nonsalary benefit for Cuban workers.

The new-type state farms (GENT) are the final component of this sector. After the creation of the UBCPs it became evident that the transition from state-farm worker to farmer was one that could be made easier if done by progressive steps. The GENTs are completely owned by the state, but worker cooperatives are built on them, and over time the cooperatives take on more of the financial and management responsibilities. At a minimum, they enter into profit-sharing schemes with the underlying state-farm structure. Rather than being state employees, the cooperative members enter into a contract with the state, and the cooperative's profits are shared among the workers according to their own internal agreements. In the GENTs, both profit and risk are shared between the state farm and the worker cooperative, but minimum salaries are guaranteed, while the ultimate responsibility for the farm, including key management decisions, lies at the state-enterprise level. There is a great deal of flexibility in these experimental arrangements, allowing each division and even particular enterprises and farms to work out their own arrangements within certain parameters. The final destiny of a given GENT might be the creation of a UBPC, or it might not.

The Non-State Sector: Collective Farming

In the non-state structure there are two principal forms of production. The largest is collective production, in which the land is worked jointly by all cooperative members, and management decisions are made through democratic processes. The other is individual production, in which each farmer's plot is worked basically on a family farm model. Most of these farmers are also members of cooperatives, in order to have access to services and credit, to purchase inputs in bulk, and to sell their produce, though production itself remains individual. Within this sector there are also two main types of land tenure, private and usufruct, which cut across both forms of production.

Agricultural Production Cooperatives (CPA). CPAs are the traditional revolutionary form of cooperative production in Cuba, founded in 1977 by farmers voluntarily choosing to unite their private individual lands and resources for increased production, marketing, and economic efficiency. In 1997 there were 1,156 CPAs with a total of 62,155 members who owned 9.4 percent of the agricultural lands (Oficina Nacional de Estadísticas 1997). The CPAs showed a steady decline in membership from the mid-1980s to the early 1990s, when they began to rebound. The recovery came about as new members joined, with backgrounds in the most diverse array of occupations but drawn to farming by the advantages of rural cooperative life with respect to income, access to affordable food, and, to a lesser degree, housing.

With many of these new members coming from other fields with different styles of workplace discipline, habits, and motivations, it would be understandable if they needed a period of adjustment and training. Although it is presently only a working hypothesis, it is likely that as a result of this influx of new blood, the present membership of the CPAs is now more heterogeneous with respect to social origin, professional characteristics, and needs and interests. At the end of the 1980s the average age of a cooperative member was 41 years old, but it is likely that the growth in numbers of new members has brought down the average in recent years.

Basic Units of Cooperative Production (UBPC). The CPAs were joined by UBPCs in the early 1990s. With their creation, a new type of cooperative was established, not by the voluntary socialization of private property, but, rather, the other way around, through the state's bestowal of the use of property and infrastructure.

UBPCs are productive units with a cooperative structure that farm state lands given free of charge to the cooperatives in permanent usufruct (the average acreage is substantially smaller than the former state farms, which were broken up to form the UBPCs). Other means of production such as buildings, machinery, animals, irrigation systems, and tools, were sold to the cooperatives at favorable prices with low-interest loans, and as such constitute private property of the cooperative. The UBPCs maintain commercial relationships with the distribution chain of the original state enterprise from which they emerged, and they negotiate prices and production plans based on a quota system. Surplus production is sold at the farmers' markets, at prices set by supply and demand, and through other outlets. The UBPCs also receive technical support from the enterprise, from which they purchase inputs and additional equipment as needed.

In terms of numbers and area, UBPCs are now the predominant type of farm in Cuban agriculture. In 1997 there were 2,654 UBPCs with 272,407 members occupying 42 percent of the land (Oficina Nacional de Estadísticas 1997). By 1995—after less than two years of existence—23 percent of the sugarcane producing UBPCs and 52 percent of the nonsugarcane producing UBPCs were profitable. This is a vast improvement over the situation among state farms prior to 1993 (Rodríguez 1996).

The new cooperative members, many of whom were workers on the previous state farms, constitute a new type of producer that must face the challenge of achieving greater economic efficiency. This social and structural transition is currently underway, and in some cases there continues to be a certain degree of ambiguity between the previous structures of state-run enterprises and the new cooperative structures. Additionally, a psychosocial transformation is also underway, as former state agricultural workers make a transition from their previous functions and mindset and become true cooperative owner-operators—in other words, become farmers.

With the appearance of the UBPCs a new economic player has emerged in Cuban agriculture: the cooperative farmer on state lands. These farmers now make up the most important sector with the largest number of people involved. They have the dual responsibility, or social duty, of achieving higher levels of production, but with fewer inputs and other resources. To do this they must break with the conventional ways of doing agriculture that were established in the former state farm sector. In some cases, the relationships between the new cooperatives and the former state enterprises have been marked by an excess of tutelage, subordination, and dependence, remnants or legacies of an enterprise management structure that has not yet fully given way to a more appropriate and participatory planning process among actors. The UBPCs demand a great deal of attention and support because they make up a new and very large grouping, which must play a key role in the new national production strategy.

Analysis of these two forms of production shows that the cooperative sector as a whole has flexibility, heterogeneity, the ability to combine diverse crops and technologies, a qualified labor force, and an unquestionable capacity to form groups with common interests (economy, ideology, community, and even family interests). These factors in combination with the large acreage, sheer number of members, and social responsibility, make it the most important part of the new social structure of Cuban agriculture.

The Non-State Sector: Individual Farming

Individual small farmers who work their land based on a family farm model can be classified into three major categories. Most of those who have private ownership of their farms are members of Credit and Service Cooperatives (CCS); then there are the individual farmers who have received lands in usufruct from the state in recent years; and finally, dispersed individual farmers who are not co-op members. After a sustained decrease in numbers in the 1980s, in the 1990s the individual farmer sector began to recover both in terms of numbers and acreage. Today they hold 55 percent of the private farmland in Cuba—up from 42 percent in 1988—and thus are economically important. While there are some dispersed individual small farmers, the majority of farmers producing in individual farms are members of CCSs.

Credit and Service Cooperatives (CCS). In 1997 there were 2,709 CCSs, with a membership consisting of 159,223 individual farmers working 11.8 percent of total agricultural land (Oficina Nacional de Estadísticas 1997). In this type of cooperative, individual farmers work their farms independently but join together to receive credit and services from state agencies. They may also share certain machinery and equipment, especially in the so-called strengthened CCSs. In any case the land continues to be individual property, independently managed by the owner. CCS members purchase inputs and sell products at fixed prices through state agencies, based on production plans and contracts established with state distribution systems. Any production above and beyond the contracted quantity may be sold in the farmers' markets at free-market prices.

During the recent period there has been an accelerated growth in the numbers of new farmers in the CCSs, even more so than in the CPAs. This may be explained by a number of factors, but in essence it is an economic phenomenon. It comes down to the fact that individual farmers have higher incomes than do members of production cooperatives. Perhaps this is because they are able to make faster decisions and because they have a greater sense of ownership, or because their management practices lead to more efficient use of limited resources. Possibly it is because they have less of a sense of social responsibility, or, more likely, it is due to a combination of these factors. As a rapidly growing group of farmers, they too have undergone a demographic shift, as most of the new members are young, lowering the average age, which had been approximately age 50 in the 1980s (Domínguez 1990).

Individual Usufruct Farmers. Beginning in 1993 individual families were given up to 27 hectares of land in free and permanent usufruct to grow specialty crops such as coffee, tobacco, and cocoa. By 1996 the number of these so-called *usufructuarios* had grown from zero to 43,015 farmers (Lage 1996). In addition to this group, in many urban areas individuals were given small plots of land (0.25 hectares) to grow food for themselves and their neighbors. These new farmers come from diverse backgrounds, although it is likely that most of them were previously workers or professionals in agricultural fields. The National Association of Small Farmers (ANAP) aims to incorporate these new farming families into the CCSs and into the association.

The Mixed Sector

Joint venture enterprises with foreign companies exist in the citrus export industry, and some other export commodities have received foreign financing for a portion of national production (rice, cotton, tomatoes), which may expand to other crops in the near future. How the agricultural labor force will be affected by this and what traits will identify and differentiate the new group of workers linked to foreign capital are topics for future research. It should be noted, however, that only state enterprises can accept and use foreign capital. Thus no private producer(s) can establish direct relations with foreign investors. This measure has been implemented by the state to regulate the sort of social and economic differentiation that might otherwise arise from these activities.

The analysis of these very different forms of organizing production, and the different social groups associated with them, shows a great socioeconomic and structural diversity in contemporary Cuban agriculture. Still, and this is very important, it is precisely this heterogeneity—conceived of as part of an articulated system—that allows for the application of distinct and varied technological alternatives. Each of the forms described above has particular characteristics to offer, that when integrated at a system level, could represent greater strength and integration in the system as a whole. Both collaboration and competition can be stimulated by a network of connections and relationships that interact and complement one another.

Flexibility and the Introduction of Market Mechanisms

Historically, distribution and marketing of agricultural commodities to the whole population at accessible prices has been the responsibility of the state, except for a brief period (1980–1986) when the earlier experiment with free-market farmers' markets was carried out. With the opening of the farmers' markets in 1994, a step was taken toward optimizing production relationships, allowing surplus production—above and beyond amounts contracted for with the state—to be sold at free-market prices based on supply and demand.

The ability to get higher prices and to raise incomes by surpassing contracted production quotas has led to the more active and efficient management of productive resources, with one outcome being the greater availability of food for the population. Sales data from 1996 from the farmers' markets reveal the dominance of individual producers in this venue.

Although the new markets have had repercussions for all producers, this change is quite significant for the former state farm workers who are now either members of UBPCs or of cooperatives within GENTs. For the first time they have the opportunity to make extra income through collective self-management. While they currently participate to a very limited degree only in the markets, there is great potential for this sector to participate more actively. The act of bringing their own production to the marketplace helps bridge the gap between producers and consumers and offers them more freedom of action and greater individual and collective incentives.

Central planning and market mechanisms are not mutually exclusive. The latter has its specific role to play—even when its negative impacts on social equity are recognized—as it currently does in the evolution from central planning toward worker self-management. The tension between the two is expressed as a necessary equilibrium. This delicate balance must simultaneously promote initiative, reduce alienation, and provide economic incentives so that agricultural production increases, without instigating a fall into anarchy, ungovernability, or the loss of the state's ability to maintain and meet the key social objectives of socialism. In concrete terms, nonsocialist forms of production must have a subordinate role, in which there is a certain level of control over windfall private profits. In the final analysis, the social and structural expression of this transformation can be described as a socioeconomic strengthening of the agricultural workforce, internally differentiated by property type and management system, and modified by the particulars of commodities produced, geographic areas, distance from markets, and availability of transport.

Participation and Initiative

The ideal of a state production system based on high-tech methods and centralized decisions was confronted with the reality of practices involving excessive use of resources and inputs (well beyond the point of diminishing returns), underutilization of expensive investments in infrastructure, a low degree of agility in decision making and provision of services, and the adoption of production norms far removed from real needs. Yet the need for transformation ran deeper still.

The changes carried out so far have, at least theoretically, enhanced participation, inspired initiative, reduced alienation, and allowed for a greater realization of the human potential of workers and farmers, though the effects to date are as yet uneven. To illustrate the impact of these changes on producers, there is the testimony of people's own varied experiences. A woman who is president of a UBPC said, ". . . [W]hen I was the head of the state farm I did not think as I do now. Only when one is here does one really know what things are really necessary, and you try to spend as little as possible so that the cooperative can be profitable." She went on to give an example: "[T]he state enterprise charged us for trucking in water twice a day and this cost us almost 30 pesos . . . and I said to myself, this cannot go on any longer . . . so I jumped on a tractor, hooked a water tank on a trailer to it, and now the whole operation doesn't cost us even two pesos."

A woman at a UBPC dairy unit was asked if she worked according to a strict, predetermined schedule. She responded, "I don't even know how to answer you; no, we don't have a schedule—if I have to bathe the animals I do it until I've finished. At the end of the day we're the ones who have to do what has to be done. I can't say I am going to quit now because it's time to go home, or think, oh, I'll let that other guy do it." Later she added, "[W]e have to worry even more about the work because since my husband is the administrator I have to help him out."

A different view was expressed by the manager of a UBPC: "[A] campesino does not understand the constraints limiting development possibilities . . . he only understands what he has in his pocket . . . today, campesinos participate more because they are under new social conditions, but they will only feel a sense of ownership when they see the benefits of their work, and this will be when there are profits—and I do not see that we will make profits in the near future." Another UBPC member expressed that, "Regardless of the fact that more efficient land use is achieved when sweet potato and maize are inter-cropped, in the past provincial officials didn't allow us to grow these crops together . . . though everybody knows that campesinos have always done this. Even today they become uneasy when we say we don't need to apply chemical formulas to soils when planting potatoes, because there is enough phosphorus and potassium available. When we applied chemical fertilizer to potatoes, the yields were no higher than when we did not."

This situation should evolve toward new forms of management and the establishment of more productive relationships among production units and between these and state enterprises. This should allow the emergence and development of production units that exercise their full rights and take advantage of the will and creativity of their members. The key is that the link with the state should not be one of dependence and subordination, but rather a two-way transmission between different mechanisms and centralized state planning.

Farmer-to-Farmer Training Techniques

For four decades the Cuban Revolution has been focused on rural development, providing free classes and workshops on both general and agricultural subjects. Cuban farmers, therefore, tend to be well educated, with both modern and traditional knowledge.

The National Association of Small Farmers (ANAP), founded in 1961, is an organization that represents the cooperatives and individual farmers that make up the non-state sector. It is also a member of La Via Campesina. Today its primary goal is to encourage and develop the use of agroecological farming techniques throughout the Cuban countryside. Some of its activities include:

- Nationwide training programs to build capacity among small farmers, cooperative members, grassroots organizations, and ANAP leaders
- Farmer-to-farmer training programs where farmers teach each other about their experiences with sustainable agriculture through direct participation and communication
- Reorientation of the National Training Center's education and training curriculum in order to emphasize agroecological knowledge

- Farmer, extensionist, and researcher participation in regional and national networks
- Ongoing discussions of topics related to food security and sustainable development

ANAP combines traditional knowledge and practices with new technologies in a participatory effort that enables farmers to educate each other. The organization is broad-based and horizontal in structure. Although its headquarters are located in the Niceto Pérez National Training Center, the majority of ANAP's activities are decentralized through provincial and municipal offices. Planning meetings and programs are held at regional locations appropriate to the topics discussed, be it at ANAP facilities, local Ministry of Agriculture (MINAG) offices, or on-site at farms or cooperatives. This ensures that meetings will be comfortable, accessible, and inclusive. This inclusive model of communication has had great success in rural Cuba.

Grassroots networking and extension dates back to the early years of the revolution, when the lack of qualified personnel in rural areas appeared to be a powerful obstacle to development. The few available technicians taught agricultural and veterinary techniques to farmers, who would then become trainers themselves. This technique, arising from necessity, was tremendously successful. In 1961, similar methods were used to combat rural illiteracy, which at that time was approximately 40 percent. Because of these early campaigns, farmers are well prepared for grassroots education.

Farmer-to-farmer programs are particularly useful when promoting ideas or techniques that contradict conventional wisdom and customs. In order to change deeply rooted habits, the teacher must establish a high level of confidence and credibility with the student. Through farmer-to-farmer contacts, ANAP has been able to maintain a strong relationship with its members. Thus, it has been very successful in disseminating teachings from scientific and technical institutions through its national structure, allowing the information to reach even farmers in remote areas.

Some of ANAP's training is conducted via the media. Nationwide, ANAP hosts regular programs on more than fifty radio stations, most of them community based. ANAP has created television shows specifically for farmers that reflect their lifestyle and cultural heritage and that provide technical information and training. ANAP's magazine reports on the recent agricultural news and scientific knowledge, including the theories and practices of agroecology. Promotional materials provide information on specific pests and diseases, biological pest controls, agroecological techniques, natural food preservation, and other topics.

The most efficient method of transmitting information and building consciousness in rural communities, however, is still direct, personal communication. During the Special Period the economic crisis limited access to printing and publication materials. Therefore, the farmer-to-farmer training schools have remained the crux of all outreach efforts.

Extension work, called the continuous teaching and education program, is part of the small farmer technical activism program. Participating farmers attend an intensive training course at the Niceto Pérez Center, during which the farmers themselves prepare the materials (both written and audiovisual) for extension work in their region. The participants then spend some time in the provincial offices, collaborating with extension agents, technical specialists, and ANAP leaders in order to develop a provincial plan. The entire team of extension agents and specialists is then dispatched throughout the area to organize meetings, teach workshops, and coordinate with local community activists. Once regional training has been completed, farmers from various regions come together in larger exchanges in order to compare experiences and discuss their work. Finally, team members evaluate the impact of their extension work in meetings with participating farmers, and a new cycle begins, as another group of farmers travels to the national center for training courses.

These extension methods, commonly called "farmer-to-farmer" exchanges, identify and emphasize many traditional farming practices that are productive and that conserve and rehabilitate farming ecosystems. Cuba's ability to survive both natural disasters and economic crises is derived from the cultural strength of its rural population. Farmers are closely connected to their land and are therefore able to observe and adapt to changing conditions. Throughout the difficulties and shortages of the 1990s, farmers had a sizeable impact by guaranteeing the food supply for Cuba's population, and they have been able to maintain, and even increase food production, in many cases using exemplary methods of sustainable agriculture.

Promoting Sustainable Agriculture

The transition to sustainable techniques has been easier for Cuban farmers than for farmers in other countries because of the security bestowed by the Cuban government: land rights; access to and ownership of equipment; avail-

ability of credit; markets; insurance; and free, quality health care and education. Sustainable technology is difficult without sustainable economic and
social structures. Cuban farmers are highly organized through the formation
of cooperatives that have real social and economic power, and the presence of
national organizations such as ANAP that can represent the interests of individual farmers at the state level.

ANAP members added sustainability as one of the farmer-to-farmer extension program's official goals at the VII International Meeting in November
1996, in the Guira de Melena municipality of Havana Province. Representatives from Mexico, Central America, and the Caribbean attended the meeting;
many had been working in solidarity with Cuba since the early 1990s to promote agricultural exchange and friendship throughout the region (ANAP
1997). ANAP defined its commitment to sustainability and agroecological agricultural through three basic goals:

- To restore and promote the practices of small farmers through direct
  farmer-to-farmer exchanges of sustainable agricultural techniques
- To support horizontal technology transfers through participatory
  methods that encourage the use of appropriate sustainable technologies
- To conduct the research necessary to carry out successful agroecological
  extension, public education, and appropriate technology transfers

ANAP initiated its agroecology program in Villa Clara province. It identified
more than two hundred small farmers who were already experienced with and
were practicing agroecological techniques, half of whom began to work as
extension agents through the farmer-to-farmer program. In 2000, similar programs began in the Cienfuegos and Sancti Spíritus provinces and have since
expanded to the rest of the country.

Cooperatives have played an important role in educating tens of thousands
of farmers about agroecology. Extensionists give workshops and classes at CPA
and CCS general assembly meetings , using existing organizational structures
to facilitate the educational process. Given that there are currently over 3,700
cooperatives with monthly meetings, this structure has been a highly effective
way to teach farmers about the values of sustainable agriculture.

ANAP has also worked with the Agrarian University of Havana (UNAH).
Since 1998, the National Training Center and UNAH have offered the
Agroecology and Sustainable Rural Development Chair at the UNAH, for professors committed to sustainable agriculture. The impact of this program has
multiplied through the national network of research institutions, and the

farms and cooperatives that provide practical and demonstrational points of reference.

Every year, UNAH trains thousands of students, administrators, and farmers in modern agroecological principles and technologies. In the first trimester of 1999, 36 ANAP employees and cooperative members received their diplomas. ANAP is currently working to make this type of certified, technical training available throughout the country by means of the decentralized training system used in their own extension work.

Conclusions: An Alternative Paradigm Emerges?

Despite the difficult circumstances of the Special Period, Cuban agriculture has undergone a positive transformation toward sustainability. An increasing number of farmers are abandoning the conventional production model that was based on excessive use of agrochemicals, wasteful use of resources, pollution of water and soil, destruction of forests and ecosystems, poor soil management, and many other misdeeds that have left our planet on the verge of ecological catastrophe. Farmers, extensionists, and researchers are collaborating to promote and apply a combination of traditional agriculture and modern scientific and technical knowledge. These alternative technologies are spreading throughout the Cuban countryside despite shortages in supplies and a deeply rooted prejudice toward the use of agrochemicals.

Cuba continues to develop and implement new technologies. Research centers have developed improved techniques for soil management such as crop rotation, integration of crops with livestock, application of animal manures, composting, green manures, and the use of animal traction instead of heavy machinery. Biological pesticides and fertilizers are becoming increasingly mainstream as Cubans recognize the need to reduce toxic chemicals. These new technologies have allowed small and medium farms to become a significant source of Cuba's food supply while protecting the surrounding environment. Farmers have gained a greater understanding of the need to protect natural resources and to practice a healthier, more harmonious and balanced agriculture.

To what extent can we see the outlines of an alternative food system paradigm in this Cuban experience? Or is Cuba just such a unique case in every way that we cannot generalize its experiences into lessons for other countries? The first thing to point out is that contemporary Cuba turned conventional wisdom completely on its head. It is commonly thought that small countries cannot feed themselves; that they need imports to cover the deficiency of their local agriculture. Yet Cuba has taken enormous strides toward self-reliance since it lost its key trade relations. It is also commonly held that a country can't feed its people without the use of synthetic farm chemicals, yet Cuba is virtually doing so. The current general opinion is that large-scale corporate or state farms are required to efficiently produce enough food, yet in Cuba, small farmers and gardeners are in the vanguard of the country's recovery from a food crisis. In fact, in the absence of subsidized machines and imported chemicals, small farms are more efficient than very large production units. We hear time and again that international food aid is the answer to food shortages—yet Cuba has found an alternative in local production.

Abstracting from that experience, the elements of an alternative paradigm might therefore be the following:

- *Agrarian Reform.* Rural peasants and urban farmers have been the most productive producers in Cuba under low-input conditions. Indeed, smaller farms worldwide produce much more per unit area than do large farms (Rosset 1999). In Cuba redistribution was relatively easy to accomplish because the major part of the land reform had already occurred, in the sense that there were no landlords to resist further change.

- *Agroecological Technology.* Instead of chemicals, Cuba has used intercropping, locally produced biopesticides, compost, and other alternatives to synthetic pesticides and fertilizers.

- *Fair Prices for Farmers.* Cuban farmers stepped up production in response to higher crop prices. Farmers everywhere lack incentive to produce when prices are kept artificially low, as they often are. Yet when given an incentive, they produce, regardless of the conditions under which that production must take place.

- *Greater Emphasis on Local Production.* People should not have to depend on the vagaries of prices in the world economy, long-distance transportation, and superpower "goodwill" for their next meal. Locally and regionally produced food offers greater security, as well as synergistic linkages to promote local economic development. Furthermore, such production is more ecologically sound, as the energy spent on international transport is wasteful and environmentally unsustainable. By promoting urban farming, cities and their surrounding areas can be made virtually self-

sufficient in perishable foods, be beautified, and have greater employment opportunities. Cuba gives us a hint of the underexploited potential
of urban farming.

The Cuban experience illustrates that a nation's population can be well fed
by means of an alternative model based on appropriate ecological technology
and in doing so can become more self-reliant in food production. Farmers
must receive higher returns for their produce, and when they do they will be
encouraged to step up production. Expensive chemical inputs—most of
which are unnecessary—can be largely dispensed with. The important lessons
from Cuba that we can apply elsewhere, then, are agrarian reform, agroecology, fair prices, and local production, including urban agriculture.

CHAPTER 13

Land for People Not for Profit in Venezuela

Gregory Wilpert

The Venezuelan government under President Hugo Chavez is the only government in Latin America, and perhaps even in the world, that is currently trying to pursue an ambitious land and agrarian reform program. The government has also introduced new agricultural policy principles, such as those of food sovereignty and the primacy of land use over landownership. Because of this, despite the fact that Venezuela has a relatively small agricultural sector, land reform has become one of the Chavez government's most controversial policy endeavors. Exactly why this land reform is so controversial, what it consists of, and its problems and prospects, are some of the issues that will be examined in the following pages.

History of Agriculture and Land Reform in Venezuela

Early in the nineteenth century Venezuela was a fairly typical Latin American country, except that during the period of colonization it was generally considered a backwater because the Spaniards did not believe Venezuela had much mineral wealth. As a result, early on agriculture became the main economic activity of the country, with the production of cocoa, coffee, sugar, cotton, and tobacco leading the way.

At least 70 percent of the population lived in the countryside at that time (Quevedo 1998). Land tenancy was mostly divided up among a handful of *caudillos* (strong men) who had fought during Venezuela's war of independence (1821–1839). This unjust land distribution was not quietly accepted in Venezuela, though. One person who fought against the unjust distribution of land shortly after independence, thus helping fuel Venezuela's post-independence civil wars, was Ezequiel Zamora (1817–1860). His famous slogan called for "Land and free men, respect for the peasant, and the disappearance of the *Godos* (Spanish colonialists)." With this slogan Zamora led numerous popular uprisings against the oligarchy of the time. Even though he was ultimately unable to reverse Venezuela's unequal land distribution, he is today one of President Chavez's main historical reference points and sources of inspiration, especially with regard to agrarian issues.

Later, a number of military rulers, such as Guzman Blanco (1880–1890), distributed land among their loyal supporters. One of the most notorious dictators in this regard was Juan Vicente Gómez (1908–1935), who simply appropriated tremendous amounts of land as his personal property. After he was overthrown his land was expropriated and became state property again.

During the Gómez dictatorship a major shift took place in which Venezuela was converted from a predominantly agricultural economy into one based primarily on mineral exploitation—especially the exploitation of oil, which was discovered in Venezuela in the early twentieth century. This shift would eventually have devastating consequences for Venezuelan agriculture. By the end of the Gómez dictatorship in 1935, agriculture made up only 22 percent of Venezuela's GDP, though it still occupied approximately 60 percent of the workforce. Meanwhile, Venezuela had become the world's largest oil exporting country.

The increasing dominance of oil production over subsequent decades caused an economic phenomenon that among economists is known as Dutch Disease, "a process whereby new discoveries on favourable price changes in one sector of the economy—for example, petroleum—cause distress in other sectors, for example manufacturing or agriculture" (Karl 1997, 5). The inflow of foreign currency as a result of oil exports has an immediate, twofold effect. First, it increases the population's purchasing power and thereby fuels inflation. Second, it makes imported products, whether industrial or agricultural, cheaper than domestic products, thus increasing the volume of imports. In Venezuela, comparatively cheaper imported goods—including food— flooded the market and practically destroyed agricultural production, while also putting a brake on industrial development in Venezuela.

By 1960 the percentage of the population living in rural areas had declined to just 35 percent, and by the 1990s this number had dropped to a mere 12 percent, making Venezuela one of Latin America's most urbanized countries. Another result of Dutch Disease is that Venezuela has been and remains the only Latin American country that is a net importer of agricultural products, and it has the smallest percentage of GDP—6 percent—that comes from agricultural production.

The relatively rapid decline of agriculture in Venezuela meant that urbanization was quite rapid, and the cities were flooded with far more people than they could accommodate. The result of this massive influx was the creation of enormous slums, *barrios*, stretching out for miles on the outskirts of Caracas and other major cities. The size of the barrios and the corresponding decline of agriculture were thus the result of the tremendous increase in oil revenues the country enjoyed in the 1960s and 1970s. This was then followed by a steady twenty-year decline in oil revenues, during the 1980s and 1990s, which meant that the state could not soften the impact of poverty with redistributive measures, and instead cut back social spending.

In addition to the overall decline of agriculture, Venezuelan farmers had to cope with the tremendous inequality in landownership. In 1937 landownership was so concentrated that the larger haciendas, with landholdings of 1,000 hectares or more, were held by only 4.8 percent of the landowners, although they constituted 88.8 percent of all agricultural land. Small farmers, meanwhile, with landholdings of 10 hectares or less, constituted 57.7 percent of all landowners, yet they occupied just 0.7 percent of agricultural land (Delahaye 2003).

Venezuela's first real experience with state-sponsored land reform began with a land reform law that passed in 1960, shortly after the defeat of the Marcos Perez Jimenez dictatorship and the 1958 introduction of liberal democracy. The social-democratic presidency of Rómulo Betancourt realized that Venezuela's land distribution was unsustainable and introduced the Agrarian Reform Law of 1960, which set up the National Agrarian Institute. Over the course of twenty years, this reform effort distributed state land to over 200,000 families. Most of this reform, however, came in the first few years after the law was passed; subsequent governments ignored the institute and the land reform program.

The intensification of Dutch Disease, especially during the country's oil boom years of the 1970s, made agricultural production quite unprofitable and urbanization nearly unstoppable. It has been estimated that the drop-out rate from this reform effort was as high as one-third of the beneficiaries. Also, as many as 90 percent of the beneficiaries never obtained full title to the land. The land reform was thus essentially a reform in land tenancy, from state to small farmer, but not in landownership. According to a 1997 agricultural census, land distribution remained almost as unequal as it had been prior to the

1960 agricultural reform law, with 5 percent of largest landowners controlling 75 percent of the land, and 75 percent of the smallest landowners controlling only 6 percent of the land.

What did change, however, was, first, that a market for landownership developed, while mostly among middle to large landholdings, as these landowners began purchasing and selling their land, often for speculative purposes. Second, the larger landowners were also increasingly inclined to expel *campesinos* from the land, either as a result of the introduction of new technologies or because they had to stop production due to the uncompetitiveness of their agricultural products, thus contributing to the already serious pressure on urbanization. Finally, a third change was that the landowners were increasingly companies rather than individuals.

Chavez and Land Reform

When Hugo Chavez came into office in 1999 it was fairly clear that one of his first priorities would be land reform. Although his political platform, aside from his emphasis on developing a new constitution, was far from clear, Chavez repeatedly stressed that one of his main heroes was Ezequiel Zamora. Also, once the new constitution was approved by referendum in December 1999, it became even clearer that land reform would be a constitutional mandate. Article 307 of the 1999 constitution states:

> The predominance of large idle estates (*latifundios*) is contrary to the interests of society. Appropriate tax law provisions shall be enacted to tax fallow lands and establish the necessary measures to transform them into productive economic units, likewise recovering arable land. Farmers and other agricultural producers are entitled to own land in the cases and forms specified under the pertinent law. The state shall protect and promote associative and private forms of property in such manner as to guarantee agricultural production. The state shall see to the sustainable ordering of arable land to guarantee its food-producing potential.

Likewise, the constitution specifies that it is the state's obligation to promote the development of agriculture in Venezuela. Article 306 states:

> The state will promote conditions for holistic rural development, with the purpose of generating employment and guaranteeing the peasant population an adequate level of well-being, as well as their incorporation into national development. Similarly, it will support agricultural activity

and the optimal use of land, by means of the provision of infrastructure works, credit, training services, and technical assistance.

It is important to note that Venezuela's 1999 constitution is replete with provisions that act as guidelines for state action. That is, the constitution is almost as much a political program as it is the country's basic legal framework. Many activists in Venezuela make this point explicitly, saying that in contrast to the past, the current constitution outlines a path for development and for social justice in Venezuela. While many might complain that the constitution is just a wish list, it is actually more than that in the sense that it acts as a focal point for galvanizing the population in the pursuit of the concrete goals that the constitution outlines. To make sense of the central role the constitution plays in contemporary Venezuela, it is useful to quote Roland Denis, a prominent Venezuelan community organizer and former vice-minister for local planning, in a conversation with the author:

> Here there was no revolutionary organization that assumed role of driving force. There were only insurrectionary movements—first of the masses (in the uprising of 1989), then of the military (in the coup attempts of 1992). These movements were heterogeneous, dispersed, fragmented. What united them was the project to develop a common foundation—that is to say the constitution. Nobody had been able to centralize this movement around a program, not even Chavez. His leadership is unquestioned, but his ideas were not sufficient to unite the movement. The constitution filled this emptiness. It is simultaneously a political program and a framework for the future of the process. In this sense, the constitution is not a dead letter. In it many values and principles are reflected. And it is a deeply libertarian and egalitarian constitution (Denis 2003).

Despite his clear interest in promoting a land reform, it was not until three years into his first term in office that Chavez presented his government's land reform law, which was passed as part of a set of decree-laws in November 2001 and went into full effect a year later, on December 10, 2002. The decree-laws were part of an "enabling act," in which the National Assembly allowed Chavez to pass a set of 49 laws by decree. When Chavez passed these 49 decree-laws, the opposition's uproar against them was immediate and resounding. As a matter of fact, it was these laws, but especially the land reform, that galvanized the opposition for the first time since its devastating defeats at the polls in 1998 and 2000. Eventually, the land reform and the other laws would provide one of the main motivations for the April 2002 coup attempt and the 2003 shutdown of the oil industry (Wilpert 2006).

The reasons the opposition was so opposed to the land reform law were varied but principally had to do with the objection that not only state-owned land but also privately held land could be redistributed. The opposition argued that since the Venezuelan state is the largest landowner in Venezuela, all redistributed land should come from state-owned land and not from privately held land. According to the opposition, Chavez was conducting an unconstitutional assault on private property. However, as is shown above, the constitution clearly states, in its opposition to *latifundios*, that privately held land is also to be part of the land reform and, thus, while generally protected, it is constitutionally eligible for redistribution.

Despite the opposition's uproar, the land reform law of 2001 is not all that radical, when compared with the history of land reform around the world. The law clearly states that large landowners are entitled to their land. Only if the land is idle and over a certain size, depending on its quality, may a portion of it be expropriated. In addition, if the government expropriates it for redistribution, then it must compensate legitimate landowners at current market rates for this land.

A change in the land reform law that was enacted in early 2005 revised the size of idle land that landowners may own. According to the law as it was first passed, the largest tract of idle low-quality agricultural land that could be held was 5,000 hectares. The 2005 reform of the land law, though, made the permissible sizes of idle agricultural land more flexible, leaving the extent up to the National Land Institute, which is in charge of land redistribution. The land institute decided to reduce the largest expansion of idle high-quality land an owner may own from 100 hectares to 50 and the largest expansion of low-quality land from 5,000 hectares to 3,000, with another four categories of land between these two extremes (Venezuela 2005).

Aside from the possibility of idle large estates being expropriated, the new land law specifies, just as required by Article 307 of the constitution quoted above, that such estates would be taxed as long as they are idle. The rate of taxation would depend, just as with the maximum size of the landholding, on the land's agricultural quality. This measure, of course, provided landowners with another reason for opposing the new land law. The government, though, decided to pass a moratorium on this tax, not requiring landowners to pay until 2006. Part of the reason for this is likely that the government does not really know who owns how much land, and needs time to sort out the land title registry.

Land Redistribution

Any Venezuelan citizen who is either the head of a family household or is single and between eighteen and twenty-five years old may apply for a parcel of land. Once the land has been productively cultivated for three years, the applicant may acquire full ownership title to it. However, even the full title does not mean that the owner can sell the land, only that it can be passed on to his or her descendants. The prohibition against selling titles acquired through the land reform is another issue that land reform critics find fault with because it can lead to a black market in land titles. And, just as with all black markets, because the trade in titles is not legal, the titles end up being traded below their true value and thus can lead to making poor farmers even poorer than they otherwise would be. The Chavez government insists, though, that land should not be a commodity to be bought and sold, and that a market in agricultural land inevitably leads to greater land concentration and inequality, and thus to rural poverty.

In an interview with the author, Olivier Delahaye, a professor of agronomy at the Central University of Venezuela and a critic of the land reform, argued, though, that "the campesino who transfers 'his' lands obtains for them a price significantly below (40–60 percent) the price he would obtain in the formal market. Such a prohibition (against selling land) cannot be implemented in practice and disadvantages the poorest." Only time will tell which side is correct in this argument about which approach to land titles is better for fighting or avoiding rural poverty (Delahaye 2002).

The implementation and management of the land reform is to take place with the help of three newly created institutions. The first is the National Land Institute (INTI), which replaced the previous National Agricultural Institute (IAN) and now manages all land held by the central government and administers all land titles. Its main duty is to determine ownership of land and to redistribute it according to the land law. Also, it certifies the quality of the land and whether it is being used productively or is idle.

The second institution is the National Institute for Rural Development (INDER), which provides agricultural infrastructure, such as technology and roads, credits, and training for farmers. The third institution is the Venezuelan Agrarian Corporation (CVA), which helps farmers and cooperatives that benefited from the land reform to bring their products to market.

Shortly before the land law entered into full effect, the Chavez government's land reform efforts were dealt a serious blow. On November 20,

2002, Venezuela's Supreme Court ruled that Articles 89 and 90 of the land law were unconstitutional and annulled them. At the time, the Supreme Court was narrowly controlled by opposition sympathizers, which led Chavez supporters to argue that this was a political move and not a legal one.

The annulled Article 89 had allowed INTI to authorize peasants to preemptively occupy land qualifying for expropriation (*ocupación previa*), while the landowners appealed their right to the land's ownership in court. Since such court proceedings generally take many years, not allowing the preemptive occupation of disputed land allows landowners to hold on to the land far longer than would have been possible with Article 89 in effect, and seriously slows down the entire land reform process. As a point of comparison, it is worth noting that *ocupación previa* is the principal tactic used by the Landless Workers' Movement (MST) in their relatively successful "land reform from below" in Brazil. To prohibit *ocupación previa*, then, is to seriously weaken the peasant movement on land reform issues.

Article 90 stated that the government did not have to compensate landowners for investments they made in the land, such as buildings, roads, and waterways, if a finding was made that this land had been acquired illegally, as many large estates were. In other words, the article's annulment required the state to compensate those large landowners who had made investments, even on land they had essentially stolen.

In April 2005 the National Assembly passed a reform of the land reform law, and essentially reinstated Article 90 with slight modifications of the text, so as to make it legal under the constitution. As for Article 89, the government has tried to get around the *ocupación previa* issue by issuing *"cartas agrarias,"* or letters granting peasants provisional land-use rights, which do not constitute land titles but allow the temporary occupation of land until legal disputes are resolved. The opposition and large landowners have challenged the legality of these titles, and numerous lower court rulings have come down against peasants and on the side of the large landowners, but as of this writing no higher court decision has yet been made on this issue.

Conflict with Land Owners

At first, the land reform program got off to a slow start, mainly because the necessary infrastructure needed to be put into place. When Chavez noticed how slow the process was moving, in 2003, he put his older brother, Adán Chavez, in charge, who instituted the Plan Ezequiel Zamora, which distributed over 1.5 million hectares to about 130,000 families over a twelve-month period. This comes to an average of 11.5 hectares per family and a total beneficiary population of 650,000 (based on an average of five persons per household). By the end of 2004 a total of 2 million hectares of state-owned land had been distributed. For 2005 the program was to be accelerated again, with the redistribution of an additional 2 million hectares of land, benefiting another 1 million Venezuelans. Venezuelan peasant organizations argue that the progress that these figures measure is not that of a "comprehensive" land reform because most of it apparently involves the legal recognition of already existing informal peasant land settlements, rather than the redistribution to the landless of previously idle, or of true *latifundio* land. So while that certainly can improve the security of land tenure for beneficiaries, and while Venezuela may have relatively fewer landless peasants than some neighboring countries, this still represents a significant pending task for the land reform.

While all of the land that had been redistributed was, until 2004, state-owned land, it was not until early 2005 that the Chavez government turned its attention to privately held land. For this task, Chavez put Eliecer Otaiza, a retired army captain who is known as a radical in the Chavez government, in charge of the INTI. Chavez apparently felt that it was necessary to put Otaiza in charge because, of the 2 million hectares slated to be redistributed in 2005, 1.5 million were to come from privately owned estates. The land reform plan for 2005 was named Mission Zamora, to indicate that it was another of the government's social programs, which, since 2003, all carry the title of "Mission." If the plan is ultimately fulfilled, the achievement will represent the government's first major challenge to Venezuela's landed elite since the passage of the land reform law in 2001.

The first effort to engage in the redistribution of private land began in March 2005, when the INTI declared that five estates currently in private hands were to be "recovered." That is, rather than declaring the land as a *latifundio* and expropriating it on the basis that too much of it is idle, the land institute said that all or part of these lands actually belong to the government because the current occupants cannot properly prove their ownership of it. This has, of course, generated much controversy, especially since some of the owners claim to be able to prove their ownership with documents dating back to the mid-nineteenth century. For its part, the government says that some of these documents are false.

One of the roots of this controversy is that landownership in Venezuela, just as in most of Latin America, is an extremely murky affair. Historically, large landowners often expanded their territory far beyond its original boundaries, claiming land that either belonged to the state or to absentee landlords. Part of the reason they could do this is that the descriptions in old land titles are very vague about demarcating the territory. Also, sometimes a landowner might have legitimately bought land, while the seller did not have a legitimate title. A main task now for the Chavez government is to sort all of this out and to develop a coherent and accurate register of land titles. This is an extremely difficult, time-consuming, and conflictive process, though. In the end, this task could prove to be so difficult and conflictive that it will be easier to simply declare any landholding over a certain size to be illegal, regardless of the land title documentation a landowner might have, or even, perhaps, whether or not the land is actually idle. The INTI, under Otaiza's brief leadership, appeared to be interested in taking the former approach. Faced with a similarly confused situation at the beginning of its revolution, Cuba eventually opted for the latter.

Many landless peasants have already challenged the ownership of large landowners on their own, saying that the latter are not the rightful owners and have illegally acquired land that historically belonged to the peasant communities. In one controversial case, for example, a large group of peasants decided to occupy the El Charcote estate, which belongs to the British cattle ranching company of Lord Vestey. The cattle ranch owners, who say that the occupation has cost them losses of beef production equal to one-third of their pre-occupation output, have said that they have ownership documentation going back to 1850. INTI's former president, Eliecer Otaiza, says that the decline in production is simply because more beef is being imported and former workers of the ranch have begun to cultivate idle sections of the ranch. INTI also argues that the owners do not have proper title to the land. However, since about two-thirds of the land is not idle, they say that the current owners may continue use that portion of the land. The other third, which INTI declared to be idle, however, would be turned over to peasants.

For the opposition this case has become emblematic, as the National Land Institute has now begun to examine property titles of estates it suspects to be *latifundios*. In early 2005 Chavez set up a special commission, the National Agricultural Commission (CAN), which included the agricultural minister, the INTI president, and the governors of various states.[1] In June 2005 Otaiza announced that the CAN had identified two hundred presumed *latifundios* throughout the country that could be available for redistribution that year. It is entirely possible that the CAN will decide that most of these *latifundios* not only consist of idle land, but that their alleged owners also do not have proper ownership titles for these lands. If this happens, it is quite likely that conflict in the countryside will intensify.

By early 2005, more than one hundred and thirty peasants had already been killed over land disputes in the previous four years. According to peasant leaders such as Braulio Alvarez, who is the director of the National Agricultural Coordinator Ezequiel Zamora (CANEZ), a coalition of progovernment peasant groups, these peasants were killed by assassins hired by the landowners. The Venezuelan Program of Action-Education on Human Rights (PROVEA), Venezuela's most important human rights group, confirms that the killers have been hired assassins, and notes that this is a distinct change from pre-Chavez years, when most of the killers were from the government's security forces (PROVEA 2003/2004). PROVEA laments, though, that these assassinations are rarely investigated, and that insufficient security measures are taken on behalf of peasant leaders.

Despite all of the protests from large landowners and the opposition, who say the Chavez government is engaging in an assault on private property, the INTI says that by 2004 less than 1 percent of the land reform's land titles had been challenged judicially (PROVEA 2003/2004).

Problems with the Land Reform

Despite the advances that have been made with the land reform, relative to the enormous expectation raised by Chavez's Bolivarian revolution and based on the country's past experiences with the issue and relative to experiences in other countries, Venezuela's peasants are quite frustrated. There are at least five problem-complexes that are the cause of this frustration and are hindering the land reform process in Venezuela. These can be summarized as problems involving the legal framework, general insecurity and impunity, weak peasant organization, poor infrastructure and support, and economic problems.

Weak Legal Framework

The combination of legal challenges to land redistribution and the poor quality of Venezuela's land title registry has made the expropriation and redistribution of privately held land extremely difficult and slow. This situation has also affected the redistribution of publicly held land because in many cases large landowners claim to own lands that the Venezuelan state also claims to own. Even though the government has been relatively rapid with the handing out of land-use rights, many feel these are legally insufficient. Recent high-profile efforts to take over land that the state considers to be illegally held (such as the Hatos Piñero and El Charcote) moved the issue of the legality of privately held land to the front burner for a while, but once press attention died down, the effort to resolve these land dispute cases seemed to die down too. This lack of *ocupación previa* is also a critical weakness in the legal framework for the land reform.

General Lawlessness and Impunity

Further complicating the land reform is the relatively lawless, insecure, and chaotic situation in Venezuela's countryside. Peasants not only have to deal with ruthless landowners who are intent on maintaining control over their *latifundios*, often with use of hired assassins and bullies, they also have to deal with drug smugglers, irregular military forces (such as Colombia's paramilitary group and an emerging Venezuelan paramilitary counterpart), and corrupt Venezuelan police and military forces.

Even though the peasant group CANEZ has tried to call attention to the more than one hundred and thirty assassinations of peasant leaders, their efforts have had little success, and the government has been very slow to deal with the problem. Only in July 2005, for the first time, did CANEZ and another organization, the Frente Ezequiel Zamora, organize a protest in Caracas to demand government action. The National Assembly finally responded shortly after the protest and formed a commission to investigate the assassinations.

Weak Peasant Organization

Complicating things further is the fact that Venezuela's peasant organizations are very weak, in part because of the history of a collapsing agricultural economy due to Dutch Disease. This means that even though they have a sympathetic government, the peasants are not in a position to exert enough pressure on the government to force it to make sure the land reform is fully implemented. Stronger peasant organizations could probably accomplish much in terms of social oversight over the land reform process. Also, more pressure would probably mean stronger law enforcement when it comes to investigating and prosecuting those responsible for the assassinations of peasant leaders.

A result of the weak level of peasant organization is that many of those who would benefit from the land reform either lack the knowledge or the resources to claim their rights. This, in turn, makes them less likely to organize politically. However, when they do organize, many times these organizations are drawn into the orbit of one political faction or another, making it difficult for the groups to work together.

Poor Infrastructure and Support

While much land has been titled in a relatively short period of time, the land reform support agencies, that is, the National Rural Development Institute (INDER) and the Venezuelan Agrarian Corporation (CVA), have not been as active as they should be in supporting the land reform. One reason for this is that most government functionaries are from pre-Chavez governments, and a great many of them belong to political factions that oppose the Bolivarian revolution and the land reform. For example, seven months after the opening of a showcase project in Chavez's home state of Barinas in 2003, nothing much had yet transpired, reports Maurice Lemoine (2003) in *Le Monde Diplomatique*:

> "Our *comandante* [Chavez] thinks everything's working great! They hide the real figures from him; no one tells him the truth. There haven't been 500 hectares opened up for farming here, only 15." The Ministry of Infrastructure (MINFRA) should have cleared 400 hectares for planting by now. It hasn't. Despite repeated demands, officials from the Rural Development Institute, responsible for drainage and irrigation, haven't appeared. Those from the environment ministry have been conspicuously absent too. "The state institutions won't see me," complains Richard Vivas, a leader of the cooperative, "only the INTI supports me" (Lemoine 2003).

In other words, while the INDER is supposed to provide training, technology, and credit to land reform beneficiaries, it has been extremely slow to do so. Other reasons for this appear to be related to problems of corruption within the institute; another reason is that the central government has paid relatively little attention to the infrastructure and support aspects of the land reform, in favor of the more controversial and visible land redistribution aspect. The CVA, which is supposed to help peasants market their new agricultural products, has not even truly gotten off the ground yet, more than three years after the official launch of the land reform program.

Another problem related to the poor governmental support is that, even though the banks are required to dedicate a certain percentage of their loans to the agricultural sector, most of these loans do not reach the small farmers, but mainly large farmers. Also, when they do reach small farmers, all too often they reach them too late, so that the farmers miss opportunities to purchase and plant seeds for the planting season.

Economic Problems

Even once peasants acquire land, training, technology, and infrastructure such as access roads and credit, they still face the next large hurdle, which is marketing their agricultural products. While the government has set up the CVA, there is no guarantee that the CVA will buy or sell the products. Venezuela has historically encountered the problem, mentioned earlier, of domestically produced products being uncompetitive compared with the cheap import market created by large inflows of foreign currency from the country's dominant oil industry. Unless the government subsidizes Venezuelan agricultural products and/or protects them against imports, it is unlikely that these products can be sold at a good price on either domestic or international markets.

This economic Dutch Disease is precisely what caused Venezuelan agriculture to decline to only 5 percent of GDP by 1998, and it seems that no government, including the Chavez government, has found a solution to this problem. Despite the Chavez government's efforts to diversify the economy by providing credit to small and medium industries, by favoring them in the state's purchasing programs (which are relatively large), and by supporting them in a variety of other measures, none of these measures addresses the problem that production prices in Venezuela are too high because the huge revenues coming in from the oil industry overvalue the Venezuelan currency. The recent oil price boom, which caused oil prices to almost quadruple during Chavez's presidency (from US$10 per barrel in 1998 to US$40 per barrel of Venezuelan crude in 2005) has only exacerbated the problem.

The government's currency control, which keeps the currency at a relatively high and steady level, while also restricting capital flight, exacerbates the problems of the Dutch Disease, in that it makes imports relatively cheap (thereby controlling inflation) and exports relatively expensive. The currency controls, however, appear to be necessary in order to control inflation and capital flight. Meanwhile, the Chavez government has publicly stated that most agricultural production should be oriented toward supplying the domestic market, so as to make Venezuela a country that enjoys food sovereignty, a goal from which it is still far removed, since it imports about 75 percent of all food products it consumes. It might make sense, therefore, if the focus on ensuring that Venezuelans consume domestically produced food products whenever they are available were intensified by imposing import tariffs on competing imported goods. So far it is unclear whether the government is pursuing such a strategy.

The international farmer and peasant movement, La Via Campesina,[2] which is advising the Chavez government, has proposed that the Venezuelan government phase out food imports at a rate of 5–10 percent per year, with a corresponding plan developed with Venezuelan peasant organizations to receive the credit, land, and other services and inputs needed to make up the deficit each year.

Prospects for the Land Reform

The land reform program under Venezuela's President Chavez essentially has two main goals: the creation of greater social justice and the establishment of food self-sufficiency in Venezuela. While the program suffers from a variety of problems, as has been described above, some initial successes have been achieved in the first few years that the land reform has been in effect.

With regard to the first goal, of creating greater social justice, over 130,000 families have benefited from the reform in the first two years of its existence, which is a substantial number of Venezuelans, relative to past land reform experiences in Venezuela and in other countries. Whether these new landowners (or tenants, as many of these only have land usage rights, not ownership, until disputes are resolved) will succeed in the long run remains to be seen. To a large extent this depends on whether the government restricts food imports, subsidizes national production, and whether the Rural Development Institute (INDER) and the Venezuelan Agrarian Corporation (CVA) are able to offer support to the new farmers for the long haul. This support will in all likelihood be necessary in light of the economic difficulties an oil-producing country such as Venezuela has in maintaining agricultural production.

With regard to the second goal, of making Venezuela more self-sufficient in terms of its food consumption, of establishing food sovereignty, here the advance is not as noticeable, but some progress has been made. Partly as a result of the land reform and partly as a result of the government's concerted effort to diversify the economy, agricultural production in Venezuela has increased from about 5 percent to 6 percent, as a percentage of GDP, during the Chavez presidency. The most concerted efforts in this area have been to recapture agricultural production in those areas where Venezuela was strong in the past, before decades of neglect made it dependent on imports. For example, Venezuelans are great consumers of beans, corn, and sugar, all of which

Venezuela could, in theory, produce for itself, while it has become an importer of these goods. These are just some of the areas in which the government hopes to become self-sufficient.

Another part of the strategy for achieving this self-sufficiency has been the social program known as the Mercal Mission. This program, which is part of a whole series of social programs the government introduced in 2003 and 2004, consists of providing food to Venezuela's poor via a network of thousands of subsidized food markets. Already 43 percent of Venezuela's population shops for food at the Mercal stores. While most of the food that is sold in the Mercal stores is still imported, the government is making a concerted effort to increase the proportion of domestically produced food in these stores. Having such a distribution network in its hands, which emerged mainly as a consequence of the 2002/2003 general strike and lockout by the management of the national oil company, puts the government in an ideal position to support the small agricultural producers that it is now creating with the land reform program (Wagner 2005).

Related to the goals of social justice and food sovereignty is the principle that land use takes priority over formal landownership. The land reform program is essentially based on this principle, which is essential for any land reform program that wants to both create social justice and food sovereignty. However, not much education of the general public has been done with regard to this issue. That is, even though there is a general consensus, even in FEDECAMARAS, the country's main chamber of commerce, that *latifundios* have no legitimacy, Venezuela's elite can still rely on the argument that a land-use principle undermines private property rights, which are held to be more or less sacred. This sacred principle of private property is still an important element in Venezuelan culture.

The opposition thus enjoys some moderate success in making the government look unreasonable and even radical whenever private property is touched in the least, thereby undermining the land reform's legitimacy both nationally and internationally. So that the land reform is not undermined in the long run, the government will have to educate the population and spearhead a general discussion about these different conceptions of property. This is especially the case as the slow pace of the reform and the growing frustration of the peasantry may lead to its radicalization, as happened in Cuba and with other revolutionary land reforms.

CHAPTER 14

Learning to Participate: The MST Experience in Brazil

Mônica Dias Martins

The Movimento dos Trabalhadores Rurais Sem Terra (Landless Worker's Movement, or MST) is one of the most combative social movements in contemporary Latin America. The MST emerged during the Brazilian military dictatorship, in 1979, with its first land occupation in Encruzilhada Natalino, in the state of Rio Grande do Sul. Supported early on during the "redemocratization" days in the aftermath of the dictatorship, by church organizations like the grassroots religious communities and the Comissao Pastoral da Terra (Land Pastoral Commission, or CPT), and by the Central Unica dos Trabalhadores (Confederation of Workers, or CUT) and the Partido dos Trabalhadores (Workers' Party, or PT), among others, the movement spread around the country as land reform was forced onto the political agenda.[1]

The MST has become an influential organization, with thousands of activists fighting for agrarian reform with revolutionary passion. Solidarity, social justice, and autonomy are their fundamental ethical values. A variety of types of cooperation characterize the MST's rural land reform settlements. Their leaders are interviewed by the media, and they negotiate with the government. The movement has established a monthly newspaper to communicate its ideas, an educational system based on a "work-and-study" methodology, and an intense process of political-ideological formation through study groups on radical theory. Within some of these groups a newly developed consciousness concerning social, rather than private, ownership of the means of production is emerging.

This chapter revises an early version published by *Latin American Perspectives* in September 2000.

The MST experience raises a crucial question in the discourse on social change, which this chapter will address: What is participation? Participation can be a social practice, a pedagogical method, and/or a political act. For the landless men, women, young people, and children of the MST, the learning process begins in the collective ways of working and living in the *acampamentos* (pre-land occupation encampments); flourishes with massive and continuous land occupations and settlements; is strengthened through the educational activities developed and carried out in MST schools; and expands in the collective construction of an alternative proposal, or "project," for all of Brazilian society. My purpose here is to examine the MST participatory practice, focusing on these four elements that make an integrated whole.

Agrarian Reform: A Contradictory Process

Agrarian reform is not necessarily radical. During the period of the Kennedy administration and the Alliance for Progress, many Latin American governments were put under pressure by the United States to carry out agrarian reform programs as part of a plan of "pacification" designed to undercut potential popular support for armed rebellion.

In Brazil at the beginning of the 1960s, landowners were frightened by a strong movement for agrarian reform led by the Ligas Camponesas (Peasant Leagues) and the Confederação Nacional de Traballhadores na Agricultura (National Confederation of Rural Workers, or CONTAG). During Joao Goulart's presidency (1962–1964), popular mobilization focused on agrarian reform as the key to democratization and modification of the social structure. This was one of the factors that led to the 1964 military coup, and the subsequent brutal repression of popular organizations. Throughout the years of dictatorship (1964–1985), agrarian reform was considered a national security issue, strategic for capitalistic development and industrialization. Reform has also been used as a state policy to restrain class struggle in rural areas and to transform potentially revolutionary peasants into conservative small farmers. But agrarian reform has also been important to more revolutionary structural changes.

Thus, agrarian reform can be better characterized as a contradictory process of transforming production and power relations that depends, in its formulation and implementation, on the correlation of political forces and the specific course of class struggle (Martins 1994). As conceived by the MST and other movements in Brazil, the concept reinforces the links among economic, social, cultural, political, and ideological conditions, as opposed to the dominant view of land reform as merely an economic issue or a social policy, or even simply an ideological problem.

Official agrarian reforms designed to establish a capitalist class of small farmers through access to rural property often occur simultaneously with an intensive proletarianization of the majority of rural people (loss of means of production, or land). This challenging contradiction helps to explain why agrarian reform cannot be labeled as conservative or revolutionary per se; it is a tool, and what makes the difference is who controls it. The reality is complex, and leads us to analyze agrarian reform as a real-world process in which social classes struggle over the direction of a contradictory process. Its character in contemporary Brazil arises in the context of a new proposal emerging from the hands and minds of thousands of *acampados* (families in temporary camps awaiting the chance to occupy land) and settlers (those who have already gained land), a proposal antagonistic to the dominant agrarian project.

The political-ideological polarization between the MST and the main organization of wealthy landowners, the Uniao Democratica Ruralista (Rural Democratic Union, or UDR)—particularly during the elaboration of the first National Plan of Land Reform in 1985 and the 1988 Constitutional Assembly—has led to the construction of two different models of land reform in Brazil.[2] Together they express the confrontation between capital and labor. Central issues include the decisions concerning the ownership of the means of production (individual or collective), and the process of distribution of wealth (private capital accumulation or social capital accumulation).

The UDR's proposal defends individual interests and private property, and, to the extent that the bourgeoisie accepts redistribution, it must be through the parceling of the land in hundreds of individual units. This "model of private appropriation" is similar to classical capitalistic agrarian redistribution, which promotes agricultural modernization under the control of agribusiness. In the 1970s, this kind of land reform was implemented in a limited way under the military dictatorship through the establishment of colonization projects, where the so-called *colono* or *parceleiro* "received" individual title to property that allowed the beneficiary to apply for credit and technical assistance. Because each beneficiary family was isolated from others, via the titling of individual parcels, and decisions concerning what and how to produce or to whom and when to sell the harvest were imposed by governmental institutions and agricultural policies, the major benefits of this so-called reform accrued to the hegemonic agro-industrial sector. This is the typical paradigm of agrarian reform accepted by various factions of the dominant classes.

The MST's more flexible "model of social appropriation," on the other hand, is based on cooperative relations among settlers and alternative patterns of land appropriation and use. Through democratic structures of decision making, settlements may vary in form from an individual family basis all the way to collective work, depending on the backgrounds and aspirations of the settlers, the quality of the soil, the kind of crops they produce, the local market structure, and many other factors. For instance, property can be individually owned, but the work and the production done collectively; or work and production can be individual on part of the land and collective on another part; or all the property can be collective. Regardless of these arrangements, families work on part of the land to produce for their own use.

Rural landowners oppose cooperative forms of possession, production, and work. They seem aware that these experiences can escalate from the local to the national sphere and may consolidate new practices of social organization and political participation that could undermine private property rights. In this context, to make a massive and radical proposal for agrarian reform is not simply to call for land redistribution to incorporate more farmers into the capitalist system; rather, it necessarily involves shifting the entire agrarian structure of production, power, and cultural relations. This means that the whole economic-social-political system would have to be changed. Even before the MST became influential, the leaders of the agrarian bourgeois were conscious that any project of collective land occupation and production would represent a challenge to their class interests and to capitalism.

The Brazilian scholar and UDR supporter Miguel Reale Junior (who was minister of justice in Cardoso's government), expressed this class position in the journal of the Sociedade Brasileira Rural (Brazilian Rural Society, or SBR) as follows: "From the end of World War II to the present, it is evident that agrarian chaos doesn't exist in Brazil, rather there is perfect coherency between the structure of landholding and use, the present economic-social system in this country, and the current neoliberal ideology" (Sociedade Rural Brasileira 1985, 9).

The MST

The MST's complex practice is designed to deal with a central question: How can a peasant organization challenge the so-called benefits of free-market capitalism and its ideology, neoliberalism? To analyze the MST's resistance to neoliberalism, it is essential to have a concept of social class. A class-struggle approach allows us to comprehend the limits and the possibilities of the MST's agrarian reform proposal vis à vis the classical agrarian reform model and Brazilian state policy and legislation.

The specific course of the battle between these two antagonistic models of agrarian reform in Brazil (which began in the 1980s and is still in flux) is the key to understanding why the MST has become the most important source of resistance to the neoliberal project. In brief, the confrontation can be expressed in terms of the duality of privatization versus occupation.

Occupying the Land

Early on the MST developed an efficient strategy of placing pressure on the state through massive and continuous land occupations. Based on the 1964 Brazilian land law, private property can be confiscated (in theory) when it is not cultivated, or when the owner is in violation of labor or environmental regulations. The MST's direct action in occupying properties that fall into these categories takes advantage of this constitutional provision, and thus strengthens it. This strategy has also been effective in publicizing land concentration, the cause of most of the present social problems.

The actual process of carrying out a land occupation, called a *festa* (party) by the movement, has a special meaning for the landless themselves. The decision, which is not an easy one, to seize and settle on a private property, requires maturity, cohesion, discipline, and hope. This action turns peasants who, in the past, had been more or less passive participants in the sociopolitical arena into powerful social actors fighting for agrarian reform and political participation. They call themselves "free workers," and they recover their capacity to create material and cultural commodities, denied to them by both the traditional *latifundios* (large estates) and the modern agribusiness complex, where they were mere workers in the service of capital.

The MST's occupations threaten the ruling classes, who react with violence, while arguing that the occupations are illegal. They believe land seizures will lead to a breakdown of authority in Brazilian society. To maintain public order, representatives of the state often respond to the occupations, which many consider to be efforts to sabotage democratic institutions, by prosecuting MST leaders.

Despite repressive violence, defamatory media campaigns, and attempts at co-optation, the MST promotes mass mobilizations to occupy unproductive properties. Land occupations increased from 119 in 1990 to 505 in 1999, a total of 2,210 occupations in nine years. In the first months of 2000, thirty thousand rural workers occupied 250 *latifundios* as well as federal government buildings in twenty-one cities, to exert political pressure for land reform. What are challenged by these radical actions are the private property rights guaranteed by dominant law, an important value of capitalist order and its neoliberal discourse. The actions also challenge the government's political performance on the national front and its commitments to structural adjustments imposed by the World Bank and the International Monetary Fund (IMF) in the international arena.

Collective Working and Living

An MST settlement is the result of a successful occupation, and is conceived of as an economic unit, not just as a legal property holding. Indeed, planning, farm production, and management have been crucial to the success of the MST's alternative proposal of agricultural cooperation. According to the MST's definition, cooperation is "the way to maximize the efforts of each individual worker by doing things together, whether buying machines and tools, raising cattle, or sharing land" (Movimento dos Trabalhadores Rurais Sem Terra 1993, 1996).

For the settlers' organizations, planning means democratic decision making concerning all the major modes of community existence: production, marketing, housing, education, health care, politics, culture, and so on. This is not a simple task, especially if hundreds of persons are involved. During their frequent assemblies, members participate in many ways by making proposals, asking questions, discussing problems, coming to decisions, and singing.[3] Normally, the meeting agenda is known in advance and some methodological tools are used to better facilitate participation. Most women and teenagers speak independently of their husbands or parents, as *companheiras de luta* (comrades in struggle). In some of the settlements, a married person is accepted only if both spouses join the organization. The participatory planning process is influenced by the families' previous experiences, the regional and ecological differences in their land, and their access to material conditions of production such as credit, technology, and training. The results vary widely, due to the heterogeneity of situations in the settlements (Medeiros 1994).

The annual balance of income and expenses is presented in a general assembly, and the distribution of profits—for maintenance and repairs of farm machinery, and investment in soil improvement, cattle feeding, computers, home building, teachers' salaries, child care, mobilization, and so on—has to be approved by the majority of the members. Increasingly, many settlers prefer their monetary income not to be divided, but rather to be invested collectively, to maintain the existing means of production, or for new investments or educational, health, and technological assistance to their families. These different kinds of *fundos* (funds) are an experiment in socialized accumulation of capital. Agrarian reform as proposed by the MST also has the potential to become a more egalitarian means of distribution of wealth.

There are two cooperative organizations in Brazil. The Organizacao das Cooperativas do Brasil (Cooperatives' Organization of Brazil, or OCB) represents the large landowners and is linked with the UDR and the SBR. The Confederacao Nacional das Cooperativas de Reforma Agraria do Brasil (National Confederation of Agrarian Reform Cooperatives of Brazil, or CONCRAB) was created in 1994 by a network of agrarian reform cooperatives, and might be thought of as the economic arm of the MST, supporting its social and political mobilizations.

As efficient as the large private farming sector, the MST settlers organize agricultural production cooperatives through CONCRAB at local, state, and national levels. Nevertheless, there is an essential difference between this system and the OCB's. The MST's cooperative structure emphasizes social needs and political results as much as economic returns to the settlers. Credit, marketing support, and technical assistance are offered by the cooperatives to increase settlers' agricultural production, profitability, the ability to market their produce, and to boost living standards (Movimento dos Trabalhadores Rurais Sem Terra 1998). The CONCRAB system has become an instrument for establishing solid relationships among producers and consumers, demonstrating the relevance of agrarian reform for the urban population and guaranteeing relative financial autonomy for the MST, at least compared with other popular organizations that do not have control over their own production.

The concept of collective working and living is the core of the MST strategy to develop sustainable actions of resistance in the settlements. If it weren't for these systems, people might become politically demobilized once they receive land. Peasants who have fought for a place to live and work now could be seduced by the supposed benefits of free-market capitalism. The MST tries to keep the people who have already gotten land politically mobilized, to support further occupations by the still landless, and to keep fighting for larger social change.

Education and Attitudes: Creating the New Man and the New Woman

The overall emphasis of the MST's proposal for changing Brazilian society starts with agrarian reform but addresses a host of other questions having to do with education, gender issues, and politics. The settlement is conceived of as a place where various forms of democratic relationships are practiced, based on direct action and on agricultural cooperation.

Education is a top priority for the MST, not only as a means to eliminate illiteracy but also to close the technological gap between rich and poor and to combat political misinformation. In a general sense, as Paulo Freire explained, a "settlement, precisely because it is a production unit (there is no production outside the man-world relation) should also be a pedagogic unit" (1983, 58).

To face the challenges posed by the MST's idea of agrarian reform, the concept of education has unfolded far beyond the formal system. Educational activities the settlers undertake include choosing their own teachers, formulating participatory rules for managing the schools, revising the subjects and methods of the official public school curriculum, organizing brigades (teams of militants who travel from settlement to settlement) for the political-ideological formation of activists, and coordinating training courses for entrepreneurial and technological improvement. The basic MST pedagogic principles are an iterative relationship of practice-theory-practice, which incorporates the lessons from the struggle for land and production and, in turn, helps build a better theoretical understanding of organizers, leaders, and teachers; and a work-and-study methodology, which bridges the dichotomy that opposes manual and intellectual labor.

The MST's two-year school for vocational level specialists in agricultural cooperation was recently accredited by the Ministry of Education, and in 1995 the movement won a UNICEF award for the quality of its educational program in its six hundred elementary schools and twenty high schools with a total of 35,000 students and 1,400 teachers. Equally as urgent as democratizing access to education for children, is training the massive number of the MST's participants, numbering more than 500,000 adults. The MST vocational and political training school, the Instituto de Capacitacao Tecnica e Pesquisa da Reforma Agraria (ITERRA), offers short courses on business management for farm enterprises, financial and human resource management, and long-term courses integrating political formation and farming techniques.

Among the many social issues MST militants consider when troubleshooting concrete problems in the settlements is the dominant cultural pattern of public and private relations between men and women. As the landless join the movement, some act as revolutionaries outside the house but maintain a conservative manner inside the family. But daily life in the *acampamentos* and set-

tlements teaches them to do things together, to observe their individual attitudes, and to make changes from inside themselves.

Although the MST believes that economic power is fundamental to achieving political power, it realizes that these aspects are intertwined, as well, with
the other strands of society; the MST has found, therefore, that most of its
efforts are aimed at nothing less than creating a "new man and a new woman
for a new society." In dialectic terms, the new emerges from the old through
a creative transformation. Much work has been done to enable women to participate fully in all aspects of settlement society; such a fundamental shift in
social relations requires a change not only in women but in men as well.

A famous and popular song at meetings teaches "Pra mudar a sociedade
do jeito que a gente quer, participando sem medo de ser mulher" [To change
society the way we want, we have to participate without fear of being women].
But what is it to be a woman according to the MST's conception? It is that,
despite any biological differences, the woman's role in the family, in production, and in society largely results from a historical process of domestication.
While this cultural role has been modified over time, most alterations have not
taken the interests of women into account. Capitalistic development imposes
new functions on her, in terms of the kind of work she can do, the way she
behaves, the type of education she can have, the size of her family, and so on.
It is necessary to study and debate these issues to strengthen women's participation and organization.

In the MST, women are typically on the front line during land occupations,
and those working at the cooperatives receive equal pay alongside the men.
Child-care centers and other community structures such as a common dining
area allow mothers and young women to become part of the active labor force.
These direct actions are the basis upon which the militants question the traditional sexual division of labor.

In 1997 a national seminar on gender held at Curitiba, Parana, was
attended by approximately one hundred landless women from all over Brazil.
Over three days they shared experiences and planned activities to increase
women's militancy around social, political, and economic issues. They formed
a national collective within the MST and created a *cartilha* (booklet) titled
Landless Woman, which addresses topics such as land reform, credit, education, health care, the Popular Project (ideas for a different, more just Brazil),
and class struggle.

The MST has developed strategies to improve the recognition of gender
issues, both within the movement and with regard to the manner in which

state agencies treat women. But changes with regard to interpersonal relations are harder to achieve. Some *companheiros* respect women in the organization, in the struggle, in the political parties, and in production, but they don't seem to think women should be given the same respect at home. The typical relationship is still mostly based on the dominant model of patriarchal family.

One may imagine the tensions within the settlers' families, especially among activist couples. In this context, it is still worth asking how we would like the new woman and the new man to be in a more egalitarian society. The Argentinean writer Jorge Luis Borges recalls in his poem "Happiness": "Praised be the love wherein there is no possessor and no possessed, but both surrender."

Constructing the Popular Project

Social scientists have tended to focus mainly on the actions of popular movements. But action and conception are equally significant in the MST's efforts to construct an alternative project for Brazil. The day-to-day practices in the land occupations and settlements, the study in MST schools of the historical experiences of other peoples, and the brigades all come together in the Popular Project, a democratic and participatory planning space through which the contribution of the MST's *amigos*—professors, politicians, technicians, students, priests, and others—is organized in a network of groups that meet regularly to work on suggestions coming from the base, and returning ideas to them.

With the underlying aim of confronting neoliberalism with its own political weapons, the MST strategy has been to realize a *consulta popular* (a sort of unofficial, alternative plebiscite) stimulating the population to participate in the formulation of proposed economic, social, and cultural policies for all Brazilians (the Popular Project). There are many ways in which the MST provokes debate about the Popular Project. For example, the movement led a march aimed at denouncing the former Cardoso administration's privatization program as a transfer of wealth to the powerful, and promoting instead the construction of a truly democratic society with social justice, income distribution, and solidarity. From August 3 to September 7, Brazilian Independence Day, in 1998, almost 6,000 workers, organized in more than eighty *colunas* (military-like columns), marched across the country, holding conversations along the way with the local populace in hundreds of small and big cities, discussing problems regarding land, employment, housing, education, health, and food. They repeated this process in 2005, during the present Lula presidency.

Building the Popular Project involves mass, direct, radical, continuous, and sustainable actions of resistance. And it has to be constructed in a process directed from the base, a base that respects its social heritage, conceives of alternatives for the majority, presents ideas in a simple and convincing way, transforms ideas into projects for structural change, makes people understand and fight for them, and mobilizes forces.

The MST has placed emphasis on the elaboration of an alternative national project on global themes such as employment, education, housing, food, and health. While the Popular Project deals with a variety of problems, agrarian reform remains an essential issue within it. However, according to João Pedro Stédile, an MST leader, the agrarian issue, while central, takes second place to the larger transformation of society, since agrarian reform itself depends on the adoption of a new model of development (interview published in *O Globo*, December 26, 1997). In this analysis, the MST's proposal of agrarian reform for all can only be thoroughly implemented within economic and power structures different from those of capitalism. The immediate challenge, however, is to demonstrate to the Brazilian people that their day-to-day problems are a consequence of neoliberal policies.

The Embryo of a New Society?

What explains the growing credibility of the MST among the Brazilian people? The movement has the declared support of important organizations such as churches and Amnesty International, and the cooperation of intellectuals and artists. Economists emphasize the production aspects of the MST, political scientists its power relations, geographers the issue of the territoriality of MST settlements, anthropologists the cultural heritage, historians the roots of the movement, pedagogues the learning process, and sociologists the organizational features. Each of these views touches on an aspect of this landless movement, but none of them represents it as a whole.

Some people attribute the MST's appeal to more symbolic or emotional sources: a combination of its mystique of militancy and its symbols: the red flag, the movement hymn, and the emblematic figure of Che Guevara. Others argue that it is due to the brigades, inspired by the revolutionary popular armies with disciplinary rules and study groups on Marxist theories.

In addition to the impressive strategy of the *festa* (land occupation), four vital concepts seem to arise from MST practice: a collective way of life that ranges across the spectrum of activities from basic food production to the artistic process, the work-and-study educational method, an expressed respect for a diversity of opinions combined with a unity of perspectives, and an insistent confrontation with the neoliberal project.

The MST practice is being closely observed by the landless themselves and by Brazilian society in general, not as a laboratory experiment in free-market policy (the manner in which Latin America has been used in the past decade) but as the embryo of a new society that can come to life through the combined efforts of the various popular sectors. The MST appears to have the capacity to transform the collective dream of the millions of Brazilians who want a better life into radical actions and perspectives. It remains to be seen whether it will do so.

CHAPTER 15

Regional Impacts of Land Reform in Brazil

Beatriz Heredia, Leonilde Medeiros, Moacir Palmeira,
Rosângela Cintrão, and Sérgio Pereira Leite

Introduction

Though a great deal of research on rural settlements in Brazil has analyzed internal conditions in land reform settlements, related policies, and the progress of settlers, few studies have examined the importance of land reform settlements for the regions in which they are located. This article tackles this issue by identifying the processes of change that the rural settlements have triggered in their local settings.[1]

The term "impact" may perhaps be an exaggerated way of expressing these changes, for it brings to mind that which is most evident and spectacular, when in reality the changes are often subtle and lead to observable results only after some time. The magnitude and characteristics of these changes depend on different geographical contexts they are examined in—for example, local, regional, and nationwide—so a linear pattern should not be sought in this transformation process. In addition, the creation of the settlements results in short-, medium-, and long-term changes, the effects of which are felt both within the settlement projects, that is, on the lives of the settlers, and beyond them.

Far from assigning them a negative or positive value or declaring them successes or failures, our analysis is designed to measure and characterize the changes, with the aim of creating indicators and identifying relationships that reflect the meaning of these experiences by comparing the settlers' before-and-

This chapter reports on the impacts of expropriative land reform in Brazil, which has typically come about as a result of pressure and direct action by the Landless Workers' Movement (MST) and other peasant organizations and unions, in contrast to the "market-led" land reform credit programs of the World Bank, discussed in part II of this volume.

TABLE 15.1 General characteristics of sample zones

Sample zones and states covered	Number of municipalities chosen	Total number of families settled in the municipalities (1985–1997)	Total area (hectares) of settlement projects in chosen municipalities (1985–1997)	Number of settlement projects studied	Number of questionnaires applied
Southern Bahia, Bahia (Cocoa-producing region)	8	734	12,919.5	14	87
Ceará Sertão, Ceará (Canindé)	4	2,999	110,401.7	10	306
Federal District and neighboring areas, Federal District,* Goiás, and Minas Gerais	6	2,409	114,8 2	14	237
Southeastern Pará, Pará (Conceição Araguaia)	2	3,320	240,929.3	10	366
Western Santa Catarina, Santa Catarina	8	1,802	27,292.9	19	185
Northeastern Sugarcane Region, Alagoas, Paraíba and Pernambuco	11	3,849	29,888.7	25	387
TOTAL	39	15,113	536,235.3	92	1,568

Source: INCRA records and data from the study.

*Located within the state of Goiás

after situations (both objectively and subjectively), as well as by comparing the social and economic conditions of settlements with those in the surrounding areas. The effects brought about by local and regional projects are also analyzed.

In broad terms, the effects of the settlements must be discussed with regard to multiple relationships, in which different avenues lead to different results. Thus, hasty generalizations should not be made. Rather than solely identifying impacts, we must analyze the economic, political, and social effects of the transformation processes triggered by the creation of the settlements. The pace and intensity of these processes vary and have a bearing not only on the families of the settlers but on the rest of the local population as well.

The focus of our study was a set of Brazilian regions, or zones, with a large concentration of land reform settlement projects and a high density of settled families per unit of land, based on the assumption that this would increase the chances of understanding the processes of change underway. The defining criterion was the existence of a set of neighboring municipalities with a relatively large concentration of settlements, in terms of number of projects, families, and occupied areas, in order to be able to consider the historical, economic, social, and organisational dynamics they have in common. We chose six large zones, reflecting the diversity of Brazilian realities: Federal District and surrounding areas, the Northeastern Sugarcane Region, the Sertão (semiarid region) of the state of Ceará, Southern Bahia, Southeastern Pará, and Western Santa Catarina.[2] Sample areas were chosen within each of these zones. The sample areas contained groups of municipalities that had the largest concentrations of settlement projects and the greatest proportion of settlers within the overall rural and urban populations.[3] We administered questionnaires to carry out a detailed analysis.

The settlements analyzed were either implemented or recognized by the Agrarian Reform Institute (INCRA) between 1985, when the National Agrarian Reform Plan (PNRA) was announced, and 1997. Table 15.1 shows some data on the sample zones in the study.[4]

Though the selected zones all have higher concentrations of settlements than the other parts of the same states (often one-third or more of the statewide number of settlements), the participation of the settlement projects (whether in terms of occupied area or number of settler families) in the municipalities and zones studied varies considerably. This factor, coupled with the fact that the dynamics of the respective regions differ, and that some settlers have greater organizational capacity than others, explains the large variation between the effects produced by different settlements.

The Land Distribution Process and the Study Zones

The structure of the zones, which is contrary to that of the isolated expropriations that characterized previous government interventions in land issues, is in itself a relevant aspect of the changes the settlements have brought upon the regions where they are located.

The original idea behind the PNRA was to establish priority areas for land reform. However, the responding outburst of antiagrarian reform pressure led to this idea being abandoned. From then on, only unplanned expropriations were carried out. These actions were indeed more frequent than during the time of the military regime, and occurred as a consequence of the social struggle and mobilization that developed at a greater pace after oppression diminished with democratization. Although the measures that resulted in the establishment of settlements during the democratic period (after 1984) were not designed to attain the massive land reform that the social movements demanded, they were clearly the result of the pressure put on the state by the land reform movements.

Furthermore, the movements gained momentum and leverage by the degree of simultaneity in the execution of the expropriations, and by the fact that these were concentrated in regions in which the movements were already active. The perceived success in achieving some expropriations stimulated workers in neighboring areas to push for the same, and new expropriations were carried out due to the force exerted by these workers; in this way settlements spread, and the movements tried to repeat this experience in other areas. This process ended up generating "reformed areas," even though the idea of such had been abandoned.

An analysis of information on land conflicts and on demands for expropriations reveals a close relationship between the initiatives of the rural workers' movements and the expropriations. Almost all of the settlements encountered had arisen out of conflicts (96 percent). In 89 percent of cases, the initiative for expropriation requests came from the workers and their movements. In our sample, only 10 percent of the settlements resulted from the initiative having been taken by the state.[5] The data clearly show the importance of the Landless Workers Movement (MST) and other peasant and union movements in driving the land reform process.

Although the workers' initiatives have taken many different forms (sometimes involving a combination of strategies and sometimes changing over time in a given place), as table 15.2 shows, 64 percent of the settlements studied

TABLE 15.2 Distribution of settlements by type of struggle used by workers in the different zones (in number of projects)

Zone	Resistance on the land (%)*	Occupation (%)†	Other (%)‡	Total percentage
Southern Bahia	6 (43)	8 (57)	—	14
Sertão of Ceará	4 (40)	6 (60)	—	10
Federal District and surrounding areas	2 (14)	9 (64)	3 (22)	14
Southeastern Pará	9 (90)	1 (10)	—	10
Western Santa Catarina	—	16 (84)	3 (16)	19
Northeastern Sugarcane Region	6 (24)	19 (76)	—	25
TOTAL	27 (29)	59 (64)	6 (7)	92

Source: Heredia et al. 2002.

* Land resistance: This includes all cases of struggle on the part of rural workers (inhabitants, partners, tenants, squatters) to stay on the land where they already lived and/or worked, but lacked title. It also includes cases of gradual occupation (four in the south of Bahia and nine in Southeastern Pará), covert actions that are usually carried out by small groups of squatters who wish to build and eventually acquire land tenure rights. In these cases, conflicts arise only when the occupation is discovered, at which point land resistance begins.

† Occupations: These are the massive and public occupations of land that have become frequent during the past fifteen years. The actions were originally initiated by the Landless Workers' Movement (MST), but have also been taken up by other movements.

‡ Others: All cases in which the initiative did not come from workers and their movements, and cases in which the actions by workers and their movements do not fit into the aforementioned categories.

were the result of land occupations. Land resistance tactics also played an important role, and were responsible for almost one-third (29 percent) of the settlements studied.

Presence of the Settlements in the Regional, Political, and Social Dynamics

Settlers and Their Families

A large part of the settler population already lived in the rural areas where they are now settled, prior to moving into the settlements: Over 80 percent of those studied in the sample came from the same municipality or from neighboring municipalities.[6] In addition, 94 percent of them had already had some sort of experience with farming.

An analysis of the type of work they carried out prior to moving to the settlements shows that 75 percent of the settlers were previously employed in farming activities, as permanent or temporary paid rural workers, squatters, sharecroppers, land tenants, or as unpaid family members.[7] As to the level of schooling of those responsible for the plots of land, the overall results for the zones show that 87 percent of them did not attend school past fourth grade; of those, 32 percent never went to school at all and only 2 percent attended beyond eighth grade. Thus, the settlements have made landownership possible for a population that has historically been excluded by society, and that, even in cases in which they were somehow incorporated into the labor market, did so in unstable and precarious conditions.

The people who go to live in the settlements do not do so alone: most of the holders of land plots move in with a family. In general, the family formations on the plots are similar to those on ordinary family farms, with a nuclear family (mother, father, and children) that finds in the settlements an important source of work as well as conditions for social and economic development. Children make up part of the families on more than 80 percent of the plots; they are mostly under the age of 14. The average number of children is three per family.[8] In approximately one-quarter of the cases (24 percent) families also included other relatives, such as parents, in-laws, siblings, grandchildren, and so forth. In most cases, these other family members did not live with the nuclear family before moving into the settlements but were incorporated into the family unit at the time of the move, which implies the settlements have played the role of reuniting families.[9] Thus the settlements contribute both to reestablishing family ties (formerly severed or threatened because sons, daughters, parents, or siblings had to leave the family household in search of means for survival), and to giving shelter to relatives.

Moving into a settlement not only involves isolated families (families living in one home with or without added relatives), but also extended family groups: 62 percent of settlers have a relative who lives on another plot in the same settlement. Thus, the settlements seem to group together (or to regroup) segments of communities, if not whole communities.

In the case of settlements in which a significant number of the settlers belonged to families already living in the expropriated area, the implementation of the settlement projects not only makes it possible to maintain existing relationships; it often also leads to a rearrangement of the families (as new neighborhood ties are formed), which fosters the coexistence of people who were strangers or near strangers, thus producing new opportunities for meeting, sharing, and determining new forms of community and organization.

The Settlements and Their Internal Organization

The internal physical organization of the settlement projects for the most part seems to obey a certain pattern already existing among local family farmers before the settlements were established, while some innovations did take place.

In most of the units studied, houses are located on the plots. Farming communities were found in almost one-fourth of the projects (most of them in Southern Bahia and in the Sugarcane Region), usually coexisting with population groupings that existed before the settlements were established. In the Ceará Sertão zone, there are communities (different-sized groupings of settlers' houses) surrounded by subsistence croplands. The pastures are often collective. In the larger projects, each community has an association, which organizes the economic activities of its members, and the whole settlement has one central cooperative that coordinates the associations.

Demographic and Land Impacts of Settlements

The rural settlements in this study did not radically alter the scenario of landownership in this country, nor in the states or regions in which they are located. The rural settlement policy, therefore, still cannot be considered a profound land reform process.

In the states studied, a comparison of the total area of rural settlements established by INCRA up to 1999 (excluding the settlements implemented by the state governments), with the total area of farming and cattle ranches listed in the 1996 census, reveals that except for in Pará, the area of the settlements ranges from 0 to 5 percent of the total area.

Nevertheless, in the sample zones studied, the ratio of settlement area to farming area in the municipalities is significantly greater, which indicates a territorial development process in the land reform. As shown in table 15.3, there are important variations among the zones (and even among the municipalities that compose a given zone), going from a mere 3.1 percent (1999 data) in the Southern Bahia zone to 40.39 percent in the Southeastern Pará zone. This means that although the impact may seem modest at the state level, it tends to be meaningful in the chosen areas, especially in certain municipalities in which it increased significantly between 1997 and 1999.

TABLE 15.3 Percentage of settlement project (SP) area over total farming area

Zone	States (up to 1999)*	Municipalities in sample (up to 1997)†	Municipalities in sample (up to 1999)†	Area strata (up to 1997)‡
Southern Bahia, Bahia	3.0	2.3	3.1	5.5
Ceará Sertão,Ceará	5.3	15.9	23.7	113.2
Federal District and surrounding areas, Goiás and Minas Gerais	1.4	3.1	5.4	57, 6
Southeastern Pará, Pará	25.3	34.6	40.4	119.5
Western Santa Catarina, Santa Catarina	1.1	9.6	11.3	18.8
Northeastern Sugarcane Region, Alagoas, Paraíba, and Pernambuco	1.5	12.1	18.4	142.7
TOTAL ZONES	5.6	8.7	12.0	62.0

Sources: Heredia et al. 2002.

* Percentage of total area of the SPs created up to 1999 in the zone state(s) over the total area of farmlands in those states. The projects belonging to the Land Title Program in Bahia, Ceará, Minas Gerais, and Pernambuco were included.

†Percentage of SP area in the municipalities studied: Percentage of total settlement area (established by INCRA up to the year shown) over the total farming area in the set of municipalities of the sample zone.

‡ Area percent of the plots in equivalent size ranges in the municipalities: The comparative size is used to determine the percentage of the total area of the settlement plots as compared with the area of farms of the same size range in the municipalities (according to data from the 1996 farming census). An average of the areas reported by the settlers was used to establish the size range that predominated in each zone, which were: 0 to 20 hectares in the Sugarcane Region; 0 to 50 hectares in Southern Bahia, Ceará Sertão, Ceará, and Western Santa Catarina; 0 to 100 hectares in Federal District and surrounding areas and Southeastern Pará.

The last column in table 15.3 gives an approximation of the impact of the settlements on land distribution in comparison with other classes of land tracts within the same size range as the settlers' plots. It indicates that there was a significant impact[10] on some zones, such as the Ceará Sertão, Southeastern Pará, and the Northeastern Sugarcane Region, where the total area of the settlements was greater than the area occupied by other farmlands in the same size stratum at the time of the IBGE census.[11] Consequently, although the implementation of the settlements has not altered the scenario of land distribution on a large scale, it has produced a significant redistribution at a local level.

As to the demographic impact, the settler population has caused a significant increase in the rural population of the municipalities, but not in the population of the regions as a whole. One possible inference is that, with some exceptions, the increase in settlements has helped to detain the migration of the rural population to the cities, if not to reverse it. In municipalities with few inhabitants, the settlement population is important, even when compared with the urban populations.[12]

Access to Public Policies and Infrastructure Conditions

In general, the infrastructure of the settlements in the zones studied is quite faulty, in keeping with the substandard conditions found in most Brazilian rural areas. However, this does not mean that nothing has changed; the creation of the settlements and the expectations of those involved necessarily has given rise to a number of demands and claims, which have been successful depending on the extent to which settlers have been able to organize themselves and on the local political state of affairs.

The initial stages of arrival in the settlements (in cases in which the population did not already live in that area) are quite difficult, because everything needs to be done on the plots, including building houses. For the families to have minimum starting conditions for their social, economic, and productive integration, they need to have access to credit. INCRA offers three different forms of credit: development, housing, and food. In the settlements studied, 81 percent of the families benefited from development credit, 72 percent from housing credit, and 74.63 percent from food credit, which represents a reasonable amount of coverage.

These data must be interpreted taking into account the fact that credit takes a long time to be granted, and generally only arrives as a result of organized pressure by the settlers and their movements. Delivery of the development and food credit took an average of nine months, counting from when the projects were officially created. The housing credit took over two years (twenty-eight months on average), which made the beginning stages more difficult and undermined the families' capacity to carry out their activities.[13]

Questioned about their current and past housing conditions, 79 percent of the settlers reported an improvement. Answers varied among regions. On average, only 8 percent of the settlers stated that their situation had become worse. Official figures regarding types of buildings match these opinions: 74 percent of the settlers' houses in the studied zones are made of brick or cinderblocks, as opposed to 39 percent—in the best of cases—of their previous houses. Credit disbursement and the changes in types of houses also served to foster local commerce (because of the demand for construction materials) and the local labor market (construction work).

With regard to the water supply, most settlements studied had problems due to the lack of water or bad water quality. In nearly 46 percent of them, interviewees reported there were plots that had problems with the amount of water available for irrigation.

On-farm electricity was present on 78 percent of the projects, while only 27 percent of them have an adequate supply. In 66 percent of the cases studied, electricity had been furnished only some time after the settlement had been established. In 53 percent of the projects that have electricity, the settlers reported having to have made demands in order to obtain it.

Public telephone systems are scarce on the settlements: only 16 percent of the projects have any at all, which means that in a medical emergency, or when in need of basic commercial information, settlers must go elsewhere, sometimes at a great cost in terms of money, time, and effort.

In the overall sample, the average distance from the settlements to the nearest city is 28 kilometers, which usually takes approximately an hour of travel.[14] Roads leading to the entrance of the settlements are usually dirt roads (46 percent of the projects), or a combination of dirt and paved roads (34 percent). In the interviews, 70 percent of the settlers reported bad roads, half of which cannot be travelled during the rainy season. The condition of the roads within the settlements is even worse: In only 18 percent of the settlements studied are all of the plots accessible year round. Therefore, the settlers usually face difficulties getting around, especially during the rainy season, which further undermines their access to health and education and makes it harder to sell their products. With regard to collective transportation, although the overall scene is bleak, field observations revealed that in several municipalities the presence of the settlements led to an increase in the number of town vehicles and machinery, such as school buses, ambulances, and tractors. The settlements' presence also caused changes in the routes of bus lines and an increase in alternative services, such as motorcycle taxis and pickup trucks, which probably benefited neighboring areas as well.

Data from the interviews show that one of the most serious concerns of settlers is whether or not there will be schools for their children. There are schools in 86 percent of the settlements researched. Most of them were built after the settlement had already been established (84 percent). This relatively large number of schools seems to have been the result of organized demands made by the settlers and their movements: in 71 percent of the cases it was necessary to fight for the construction of schooling facilities. Most settlement schools are maintained by the local authorities (87 percent). In some cases, they are set up, supported, and even run by social movements (for example, the MST or rural workers' unions), sometimes in partnership with nongovernmental organizations (NGOs) and the government.

Living on a settlement seems to improve the chances of children going to school. A large percentage of the school-age settlement population goes to school: approximately 90 percent of the children between ages seven and fourteen, and 60 percent of the youths between fifteen and nineteen. In a comparative assessment by the settler interviewees who were asked to compare the current versus previous schooling situations, they acknowledged shortcomings, but 70 percent considered the situations had improved, 20 percent that they had not changed much, and 9 percent that they had become worse.

On the other hand, in terms of grade levels, school arrangements are not so favorable: 77 percent of the projects with schools have multiple-grade classrooms; in 73 percent of these, the schools go up to only fourth grade. Only 19 percent of the projects that have schools offer education up to eighth grade. We found no high schools or technical schools in our sample.

There are also youth and adult education programs in 64 percent of the cases studied. This has made literacy possible for part of the adult population on the settlements: in the projects studied, 6 percent of the adults over 30 years of age attended these programs.

As to health services, while there are a good number of community health workers in most of the projects (78 percent), there are community health centers in only 21 percent of the settlements studied, most built after settlers and their organizations pushed for them. Even when there are medical facilities, there are usually no doctors on a regular basis.[15] Given this bleak situation, most of the settlers seek health services in the same municipality (in 92 percent of the projects), in neighboring municipalities (42 percent), or in cities that have general hospitals (25 percent).

This means that the establishment of settlements, especially when it involves populations from other municipalities or regions, puts a great deal of strain on those health services, and it is a known fact that these services already provide an insufficient level of health care. The presence and effect of the settlers in this case, therefore, tends to cause new demands, or to add upon existing ones. Additionally, settlements are normally far from urban centers, and access roads and/or collective transportation services are inadequate, adding a further burden on settlers who must go outside the settlements for health care, having a serious effect on their lives.

The Principles of Association and Political Participation

Given the precarious infrastructure, coupled with the difficulties found in getting settled on the land and, in more general terms, in reproducing family farms, the establishment of the settlements is not as much the end point of a process of struggle as the starting point for new social and economic demands. Their new situation forces the settlers into life experiences that they would hardly have encountered in their previous situations. They begin to organize themselves, establish dialogues with the government, make demands, exert pressure, negotiate; in sum, they begin a number of activities that put them at the front line of political participation.

The study showed that in the various zones, the presence of the settlements brought about changes in the relationships between the workers who live in them and the local authorities, either requiring new forms of action, strengthening traditional patronage systems (which are common in precarious situations), or empowering new leaders to run for public office.

Associations are a predominant form of organization representing the settlers and are present in 96 percent of the settlements studied. They represent the settlements legally and in formal connections with government departments and other agencies. In some cases noted in the study, settlers' representatives sat on municipal management councils (rural development, health, education, and agriculture councils) or in municipal agriculture secretariats, or they were candidates for local public office (aldermen or mayors).

These data indicate that the political experience acquired in the struggle for the land (in whichever form or forms it took place) resulted in producing new leaders and forms of representation, as well as in providing the opportunity for lessons on the importance of different forms of organization and their capacities to produce demands. Thus, the existence of the settlements has to some degree modified surrounding local political scenarios.

The Presence of the Settlements Within the Dynamics of Regional Economies

Employment

In the current context of crisis in the farming sector and of difficulties in reproducing family farming, along with the fact that the labor market has become more and more difficult for the less educated segment of the population, the settlements provide an important source of employment and access to land tenure.

As mentioned, in the areas studied, most of the settlement population comes from the same municipality or from neighboring municipalities, and the plot owners have a low level of formal education and have previously had a precarious position in the rural/farming labor market. With the establishment of the settlements, it has become possible for these people to center their family development and financial livelihood strategies on their own plot, combining the activities they carry out there with other activities related to the existence of the settlement.

In the total population above the age of fourteen in the settlement projects studied, 79 percent worked only on the plot, 11 percent on the plot and also elsewhere, 1 percent only elsewhere, and 9 percent declared they did not work. This means that 90 percent of the settlers over fourteen years old worked or helped on the plot. There was an average of three people per plot. Of those who did any type of work in other places (12 percent in all),[16] 44 percent did so occasionally, 24 percent temporarily, and 31 percent on a permanent basis. It is worth mentioning that of those who worked in other places, more than half (56 percent) carried out activities only within the settlement itself, which included nonfarming work created by the implementation of the settlement project (construction of roads and collective infrastructure, teaching, food and health services, collective work, product processing, and so forth).

Although the settlements are evidently job creators, some of the settlers end up leaving (temporarily or definitively): 28 percent of the families in the settlements of the zones studied reported having had a family member leave the plot (there are regional variations, the highest percentage being that of the Southeastern Pará (38 percent), and the lowest that of the Northeastern Sugarcane Region (approximately 15 percent). Overall, 42 percent of the departures were due to the need to search for employment and/or another land property (the highest percentage being 60 percent, in Ceará).[17] In all, 12 percent of the plots in the settlements studied had lost members who left in order to find employment elsewhere.

Agricultural Production

The settlements produce a wide variety of products. Table 15.4 shows for each zone the five top farm products produced (P), sold (S), and considered important (I) in the 1998–1999 harvest. It also includes the five products that contributed the most to the plots' gross value of production (GP).[18]

It is evident that there is not necessarily a match between the products most grown, sold, and considered important, nor between these and the products with the greatest GP. Corn, cassava, and beans are clearly the most commonly grown products and are those considered important by the greatest number of settlers, with exceptions in some zones. This choice has strategic value: these products are easily sold and are crucial in the families' daily diet. These are followed by taro root, bananas, and rice. Other, mainly cash crops, such as cotton, sugarcane, pineapples, and tobacco, are also high on the lists.

Analysis of the share of different farming products in the overall GP (the only animal products included are milk and eggs),[19] showed that milk, cassava, corn, beans, eggs, rice, pineapples, soybeans, taro root, and cassava flour were in the top ten positions (representing 78 percent of the GP). Of these, the first three account for 48 percent of GP and the first five for 61 percent.

Table 15.5 shows the top ten animal products raised, sold, and considered important.

Both dairy and beef cattle are important in all of the zones except for Southern Bahia and the Sugarcane Region. It is especially important in Southeastern Pará (sale of calves and milk production), Western Santa Catarina, and Federal District and surrounding areas. Poultry for meat is considered important by many producers, but it seems to be reserved mostly for subsistence rather than commercial use (meat and eggs), except for in the zones in Southeastern Pará and Federal District and surrounding areas, in which they are also sold. Pork is common (except for in the Southern Bahia and Sugarcane Region zones) and is almost exclusively used

TABLE 15.4 Main plant products grown in the 1998–1999 crop season

Zone	Category*	Highest percentage	2nd highest percentage	3rd highest percentage	4th highest percentage	5th highest percentage
Southern Bahia	P	cassava	Corn	bananas	beans	pineapples
	S	cassava	pineapples	bananas	corn	cocoa/coconuts
	I	cassava	Bananas	coconuts	corn	pineapples/coconuts
	GP	cassava	pineapples	cocoa	rubber	coconuts
Ceará Sertão	P	corn	Beans	cotton	squash	watermelon
	S	cotton	Corn	beans	squash	bananas
	I	cotton	corn	beans	bananas	—
	GP	corn	beans	cotton	watermelon	rice
Federal District and surrounding areas	P	corn	rice	cassava	sugarcane	beans
	S	corn	rice	cassava	beans	sugarcane
	I	corn	rice	cassava	sugarcane	beans
	GP	cassava	beans	corn	rice	soybeans
Southeastern Pará	P	corn	rice	cassava	squash	watermelon
	S	rice	corn	pineapples	bananas	cassava
	I	rice	corn	pineapples	cassava	bananas
	GP	cassava	pineapples	rice	corn	squash
Western Santa Catarina	P	corn	beans	cassava	rice	sweet potatoes
	S	corn	beans	tobacco	soybeans	rice
	I	corn	beans	tobacco	soybeans	—
	GP	corn	beans	tobacco	soybeans	matte
Northeastern Sugarcane Region	P	cassava	beans	corn	taro root	bananas
	S	cassava	beans	corn	taro root	bananas
	I	cassava	taro root	beans	sugarcane	corn
	GP	cassava	taro root	beans	potatoes	sugarcane

*P = produced, S = sold, I = considered important to the settlers, GP = contributed most to the gross value of production

for subsistence. Goats and sheep are considered important only in the Ceará Sertão.

Gathering activities are important in some zones: *piaçava* palm, in Southern Bahia (where 44 percent of the interviewees produce and sell it) and *matte* in Western Santa Catarina (sold by 14 percent of the settlers and placed among the products with the greatest GP). Timber for fence posts is considered important in Southeastern Pará (17 percent declared selling) and firewood for charcoal in Western Santa Catarina. Other forest products mentioned as important for household use in different zones include firewood, clay, timber (for fences and for construction), and medicinal plants.

TABLE 15.5 Animals raised, sold, and considered important by settler families in each zone (by percentage)*

Zone	Beef cattle†			Dairy cattle†			Poultry			Goats / Sheep			Pork		
	Raised	Sold	Important††	Raised	Sold	Important	Raised	Sold	Important	Raised	Sold	Important	Raised	Sold	Important
Southern Bahia, Bahia	20	13	15	10	8	8	9	7	6	0	0	0	3	3	2
Ceará Sertão	29	25	17	76	10	5	88	19	12	74	26	22	44	7	3
Federal District and surrounding areas	34	34	21	77	26	18	95	34	14	7	0,4	0	54	5	3
Southeastern Pará	58	57	43	52	40	30	89	37	13	3	2	0,6	30	8	4
Western Santa Catarina	39	36	26	83	34	21	97	14	4	6	0	0	83	11	7
Northeast Sugarcane Region	30	16	13	12	2	2	64	9	6	19	6	3	3	1	1
TOTAL	38	32	24	52	20	14	80	22	10	21	7	5	34	6	3

Source: Heredia et al. 2002.

* The figures in the table represent percentage of the total number of interviewees in the sample. Besides those mentioned, 83 settlers (5.3 percent of the total) declared other animal production, such as beekeeping and fish farming.

† In the cattle sector, the idea was to know which type of cattle product was most important: dairy or beef.

††Raised, Sold, Important:

  Raised: percentage of settlers interviewed who declared they raised animals.

  Sold: percentage of settlers who declared having sold animals during the previous year.

  Important: percentage of the settlers who declared considering the product important. In the case of poultry, the percentage of sales covers both meat and eggs.

Impacts on Local Production

A comparison between the data on production obtained from the study and secondary data may provide some indication of the impacts of the settlements studied in the municipalities where they are located.[20]

Comparing the settlers' overall production (based on an estimate of the settlements' farming products in 1998–1999) and the municipalities' overall production (obtained from data of the 1999 PAM/PPM and of the 1996 farming census), we observe that the settlements definitely contribute to diversifying the farming products in their areas by introducing new crops and significantly increasing the production of some secondary crops. Moreover, the settlements are leading producers of many of the products that are already traditional in various locations.

Thus, in Southern Bahia, even with only 2.3 percent of the total area of farms in that municipality, the settlements topped the local production of pineapples, oranges, milk, passion fruit, corn, rice, sweet potatoes, tobacco, and papayas, as well as squash, *acerola*, eggs, cucumbers, okra, and tomatoes (in the comparison with the 1996 census). In the Ceará Sertão zone, the settlements (23.7 percent of the area) had an important participation in the production of eggs and, according to the 1996 census comparison, in the production of cotton as well. In that region, however, they did not have a major impact on bolstering the region's production. In the zone of the Federal District and surrounding areas, where the settlements account for only 5.4 percent of the total farming area, they introduced sweet potatoes and became leaders in the production of passion fruit, eggs, sorghum, and (in the 1996 census comparison) cassava flour and root. In the Southeastern Pará zone, where the settlements occupy 40.4 percent of the area, they topped the production of rice, milk, eggs, soybeans, and (in the 1996 census comparison) of squash, acerola, sugarcane, *cupuaçu*, lima beans, sesame seeds, taro root, firewood, honey, watermelon, cassava starch, and okra. Settlements were also responsible for introducing ginger and orange. Though they had an important role in introducing pineapple crops in the region as a commercial product, their relative position as producers has declined.[21] In the Western Santa Catarina zone, the settlements (11.2 percent of the area) were shown to be leaders in the production of beans, cassava, and eggs. In the 1996 comparison, the production of squash, peanuts, rice, potatoes, sweet potatoes, onions, matte, and wood for charcoal were considered important. It is noteworthy that the settlements in this zone have been on the forefront of the creation of collective approaches to transforming the agro-industry. In the Northeastern Sugarcane Region zone, the settlements (18.4 percent of the area) introduced products such as saffron, cashew nuts, and sesame seeds, and became leading producers of peanuts, beans, passion fruit, corn, pineapples, and (in the 1996 census comparison) squash, firewood, cabbage, sweet potatoes, watermelon, and cassava flour. Sugarcane, which is still the predominant crop in the region, is not important in the settlements, except in some specific projects.

As to livestock, the chief products are cattle (26 percent of the region's production, in heads of cattle) and pork (22 percent) in the Southeastern Pará zone; goats and sheep in the Ceará Sertão (27 percent), Southeastern Pará (24 percent), and the Northeastern Sugarcane Region (45 percent). The settlements are also leaders in poultry production in the Ceará Sertão (32 percent of municipalities' production), in Federal District and surrounding areas (48 percent), and in Southeastern Pará (56 percent).

Clearly, there has been a diversification and intensification of production in areas where monocultures or extensive cattle grazing have been predominant, leading to changes in the forms of production and often in the reorganization of land use, in regions afflicted by the crises caused by the patronage farming systems. Product diversification has also had an effect on the lives of the settlers themselves, since the coexistence of subsistence and commercial production serves as a safeguard for the families at times when sales are difficult (besides the fact that it represents a quantitative and qualitative improvement).

Productivity, Technical Assistance, and Level of Technology

Relevant products were compared in terms of productivity by comparing the average productivity in the settlements (1998–1999 harvest) with the average productivity in their respective municipalities, according to the 1996 farming census.[22] This analysis revealed that in 42 percent of cases, the projects attained greater productivity than the average farms in the region. In 11 percent, their productivity was roughly the same, and in 48 percent it was below that of the other farms. These figures varied among zones.

Access to Credit

Only by becoming settlers did this segment of rural workers begin to have access to rural credit to finance production, difficult as this process may be: 93 percent of the families interviewed had never had access to credit before. Moreover, as the financial resources for credit foster a set of local activities, they also increase the circulation of currency in the municipality. Moreover, a direct dialogue is established with the state government authorities, i.e., with policy makers and financial agents.

In the 1998–1999 harvest, 66 percent of the families interviewed received rural credit, on average 2,200 reals each, which represents a reasonable amount of coverage.[23] The main source of financial resources was the Program of Special Credit for Agrarian Reform (PROCERA), according to 88 percent of the interviewed families who had access to credit. However, more than half (59 percent) of the interviewees who received credit reported difficulties in obtaining it. The main complaint (78 percent of the complaints) had to do with the delay in the disbursement of the money, which in agriculture significantly undermines the results, for it is not available at the moment of the planting cycle in which it is most needed.

Several statements collected by the researchers suggested that the credit received by the settlements has a direct repercussion on the dynamics of the local commerce of neighboring municipalities, where a good number of the settlers buy their goods. One estimate of the total amount of loans taken out by settlers in the municipalities studied (1998–1999 harvest) puts this figure at 12.5 percent of the total rural credit extended in the same municipalities. This figure varies greatly among regions: while in the Western Santa Catarina, Federal District, and Southern Bahia zones the percentage was below 8 percent, in the other three zones it represented more than 30 percent, the highest being 80 percent in the Sugarcane Region.

Impacts on Sales

With regard to the sale of products, the study showed that the settlements sometimes reproduce preexisting local situations, without innovating new marketing channels, or they may create new possibilities or alter existing channels. It must be kept in mind that the poor condition of the roads, and other negative aspects of the infrastructure, affect the conditions and possibilities for selling products.

In all of the zones, middlemen are very important. The presence of the settlements brought up the volume of production and/or introduced new crops, in some cases facilitating the creation of new circuits of middlemen, which, even when they operate in the traditional manner or represent channels, also benefits local farming.

In several of the municipalities analyzed, the presence of the settlements caused an increase in the supply and diversification of food products and, consequently, a reduction in their prices. This has affected mainly open food markets, increasing the physical space occupied and the number of days per week they operate. The large numbers of registered or unregistered vendors from the settlements compete with local professional vendors. The study also showed that sales play an important role within the settlements themselves (to other settlers), and that the settlement projects may, in some cases, provide a market for the settlers' products, especially when there are large numbers of families.

Marketing through associations (and of product processing) has also been done in several places, often by establishing new points of sale (farmers' fairs or alternative roadside stands) or marketing cooperatives, by implementing small agro-industries, or by creating new brand names for the products sold, as the MST as done. These associative enterprises are often an important factor for the sale of products, but beyond their commercial importance lies the fact that they serve the purpose of turning sales transactions into a social and political reaffirmation of the settlers' identity and of the success of the settlement experience.[24]

Impacts on the Living Conditions of the Settlers

The sale of products grown on the plots is not the only source of family income, though it has a great relative importance in all the zones studied. As several studies (not only on the settlements) have shown, the reproduction of rural family units goes beyond the sphere of farming, combining a set of other activities that bolster the household economies.

Due to the size of the study and the complexity of the analysis of family farming income, this study was conducted utilizing the concept of income generation. This is an approximation and must be viewed as such.[25] Three sorts of income were considered: income derived from the sale of products from the plots, from work carried out outside the plot, and from other forms of income and financial aid received (retirements, pensions, and so forth). We sought to complement this analysis with aspects of the settlers' living conditions in order not to use income as the sole measurement variable.

Access to the land gives families greater stability and enables them to rearrange their family development strategies. In most cases, this leads to an improvement in income and in living conditions, in clear contrast with the poverty and social exclusion that many of these families suffered before entering the settlement projects.

An analysis of income components (or, rather, of the capacity to generate income) for the 1998–1999 harvest shows the importance of not only the income derived from the plots in all zones, but also that of other sources of income, such as retirement and pension, and the diverse forms of employment outside the plots. The average percentage for each type of income is 69 percent for income derived from the plot, 14 percent for external employment, and 17 percent for social security benefits. These percentages vary from one region to another.

The average monthly gross income per family in the sample was 312.42 reals, the lowest average being 116.74 reals in the Ceará zone and the highest 438.72 reals in the Santa Catarina zone. Of course, there are differences within each zone. Comparing the estimated monthly per capita income based on this data, with an acceptable parameter to define the threshold of poverty that takes into account the specifics of the settlers' conditions (adopting half the minimum wage for this purpose), it turns out that the average income in the sample is greater than this poverty level, reflecting the successful situation of the families of settlers. There are, however, important regional variations.

Although the issue of the settlers' income has constantly been raised—by some in order to support success and by others to show the supposed failure of the land reform settlements—we chose a different avenue, so as to break down that variable. Our concern was to go a little further and try to obtain a qualitative measurement of the settlers' living conditions, of their chances of having access to services and to goods, and of the way they view this new situation and the opportunities it offers.

Comparing their previous living conditions with their current ones, 91 percent of the settlers interviewed said they considered their situation had improved since arriving at the settlement. A more global analysis would seem to confirm this perception. The Ceará Sertão and the Northeastern Sugarcane Region zones (whose incomes were below the threshold of poverty in the previous analysis) are among the zones that had the highest rates of perceived improvement: 95 percent and 92 percent, respectively.

As far as food is concerned, 66 percent of the settlers reported an improvement. This percentage was highest in the Northeastern Forest Region (82 percent). Overall, access to the land and being able to cultivate crops and raise animals for subsistence, which resulted in the aforementioned diversity of products, is in itself enough to ensure the families' food is provided.

Upon inquiry as to their purchasing power, 62 percent of the settlers reported an improvement (23 percent considered that it remained the same), with regional variations. In this case the highest rates were also found in the Ceará and Northeastern Sugarcane Region zones, in which 68 percent of the settlers stated that their purchasing power increased. An analysis of the durable goods owned corroborated that perception. Though there were variations, there was a rise, in all of the zones, in the number of families that owned gas stoves, refrigerators, television sets, parabolic antennas, washing machines, and their own means of transportation. The most common types of transportation are bicycles and animals, but there was an increase in the number of people who own cars and motorbikes, though the percentages are still low—8 percent and 7 percent, respectively. The improvements in housing conditions and in durable goods also contributed significantly to boosting local commerce.

Despite the relatively poor conditions, settlers expressed much hope when assessing their families' future. Overall, 87 percent of the interviewees stated that they believed that the future would be better, with very little variation between the zones. As other studies indicate—and the data from the present study confirm—the settlers appear confident about their future; their access to the land has given them a perspective of greater long-term stability.

Final Considerations

Factors such as the extent of social conflicts that crop up in the struggle for land, the adoption by the social movements of forms of struggle that have turned out to be effective (such as the collective occupation of land), and the greater concentration of settlements in certain regions—many of whose large properties are undergoing crises in their production systems—all ended up forcing the government to carry out relatively concentrated actions of expropriation in specific zones. This process generated the zones analyzed in the study, some of which are fundamentally reformed areas, in contrast with the individual phenomena left behind by the previous method of isolated expropriations; this, in itself, created a new paradigm in the regions in which these settlements are established.

As we show in this chapter, the changes brought about by the existence of the settlements are multiple, given the specific contexts in which they arise, the density of the different projects, and the trajectories of the settlers and regional differences in public policy.

It would be safe to say that the establishment of the land reform settlements has led to land redistribution and made land tenure possible for rural workers who usually come from the same region, but this development has still not drastically altered the overall scenario of land concentration in the larger zones:

the changes in the agrarian structure are noticeable only locally. The settlements are the result of struggle for the land, they are a point of reference for public policy, and they lack infrastructure. For all of these reasons, we may view the settlements as starting points for other demands, as fostering the affirmation of new identities and interests and the formation of new forms of organization within the settlement projects, and as searching for places where the settlers will be heard. Thus, the settlements end up bringing about changes in local political scenarios, enabling settlers to move into political spheres and to electoral campaigns.

In some of the zones analyzed, the settlements have caused a rearrangement of the rural areas, modifying the landscape, the patterns of distribution of the population, and the course of roads and highways. This has led to the formation of new clusters of populations and has changed the levels of production, often stimulating the autonomy of districts and even the creation of new districts.

In the zones studied, the creation of the settlement projects has provided a population disadvantaged by low levels of education and an unstable position in the labor market, with the possibility to centralize strategies for family farm reproduction on the land plots, even when they may seek other complementary sources of income elsewhere. The presence of the settlements also generates nonfarming employment (construction projects, teaching positions, alternative transportation, and so forth). In addition to generating jobs, the settlement projects serve as a social shelter for settlers' relatives, acting in come cases as a mechanism for the reconstitution of families. As to farming activities, one of the main changes brought about by the settlements has been an increase in the diversity of goods in the local markets, especially in areas that used to have monocultures or extensive cattle grazing. Some settlers and their movements also introduced innovations in product processing and in forms of marketing. Their status as organized settlers enabled this population to gain access to agricultural credit for the first time in their lives, though their integration into the financial market has been difficult. The volume of credit put in play as the result of the settlements also has noticeably boosted surrounding local and regional commerce and has stimulated other activities, such as construction.

The establishment of the settlements has provided greater stability of and shifts in livelihood strategies, and this has led to an improvement in the settlers' living conditions, increasing their purchasing power not only of foodstuffs but of consumer goods in general, such as home appliances, farming inputs, and equipment. In this manner, as well, settlements have bolstered local commerce, especially when there is a great concentration of settlements.

In many areas, the settlers have obtained the social and political recognition of other social groups, overcoming tensions often arising from initial concerns that the settlers were foreigners or troublemakers (especially in the areas where the settlements resulted from land occupations). Beyond the economic issues, a new social activism has emerged, and the dignity of a previously excluded population has been reestablished. Many settlers have provided testimonials about what it means to be a settler, especially in previously monocultural areas with the power relations that characterize them. To be relieved of paying land rental, to feel emancipated, to live in freedom and able to control their own lives, to stop being a slave, these have been common themes in the discourse of the settlers, when they compare their present lives with their lives in the past. No matter how many difficulties they may currently face, access to the land has helped break many chains and has clearly brought about a feeling of improvement.

Important changes have emerged from the settlements in the zones studied. Nonetheless, health care, schools, infrastructure, access to technical assistance, and other vital social services are clearly lacking, and this indicates inadequate government intervention in the process of agrarian transformation and a marked continuity of the substandard conditions that afflict the Brazilian rural landscape.

CHAPTER 16: CONCLUSION

Moving Forward: Agrarian Reform as a Part of Food Sovereignty

Peter Rosset

Food sovereignty implies the implementation of radical processes of comprehensive agrarian reform adapted to the conditions of each country and region, which will provide peasant and indigenous farmers—with equal opportunities for women—with equitable access to productive resources, primarily land, water, and forests, as well as the means of production, financing, training, and capacity building for management and interlocution.

   Agrarian reform, above all, should be recognized as an obligation of national governments . . . within the framework of human rights and as an efficient public policy to combat poverty. These agrarian reform processes must be controlled by peasant organizations . . . and must guarantee both individual and collective rights of producers over shared lands, and be articulated within coherent agricultural and trade policies. We oppose the policies and programs for the commercialization of land promoted by the World Bank instead of true agrarian reforms by governments.

— *Final Declaration, World Forum on Food Sovereignty, Havana, Cuba, September 7, 2001 (civil society preparatory meeting for World Food Summit +5)*

The right to food is a human right that is protected by international law. It is the right to have regular, permanent, and unobstructed access, either directly or by means of financial purchases, to quantitatively and qualitatively adequate and sufficient food corresponding to the cultural traditions of the people to which the consumer belongs, and ensuring a physical and mental, individual and collective, fulfilling and dignified life free from anxiety. Governments have a legal obligation to respect, protect and fulfill the right to food . . .

   While the Special Rapporteur believes that international cooperation is fundamental, the primary obligation to realize the right to food rests with national governments. At this level, access to land is fundamental, and agrarian reform must be a key part of government strategies aimed at reducing hunger. In many parts of the world, people are struggling to survive because they are landless or because their properties are so small that they cannot make a decent living. Agrarian

reform must be just, fair, and transparent . . . [and] more attention
should be paid to the alternative models proposed by civil society,
particularly the concept of food sovereignty. Access to land and agrarian reform, in particular, must be key elements of the right to food.
—*Jean Ziegler, Special Rapporteur of the United Nations Commission on
Human Rights on the Right to Food, 2002*

Introduction: A Rural World in Crisis

At the start of the new millennium we find the rural world everywhere to be
in a state of crisis. The historical origins of this crisis, in the nations of the
South, can be found in colonial land grabs and in the displacement of farming peoples from fertile lands with adequate rainfall, toward steep, rocky
slopes; desert margins; and infertile rainforest soils; and the progressive incorporation of these displaced peoples into poorly paid seasonal labor forces
for export agriculture. As a result of this legacy, only slightly modified in the
postcolonial period, the landless and near-landless have long made up the
poorest of the poor. In recent decades, neoliberal economic policies have typically made the conditions in rural areas even worse, as national governments,
often with urging from international financial institutions like the World Bank,
International Monetary Fund (IMF), and World Trade Organization (WTO),
have:

- Presided over a set of trade, macroeconomic, and sectoral policies that
  have conspired to undercut the economic viability of peasant, small, and
  family farmers and cooperative/collective agriculture. These policies have
  included trade liberalization and the subsequent flooding of local markets with dumped, cheap food imports, against which local farmers can
  scarcely compete; cutting of price supports and subsidies for food producers; the privatization of credit, commercialization, and technical
  assistance; excessive export promotion; the patenting of crop genetic
  resources; and a bias in agricultural research toward expensive technologies such as genetic engineering. Increasingly, smaller and poorer farmers find that credit is inadequate or too expensive to cover rising production costs, buyers are more scarce and monopsonist than ever, and prices
  are too low to cover credit and production costs (Hellinger, Hansen-
  Kuhn, and Fehling 2001; Lappé et al. 1998). The net result has been a
  significant and continued deterioration in the access of the poor to land,
  as they are forced to sell off land they own, cannot afford land rentals or

similar arrangements, or lose land by defaulting on credit (European Commission 1999; Rosset 2001a; Ziegler 2002).

- Dragged their feet in implementing already existing land reform and land redistribution policies, and by and large resisted—sometimes using force—efforts by civil society organizations, such as movements of the landless, to push the implementation of these policies (Langevin and Rosset 1997; Agencia EFE 2000; Rosset 2001a; Ziegler 2002).

- Stood by as land has increasingly been commercialized, and watched passively as business interests—both agricultural (i.e., plantations) and nonagricultural (i.e., petroleum and mining)—and large infrastructure projects (i.e., hydroelectric dams) have encroached on communal and public lands and territories of indigenous peoples (Bryant 1998; European Commission 1999; Rosset 2001a).

- Done nothing as agricultural commodity chains—on both the input (i.e., seeds) and output (i.e., grain trading) sides—have become increasingly concentrated in the hands of very few transnational corporations, which, by virtue of their near-monopoly status, are increasingly setting costs and prices unfavorable to farmers, putting all, especially the poorest, in an untenable cost-price squeeze, thus further encouraging the abandonment of agriculture (ETC Group 2001; Heffernan 1999; Rosset 2001a; Ziegler 2004).

As we saw in part II of this volume, governments and multilateral institutions have taken up only one policy initiative on a more or less global scale, which they have presented as a positive step to redress land access issues. This initiative, or series of initiatives, consists of accelerating, building upon, and featuring World Bank–designed and supported policies to title lands, facilitate land markets, and, increasingly, to promote "land-bank" credit for land purchases by the poor. This is so-called market-assisted or negotiated land reform (Deininger 2001). Unfortunately, as is detailed in this volume, there is mounting evidence that these policies are unlikely to significantly improve access by the poor to land or give them more secure tenure. In fact there is good reason to believe these policies will actually worsen the situation in many cases.

Thus, it should come as no surprise that it is in rural areas where the worst poverty and hunger are still to be found. The expansion of agricultural production for export, controlled by wealthier producers who own the best lands, continually displaces the poor to ever more marginal areas for farming. They are forced to fell forests located on poor soils, to farm thin, easily eroded soils on steep slopes, and to try to eke out a living on desert margins and in rain-forests (Lappé et al. 1998).

But the situation is often worse on the most favorable lands. The better soils of most countries have been concentrated into large holdings used for mech-anized, pesticide-laden, and chemical fertilizer–intensive monocultural pro-duction for export. Many of our planet's best soils—which had earlier been sustainably managed for millennia by precolonial traditional agriculturalists—are today being rapidly degraded, and in some cases abandoned completely, in the short-term pursuit of export profits and competition. The productive capacity of these soils is dropping rapidly due to soil compaction, erosion, waterlogging, and fertility loss, together with growing resistance of pests to pesticides and the loss of biodiversity (Lappé et al. 1998; Pingali, Hossain, and Gerpacio 1997).

The products harvested from these more fertile lands flow overwhelmingly toward consumers in wealthy countries. Impoverished local majorities cannot afford to buy what is grown, and, because they are not a significant market, the elite classes essentially see local people as a labor source—a cost of produc-tion to be minimized by keeping wages down and breaking up unions. The overall result is a downward spiral of land degradation and deepening poverty in rural areas. Even urban problems have rural origins, as the poor must aban-don the countryside in massive numbers and migrate to cities, where only a lucky few make a living wage, while the majority languish in slums and shanty towns (Lappé et al. 1998).

If present trends toward greater land concentration and the accompanying industrialization of agriculture continue unabated, it will be impossible to achieve social or ecological sustainability. On the other hand, research shows the potential that could be achieved by redistribution of land. Small farmers are more productive, more efficient, and contribute more to broad-based regional development than do the larger corporate farmers who hold the best land (Rosset 1999). Small farmers with secure tenure can also be much bet-ter stewards of natural resources, protecting the long-term productivity of their soils and conserving functional biodiversity on and around their farms (Altieri, Rosset, and Thrupp 1998).

A Clash of Models in the Rural World

Many of the world's organizations of family farmers, peasants, the landless, rural workers, indigenous people, rural youth, and rural women have joined together in global alliance, La Via Campesina. According to La Via Campesina, we are facing a historic clash between two models of economic, social, and cultural development for the rural world. The dominant model and its negative impacts have been described above, and La Via Campesina counterposes an alternative paradigm called *food sovereignty*. Food sovereignty starts with the concept of economic and social human rights, which include the right to food (La Via Campesina 2002). But it goes further, arguing, as does the UN Special Rapporteur for the Right to Food Jean Ziegler, that there is a corollary right to land, and, even, the "right to produce" for rural peoples (Ziegler 2002, 2004).

Proponents of food sovereignty argue that feeding a nation's people is an issue of national security—of sovereignty, if you will. If the population of a country must depend for their next meal on the vagaries of the global economy, on the goodwill of a superpower not to use food as a weapon, on the unpredictability and high cost of long-distance shipping, then that country is not secure, neither in the sense of national security nor in the sense of food security. Food sovereignty thus goes beyond the concept of food security, which has been stripped of real meaning (Rosset 2003).

Food security means that every child, woman, and man must have the certainty of having enough to eat each day; but the concept says nothing about where that food comes from or how it is produced. Thus Washington is able to argue that importing cheap food from the United States is a better way for poor countries to achieve food security than producing it themselves. But massive imports of cheap, subsidized food undercut local farmers, driving them off their land. These people then swell the ranks of the hungry, and their food security is placed in the hands of the cash economy, just as they migrate to urban slums where they cannot find living-wage jobs. To achieve genuine food security, people in rural areas must have access to productive land and receive prices for their crops that allow them to make a decent living (Rosset 2003).

Real food security also means that access to land and productive resources is not enough. The current emphasis in trade negotiations on market access for exports, to the detriment of protection of domestic markets for domestic producers, is a critical problem. According to La Via Campesina (2002), "food sovereignty gives priority of market access to local producers. Liberalized agricultural trade, which gives access to markets on the basis of market power and low, often subsidized, prices, denies local producers access to their own markets," and thus violates the right to produce, while undercutting local and regional economic development. One way to promote local economic development in rural areas is to create local circuits of production and con-

TABLE 16.1. Dominant model versus food sovereignty model

Issue	Dominant model	Food sovereignty
Trade	Free trade in everything	Food and agriculture exempt from trade agreements
Production priority	Agro-exports	Food for local markets
Crop prices	"What the market dictates" (i.e., leave intact the mechanisms that enforce low prices)	Fair prices that cover costs of production and allow farmers and farm workers a life with dignity
Market access	Access to foreign markets	Access to local markets; an end to the displacement of farmers from their own markets by agribusiness
Subsidies	While prohibited in the Third World, many subsidies are allowed in the United States and Europe but are paid only to the largest farmers	Subsidies that do not damage other countries via dumping are OK (i.e., grant subsidies only to family farmers, for direct marketing, price/income support, soil conservation, conversion to sustainable farming, research, etc.).
Food	Chiefly a commodity; in practice, this means processed, contaminated, food that is full of fat, sugar, high fructose corn syrup, and toxic residues	A human right: specifically, should be healthy, nutritious, affordable, culturally appropriate, and locally produced
Being able to produce	An option for the economically efficient	A right of rural peoples
Hunger	Due to low productivity	Problem of access and distribution due to poverty and inequality
Food security	Achieved by importing food from where it is cheapest	Greatest when food production is in the hands of the hungry or when produced locally

Control over productive resources (land, water, forests)	Privatized	Local, community controlled
Access to land	Via the market	Via genuine agrarian reform
Seeds	Patentable commodity	Common heritage of humanity, held in trust by rural communities and cultures; "no patents on life"
Rural credit and investment	From private banks and corporations	From the public sector, designed to support family agriculture
Dumping	Not an issue	Must be prohibited
Monopoly	Not an issue	The root of most problems
Overproduction	No such thing, by definition	Drives prices down and farmers into poverty; we need supply-management policies in the United States and the European Union
Farming technology	Industrial, monocultural, chemical-intensive; uses GMOs	Agroecological, sustainable farming methods, no GMOs
Farmers	Anachronism; the inefficient will disappear	Guardians of culture and crop germplasm; stewards of productive resources; repositories of knowledge; internal market and building block of broad-based, inclusive economic development
Urban consumers	Workers to be paid as little as possible	Need living wages and healthful, locally produced, affordable food
Genetically modified organisms (GMOs)	The wave of the future	Bad for health and the environment; an unnecessary technology, should be prohibited
Another world (alternatives)	Not possible/not of interest	Possible and amply demonstrated

Source: Rosset 2003.

sumption, where family farmers sell their produce in local towns and villages and buy other necessities from artisans and merchants in those towns. As we saw in chapter 15 (Heredia et al.), the presence of agrarian reform settlements boosts local economies in Brazil, despite the fact that the country lacks a "real" agrarian reform policy.

In this way money circulates several times in the local economy, generating town employment and enabling farmers to make a living. If, instead, all that farmers produce is exported to faraway countries that pay international market (i.e., low) prices, and all that they buy is also imported, all profits from the system are extracted from the local economy and can only contribute to economic development in remote locations like Wall Street. Food sovereignty places the emphasis on local markets and local economies as the sine qua non of fighting hunger and poverty (Rosset 2003).

Only by changing development tracks from the export-led, free trade–based, industrial agriculture model of large farms/land concentration/displacement of peoples can we stop the downward spiral of poverty, low wages, rural-urban migration, and environmental degradation. Redistributive land reform and a reversal of dominant trade policy hold the promise of change toward a smaller farm, family-based or cooperative model, with the potential to feed the poor, lead to broad-based economic development, and conserve biodiversity and productive resources (Rosset 1999, 2001b).

This brings us back to the argument of La Via Campesina, that we are facing a clash of models for the rural world, a clash of economic development models. The contrast between the dominant model, based on agro-exports, neoliberal economic policies, and free trade versus the food sovereignty model, could not be more stark (see table 16.1). On virtually every issue related to food, agriculture, and rural life, the positions are contrary. Where one model sees family farmers as a quaint but inefficient anachronism that should disappear with development (unless some farmers stay on as Disneyland-like attractions for bucolic rural tourism), the other sees them as the basis of local economies, as the internal market that enabled today's industrial economic powerhouses like the United States, Japan, China, and South Korea to get off the ground in times past (Rosset 1999; Lappé, Collins, and Rosset 1998).

As for hunger, one model sees boosting exports from the giant plantations of the wealthy as the way to generate the foreign exchange needed to import cheap food for the hungry, while the other sees the conversion of farmland that once belonged to family farmers, peasants, and indigenous peoples to export cropping, as precisely the driving force behind the growth of hunger and immiseration in rural areas. Finally, while the dominant model is based on chemical-intensive, large-scale monoculture, with genetically modified crops (GMOs), the food sovereignty model sees these industrial farming practices as eventually destroying the land for future generations, and it counterposes a mixture of traditional knowledge and sustainable, agroecologically based farming practices (Rosset 2003). Overall, this is why the Landless Workers' Movement (MST) of Brazil, a La Via Campesina member, says that "the enemy is the model," and the goal of the struggle is "mudança do modelo," or a transition of models. They argue that while agrarian reform is a critical piece in this transition, it is not enough. To be successful, agrarian reform must be embedded with a larger policy emphasis on food sovereignty.[1]

Ongoing Agrarian Reforms

The Official Reforms

The World Bank is taking the lead in promoting, and, in some cases, financing, comprehensive reforms of land tenure, including titling, cadastres and land registries, land-market facilitation, market-assisted or negotiated redistributive reforms, and credit, technical assistance, and marketing support (Rosset 2004; Deininger and Binswanger 2001; Deininger 2001; Bond 2000; figure 1 in the introduction to part II of this volume). Here the Bank has followed the lead of its own development economists, who have found that severe inequality in land tenure retards economic growth, poverty alleviation, and efforts to use soils sustainably (Deininger and Binswanger 2001). In this policy environment, other institutions, including governments, aid agencies, and other development banks are following the lead of the World Bank and aggressively implementing some, or in some cases, all of these reforms (de Janvry et al. 2001; Burns et al. 1996).

While one might applaud the fact that it is no longer taboo to propose land reform as a key element in sustainable development (de Janvry et al. 2001), we have seen in this volume how far short they fall. Land titling programs can lead to new land loss (Thailand) and conflicts (Mexico); their cost makes their potential scope woefully inadequate when compared to the magnitude of landlessness (Brazil and Colombia), while so-called beneficiaries are strapped with heavy debts for expensive land of dubious quality (Brazil). Furthermore, they tend to depoliticize the problem of landlessness, which by its nature can be addressed only by structural changes of a kind that fall squarely in the sphere of politics, rather than that of the market (Rosset 2002b, 2004, chapter 9).

Finally, these alleged reforms are carried out leaving the neoliberal policy environment, so inimical to family agriculture, and the "model," intact. We can hope for little real change, then, from these efforts (Barraclough 1999; Borras, chapter 5 in this volume).

State-Led Land Reforms

"In every Latin American case where significant land redistribution benefiting the rural poor took place, the state played a decisive role," wrote the late Solon Barraclough (1999, 33). He also noted that, unfortunately, in every case where reform was denied or deformed, the state also played a critical role.

Only two contemporary governments, in Latin America or elsewhere, can truly be said to have a sincere commitment to genuine land reform, including a transition to models geared to making family-scale and cooperative agriculture more viable. These are Cuba and Venezuela, discussed in part III of this book.

While Cuba's original revolutionary land reform took place in the 1960s, in chapter 12 we show how a second "reform within the reform" allowed Cuba to escape from a food crisis in the 1990s, in what might be the closest example to a true transition from an agro-export toward a more food sovereignty–like model of the kind called for by La Via Campesina. Figure 16.1 summarizes key elements that made such a transition possible. The sine qua non factors were, first of all, access to land by the rural majority, shown in the center of the schematic model. Cuba's second land reform, to break up state farms into smaller, cooperative, and individual production units, was possible because the earlier expropriation of landlords had already taken place. Second, the de facto protection from dumping provided by the trade embargo, provided a positive condition (albeit for a very negative reason), in that higher prices paid to farmers provided the economic viability and incentives needed for agriculture itself to survive the crisis. The other key factors were state support for the transition (shifts in credit, research, extension, education, etc., to support the new model), a highly organized rural sector that made the rapid dissemination of change possible, and the existence of autoctonous, agroecological technology (from both accumulated peasant knowledge and from scientific institutions) to help break dependence on unavailable imported inputs.

The case of Venezuela is still very much up in the air. While the government of President Chavez has made clear its commitment to genuine agrarian reform, a number of factors—including the resistance of landlords and bureaucrats, the failure (so far) to address the dumping effects of massive food imports, and the relative lack of organization of the peasantry into an actor, or at least active subject, to push land reform—have so far conspired to keep progress uneven at best (chapter 13 in this volume).

FIGURE 16.1. Keys to the Cuban transition toward a more food sovereignty–style model, during the 1990s

Land Reform from Below

Barraclough also noted that, "in every case where significant land reforms occurred, protests and demands by organized peasant producers and rural workers made crucial contributions to bringing them about" (1999, 36). Today movements around the world are engaged in a wave of land occupations that are putting the pressure on governments to respond. The mid to late 1980s and 1990s saw the appearance, and, in some cases, the coming of age, of a new generation of well-organized movements of landless peasants and rural workers. While the landless have always engaged in takeovers, or recuperations, of idle lands, there has been a qualitative change in the organization and political savvy of contemporary groups. Landless movements are bringing land reform to national and international policy debates—even as they seize, occupy, and plant idle lands—often at tremendous cost of life or liberty. These movements are growing rapidly around the world, from Brazil, Paraguay, Bolivia, Honduras, and Nicaragua to South Africa, Zimbabwe, Indonesia, Thailand, India, and countless other countries. Indeed, across most of the Third World, we are seeing the emergence of a new source of hope and dynamism, from these largely nonviolent poor people's movements that sidestep government inaction and take matters firmly into their own hands (Rosset 2001b).

As we saw in part III of this volume, Brazil and the very successful Landless Workers' Movement (MST) are a case in point. While large landowners in Brazil on the average leave more than half of their land idle, twenty-five million peasants struggle to survive in temporary agricultural jobs. Founded in 1985, the MST organizes landless workers to occupy idle lands, using the "social function of land" clause in the Brazilian constitution to legalize their claims, though they must defend themselves against the hired guards of the landowners and government security forces. Today more than 300,000 families—which means more than 1 million people—have won title to over 8 million hectares of land through MST-led actions, a veritable reform from below (Langevin and Rosset 1997; Mançano Fernandes 2001; Wolford 2001; Wright and Wolford 2003).

The Case for Redistributive Land Reform

The redistribution of land can fulfill a number of functions in more sustainable development (Barraclough 1999; Ziegler 2002; Boyce, Rosset, and Stanton 2005). Dozens of land reform programs were carried out after World War II. In looking back at the successes and failures, we can distinguish between what might be called genuine land reforms, and the more window-dressing or even fake reforms (Lappé et al. 1998; Sobhan 1993, chapter 5).

When a significant proportion of quality land was really distributed to a majority of the rural poor, with trade, macroeconomic, and sectoral policies favorable to successful family farming in place; and when the power of rural elites to distort and "capture" policies was broken, the results have invariably been real, measurable poverty reduction and improvement in human welfare (Sobhan 1993). The economic successes of Japan, South Korea, Taiwan, China, and Cuba resulted from such reforms (Sachs 1987; Ziegler 2002). In contrast, when alleged reforms gave only poor-quality land to poor families and failed to support them with favorable policies, credits, prices, and access to markets, or failed to alter the rural power structures that work against the poor, land reform failed to affect broad-based changes (Sobhan 1993; Lappé et al., 1998; Thiesenhusen 1995; Barraclough 1999).

The more successful reforms triggered relatively broad-based economic development. By including the poor in economic development, these reforms built domestic markets to support national economic activity (Sachs 1987). The often-tragic outcome of failed reforms was to condemn the beneficiaries to marginalization from national economic life, as they frequently assumed heavy debts to pay for the poor-quality land they received in remote locations, without credit or access to markets and in policy environments hostile to small farmers (Sobhan 1993; Thiesenhusen 1995).

Today we have a new opportunity to learn the lessons of past reforms and apply them to the practical goals of development. Land reform is no longer a taboo subject in the discourse on development, thanks in part to the 1996 World Food Summit, and to the somewhat unfortunate initiatives of the World Bank. We are witnessing a worldwide upsurge in people taking matters into their own hands via land occupations, both spontaneous and organized, on both a small and large scale. From the land crisis in Zimbabwe (Moyo and Yeros 2005), to the massive land takeovers in Chiapas in the wake of the Zapatista rebellion (Rosset 1995), to the MST in Brazil (Langevin and Rosset 1999; Wolford 2001), "land reform from below" is increasingly a reality even as policy makers dither. These grassroots movements, together with a wide array of civil society organizations, are increasingly challenging national governments and World Bank land reform policies, and putting forth alternatives.

Here we look at the important roles redistributive land reform can play in the move toward food sovereignty and more sustainable development.

Land Reform and Poverty

History shows that the redistribution of land to landless and land-poor rural families can be a very effective way to improve rural welfare (Ziegler 2002). Sobhan (1993) examined the outcome of virtually every land reform program carried out in the Third World since World War II. He is careful to distinguish between what he calls "radical" redistribution (called "genuine land reform" by Lappé et al. 1998), and "nonegalitarian" reforms (or "fake land reform" in the terminology of Lappé et al.). When quality land was actually distributed to the poor, and the power of the rural oligarchy broken, real, measurable poverty reduction and improvement in human welfare has invariably been the result. In contrast, countries with reforms that gave only poor-quality land to beneficiaries, and/or failed to alter the rural power structures that work against the poor, have failed to make a major dent in rural poverty (Sobhan 1993; Lappé et al. 1998).

While Sobhan looked at national-level statistics to derive his conclusions, Besley and Burgess (2002) recently looked at the history of land reform in sixteen individual Indian states from 1958 to 1992. While these were by and large not radical reforms in Sobhan's sense, many did abolish tenancy and reduce the importance of intermediaries. The authors found a strong relationship between the degree of land reform and the reduction of poverty. Chapter 15 in this volume shows that settlers in land reform settlements in Brazil earn more than they did before and than still-landless families; they eat better, they have greater purchasing power, they have greater access to educational opportunities, and they are more likely to be able to unite their families in one place (rather than lose family members to migration). In fact, land reform holds promise as a means to stem the rural-urban migration that is causing Third World cities to grow beyond the capacity of urban economies to provide enough jobs. Even in Zimbabwe, where earlier land reforms were ended prematurely, the evidence shows that beneficiaries are quite substantially better off than others (Deininger et al. 2000).

Another way of looking at it is in terms of the cost of creating a new job. Estimates of the cost of creating a job in the commercial sector of Brazil range from two to twenty times more than the cost of establishing an unemployed head of household on farmland, through agrarian reform. Land reform beneficiaries in Brazil have an annual income equivalent to 3.7 times the minimum wage, while still-landless laborers average only 0.7 of the minimum. Infant mortality among families of beneficiaries has dropped to only half of the national average (Stédile 1998). This provides a powerful argument that land reform, for the creation of a small-farm economy, is not only good for local economic development, but is also more effective social policy than allowing business as usual to keep driving the poor out of rural areas and into burgeoning cities.

Sobhan (1993) argues that only land reform holds the potential to address chronic underemployment in most Third World countries. Because small farms use more labor—and often less capital—to farm a given unit of area, a small-farm model can absorb far more people into gainful activity and reverse the stream of out-migration from rural areas.

Land Reform and Productivity

In the past there was a longstanding debate concerning the likely impacts of the redistribution of farm land to the poor, which almost inevitably leads, on the average, to smaller production units. One concern was that, when freed from exploitative sharecropping, rental, or labor relationships, the poor would retain a greater proportion of their own production for their own consumption (not necessarily a bad thing), thus leading to a net decrease in food availability for other consumers. However, this argument has been put to rest by the evidence (Sobhan 1993), and by the productivity gains that can be achieved by shifting to smaller-scale, more intensive styles of production.

In Brazil, family farm agriculture produces 24 percent of the total national value of production of beef, 24 percent of milk, 58 percent of pork, and 40 percent of poultry and eggs. It also generates 33 percent of cotton, 31 percent of rice, 72 percent of onions, 67 percent of green beans, 97 percent of tobacco, 84 percent of cassava, 49 percent of maize, 32 percent of soya, 46 percent of wheat, 58 percent of bananas, 27 percent of oranges, 47 percent of grapes, 25 percent of coffee, and 10 percent of sugar. In total, family farm agriculture accounts for 40 percent of the total national value of production, while occupying just 30.5 percent of the cultivated land area. It generates fully 76.9 percent of the national employment in agriculture, all while receiving only 25.3 percent of farm credit (Pengue 2005).

In fact, data show that small farms almost always produce far more agricultural output per unit area than larger farms, and do so more efficiently (Rosset 1999). This holds true whether we are talking about industrial countries or any country in the Third World. This is widely recognized by agricultural economists as the "inverse relationship between farm size and output" (Tomich, Kirby, and Johnston 1995; Rosset 1999). A recent report (Rosset 1999) examined the relationship between farm size and total output for fifteen countries in the Third World. In all cases, relatively smaller farm sizes were much more productive per unit area—two to ten times more productive—than larger ones. Thus redistributive land reform is not likely to run at cross-purposes with productivity issues.

Land Reform and Economic Development

Agrarian reform that is truly transformative and redistributive
has proved to be fundamental in reducing poverty and hunger
in many countries, and can be a key to generating economic
growth that benefits the poorest.
—*Jean Ziegler, Special Rapporteur of the Commission*
  on Human Rights on the Right to Food, 2002

Surely more tons of grain is not the only goal of farm production; farm resources must also generate wealth for the overall improvement of rural life—including better housing, education, health services, transportation, local economic diversification, and more recreational and cultural opportunities.

In the United States, the question was asked more than a half-century ago: what does the growth of large-scale industrial agriculture mean for rural towns and communities? Walter Goldschmidt's classic 1940's study of California's San Joaquin Valley compared areas dominated by large corporate farms with those still characterized by smaller, family farms (see Goldschmidt 1978; Lappé, Collins, and Rosset 1999).

In farming communities dominated by large corporate farms, nearby towns died off. Mechanization meant that fewer local people were employed, and absentee ownership meant that farm families themselves were no longer to be found. In these corporate-farm towns, the income earned in agriculture was drained off into larger cities to support distant enterprises, while in towns surrounded by family farms, the income circulated among local business establishments, generating jobs and community prosperity. Where family farms predominated, there were more local businesses, paved streets and sidewalks, schools, parks, churches, clubs, newspapers, better services, higher employment, and more civic participation. Studies conducted since Goldschmidt's original work confirm that his findings remain true today (see Fujimoto 1977; MacCannell 1988; Durrenberger and Thu 1996).

The Amish and Mennonite farm communities, found in the eastern United States, provide a strong contrast to the virtual devastation described by Goldschmidt in corporate-farm communities. Lancaster County in Pennsylvania, which is dominated by these small farmers, who eschew much modern technology and, often, bank credit as well, is the most productive farm county east of the Mississippi River. It has annual gross sales of agricultural products of US$700 million, and receives an additional US$250 million from tourists who appreciate the beauty of traditional small-farm landscapes (D'Souza and Ikerd, 1996).

If we turn toward the Third World we find a similar situation. On the one hand there is the devastation caused by land concentration and the industrialization of agriculture, while on the other we find local benefits to be derived from a small farm economy—in one case, created by land reform from below.

Chapter 15 in this volume describes how local towns benefit from the commerce that is generated when estates belonging to absentee landlords are turned into productive family and cooperative farming enterprises through land reform driven from below. A study of one such municipality, Julho de Castilhos, found that while the MST settlement possessed only 0.7 percent of the land, its members paid 5 percent of the taxes, making the settlement into the municipality's second largest rural tax payer (Movimento dos Trabalhadores Rurais Sem Terra 2001a, 2001b).

It is clear that local and regional economic development can benefit from a small-farm economy, as can the life and prosperity of rural towns. But what of national economic development?

History has shown us that a relatively equitable, small farmer–based rural economy provides the basis for strong national economic development. This "farmer road to development" is part of the reason, for example, the United States, early on in its history, developed more rapidly and evenly than did Latin America with its inequitable land distribution characterized by huge haciendas and plantations interspersed with poverty-stricken subsistence farmers (de Janvry 1981). In the early decades of the United States, independent "yeoman" farmers formed a vibrant domestic market for manufactured products from urban areas, including farm implements, clothing, and other necessities. This domestic demand fueled economic growth in the urban areas, and the combination gave rise to broad-based growth (Sachs 1987).

The post-war experiences of Japan, South Korea, and Taiwan, in the capitalist world, and China, Cuba, and, more recently, Vietnam, in the socialist world, also demonstrate how equitable land distribution fuels economic development. At the end of the Second World War, circumstances, including devastation and foreign occupation, conspired to create the conditions for radical land reforms in the former countries—while revolutions did the same in the latter—breaking the economic stranglehold of the landholding class over rural economic life. Combined with trade protection to keep farm prices high, and targeted investment in rural areas, farm families rapidly achieved a high level of purchasing power, which guaranteed domestic markets for fledging industries (Rosset 1999; Lappé et al. 1998; Sachs 1987; International Fund for Agricultural Development 2001).

The post-war economic miracles of the three capitalist countries were each fueled at the start by internal markets centered in rural areas, long before the advent of the much-heralded export-orientation policies, which much later on pushed those industries to compete in the global economy. This was a real triumph for "bubble-up" economics, in which redistribution of productive assets to the poorest strata of society created the economic basis for rapid, relatively inclusive development. While this analysis in no way is meant to suggest that all policies pursued by these countries were positive, or should be blindly replicated, their experience does stand in stark contrast to the failure of trickle-down economics to achieve much of anything in the same time period in areas of US dominance, such as much of Latin America (Sachs 1987). More generally, there is now a growing consensus among mainstream development economists, long called for by many in civil society, that inequality in asset distribution impedes economic growth (Solimano 2000).

A key distinction that Sobhan (1993) makes is between transformative agrarian reforms and other types. In most redistributive reforms those who actually receive land are at least nominally better off than those who remain landless (unless and until policies inimical to small-farm agriculture lead them to lose their land once again). However, certain agrarian reforms have been the key step in allowing entire nations to change development tracks. In these cases countries have "jumped" from the alienating, downward spiral into poverty and environmental degradation, to the upward spiral of broad-based improvements in living standards, producing strong internal markets, which in turn lead to more dynamic and inclusive economic development—the Japans, South Koreas, Chinas, Taiwans, and others. Sobhan shows by comparative analysis what the transformative reforms, those that led to real social transitions, have had in common. In brief, the majority of the landless and land poor benefited; the majority of the arable land was affected; the stranglehold of entrenched power structures over rural life and economy was broken; and favorable, enabling economic policies were put in place. A key feature of the more successful reforms is that farm families were seen as key actors to be mobilized in national economic development—whereas in failed reforms they have typically been seen as indigents in need of charitable assistance.

Land Reform and the Environment

The benefits of small-farm economies extend beyond the merely economic sphere. Whereas large, industrial-style farms impose a scorched-earth mentality on resource management—no trees, no wildlife, endless monocultures—small farmers can be very effective stewards of natural resources and the soil. To begin with, small farmers use a broad array of resources and have a vested interest in their sustainability. At the same time, their farming systems are diverse, incorporating and preserving significant functional biodiversity within the farm. By preserving biodiversity, open space, and trees, and by reducing land degradation, small farms provide valuable ecosystem services to the larger society (Rossett 1999).

In the United States, small farmers devote 17 percent of their area to woodlands, compared to only 5 percent on large farms. Small farms maintain nearly twice as much of their land in "soil-improving uses," including cover crops and green manures (D'Souza and Ikerd 1996). In the Third World, peasant farmers show a tremendous ability to prevent and even reverse land degradation, including soil erosion (Templeton and Scherr, 1999). They can and/or do provide important services to society at large, including sustainable management of critical watersheds, thus preserving hydrological resources and the in situ conservation and dynamic development and management of the basic crop and livestock genetic resources on the which the future food security of humanity depends.

Compared with the ecological wasteland of a modern export plantation, the small-farm landscape contains a myriad of biodiversity. The forested areas from which wild foods and leaf litter are extracted; the wood lot; the farm itself with intercropping, agroforestry, and large and small livestock; the fish pond; the backyard garden—all these allow for the preservation of hundreds if not thousands of wild and cultivated species. Simultaneously, the commitment of family members to maintaining soil fertility on the family farm means an active interest in long-term sustainability not found on large farms owned by absentee investors. If we are truly concerned about rural ecosystems, the preservation and promotion of small, family farm agriculture is a crucial step we must take (Rossett 1999).

Moving Forward: Guidelines for the Future

Rather than following the World Bank's market-based approach, policy makers and social movements should learn from the successes and failures of the post–World War II period and from ongoing reforms. A set of useful guidelines should include the following:

- Severe inequality in landholdings—such as the *latifundia/minifundia* pattern in many parts of Latin America—is inefficient, environmentally and socially destructive, immoral, and impedes broad-based development. A range of perspectives and concerns—from economic and social human rights to economic growth—all lead to the conclusion that we must once and for all eliminate the *latifundia* (Rosset 2001b; Repartir a Terra 2001; Ziegler 2002).
- When families receive land they must not be saddled with heavy debt burdens. This can be accomplished by government expropriation of idle

lands, with or without compensation to former owners (Sobhan 1993; Borras, chapter 5 in this volume).

- Secure tenure and/or access rights are critical to ensuring long-term food security for families and communities. Without such security and/or rights it is also difficult for families and communities to invest in land improvement, means of production, and/or conservation measures (Lastarria-Cornhiel and Melmed-Sanjak 1998).

- Women must have the right to hold title to land or participate as equals in communal ownership. When titles are vested exclusively in male heads of household, the departure or premature death of a male spouse often leads to the destitution of women and children (Deere and León 2001a, b; Monsalve Suárez, chapter 10 in this volume).

- The land distributed must be of good quality, rather than ecologically fragile soils that should never be farmed, and it must be free of disputed claims by other poor people (Rosset 2001b).

- The rights of indigenous and other peoples to land, forests, water, and other common property resources must be guaranteed and protected, as must be their right to manage them using customary law and tradition. Provision must be made for individual and/or collective rights, depending on each socio-cultural situation. No one recipe can be applied everywhere (Hall 1998; Stavenhagen, chapter 11 in this volume).

- People need more than land if they are to be successful. There must also be a supportive policy environment and essential services such as credit on reasonable terms, infrastructure, support for ecologically sound technologies, and access to markets and fair prices (Sobhan 1993; Sachs 1987; Adams 2000; IFAD 2001). Perhaps most critical is to step back from damaging free-trade policies and dumping—which drive down farm prices and undercut the economic viability of farming—and apply a food sovereignty perspective that places the highest priority on national production for national markets (World Forum on Food Sovereignty 2001; Rosset 2003).

- Truly transformative reforms will also require investment in rural areas to ensure basic services such as schools, health clinics, potable water, and basic infrastructure (Sobhan 1993, chapter 15).

- The power of rural elites to distort and capture policies, subsidies, and windfall profits in their favor must be effectively broken by the reforms (Sobhan 1993).

- The vast majority of the rural poor must be actual, not token, beneficiaries of the reform process (Sobhan 1993).

- Successful reforms are distinguished from failed ones by a motivation and perception that the new small family farms that are created will be the centerpiece of economic development, as was the case in Japan, Taiwan, China, and Cuba. When land reform is seen as welfare or as a charitable policy for the indigent, failure has been the inevitable result (Sobhan 1993; Sachs 1987; Rosset 2001b).

- In today's conservative, neoliberal political environment, strong grassroots poor people's movements are critical to pushing the reform process, stopping government foot-dragging and, when necessary, taking matters into their own hands. Land occupations are one of the most effective, proven methods of pressuring governments to act (Wolford 2001; Langevin and Rosset 1997; Barraclough 1999; Wright and Wolford 2003).

Notes

Introduction and Overview. The Resurgence of Agrarian Reform
in the Twenty-first Century

1. Indeed, many urban problems as well have their origins in displacement and in rural–urban migration due to landlessness in the countryside.

2. Those regions outside of the large industrial nations of the northern hemisphere; also referred to as the Third World or less developed countries (LDCs).

3. The early small farmers of the US came from privileged European stock and/or took land that had not been held by colonial powers prior to their arrival. These farmers' tie to the land was one of convenience and legal maneuvering against Native Americans. There was no landed aristocracy and there was no relationship that resembled, even remotely, the European feudalism that was exported to the Global South. See Clark (1990).

4. Figures for landlessness are often based on estimates and are difficult to measure due to problems with sampling, rural–urban migration, and the informal relationships between landless dwellers and land. In 2000, estimates of landlessness around the world were reported at about 100 million.

5. At its core, "food sovereignty" is defined throughout this volume as the prioritization of food production by peasant and family farms for domestic and local market, using diverse ecological production methods. In addition to this focus on small producers, Rosset (see conclusion in this volume) elaborates on the importance of ensuring access to natural resources, fair prices, gender equity, seed protection and public expenditure toward these ends.

6. "Economism" is defined here as a reduction of society and human interaction to a series of cost-benefit analyses, and the conscious efforts by individuals, groups, and nations to maximize their utility through market exchange.

7. The categories of small producer, small farmer, and peasant farmer are used interchangeably within the literature on rural development and land reform.

While the literature does not always distinguish among the three groupings, there is a general consensus that these refer to those producers who are dependent on the smallest landholdings (usually less than 10 hectares of land) within a given society.

8. These calculations are based on data from INE 2003 only.

9. Two central definitions of efficiency inform economic thinking. Pareto efficiency, or Pareto optimality, is a situation in which no change in resources can be made without making someone worse off. This situation clearly tilts against redistributive land reform; any case in which a landowner, deprived of land for redistributive purposes, can claim to be worse off, makes the system non-Pareto efficient. The second kind of efficiency, allocative efficiency, has a broader definition: a system is allocatively efficient if resources are optimized in such as way as to maximize the net benefit attained through their use. Again, though, the World Bank's understanding of the benefit to be achieved in the domain of land redistribution tends to remain narrowly defined and short in scope, excluding broader values of equity, justice, or social change.

10. www.viacampesina.org.

11. For a good discussion of this issue, see Williams (1994) and Brockett (1998, 101–6).

12. It is not sufficient to explain the Soviet experience as simply a cause and effect relationship between "large-scale bias" and the destruction of the peasantry. Resnick and Wolff (2002) have made a good case for considering the distorted class analysis of the Soviet Communist Party during the early part of the twentieth century in any evaluation of the policies that took place during that time. The problem was not just one of anti-peasant bias, but a distorted view of how the full transition to socialism was accomplished. An inaccurate analysis of the rural sector led to a great deal of misdirected policies that originated with, and were perpetuated by, a false belief that the Soviet Union had already arrived at communism (i.e., a "classless" society with a proletarian majority).

13. This team, led by Raj Patel, included Michael Courville, Julia Clarke, and Paulina Novo, with expertise contributed by Peter Rosset.

14. Land reform was conceptualized as a systematic redistribution or retitling of land on a large scale, which transfers arable land to landless beneficiaries and serves as a leveling mechanism for wealth concentration in rural areas.

15. These nations were selected for their historical importance. Time constraints prevented a full global examination of land reform, with attention focused on states that are either directly involved in the LRAN project or are of importance to LRAN partners. Resource constraints also prevented the exploration of units of analysis that were not nation states. For this reason, certain kinds of land reform remain invisible to this analysis, and there are important omissions, including but not limited to Nicaragua, Tanzania, West Africa, and the Middle East. Despite these limitations, the authors believe the analysis to be of some merit.

16. While the primary period of our evaluation begins in 1945, China,

Guatemala, Mexico, and the former Soviet Union had ongoing reform movements and policies prior to the World War II period. They have been included because of the scope of land reform efforts and continued significance of land reform in economic and political planning during the period of study.

17. In the summer of 2005, Zimbabwe's President Mugabe had implemented a sweeping forced eviction in urban areas known as "Operation Murambatsvina" ("Clean up the Filth"). The professed goal of this initiative was to relocate poor urban dwellers to rural areas through force, if necessary. In an instant, thousands of Zimbabweans became homeless, landless dwellers. The implications of this forced relocation were only beginning to be observed in the fall of 2005. Many of those evicted from urban homes were those who had left rural areas in earlier years to flee from violence during the 2000 national elections and to escape persistent drought. The immediate results of the Mugabe administration's policy were observable human rights abuses, increased landlessness, hunger, and rural poverty. This incident further highlights the persistent struggle of the landless to find stable, safe residence within their own nation, even after sweeping land reform policy was implemented only a few years earlier.

Chapter 1: The Agrarian Question in Guatemala

1. Referring to those farmers who have made investments in land, machinery, agricultural technology, and/or fixed irrigation systems.

2. Estimates of poverty in Guatemala vary. The World Bank (WB) estimates that in 2000, 66 percent of the total population lived in poverty, including 86 percent of the rural population and 93 percent of the indigenous population. The figures given here are the most recent figures cited by the UN Mission in Guatemala, May 2000.

3. Perera (1993) notes the link in Guatemala between land tenure and health, in which landless families were shown to have much higher infant mortality rates (278).

4. Migration due to insufficient landholdings has also been cited as a source for loss of cultural identity and community (Katz 2000).

5. Descendents of Spanish colonial families who married indigenous Guatemalans and come from a mixed ethnic heritage.

6. Large landed estates held by one owner or a family, and specializing in agricultural export production.

7. Coffee, cotton, citronella, lemon, tea, bananas, sugarcane, tobacco, rubber, quinine, fruit, hay, beans, cereals, and other commercial crops.

8. Leading up the 1952 reform, tax evasion, undervaluation of land for tax purposes, overvaluation for forced sales, and the nonenforcement of progressive taxation of idle lands were common problems. As will be discussed below, these problems remain in present-day Guatemala, and present serious obstacles for the successful implementation of a market-based land reform.

9. Thiesenhusen (1995) characterized the potential beneficiaries of the Arbenz

reform as "unorganized"; this notion is disputed by Forster (1998) who argues that the 1944–54 period was a time of growing mobilization for land and labor rights among labor, campesino, and indigenous organizations.

10. For the larger discussion and details of the implementation of Arbenz's land reform program, his subsequent overthrow, and the reversal of land awards, see especially Schlesinger and Kinzer (1982); Paz C (1986); Cambranes (1992), Handy (1994); and Thiesenhusen (1995).

11. The wording of the law's title, "transformation" (rather than "land reform"), reflects the relative taboo on discussion of agrarian reform in the post-Arbenz era.

12. Farmers were expected to compensate the government at a rate of 5 percent of total crop value for a period of twenty-five years.

13. Figures do not include permanently employed plantation workers.

14. Even though he was known as a reformer, Cerezo recognized his lack of power vis-à-vis the military and the rural landowning elite, commenting that "if we institute reform measures that affect private enterprise and don't take the army into account, we shall be overthrown; and if we attack the army without having the business sector on our side, the result would be the same" (Perera 1993, 282).

15. The 1956, 1965, and 1985 constitutions took a step back on authorizing land expropriation for agrarian reform, limiting the application of provisions to expropriate unused lands (Sandoval 1987).

16. Between 1970 and 1981, INTA received 5,334,000 Quetzales in payment for distributed frontier lands, while only receiving 602,000 Quetzales in idle land tax. In any case, only 263 large landholdings were assessed the idle land tax between 1963 and 1972, most of which were exonerated from payment by 1972 and 1973 government decrees (Sandoval 1987).

17. The political climate against discussion of agrarian issues was so harsh that even a 1988 Episcopal letter from the Archbishops of Guatemala that called for a study of the land distribution problem faced extreme censure from the large landowner organizations (Stringer and Lambert 1989, 16).

18. The failures of FONTIERRAS have been chronicled by Byron Garoz and Susana Gauster at www.landaction.org/category.php?section=25.

Chapter 2: An Introduction to Land and Agrarian Reform in Zimbabwe

1. A term from Zimbabwean history that refers to a struggle for justice, a large uprising of popular sentiment, or a struggle for independence.

Chapter 3: Land and Agrarian Reform in South Africa

1. Tribal homelands of indigenous Africans as designated by the South African government during the apartheid era.

2. The population estimates by the Central Statistical Services (CSS) and the Development Bank of South Africa (DBSA) were 41.9 million and 44.7 million respectively. The reason for the disparities has been that the DBSA adjusted its figures to take into account an undercounting in the 1991 census. The 1994 estimates by CSS and DBSA were similar, 40.7 million and 40.6 million respectively.

3. CSS claims that the previous population estimates were overstated and that the current estimates have corrected for the overestimation.

4. The Development Bank of South Africa (DBSA) estimated the rural population to be 21.05 million in 1993, and the October Household Survey (by CSS) put the rural population at 21.01 million.

5. The CSS preliminary estimates for 1996, however, indicated a higher figure of 88 percent of the population in Northern Province as rural.

6. Until 1995, South Africa was divided into four states: Transkei, Bophuthatswana, Venda, and Ciskei. Better known as TBVC states, they were essentially self-governing territories or homelands. The TBVC states had independent status within the apartheid government of South Africa, but they were usually not recognized by the international community.

7. A Gini-coefficient of 1 implies absolute concentration of income and a coefficient of 0 implies absolute equality.

Chapter 4: Land Reform in India: Issues and Challenges

1. A system of land tenure in which the agricultural land of a village or group of villages is owned by one person or a group of joint owners. The owners were known as zamindars, and they were the primary link between the colonial government and the farmers working the land. Historically, the zamindars were tied to the interests of the British Crown and usually negotiated work agreements that aimed to strengthen the profitability of the colonial enterprise.

2. Jajmani is an informal system of personal obligations, hereditary occupational duties, obligatory payments, and familial relationships that is often bounded by caste and class status. There has been some disagreement over the degree of formality that should be related to the practices of jajmani, and the function of these relationships in the rural class structure across different regions and areas throughout India (Mayer 1993).

3. This includes, but is not limited to, such methods as increased mechanization; development and widespread use of artificial fertilizers, pesticides, and herbicides; an emphasis on economies of scale through larger field and farm size; continuous cropping; and developments in livestock, plant breeding, and biotechnology.

4. The World Bank's involvement in the green revolution began in 1964 when it sent a mission headed by Bernard Bell to India. The Bell mission called for a devaluation of Indian currency, the liberalization of trade controls, and greater emphasis on chemical- and capital-intensive agriculture.

5. The World Bank started to fund the construction of the Sardar Sarovar Dam Project in 1985. However, in 1993 the World Bank announced a withdrawal of all their funding for the dam citing "project irregularities" as the impetus for their decision. For a good discussion of the dam project see Gadgil 1995.

6. The World Bank currently has outstanding commitments worth about US$20 billion in water projects, of which US$1.7 billion is marked for rural water schemes, US$5.4 billion for irrigation, and the rest for other purposes, such as

urban water supply and hydropower development. South Asia receives 20 percent of Bank water loans.

7. The International Development Bank (IDA) is the soft-lending arm of the World Bank, providing interest-free assistance to the poorest countries.

8. Approximately one billion inhabitants in India as of 2000.

9. It is generally accepted that, in many countries, inequities associated with land have led to rebellions by the oppressed. Feudal land tenure systems and the struggle of peasants for rights to land were the key factors in the French Revolution, for example, while the American Civil War was a conflict over land and slavery.

Chapter 5: The Underlying Assumptions, Theory, and Practice of Neoliberal Land Policies

1. See, e.g., Griffin, Khan, and Ickowitz 2002; Lipton 1974.

2. See, e.g., Byres 1974b, 2004b; Bernstein 2002, 2004b.

3. See, e.g., Paige 1975; Migdal 1988.

4. See, e.g., Ross 1998; Putzel 1992; Walinsky 1977.

5. See Ghose 1983; Kay 1983; Herring 1983; Harriss 1993.

6. Tannenbaum 1929; Sanderson 1984; Salamini 1971; Urioste 2001; Handy 1994.

7. Refer to the discussions in World Bank 2003. De Soto (2000) has also inspired this mainstream thinking.

8. See, e.g., Korovkin 2000; Yashar 1999; Tauli-Corpuz and Cariño 2004; Vidal 2004.

9. For a general background, refer to the important works of Deere and León 2001a; Agarwal 1994; Razavi 2003a; Kabeer 1995.

10. For a general background on the Salvadoran case, see J. Pearce 1998; Foley 1997; Diskin 1989. For the South African experience, see Levin and Weiner 1997; Cousins 1997.

11. For fresh analytic insights, see Pons-Vignon and Lecomte 2004.

12. For Indonesia, see Aspinal 2004; Lucas and Warren 2003; Tsing 2002. For the Philippines, see Franco 2001; Riedinger 1995; Lara and Morales 1990. For Brazil, see Houtzager 2000. For other Latin American cases, see Fox 1990.

13. For further discussion on the changing global context of land reform today, see Herring 2003; Ghimire 2001a, 2005; de Janvry, Platteau et al. 2001; Zoomers and van der Haar 2000; Fortin 2005.

14. This can also be seen as part of the state's continuing effort to, in the words of James Scott 1998, "simplify" or make "legible" complex social relationships, data, and information especially in "non-state spaces."

15. For general background, see Banerjee 1999; Gordillo 1997, 12–19; Carter 2000; Carter and Salgado 2001; and Carter and Mesbah 1993.

16. For Brazil, see Deere and Medeiros 2005; Sauer 2003; Borras 2002. For Colombia, see Mondragón 2003. For South Africa, see Levin and Weiner 1997; Lahiff 2003; Greenberg 2004. For the Philippines, see Borras 2005. For related dis-

cussion in Zimbabwe, see Moyo 2000; Lahiff and Cousins 2001. For Egypt, see Bush 2002. For general global critical discussions, see Herring 2003; Putzel 2002; Riedinger, Yang, and Brook 2001; El-Ghonemy 2001; Ghimire 2005; Borras, Kay, and Akram Lodhi 2005; Borras 2003b, 2003c.

17. See FoodFirst Information and Action Network and La Via Campesina 2003a; Baranyi, Deere, and Morales 2004; Paasch 2003; and Borras 2004b. The World Bank land policies have also influenced, to varying degrees, the land policies of other international development institutions such as the European Union see, e.g., Monsalve Suárez 2004.

18. See, e.g., Spoor 1997, 2003; Akram Lodhi 2004, 2005.

19. Refer to, e.g., Borras 2003a; Borras, Reyes, and Carranza 2005.

20. See, e.g., Nuijten 2003 for Mexico's ejido; see also Carter and Salgado 2001.

21. For a more elaborate conceptual discussion, see Borras 2004a.

22. See, e.g., El-Ghonemy 2001; Thiesenhusen 1995; Kay 1998; Griffin, Khan, and Ickowitz 2002; Wright and Wolford 2003; Wolford 2003.

23. Refer to the works of Bratton 1990; Moyo 2000; Matondi and Moyo 2003; Palmer 2000.

24. For a recent discussion, see Borras, Kay, and Akram Lodhi 2005.

25. See, e.g., Kay 2002b; Griffin, Khan, and Ickowitz 2002; Tai 1974; also see Spoor 2002.

26. Refer to Borras 2005; Franco 2005; de la Rosa 2005; Feranil 2005.

27. See Deere and Medeiros 2005; Barros, Sauer, and Schwartzman 2003; see also Buainain et al. 1999; Rosset 2001b.

28. See, e.g., Kay 2001; Scott 1985; Scott and Kerkvliet 1986; Kerkvliet 1993.

29. For a background on this case, see Gutierrez and Borras 2004.

30. See, e.g., Griffin, Khan, and Ickowitz 2002; Stiglitz 2002, 81; El-Ghonemy 1990; Ghose 1983; Borras, Kay, and Akram Lodhi 2005; Kay 2002b.

31. But see also Forero 1999, Mondragón 2003, and Borras 2003b.

32. Refer to the critical works of Griffin 1980; Slater 1989; Bernstein 1998; Mamdani 1996; Boone 1998.

33. See, e.g., Tannenbaum 1929; Sanderson 1984; Salamini 1971; Grindle 1986; Herring 1983, 1990.

34. See, e.g., Thiesenhusen 1995; Griffin, Khan, and Ickowitz 2002; King 1977; Herring 1983; Tuma 1965.

35. See, e.g., Carter and Mesbah 1993; Carter and Salgado 2001.

36. See, e.g., Griffin 1976; Byres 1974, 224; Kay 1998, 2002b; Lehmann 1974; Lipton 1974, 1993.

37. See, e.g., Putzel 2002; Franco 1999, 2000.

38. See, e.g., Buainain et al. 1999; Navarro 1998; Barros, Sauer, and Schwartzman 2003; Borras 2002.

39. See, e.g., Deere and Medeiros 2005; Sauer 2003; Borras 2002, 2003b.

40. See, e.g., Griffin, Khan, and Ickowitz 2002; Putzel 1992.

41. Refer also to Bello with de Guzman 2001.

42. See, e.g., the persuasive arguments by Harriss 1982, 16; see also 2002.

43. Refer to Putzel 1992; Sobhan 1993; Christodoulou 1990; Walinsky 1977; Lehmann 1974; Bernstein 2002; Thiesenhusen 1995; King 1977; Tuma 1965.

44. For further discussion on this argument, see Borras 2004a.

45. Among the relevant critical works in this regard are Deere 1985; Deere and León 2001a; Bernstein 2002, 2003, 2004; Byres 1974, 2004b; Lipton 1993; Ghimire 2001a; Dorner 1992; de Janvry 1981; Kay 1998, 2004; Thiesenhusen 1989, 1995; Hirtz 1998; Herring 1983, 2003; Grindle 1986; Razavi 2003a; Borras, Kay, and Akram Lodhi 2005.

Chapter 6: Thailand's Land Titling Program: Securing Land for the Poor?

1. The program was awarded a World Bank Award for Excellence in 1997.

2. CIA, *The World Factbook*, www.cia.gov/cia/publications/factbook/geos/th .html.

3. The phases and regions covered by the land titling project are: Phase 1: Northeastern region (southern 33 percent of the area) and Upper Northern region (western 50 percent). Phase 2: Lower Northern and Central region (16 provinces of high-value rural land), Northeastern region (6 provinces), and Eastern Seaboard region. Phase 3: Northeastern (remaining 10 provinces, Northern (remaining 7 provinces), and Central regions (2 provinces). Phase 4: Southern region, yet to begin implementation. The World Bank has suspended loans for the fourth phase, as the government will use own revenue for future implementation of the program.

4. An estimated 10 million people are living and farming in the national forest reserve areas as well as in many protected forest areas. A draft community forestry bill, giving legal recognition to the role of these forest-dependent communities and their sustainable management of forests, has been an issue of debate in parliament since the early 1990s.

5. The Rally for Rights (by the Assembly of the Poor, a broad coalition of farmers and village groups from all over Thailand) in front of Government House in Bangkok in 1997 highlighted 121 cases of state officials issuing illegal titles all over the country. A committee of the Assembly of the Poor has investigated these cases and submitted the evidence to the government.

6. Women do not appear to have been prejudiced by the process of the formalization of land rights in Thailand. The civil and commercial code protects women by requiring each spouse to consent in the sale of property. The Department of Lands registration processes have respected this position, requiring spousal consent to a transfer of rights regardless of who is registered on the title. However, no formal studies have been undertaken to investigate the impact of the program on women.

7. The full quote reads: "The findings of a 1980 sector strategy review might suggest that land administration was not a priority area for Bank intervention. First, land tenure in Thailand was relatively secure, based on a homesteading tradition that allows any citizen to claim up to four hectares to provide for his family. Second, landholdings were relatively equal, with many small and few large land-

holders, and no apparent trend toward increasing property concentration. Third, as a result of these factors, the country did not have a large landless population. And fourth, farmers' access to credit was relatively good and getting better. Thus, based on the sector review, there was little scope or justification for the Bank to give priority to land administration."

8. The property boom has resulted in a major rise in government revenue from registration (in 2001 the Department of Lands received an average revenue of approximately US$90 per transaction). Burns, a consultant to the LTP program, stated that a key indicator of the program's success was that better land records systems and new technology such as the Internet have contributed to increased land market activity. He cites an article in the *Far Eastern Economic Review* (Kanwerayotin 2001), which observed that "[b]uyers are demanding better quality, and can do their research more thoroughly, thanks to online registration records and home-buying guides on the [W]eb. Buyers who used to spend six months driving around to make inquiries can now find the information online within hours. And they bargain hard, their purchasing power enhanced by low interest rates and cutthroat competition among banks to give them housing loans." If such indicators are indeed key, it seems the program's focus on empowering the poor was lost somewhere after the initial planning stages.

Chapter 7: Land Concentration in Mexico after PROCEDE

1. Despite the importance of the topic—for it is the axis of the new agrarian structure, and as such it is essential to an understanding the current situation of peasants and of the countryside—the available quantitative official information neither allows for a complete analysis nor a thorough examination of more detailed aspects. The main evaluations of PROCEDE, using data from 1994 and 1997 (de Janvry, Gordillo, and Sadoulet 1997, 1998) and in 2001 (Deininger et al. 2001; Lavadenz and Deininger 2001) using privileged information inaccessible to the public, have been written from the perspective of the reform's planners and promoters, with very little self-criticism. The independent studies that address particular aspects of PROCEDE, such as those of Appendini (2001) and others, published in the magazine *Estudios Agrarios*, or the study coordinated by Concheiro and Roberto Diego (2001), which explain PROCEDE's impact on the land market through case studies, have been used as this paper's main secondary sources of information.

2. And 65 percent of the country's forests are property of ejidos and indigenous communities. Gonzalez Pacheco (1981), cited in Merino (2001).

3. A 75 percent quorum is necessary for making the decision to privatize, but this number is reduced to 50 percent if the matter is taken to a second or third assembly. Once the legal quorum is reached, only 50 percent plus one, among members of an ejido, is required to permit privatization.

4. Material in this section is taken from *Estructura Agraria* based on information generated by PROCEDE through July 1996. The data pertain to more than 725,000 ejidatarios from 10,000 ejidos, which represent 20.5 percent of the coun-

try's ejidatarios and 37.5 percent of the ejidos. PROCEDE's results attest to the agrarian diversity that is present in the countryside, given that it has information of at least one certified ejido in each of the 1,448 municipalities, in the 196 Districts of Rural Development (DDR).

Chapter 9: The World Bank's Market-Based Land Reform in Brazil

1. The research was carried out by Francisco Amaro Alencar, Guiomar Germani, João Francisco de Souza, Paulo Roberto Faccion, and Romildo dos Santos Silva, who coordinated the survey of data and the drafting of state reports.

2. The study presents calculations of the potential number of beneficiaries of land reform done by several agents involved in the struggle: in 1971, José Gomes da Silva estimated there were 2.43 million families; the 1985 PNRA proposal put the number between 6 and 7 million families; and in 1993 the MST estimated there were 3.039 million families that would be potential beneficiaries of land reform.

3. Under pressure from social movements and from international public opinion, the present government created the Ministry of Agrarian Development (MDA) and implemented a settlement policy that granted land to approximately 240,000 families in the course of four years, according to official data, although this figure is contested by rural social movements.

4. These funds, worth €218.2 million, were approved through the project appraisal document under the title Land-Based Poverty Alleviation Project I.

5. *Cédula* loans are composed of two subprojects, one with funds to purchase land (SAT) and the other to implant community social infrastructure (SIC). The latter uses World Bank grant funds for community projects, meaning that the families are not obliged to pay—but since it is a loan, Brazil has to pay the World Bank.

6. This imposition of collective areas was not observed in projects studied in the state of Ceará. On the contrary, collective areas were created by the decisions of families that acquired land through the Cédula da Terra program (as in the case of land reform settlements) and that included a cultural element in the organization of their projects.

7. In addition to organizing production (through division of land into individual lots and collective areas), the implementing agencies impose a certain form of social organization by building *agrovilas* (with houses not located on the lots as peasants are accustomed) to facilitate (make cheaper) the building of infrastructure (electric power, roads, schools, etc.).

Chapter 10: Gender and Land

1. The lengthier original version of this chapter, with a fuller treatment of institutional politics, is available online in Spanish and English at www.landaction.org.

2. This section is based primarily on Desmarais 2003a. Currently, La Via Campesina brings together close to 150 organizations from eight regions: Africa, Central America, North America, South America, the Caribbean, South Asia, Northeast and Southeast Asia, and Europe. Each region elects two representatives,

a woman and a man, to La Via Campesina's International Coordinating Committee, the executive organ of the movement, in addition to the International Operative Secretary.

3. It could be said that food sovereignty is a political concept, while the right to food is a juridical concept. For a detailed comparison of these two concepts, see Windfuhr and Jonsén 2005.

4. For an account of the GCAR and its principal forms of action, see Borras 2004a.

5. The GCAR has been supported by the Land Research Action Network (LRAN) since the year 2000. Recently, LRAN and the GCAR have intensified their cooperation, through the representation of GCAR staff within LRAN and vice versa.

6. The Emergency Network is one of the main instruments of the GCAR for promoting solidarity with all peasant women and men who are victims of human rights violations. The Network intervenes internationally with letters of protest when peasant groups suffer violations of their right to food or their civil rights due to their struggle for land. The Network comprises members of La Via Campesina, sections and coordinating offices of FIAN, and organizations and people who sympathize with the GCAR. See FoodFirst Information and Action Network and La Via Campesina 2003b.

7. Land administration policies cadastre, registry, demarcation, entitlement, etc., enforced in the past few years with the endorsement of the World Bank, have not contributed to a higher degree of security in the tenancy of land by women or poor rural communities. On the contrary, in many cases such policies have made them more vulnerable to the loss of their land. In order to fully understand the effects of these land administration policies, it is necessary to analyze them in conjunction with agrarian and agricultural policies and with the general macroeconomic context; what we then observe is that with the promise of regularizing, formalizing, and making the tenancy of land more secure, processes of land entitlement were initiated—in most cases on an individual basis—while, simultaneously, agrarian commerce was liberalized and the state began to dismantle its support services for small- and medium-scale agriculturalists. The consequent bankruptcy of many farmers, who had counted on title deeds now alienable and subject to embargo, allowed creditor banks to keep those lands. In other cases, adverse conditions for the peasant family economy, the impossibility of producing, and, concomitantly, the dramatic deterioration of living conditions have forced many peasants to sell their lands to large agro-exporters to have a few ephemeral pesos in their pockets. On the effects of titling programs, see El-Ghonemy 2001 and chapter 6 in this volume.

8. The Cochabamba Declaration picked up this debate in the following form: "During the last few years women's movements have achieved in some countries a formal advancement in terms of gender equity within policies of access to land, which shaped processes of constitutional and legal reform. However, the neoliberal policies that unleashed processes of reconcentration of lands and resources in

few hands pulverized this achievement. We observed that in many cases formal advancements in gender equity tend to benefit middle-class women; thus the importance of understanding how race, class, ethnicity, and gender combine to impede the fulfillment of our rights, as poor, indigenous, peasant, and black women" (FoodFirst Information and Action Network and La Via Campesina 2003b).

9. In Colombia, for example, "peasant reserves" are a particular form of land tenancy inspired by the experience of indigenous peoples. The 2002 Proyecto de Ley 107, drafted by peasant organizations to promote new policies for agrarian reform and the reconstruction of the agrarian sector, sought to strengthen and broaden peasant reserves as a central element of that strategy.

10. The Cochabamba Declaration states in this respect: "The human right to land and to feed oneself is a consecrated right of every woman and man. To guarantee women's access to and control over land we will struggle for the coownership of land, or the individual guarantee to the man and the woman, be it within collective/communal or individual forms of land tenancy. The effective guarantee of women's access to land has to address legal, institutional, cultural, and structural exclusion mechanisms."

11. The Movimiento de Mujeres Campesinas de Brasil (MMC), for example, has developed a clear vision of gender, class, and popular project (see Movimiento de Mujeres Campesinas de Brasil 2004).

12. Agarwal pinpoints four basic concepts regarding the importance of gender and the right to land: efficiency, welfare, equality, and empowerment (Agarwal 1994). Different authors emphasize and elaborate on one or another justification.

13. The International Covenant on Economic, Social and Cultural Rights, for example, demands that states apply basic criteria in the observance of economic, social, and cultural rights. Among these criteria are the immediate guarantee of the core content of rights. In the case of the right to food, the core content is to be free from hunger, nondiscrimination, the participation of affected groups in the design of public policies, the obligation to identify and protect vulnerable groups, the use of maximum available resources to meet rights obligations, and the obligation of progressiveness as opposed to retrogressiveness in the observance of rights. Based on these criteria, it could be demanded that the state identify sex-specific need for land; that it draft, with the real and effective participation of those affected, an agrarian reform plan with verifiable goals of how many women and men will be provided land within what period of time; and that it create independent monitoring mechanisms and organizations to keep vigilance over the implementation of the programs, guaranteeing the equal participation of women in those organisms.

14. In the opinion of the Italian jurist, Luigi Ferrajoli, "[. . .] the simultaneous crisis of the state of rights the welfare state, and the nation state today requires a rethinking of the bases of constitutionalism, that is, of the bases of the rigid guarantees imposed constitutionally on all powers in defense of fundamental rights.

It is true that historically the guarantees of these rights were born into and, until now, have remained bound to the form [. . .] of the sovereign state as 'the state of rights.' But this historical nexus between state and fundamental rights is contingent, because the paradigm of the state of rights as guarantor is applicable to any legal code. This crisis can be overcome in a progressive sense only if the seats of constitutional guarantees are transferred to the new political and decisional seats, and the entire system of legal sources is correlatively reformed, reinforcing local autonomies with an inversion of the hierarchy of legal sources that guarantees the system's primacy with respect to that of the state; democratizing and subjecting to new constitutional bonds the various seats of international power; placing the guarantees of fundamental rights at the summit of the entire system of legal sources, and therefore definitively withdrawing them from the market as well as from politics—local, state, international[. . .]" (Ferrajoli 1999; author's translation).

Part Three: Introduction

1. Henry Seragih (Indonesian Federation of Peasant Unions (FSPI), personal communication, 2005.

2. João Pedro Stédile, MST leader, personal communication, 2003.

Chapter 13: Land for People Not for Profit in Venezuela

1. Chavez launched this commission with Decree 3,408.

2. www.viacampesina.org

Chapter 14: Learning to Participate: The MST Experience in Brazil

1. Particularly important, among the literature that examines the significance and the viability of Brazilian land reform in that period, are the works that reflect the dynamics of the debate among intellectuals and worker leaders (Carvalho and da Conceição D'incao 1982; CONTAG 1982; Figueredo 1984). During the so-called Nova Republica (New Republic), this debate intensified and the Campanha Nacional da Reforma Agraria (National Campaign for Agrarian Reform, or CNRA) was organized to coordinate the proposals and the popular mobilizations (CNRA 1987).

2. The UDR, the Brazilian rural entrepreneurs' organization, was created in 1986 (Bruno 1987). Due to its violent methods, such as using hired gunmen and maintaining a private army to defend the rural property, it lost its political support in the 1990s. Its leader, Ronaldo Caiado, made a weak impression as a candidate in the 1990 presidential election.

3. Meetings start and end with the MST hymn and popular songs about the struggle for land, the alliance with the proletariat, and women's participation. Before making decisions, members sometimes dramatize or draw "pictures of life," and they use seeds to indicate their approval of statutes or to elect representatives, rather than raising their hands.

Chapter 15: Regional Impacts of Land Reform in Brazil

1. This chapter summarizes some of the results of the study *Os impacts regionais da reform agrária: um estudo sobre areas selecionadas* (The regional impacts of land reform: A study on selected areas), carried out from January 2000 through December 2001, by CPDA/UFRRJ and Nuap/PPGAS/MN/UFRJ, with the financial support of Nead and IICA (Heredia et al. 2002). The study was headed by Beatriz Heredia (IFCS/UFRJ), Leonilde Servolo de Medeiros (CPDA/UFRRJ), Moacir Palmeira (Nuap/PPGAS/MN/UFRJ), Sérgio Leite (CPDA/UFRRJ), and Rosângela Cintrão. The summary, on which this article is based, was prepared by Rosângela Cintrão and John Comerford, under the orientation of the project coordinators, and can be found at www.nead.gov.br.

2. The zones were also chosen taking into account the data from previous studies on the settlement projects, as well as the fact that there already are teams who have experience with studies on these regions. We avoided the regions already covered in the study *Impactos regionais dos assentamentos rurais: dimensões econômicas, políticas e sociais* (Regional impacts of rural settlements: Economic, political and social dimensions), which included the states of Acre, Mato Grosso, Rio de Janeiro, Rio Grande do Sul, São Paulo, and Sergipe (Medeiros and Leite 2002). The coordinators of the regional teams were Aloísio Lopes Melo (Southeastern Para), Ana Cláudia Silva and Rodrigo de Ávila (Southern Bahia), José Ambrósio Ferreira Neto (Federal District and surrounding areas), César Barreira and Francisco Amaro de Alencar (Ceará Sertão), Emília de Rodat Moreira and Marilda Menezes (Northeastern Sugarcane Region), and Renato Maluf (Western Santa Catarina).

3. The choice of which municipalities would be studied in each zone was made with consideration of the fact that the sample should cover 10 percent of the settler families in each municipality and that 100 to 300 questionnaires should be administered in each zone, so that the final count for all zones should not be too much more than 1,500 questionnaires, representing 15,000 families settled there between 1985 and 1997.

4. A profile was drawn up for each settlement project to collect general information on the settlements. Not all projects implemented in a given state between 1985 and 1997 were included in the application of the questionnaires. Nonetheless, the sample of questionnaires covers 10 percent of the families settled in all of the projects. An ample questionnaire was administered to the person responsible for each plot of land (i.e., the person managing it; usually the head of the household, regardless of whether or not he or she was legally the owner). This ensured that each questionnaire represented one production family unit. The study also used qualitative interviews, with representatives of different local and regional institutions; geographic data; technical reports; and secondary data statistical sources.

5. Besides these, there was one case, in the Abelardo Luz Municipality (SC), in which the expropriation request initiative was taken by the local authorities, with no prior conflicts.

6. The only exception is the Western Santa Catarina zone, where many of the settlers used to live in other parts of the same state (29 percent), which may be

explained by the singularities of the struggle for the land in that region. In Federal District and Southeastern Pará there is a large percentage of settlers who were born in other states, which probably indicates that the settlements are receiving populations that had resulted from previous migrations. The lowest numbers of plot holders who used to live in rural areas are to be found in Federal District (62 percent) and Southern Bahia (66 percent) zones.

7. These figures represent the total number of working-age settlers, and therefore include both the plot holders and the other family members over the age of 14 at the time the settlement projects were created. The category "unpaid family members" includes people who worked with their parents (or other relatives), family farmers, and housewives.

8. Only plots inhabited by families with children are considered here.

9. The percentages of other relatives who lived in urban areas before going to the settlements were 52 percent in the zone of Federal District and surrounding areas, 42 percent in Southern Bahia, around 30 percent in the Sugarcane Region, 33 percent in Santa Catarina, and 22 percent in Ceará.

10. One good example occurred in the municipality of Paracatu, in the state of Minas Gerais: In 1996, before the settlements existed, there were 500 farms with an area smaller than 50 hectares (31.57 percent of the total number of farms and 1.8 percent of the total area). Adding to these figures the number and area of settlements established up to 1999, all of which stemmed from the dismemberment of properties larger than 1,000 hectares, we will observe an increase of 239.8 percent in the number of farms and of 400.48 percent in the total area, bringing their participation in the total overall number of farms in that municipality up to 52.52 percent of all farms and 7.39 percent of the area occupied by farms.

11. Another way of analyzing the impact of the settlements on land distribution would be to use the Gini-coefficient, which is a specific indicator. One of the greatest problems with using this indicator was the lapse between the last land census (1995–1996) and the period in which most of the settlements in the studied zones were established.

12. The idea was to establish a parallel between the rural settlement implementation process and the impact on the demographic and migratory dynamics in the studied regions, based on the population census analyses. However, this was met with difficulties because there was the risk of attributing to the settlements effects that would have occurred anyway or, inversely, of denying any participation of the settlements in the demographic changes because of the ampler dynamics presented.

13. These figures are, in fact, even worse, considering the dates on which the families effectively entered the project areas: then the average time until the development credit was received was four years after and the housing loans, five years. The figures for Western Santa Catarina considerably lowered the averages, perhaps because the farmers there had a greater capacity to exert pressure.

14. The longest average distances are in Federal District zones and surrounding areas (45 kilometers) and in Southeastern Pará (40 kilometers), but in the lat-

ter it takes much longer to get to the city (90 minutes versus 66 minutes for Federal District and surrounding areas).

15. In only four cases in the entire sample was a daily presence of doctors in the settlements reported. In most of the cases, they were reported to come in a few times a week; in seven settlements, once a month. The doctors who come in are usually general practitioners. In two cases isolated specialists were mentioned; one gynecologist and one pediatrician. Only one of the settlements (in the municipality of Goiana, in Pernambuco) enjoyed a full medical team, including general practitioner, pediatrician, gynecologist, and dentist.

16. Including those who only worked elsewhere and those who worked both on the plot and elsewhere.

17. Other reasons for departure included getting married (35 percent), going away for study (18 percent); the rest left for reasons due to health problems or to conflicts with the family or other settlers.

18. The GP was calculated by multiplying the total reported production by the prices in the different regions. It is an approximation, for not all of the products are sold, and the prices effectively charged by the settlers are not always the same as those in the rest of the region.

19. The GP for all animal products but milk and eggs could not be calculated because there were not enough data available for the year prior to the field study.

20. The data were extracted from the 1996 farming census and the PAM/PPM (Municipal Farming Study and Municipal Livestock Study, respectively), both conducted by the IBGE. There is a lapse between the years the data were collected (on the different harvests) and the IBGE census and sample studies. The latter are not specific enough regarding data on the settlements.

21. In the Pará zone, the significant participation of the total settlement area coupled to innovations and changes brought about by the settlements resulted in an important impact on the regional productive profile. Besides diversification and an increase in the offer of products for the local markets (including basic items such as rice, beans, cassava, and corn, for pork and poultry feed, as well as vegetables, fruit, poultry, forest products, and animal products), the settlers were responsible for the implementation of agro-industrial units that produced for the local markets (rice and dairy processing) and for the regional and national markets (dairy products, meat, and pineapple concentrate).

22. The productivity of each product was compared in each zone and in each municipality (by number of settlers who produce them, sell them, and consider them important, and by the product's participation in the GP), in a total 146 cases.

23. There are differences between zones: in the Ceará Sertão, 83 percent of the families received credit (however, this zone had the lowest average credit: 553.81 reals); in Southern Bahia only 43 percent of the families received credit (the average amount was 1,608.14 reals). The highest average amounts were received in Pará: 5,698.00 reals.

24. One example is a regional cooperative run with the help of the MST in Western Santa Catarina, in which commercial, credit, and agro-industrial activities

(for example, long-lasting milk) have great importance for the settlers' economic prospects.

25. Given the complexity involved in calculating the income per plot in a study such as this one (with an early deadline, large span of research, and in which income was just one of the elements analyzed), and in order not to make the questionnaire too long, it was decided that only items produced, items sold, and overall production would be asked. No data were collected on the amount sold, on the actual price charged during each season of the year in question, nor on production costs. Since the amount sold is the same as the total production, plot income (or income generation capacity) was calculated based on the average local prices (based on secondary statistics sources, such as the PAM/PPM). On one hand, this resulted in an overrated income estimate, since the entire production is not always sold (especially in the case of products that are both commercial and subsistence products) when calculating gross income (as production costs are not considered). On the other, there was an underrated estimate of income potential because products that are exclusively for subsistence were included, which balances out the end result.

Chapter 16: Conclusion.
Moving Forward: Agrarian Reform as a Part of Food Sovereignty

1. João Pedro Stédile, MST leader, personal communication, 2003.

References

Acosta, J. 1972. Las leyes de reforma agraria en Cuba y el sector privado campe-sino. *Revista Economía y Desarrollo* 12.

Adams, Martin. 2000. *Breaking Ground: Development Aid for Land Reform*. London: Overseas Development Institute.

Agarwal, Bina. 1994. *A Field of One's Own: Gender and Land Rights in South Asia*. Cambridge: Cambridge University Press.

———. 2003. Gender and Land Rights Revisited: Exploring New Prospects via the State, Family and Markets. In Razavi 2003a.

Agencia EFE. 2000. More have died in Brazil land struggle than at dictators' hands. Wire story. September 6.

Akram Lodhi, Haroon. 2004. Are landlords taking back the land: An essay on the agrarian transition of Vietnam. *European Journal of Development Research* 16 (2): 757–789.

———. 2005. Vietnam's agriculture: Processes of rich peasant accumulation and mechanisms of social differentiation. *Journal of Agrarian Change* 5 (1): 73–116.

Altieri, Miguel. 1996. *Agroecology: The Science of Sustainable Agriculture*. Boulder, CO: Westview Press.

Altieri, Miguel, Peter Rosset, and Lori Ann Thrupp. 1998. The Potential of Agroecology to Combat Hunger in the Developing World. Food First Policy Brief no. 2. Oakland, CA: Institute for Food and Development Policy.

ANAP. 1997. Promoción productiva agroecológica de *campesino a campesino*. Proyecto de Cooperación al Desarrollo ANAP-Pan para el Mundo, CUB-9710-004. Dirección de Cooperación ANAP (October).

Appendini, Kirsten. 2001. *Land regularization and conflict resolution: The case of Mexico*. Food and Agriculture Organization of the United Nations, www.fao.org/REGIONAL/LAmerica/prior/desrural/tenencia/pdf/mexico.pdf.

Asociación para el Avance de las Ciencias Sociales. 2001. *Regiones y Zonas*

Agrarias de Guatemala: Una visión desde la reproducción social y económica de los campesinos. Guatemala City: AVANCSO.

Aspinal, Edward. 2004. Indonesia: Transformation of Civil Society and Democratic Breakthrough. In *Civil Society and Political Change in Asia*, ed. M. Alagappa, 61–96. Stanford: Stanford University Press.

Balisacan, A. M. 2002. Pathways to Sustained Poverty Alleviation: Agrarian Reform Communities and Beneficiaries and the New Economic Paradigm. Agrarian Reform Communities Development Project. Washington DC: The World Bank.

Bamford, C. C. 2000. Micro Credit Equals Micro Debt. In *The Transfer of Wealth: Debt and the Making of a Global South.* Bangkok: Focus on the Global South, www.focusweb.org/content/blogsection/20/30/9/9/.

Banerjee, Abhijit V. 1999. Land Reforms: Prospects and Strategies. Paper prepared for the annual bank conference on development economics, Washington, DC; MIT Department of Economics Working Paper no. 99-24, Social Science Research Network, http://ssrn.com/abstract=183711.

Baranyi, Stephen, Carmen Diana Deere, and Manuel Morales. 2004. *Scoping Study on Land Policy Research in Latin America.* Ottawa: The North-South Institute; International Development Research Centre.

Barraclough, Solon L. 1999. Land Reform in Developing Countries: The Role of State and Other Actors. Discussion Paper no. 101, United Nations Research Institute for Social Development, Geneva.

———. 2001. The Role of the State and Other Actors in Land Reform. In Ghimire 2001a, 26–64.

Barret, Christopher B. 1993. On Price Risk and the Inverse Farm Size–Productivity Relationship. Staff Paper Series no. 369, Department of Agricultural Economics, Univ. of Wisconsin–Madison.

Barrios, Lina. 1996. *La Alcaldía Indígena en Guatemala: Época Colonial (1500-1821).* Guatemala City: Instituto de Investigaciones Económicas y Sociales, Universidad Rafael Landivar.

Barros, Flavia, Sérgio Sauer, and Stephan Schwartzman, eds. 2003. *The Negative Impacts of World Bank Market-Based Land Reform.* São Paolo: Comissao Pastoral da Terra (CPT) / Movimento dos Trabalhadores Rurais Sem Terra (MST) / FoodFirst Information and Action Network (FIAN).

Bello, Walden. 1994. *Dark Victory: The United States, Structural Adjustment, and Global Poverty.* With Shea Cunningham and Bill Rau. Transnational Institute Series. xii, 148. London: Pluto Press in association with the Institute for Food and Development Policy and Transnational Institute (TNI).

Bello, Walden, with Marissa de Guzman. 2001. Why Land Reform Is No Longer Possible Without Revolution. In *The Future in the Balance: Essays on Globalization and Resistance*, 192–99. Quezon City: University of the Philippines Press.

Berger, Susan. 1992. *Political and Agrarian Development in Guatemala.* Boulder, CO: Westview Press.

Bernstein, Henry. 1998. Social change in the South African countryside? Land and production, poverty and power. *Journal of Peasant Studies* 25 (4): 1–32.

———. 2002. Land reform: Taking a long(er) view. *Journal of Agrarian Change* 2 (4): 433–63.

———. 2003. Land reform in southern Africa in world-historical perspective. *Review of African Political Economy* 30 (96): 203–26.

———. 2004. Changing before our very eyes: Agrarian questions and the politics of land in capitalism today. *Journal of Agrarian Change* 4 (1–2): 190–225.

Berry, R. Albert, and William R. Cline. 1979. *Agrarian Structure and Productivity in Developing Countries*. Baltimore: Johns Hopkins University Press.

Besley, Timothy, and Robin Burgess. 2002. Land reform, poverty reduction and growth: Evidence from India. *Quarterly Journal of Economics* 115 (May): 389–430.

Binswanger, Hans P. 1996. The Political Implications of Alternative Models of Land Reform and Compensation. In van Zyl, Kirsten, and Binswanger 1996, 139–46.

Binswanger, Hans P., and Klaus Deininger. 1996. South African Land Policy: The Legacy of History and Current Options. In van Zyl, Kirsten and Binswanger, 1996, 64–103.

———. 1997. Explaining Agricultural and Agrarian Policies in Developing Countries. Paper presented at the FAO Technical Consultation of Decentralization and Rural Development, Rome, December 16–18.

Binswanger, Hans P., Klaus Deininger, and Gershon Feder. 1995. Power, Distortions, Revolt and Reform in Agricultural Land Relations. In *Handbook of Development Economics*. Vol. 3B. Ed. J. Behrman and T. N. Srinivasan. Amsterdam: Elsevier Science BV.

Bobrow-Strain, Aaron. 2004. (Dis)accords: The politics of market-assisted land reforms in Chiapas, Mexico. *World Development* 32 (6): 887–903.

Bond, Patrick. 2000. *Elite Transition: From Apartheid to Neoliberalism in South Africa*. London and South Africa: Pluto Press and University of Natal.

Boone, Catherine. 1998. State-building in the African countryside: Structure and politics at the grassroots. *Journal of Development Studies* 34 (4): 1–31.

Borras, Saturnino Jr. 2001. State-society relations in land reform implementation in the Philippines. *Development and Change* 32 (3): 545–75.

———. 2002. Toward a better understanding of market-led agrarian reform in theory and practice: Focusing on the Brazilian case. *Land Reform, Land Settlements and Cooperatives* 1: 33–50.

———. 2003a. Inclusion-exclusion in public policies and policy analyses: The case of Philippine land reform, 1972–2002. *Journal of International Development* 15 (8): 1049–65.

———. 2003b. Questioning market-led agrarian reform: Experiences from Brazil, Colombia and South Africa. *Journal of Agrarian Change* 3 (3): 367–94.

———. 2003c. Questioning the pro-market critique of state-led agrarian reform. *European Journal of Development Research* 15 (2): 105–28.

———. 2004a. Rethinking Redistributive Land Reform: Struggles for Land and Power in the Philippines. PhD diss., Institute of Social Studies, The Hague.

———. 2004b. La Via Campesina: An Evolving Transnational Social Movement. Transnational Institute Briefing Series no. 6. Amsterdam: TNI, www.tni.org.

———. 2005. Can redistributive reform be achieved via market-based land transfer schemes? Lessons and evidence from the Philippines. *Journal of Development Studies* 41 (1): 90–134.

Borras, Saturnino Jr., and Jennifer C. Franco. 2005. Struggles for land and livelihood: Redistributive reform in agribusiness plantations in the Philippines. *Critical Asian Studies* 37 (3).

Borras, Saturnino Jr., Cristobal Kay, and Haroon Akram Lodhi. 2005. Property Rights Reforms and State-Society Interaction for Poverty Eradication and Development: Historical Overview and Alternative Perspectives. ISS/UNDP Land, Poverty, and Public Action Policy Paper no. 1, Institute of Social Studies, The Hague, www.iss.nl/land/.

Borras, Saturnino Jr., Ricardo Reyes, and Danilo Carranza. 2005. Land, Poverty, and State-Society Interaction in the Philippines. ISS/UNDP Land, Poverty, and Public Action Policy Paper no. 5, Institute of Social Studies, The Hague, www.iss.nl/land/.

Boyce, James K., Peter Rosset, and Elizabeth A. Stanton. 2005. Land Reform and Sustainable Development. Working Paper no. 98, Political Economy Research Institute, University of Massachusetts at Amherst.

Branford, Sue, and Jan Rocha. 2002. *Cutting the Wire: The Story of the Landless Movement in Brazil*. London: Latin America Bureau.

Bratton, Michael. 1990. Ten Years After Land Redistribution in Zimbabwe, 1980–1990. In *Agrarian Reform and Grassroots Development: Ten Case Studies*, ed. R. Prosterman, M. Temple, and T. Hanstad, 265–91. Boulder, CO / London: Lynne Rienner Publishers.

Brits, A-M., C. Grant, and T. Burns. 2002. Comparative Study of Land Administration Systems with Special Reference to Thailand, Indonesia and Karnataka (India). Draft report for Regional Workshops on Land Policy Issues, Asia Program. Washington DC: The World Bank.

Brockett, Charles D. 1998. *Land, Power, and Poverty: Agrarian Transformation and Political Conflict in Central America*. 2nd ed. Boulder, CO: Westview Press.

Brown, Richard. 1988. *Modernization: The Transformation of American Life 1600–1865*. Prospect Heights, IL: Waveland Press.

Bruno, Regina. 1987. UDR: para além da violência. *Tempo e Presenca/CEDI* 221 (June).

Bryant, Coralie. 1996. Strategic change through sensible projects. *World Development* 24 (9): 1539–50.

———. 1998. Property rights for the rural poor: The challenge of landlessness. *Journal of International Affairs* 52 (1): 181–205.

Buainain, Antônio Márcio, José Maria Silveira, Marcelo Marques de Magalhães, Rinaldo Artes, and Hildo Meirelles Souza Filho (Economista Agrícola). 1999.

Avaliação preliminar do Cédula da Terra. Mimeograph, Campinas: Núcleo de Estudos Agrários e Desenvolvimento Rural (NEAD) (June 7).

Burns, Tony, Bob Eddington, Chris Grant, and Ian Lloyd. 1996. Land Titling Experience in Asia. Prepared for the International Conference on Land Tenure and Administration, Orlando, Florida, November.

Bush, Ray, ed. 2002. *Counter-Revolution in Egypt's Countryside: Land and Farmers in the Era of Economic Reform*. London: Zed Books.

Byres, Terence J. 1974. Land Reform, Industrialization and the Marketed Surplus in India: An Essay on the Power of Rural Bias. In *Peasants, Landlords and Governments: Agrarian Reform in the Third World*, ed. D. Lehmann. New York: Holmes and Meier Publishers.

———. 1996. *Capitalism from Above and Capitalism from Below*. London: Macmillan.

———. 2004a. Introduction: Contextualizing and interrogating the GKI case for redistributive land reform. *Journal of Agrarian Change* 4 (1–2): 1–16.

———. 2004b. Neo-classical Neo-Populism 25 Years on: Déjà Vu and Déjà Passé: Towards a Critique. *Journal of Agrarian Change* 4 (1–2):17–44.

Caja Agraria.1998. *Informe al Comité de Revisión de la Ley 16* (May) .

Cambio para construir la paz. 1998. Plan Nacional de Desarrollo 1998–2000, Bases, 1998. Bogotá: Imprenta Nacional.

Cambranes, José C., ed. 1992. *500 Anos de Lucha por la Tierra: Estudios sobre propiedad rural y reforma agraria en Guatemala*. Guatemala City: FLACSO.

Carter, Michael R. 2000. Old Questions and New Realities: Land in Post-Liberal Economies. In *Current Land Policy in Latin America: Regulating Land Tenure Under Neo-Liberalism*, ed. A. Zoomers and G. van der Haar, 29–44. Amsterdam: Royal Tropical Institute (KIT).

Carter, Michael R., and Bradford L. Barham. 1996. Level playing fields and laissez faire: Postliberal development strategy in inegalitarian agrarian economies. *World Development* 24 (7): 1133–49.

Carter, Michael R., and Dina Mesbah. 1993. Can land market reform mitigate the exclusionary aspects of rapid agro-export growth? *World Development* 21 (7): 1085–1100.

Carter, Michael R., and Ramón Salgado. 2001. Land Market Liberalization and the Agrarian Question in Latin America. In *Access to Land, Rural Poverty, and Public Action*, ed. Alain de Janvry, Gustavo de Anda Gordillo, Jean-Philippe Platteau, and Elisabeth Sadoulet, 246–78. Oxford: Oxford University Press.

Castro, F. 1959. Discurso pronunciado en clausura del I Congreso Campesino. Havana, Cuba.

Chayanov, Alexander V. 1966. On the Theory of Non-Capitalist Economic Systems. In *The Theory of the Peasant Economy*, ed. Daniel Thorner, Basile Kerblay, and R.E.F. Smith. Homewood, IL: Richard D. Irwin.

Christodoulou, D. 1990. *The Unpromised Land: Agrarian reform and Conflict Worldwide*. London: Zed Books.

Clark, Christopher. 1990. *The Roots of Rural Capitalism: Western Massachusetts, 1780–1860*. Ithaca, NY: Cornell University Press.

Clunies-Ross, Tracy, and Nicholas Hildyard. 1992. *The Politics of Industrial Agriculture*. London: Earthscan.

Collins, Joseph, Frances Moore Lappé, and N. Allen. 1982. *What Difference Could a Revolution Make: Food and Farming in New Nicaragua*. San Francisco, CA: Institute for Food and Development Policy.

Concheiro Bohorquez, Luciano, and Roberto Diego Quintana. 2001. *Una perspectiva campesina del mercado de tierras ejidales: Siete esudios de caso*. Iztapalapa, Mexico: Casa Juan Pablos, UAM.

Cornelius, W., and D. Mhyre, eds. 1998. *The Transformation of Rural Mexico: Reforming the Ejido Sector*. La Jolla, CA: Center for US–Mexican Studies, University of California–San Diego.

Cornia, Giovanni Andrea. 1985. Farm Size, Land Yields and the Agricultural Production Function: An Analysis for Fifteen Developing Countries. *World Development* 13 (4): 513–34.

Corpuz, O. D. 1997. *An Economic History of the Philippines*. Quezon City: University of the Philippines Press.

Courville, Michael. 2005. Free Markets, Land Reform and Peasant Welfare: An Exploration of Rural Development in Honduras 1993–2004. Master's thesis, University of California, Berkeley.

Cousins, Ben. 1997. How do rights become real? Formal and informal institutions in South Africa's land reform. *IDS Bulletin* 28 (4): 59–67.

Daoas, David A. 1995. The rights of the cultural communities in the Philippines . . . Vines that won't Bind. . . . Conference proceedings. International work group for indigenous affairs (IWGIF) document. 80, 97–107, 102–103. Chiang Mai, Thailand.

Deere, Carmen Diana. 1985. Rural women and state policy: The Latin American agrarian reform experience. *World Development* 13 (9): 1037–53.

———. 2000. Towards a Reconstruction of Cuba's Agrarian Transformation: Peasantization, De-peasantization and Re-peasantization. In *Disappearing Peasantries?—Rural Labour in Africa, Asia and Latin America*, ed. D. Bryceson, C. Kay, and J. Mooij, 139–58. London: Intermediate Technology Publications.

Deere, Carmen Diana, and Magdalena León. 1999. *Mujer y Tierra en Guatemala*. Invited Author Series no. 4, Asociación para el Avance de las Ciencias Sociales, Guatemala City.

———. 2001a. *Empowering Women: Land and Property Rights in Latin America*. Pittsburgh and Bogotá: University of Pittsburgh Press.

———. 2001b. Who owns the land: Gender and land-titling programmes in Latin America. *Journal of Agrarian Change* 1(3): 446–67.

———. 2002. *Género, propiedad y empoderamiento: Tierra, estado y mercado en América Latina*. Mexico City, Quito: UNAM, FLACSO Ecuador.

Deere, Carmen Diana, and Leonilde Servolo de Medeiros. 2005. Agrarian Reform and Poverty Reduction: The Experience of Brazil. ISS/UNDP Land, Poverty, and Public Action Policy Paper no. 2, Institute of Social Studies, The Hague, www.iss.nl/land/.

de Guzman, Marissa, M. Garrido, and M. A. Manahan. 2004. Agrarian Reform: The Promise and the Reality. In *Anti-Development State: The Political Economy of Permanent Crisis in the Philippines*, ed. W. Bello, M. L. Malig, H. Docena, and M. de Guzman. Quezon City, Philippines: Focus on the Global South.

Deininger, Klaus W. 1995. Collective agricultural production: A solution for transition economies? *World Development* 23 (8):1 317–34.

———. 1999. Making negotiated land reform work: Initial experience from Colombia, Brazil and South Africa. *World Development* 27 (4): 651–72.

———. 2001. Negotiated land reform as one way of land access: experiences from Colombia, Brazil and South Africa. In de Janvry et al., 2001, chap. 13.

———. 2002. Agrarian reforms in Eastern European countries: Lessons from international experience. *Journal of International Development* 14 (7): 987–1003.

Deininger, Klaus W., and Hans Binswanger. 1999. The evolution of the World Bank's land policy: Principles, experience and future challenges. *The World Bank Research Observer* 14 (2): 247–76.

———. 2001. The Evolution of the World Bank's Land Policy. In de Janvry et al., 2001, chap. 17.

Deininger, Klaus W., and G. Feder. 1999. *Land Policy in Developing Countries*. Rural Development Note no. 3., Washington, DC, World Bank.

Deininger, Klaus W., G. Feder, Gustavo de Anda Gordillo, and P. Munro-Faure. 2003. Land Policy to Facilitate Growth and Poverty Reduction. In *Land Reform: Land Settlement and Cooperative*. Rome, Italy: Food and Agricultural Organization of the United Nations.

Deininger, Klaus W., Isabel Lavadenz, Fabrizio Bresciani, and Manuel Diaz. 2001. *Mexico's "Second Agrarian Reform": Implementation and Impact*. Washington DC: The World Bank.

Deininger, Klaus W., and J. May. 2000. Can There be Growth with Equity? An Initial Assessment of Land Reform in South Africa. World Bank Working Paper no. 2451, Washington DC.

Deininger, Klaus W., Roger van den Brink, Hans Hoogeveen, and Sam Moyo. 2000. How land reform can contribute economic growth and poverty reduction: Empirical evidence from international and Zimbabwean experience. Southern African Research Institute for Policy Studies (SARIPS).

Deininger, Klaus W., and the World Bank. 2003. *Land Policies for Growth and Poverty Reduction, A World Bank Policy Research Report*. Washington DC: The World Bank / Oxford and New York: Oxford University Press.

de Janvry, Alain. 1981. *The Agrarian Question and Reformism in Latin America*. Baltimore: John Hopkins University Press.

de Janvry, Alain, Gustavo de Anda Gordillo, and Elizabeth Sadoulet. 1997. *Mexico's Second Agrarian Reform: Household and Community Responses, 1990–1994*. La Jolla, CA: Center for US–Mexican Studies, University of California–San Diego.

———. 1998. *Access to Land and Land Policy Reforms*. La Jolla, CA: Center for US–Mexican Studies, University of California–San Diego.

de Janvry, Alain, Jean-Philippe Platteau, Gustavo de Anda Gordillo, and Elizabeth Sadoulet. 2001. Access to Land and Land Policy Reforms. In de Janvry et al., 2001.

de Janvry, Alain, Gustavo de Anda Gordillo, Jean-Philippe Platteau, and Elisabeth Sadoulet, eds. 2001. *Access to Land, Rural Poverty, and Public Action*. Oxford: Oxford University Press.

de Janvry, Alain, and Elizabeth Sadoulet. 1989. A study in resistance to institutional change: The lost game of Latin American land reform. *World Development* 13 (4): 513–34.

———. 2001. The Changing Role of the State in Latin American Land Reform. In de Janvry et al., 2001, 279–303.

Delahaye, Olivier. 2002. La discusión sobre la ley de tierras: Espejismos y realidades. *Revista SIC* (Caracas) no. 647 (August): 351–54, www.gumilla.org.ve/SIC/SIC2002/SIC647/SIC647_Delahaye.htm.

———. 2003. La privatización de la tenencia de la tierra. *Agroalimentaria* no. 16 (January–June).

de la Rosa, Romulo. 2005. Agrarian Reform Movement in Commercial Plantations: The Experience of the Banana Sector in Davao del Norte. In *On Just Grounds: Struggling for Agrarian Justice and Exercising Citizenship Rights in the Rural Philippines*, ed. J. Franco and S. Borras. Amsterdam: Transnational Institute, 45.

Denis, Roland. 2003. Interview with Roland Denis: To Destroy and to Reconstruct. The New State in Venezuela and the Popular Movement. By Raul Zelik, trans. Gregory Wilpert.Venezuelanalysis.com. September 3 2005, www.venezuelanalysis.com/articles.php?artno=1006.

Desmarais, Annette-Aurélie. 2003a. The Via Campesina: Peasants Resisting Globalization. PhD diss., Department of Geography, University of Calgary, Alberta.

———. 2003b. The Vía Campesina: Peasant Women on the Frontiers of Food Sovereignty. *Canadian Woman Studies/les cahiers de la femme* 23 (1): 140–45.

De Soto, Hernando. 2000. *The Mystery of Capital: Why Capitalism Triumphs in the West and Fails Everywhere Else*. New York: Basic Books.

Diskin, Martin. 1989. El Salvador: Reform Prevents Change. In *Searching for Agrarian Reform in Latin America*, ed. William C. Thiesenhusen. Boston: Unwin Hyman, 429–50.

Domínguez, M. I. 1990. *Diferencias y relaciones generacionales en el campesinado*. Havana: Centro de Investigaciones Psicológicas y Sociológicas.

Dorner, Peter. 1992. *Latin American Land Reforms in Theory and Practice: A Retrospective Analysis*. Madison, Wisconsin: Univ. of Wisconsin Press.

———. 2001. Technology and Globalization: Modern-Era Constraints on Local Initiatives for Land Reform. In Ghimire 2001a, 86–104.

Dovring, Folke. 1969. Land Reform and Productivity: The Mexican Case, Analysis of Census Data. Land Tenure Center Paper no. 63, Univ. of Wisconsin at Madison.

D'Souza, Gerard, and John Ikerd. 1996. Small farms and sustainable development: Is small more sustainable? *Journal of Agricultural and Applied Economics* 28 (1): 73–83.

Durrenberger, E. Paul, and Kendall M. Thu. 1996. The expansion of large-scale hog farming in Iowa: The applicability of Goldschmidt's findings fifty years later. *Human Organization* 55 (4): 409–15.

Economist Intelligence Unit (EIU). 2004. *Country Profile: Philippines*. www.store .eiu.com.

———. 2004. *Country Profile: Tanzania*. www.store.eiu.com.

El-Ghonemy, M. Riad. 1990. *The Political Economy of Rural Poverty: The Case for Land Reform*. New York: Routledge.

———. 2001. The Political Economy of Market-Based Land Reform. In Ghimire 2001a, 105–33.

Ellis, Frank. 1993. *Peasant Economics: Farm Households and Agrarian Development*, 2nd ed. Cambridge: Cambridge University Press.

Enríquez, Laura J. 1994. *The Question of Food Security in Cuban Socialism*. Berkeley: Institute of International and Area Studies, Univ. of California.

———. 2003. Economic reform and repeasantization in post-1990 Cuba. *Latin American Research Review* 38 (1): 202–18.

———. 2004. The Role of the Small Farmer in the Retreat From and the Reconfiguration of Socialism. Paper presented at the ninety-ninth meeting of the American Sociological Association, San Francisco, California.

Espinosa, E. 1997. La economía Cubana en los 1990: De la crisis a la recuperación. *Carta Cuba*. Havana: FLACSO / University of Havana.

ETC Group. 2001. Globalization, Inc. Concentration in corporate power: The unmentioned agenda. ETC Group Communique no. 71, www.etc.org.

European Commission. 1999. Agriculture and Rural Development Policy in Developing Countries. Phase I, Task A, Diagnostic Report. http://europa.eu/ index_en.htm.

Fajardo, Darío, and Héctor Mondragón, 1997. *Colonización y Estrategias de Desarrollo*. Bogotá: Inter-American Institute for Cooperation on Agriculture (IICA) / Ministerio del Ambiente/Instituto de Estudios Políticos y Relaciones Internacionales (IEPRI), Universidad Nacional de Colombia.

Feder, Ernest. 1970. Counterreform. In *Agrarian Problems and Peasant Movements in Latin America*, ed. Rodolfo Stavenhagen. New York: Anchor Books.

Feder, Gershon. 1985. The relationship between farm size and farm productivity. *Journal of Development Economics* 18:297–313.

Feder, Gershon, Tongroj Onchan, Yongyuth Chalamwong, and Chira Hongladarom. 1988. *Land Policies and Productivity in Thailand*. Baltimore: Johns Hopkins University Press.

Feranil, Salvador. 2005. Evolving Peasant Movements in the Negros Occidental. In Franco and Borras 2005.

Ferguson, James. 1990. *The Anti-Politics Machine: "Development," Depoliticization, and Bureaucratic Power in Lesotho*. Cambridge and New York: Cambridge University Press.

Ferrajoli, Luigi. 1999. *Derechos y garantías. La ley del más débil*. Madrid: Editorial Trotta.

Figueredo, Vilma, ed. 1984. *A questão da reforma agrária nos anos oitenta*. (April/ June). Rio de Janeiro: Tempo Brasileiro.

Figueroa, V. 1996. El nuevo modelo agrario en Cuba bajo los marcos de la Reforma Económica. *UBPC, Desarrollo rural y participación*. Havana: Colectivo de Autores.

Foley, Michael. 1997. Land and Peace in Postwar El Salvador: Structural Adjustment, Land Reform and Social Peace in the Salvadoran Countryside. Research for the Washington Office on Latin America (WOLA).

Food and Agriculture Organization of the United Nations. 1998. *Contemporary Thinking on Land Reforms*. Rome: FAO, Land Tenure Service in Rural Development Division.

———. 2001. *Plan de Acción sobre Género y Desarrollo (2002–07)*. 31 período de sesiones. C 2001/9.

FoodFirst Information and Action Network and La Via Campesina. 2002. *Informe de la misión investigadora a Bolivia*. La Paz: FIAN.

———. 2003a. Commentary on Land and Rural Development Policies of the World Bank. Heidelberg and Tegucigalpa: FIAN.

———. 2003b. *Declaración de Cochabamba*. Seminario Internacional sobre Reforma Agraria y Género. Campaña Global por la Reforma Agraria. Heidelberg and Tegucigalpa: FIAN/Campaña Global.

———. 2003c. Red de Emergencia No. 03–01, 03–03. Campaña Global por la Reforma Agraria. Heidelberg and Tegucigalpa: FIAN/Campaña Global.

———. 2004. *La reforma agraria en Brasil. Informe de la misión investigadora sobre el estado de la realización de la reforma agraria en tanto obligación de derechos humanos*. Heidelberg and Tegucigalpa: FIAN/Campaña Global.

Forero, Roberto. 1999. Evaluacion de Proyectos Piloto de Reforma Agraria en Colombia: Informe Preliminar, Junio 15 de 1999. Unpublished World Bank document, Washington DC.

Forster, Cindy. 1998. Reforging National Revolution: Campesino Labor Struggles in Guatemala, 1944–1954. In *Identity and Struggle at the Margins of the Nation State*, ed. Aldo Lauria-Santiago, 196–228. Durham: Duke University Press.

Fortin, Elizabeth. 2005. Reforming land rights: The World Bank and the globalisation of agriculture. *Social and Legal Studies* 14(2).

Fox, Jonathan. 1990. The challenge of rural democratisation: Perspectives from Latin America and the Philippines. *Journal of Development Studies* 26 (4): 143–62.

———. 1993. *The Politics of Food in Mexico: State Power and Social Mobilization*. Ithaca, NY: Cornell University Press.

———. 1994. The difficult transition from clientelism to citizenship: Lessons from Mexico. *World Politics* 46 (2): 151–84.

———. 1995. Governance and rural development in Mexico: State intervention and public accountability, *Journal of Development Studies* 32 (1): 1–30.

Franco, Jennifer. 1999. *Organizational Strength Appraisal of Organizations in Top Agrarian Reform Communities (ARCs)*. Quezon City: FAO.

———. 2000. *Agrarian Reform Communities and Rural Democratization in Quezon Province.* Quezon City: Institute for Popular Democracy/United Nations Development Programme-SARDIC Programme.

———. 2001. *Elections and Democratization in the Philippines.* New York: Routledge.

———. 2005. Making property rights accessible: Social movements and legal innovation in the Phillipines. Institute of Development Studies Working Paper no. 244.

Franco, Jennifer, and Saturnino Borras Jr., eds. 2005. *On Just Grounds: Struggling for Agrarian Justice and Exercising Citizenship Rights in the Rural Philippines.* Quezon City: Institute for Popular Democracy; Amsterdam: Transnational Institute.

Fraser, Nancy, and Axel Honneth. 2003. *Redistribution or Recognition? A Political-Philosophical Exchange.* London: Verso.

Freire, Paulo. 1983. *Extensão ou comunicacão,* 7th ed. Rio de Janeiro: Paz e Terra.

Friedmann, Harriet. 1982. The political economy of food: The rise and fall of the postwar international food order. *The American Journal of Sociology, Supplement: Marxist Inquiries; Studies of Labor, Class, and States* v88, S248–286.

Fujimoto, Isao. 1977. The Communities of the San Joaquin Valley: The Relationship between Scale of Farming, Water Use, and the Quality of Life. Testimony before the House Subcommittee on Family Farms, Rural Development, and Social Studies, Sacramento, CA. October 28.

Gadgil, Madhav. 1995. *Ecology and Equity: The Use and Abuse of Nature in Contemporary India.* New York: Routledge.

Ghimire, Krishna B., ed. 2001a. *Land Reform and Peasant Livelihoods: The Social Dynamics of Rural Poverty and Agrarian Reform in Developing Countries.* Geneva: United Nations Research Institute for Social Development/London: ITDG.

———. 2001b. Regional Perspectives on Land Reform: Considering the Role of Civil Society Organizations. In *Whose Land? Civil Society Perspectives on Land Reform and Rural Poverty Reduction: Regional Experiences from Africa, Asia and Latin America,* ed. Krishna B. Ghimire and Bruce H. Moore. Rome: United Nations Research Institute for Social Development.

———, ed. 2005. *Civil Society and the Market Question: Dynamics of Rural Development and Popular Mobilization.* London: Palgrave.

Ghose, Ajit Kumar, ed. 1983. *Agrarian Reform in Developing Countries: Issues of Theory and Problems of Practice.* London: Croom Helm/New York: St. Martin's Press.

GNAU (Grupo National de Agricultura Urbana). 2000. *Manual Técnico de Organopónicos y Huertos Intensivos.* Havana: ACTAF, INIFAT, MINAG.

Goldschmidt, Walter. 1978. *As You Sow: Three Studies in the Social Consequences of Agribusiness.* New York: Allenheld, Osmun.

Gómez, Alfredo Ramírez. 2001. Las comunidades indígenas: Entre la Ley Indígena y la Ley Agraria. Avances del PROCEDE en comunidades del Valle de Oaxaca 1996–2001. *Studios Agrarios* 18.

Gonzales, Gerardo. 1996. *En Busca del Horizonte*. Bogotá: Alekos Publicaciones.

Gordillo, Gustavo de Anda. 1997. The Reconstruction of Rural Institutions. Paper presented at the FAO Technical Consultation on Decentralisation and Rural Development, Rome.

Greenberg, Stephen. 2004. *The Landless People's Movement and the Failure of Post-Apartheid Land Reform*. Centre for Civil Society Research Reports Series, Durban: University of KwaZulu-Natal, School of Development Studies.

Griffin, Keith. 1976. *Land Concentration and Rural Poverty*. London: Macmillan Press.

————. 1980. Economic development in a changing world. *World Development* 9 (3): 221–26.

Griffin, Keith, Azizur Rahaman Khan, and Amy Ickowitz. 2002. Poverty and distribution of land. *Journal of Agrarian Change* 2 (July): 279–330.

————. 2004. In defence of neo-classical neo-populism. *Journal of Agrarian Change* 4 (3): 361–86.

Grindle, Merilee. 1986. *State and Countryside: Development Policy and Agrarian Politics in Latin America*. Baltimore: Johns Hopkins University Press.

Groppo, Paolo, H. M. Corrales, A. Hurtado, C. L. Vegro, J. K. Costa Pereira, L. C. de Aquino Pereira, M. L. Candido, and A. G. Marques. 1998. Avaliacão Sintètica do Projeto Cédula da Terra. Fortaleza-CE, Brazil: Convêvio FAO/INCRA.

Guanzirole, E. 2000. Agrarian Reform and Economic Globalization: The Case of Brazil. Paper presented at the 10th Congress of Rural Sociology, Rio de Janeiro, Brazil, July 30–August 5.

Guatemala. 1996. Presidencia de la Republica, Comisión de la Paz. Agreement on Socio-Economic Aspects and the Agrarian Situation (Acuerdo Sobre Aspectos Socioeconomicos y Situación Agrária) in Guatemalan Peace Accords. English translation.

Gutierrez, Eric, and Saturnino Borras Jr. 2004. The Moro Conflict: Landlessness and Misdirected State Policies. *Policy Studies Series* 8: 1–89. Washington, DC: East-West Center. www.eastwestcenterwashington.org.

Hall, Anthony. 1990. Land Tenure and Land Reform in Brazil. In *Agrarian Reform and Grassroots Development: Ten Case Studies*, ed. R. Prosterman, M. Temple, and T. Hanstad, 205–32. Boulder, CO: Lynne Rienner Publishers.

Hall, Ruth. 1998. Design for Equity: Linking Objectives with Practice in Land Reform. Proceedings of the International Conference on Land Tenure in the Developing World, University of Capetown, South Africa, January 27–29.

Handy, Jim. 1994. *Revolution in the Countryside: Rural Conflict and Agrarian Reform in Guatemala, 1944–1954*. Chapel Hill: University of North Carolina Press.

Harnecker, Marta. 2003. *Landless People: Building a Social Movement*. São Paulo: Editora Expressão Popular.

Harriss, John, ed. 1982. *Rural Development: Theories of Peasant Economy and Agrarian Change*. London: Routledge.

————. 1993. What is happening in rural West Bengal? Agrarian reform, growth and distribution. *Economic and Political Weekly* 28:1 237–47.

─────. 2002. *Depoliticizing Development: The World Bank and Social Capital.* London: Anthem Press.

Hart, Gillian. 2002. *Disabling Globalization: Places of Power in Post-Apartheid South Africa.* Berkeley: University of California Press.

Harvey, Neil. 1998. *The Chiapas Rebellion: The Struggle for Land and Democracy.* Durham, NC: Duke University Press.

Heath, John Richard. 1990. Enhancing the Contribution of Land Reform to Mexican Agricultural Development. Policy, Research, and External Affairs Working Paper no. 285, www-wds.worldbank.org/external/default/WDSContentServer/IW3P/IB/1990/02/01/000009265_3960928232451/Rendered/PDF/multi_page.pdf.

Heffernan, William. 1999. Consolidation in the Food and Agriculture System. Report to the National Farmers Union. Columbia: University of Missouri.

Hellinger, Douglas, Helen Hansen-Kuhn, and April Fehling. 2001. *Stripping Adjustment Policies of Their Poverty-Reduction Clothing: A New Convergence in the Challenge to Current Global Economic Management.* Washington, DC: Development Group for Alternative Policies (D-GAP), www.developmentgap.org/UN%20paper.pdf.

Henriques, Gisele, and Raj Patel. 2003. Agricultural Trade Liberalization and Mexico. Food First Policy Brief No. 7. Oakland, CA: Institute for Food and Development Policy.

Heredia, Beatriz, Leonilde Servolo de Medeiros, Moacir Palmeira, Sérgio Leite, and Rosângela Cintrão. 2002. *Os impactos regionais da reforma agrária: um estudo sobre áreas selecionadas (Regional impacts of land reform: A study on selected areas).* Mimeograph. Rio de Janeiro: CPDA/UFRRJ-Nuap/PPGAS/ UFRJ.

Heredia, Beatriz, Leonilde Servolo de Medeiros, Moacir Palmeira, Sérgio Leite, and Rosângela Cintrão. 2004. *An Analysis of the Regional Impacts of Land Reform in Brazil.* Brasília: Agrarian and Rural Development Studies Centre.

Hernández Alarcón, Rosalinda. 2000. *Problemática de la tierra reclama soluciones efectivas: (deuda histórica, capacidad de propuesta, negociaciones y participación social).* Guatemala: Inforpress Centroamericana.

Herring, Ronald J. 1983. *Land to the Tiller: The Political Economy of Agrarian Reform in South Asia.* New Haven: Yale University Press.

─────. 1990. Explaining Anomalies in Agrarian Reform: Lessons from South India. In *Agrarian Reform and Grassroots Development: Ten Case Studies,* ed. R. Prosterman, M. Temple, and T. Hanstad, 49–76. Boulder, CO: Lynne Rienner Publishers.

─────. 2000. Political Conditions for Agrarian Reform and Poverty Alleviation. Institute for Development Studies Discussion Papers no. 375.

─────. 2002. State Property Rights in Nature (With Special Reference to India). In *Land, Property, and the Environment,* ed. F. Richards, 263–97. Oakland, CA: Institute for Contemporary Studies.

─────. 2003. Beyond the Political Impossibility Theorem of Agrarian Reform. In *Changing Paths: International Development and the New Politics of Inclusion,* ed. P. Houtzager and M. Moore, 58–87. Ann Arbor, MI: University of Michigan Press.

Hirtz, Frank. 1998. The discourse that produces silence: Farmers' ambivalence toward land reform in the Philippines. *Development and Change* 29 (1) 247–75.

Hobsbawm, Eric J. 1994. *The Age of Extremes: The Short Twentieth Century 1914–1991*. London: Abacus.

Holt-Giménez, Eric. 2002. Measuring farmers' agroecological resistance after Hurricane Mitch in Nicaragua: A case study in participatory, sustainable land management impact monitoring. *Agriculture, Ecosystems and Environment* 93: 87–105.

Hough, Richard L., J. C. Kelly, S. Miller, D. DeRossier, and F. L. Mann. 1982. *Land and Labor in Guatemala: An Assessment.* Washington, DC: Agency for International Development, Development Associates, Inc.

Houtzager, Peter. 2000. Social movements amidst democratic transitions: Lessons from the Brazilian countryside. *Journal of Development Studies* 36 (5): 59–88.

Houtzager, Peter, and Jennifer Franco. 2003. When the Poor Make Law: Comparisons Across Brazil and the Philippines. Research Note, Law, Democracy, and Development Program, Institute of Development Studies, Sussex, England.

IFAD (International Fund for Agricultural Development). 2001. *Rural Poverty Report 2001: The Challenge of Ending Rural Poverty.* New York and Oxford: Oxford University Press.

IGAC (Instituto Geográfico Agustín Codazzi). 1998. *Suelos y Bosques de Colombia.* Bogotá, Colombia.

INE (Instituto Nacional de Estadística. 2003. *Encuesta Agropecuria Básica.* Tegucigalpa, Honduras: Instituto Nacional de Estadistica.

Jones, P. M. 1991. The "agrarian law": Schemes for land redistribution during the French Revolution. *Past and Present* 133: 96–133.

Jungmann, Raul. 1999. *Banco da Terra: Relatório de recomendações do Painel de Inspeção do Banco Mundial sobre o Projeto Piloto Cédula da Terra.* Brasília: Ministério do Desenvolvimento Agrário.

Kabeer, Naila. 1995. *Reversed Realities: Gender Hierarchies in Development Thought.* London: Verso.

Kanwerayotin, Supapohn. 2001. "Talking up the market in Thailand." *Far Eastern Economic Review.* 164(9): 51.

Karl, Terry Lynn. 1997. *The Paradox of Plenty: Oil Booms and Petro-States.* Berkeley, CA: University of California Press.

Katz, Elizabeth G. 2000. Social capital and natural capital: A comparative analysis of land tenure and natural resource management in Guatemala. *Land Economics* 76: 114–32.

Kautsky, Karl. 1988. *The Agrarian Question.* London: Zwan Publications.

Kay, Cristóbal. 1983. The Agrarian Reform in Peru: An Assessment. In *Agrarian Reform in Contemporary Developing Countries*, ed. Ajit Kumar Ghose, 185–239. London/New York: Croom Helm Ltd./St. Martins Press.

———. 1997. Globalisation, peasant agriculture and reconversion. *Bulletin of Latin American Research* 16 (1): 11–24.

———. 1998. Latin America's agrarian reform: Lights and shadows. *Land Reform, Land Settlements and Cooperatives*. 1998 (2): 9–31.

———. 2001. Reflections on rural violence in Latin America. *Third World Quarterly* 22 (5): 741–75.

———. 2002a. Chile's neoliberal agrarian transformation and the peasantry. *Journal of Agrarian Change* 2 (4): 464–501.

———. 2002b. Why East Asia overtook Latin America: Agrarian reform, industrialization and development. *Third World Quarterly* 23 (6): 1073–1102.

———. 2004. Rural Livelihoods and Peasant Futures. In *Latin America Transformed: Globalization and Modernity*, 2nd ed. Ed. R. Gwynne and C. Kay, 232–50. London: Arnold.

Kay, Cristóbal, and Patricio Silva, eds. 1992. *Development and Social Change in the Chilean Countryside: From the Pre-Land Reform Period to the Democratic Consolidation*. Amsterdam: CEDLA (Centro de Estudios y Documentación para América Latina).

Kelsey, Jane. 1995. *The New Zealand Experiment: A World Model for Structural Adjustment?* Auckland: Auckland University Press.

Kanwerayotin, Supapoh. 2001. "Talking up the market in Thailand." *Far Eastern Economic Review*. 164(9):51.

Kerkvliet, Benedict J. Tria. 1977. *The Huk Rebellion: A Study of Peasant Revolt in the Philippines*. Berkeley: University of California Press.

———. 1979. Land Reform: Emancipation or Counterinsurgency? In *Marcos and Martial Law in the Philippines*, ed. D. A. Rosenberg. Berkeley: University of California Press.

———. 1993. Claiming the land: Take-overs by villagers in the Philippines with comparisons to Indonesia, Peru, Portugal, and Russia. *Journal of Peasant Studies* 20 (3): 459–93.

Kerkvliet, Benedict J. Tria, and Mark Selden. 1998. Agrarian transformation in China and Vietnam. *The China Journal* 40 (July): 37–58.

Keynes, John M. 1958. *Teoría general de la ocupación, el interés y el dinero*. 5th ed. Mexico City: Fondo de Cultura Económica.

Kilusang Magbubukid ng Pilipinas (KMP). 2000. *The World Bank's Market-Assisted Land reform, Obstacle to Rural Justice* Philippines: KMP Research Desk.

King, Russell. 1977. *Land Reform: A World Survey*. London: B. Bell and Sons Ltd.

Kinsey, B. 2000. Allowing land reform to work in Southern Africa: A long-term perspective on rural restructuring in Zimbabwe. Unpublished manuscript.

Korovkin, Tanya. 2000. Weak weapons, strong weapons: Hidden resistance and political protest in rural Ecuador. *Journal of Peasant Studies* 27 (3): 1–29.

La Via Campesina. *See* Via.

Lage, C. 1996. Informe al IV Pleno del Partido Comunista de Cuba. *Granma* 26: 3.

Lahiff, Edward. 2003. Land Reform and Sustainable Livelihood in South Africa's Eastern Cape Province. Institute of Development Studies Research Paper no. 9. Brighton: IDS, University of Sussex, March.

Lahiff, Edward, and Ben Cousins 2001. The land crisis in Zimbabwe viewed from south of the Limpopo. *Journal of Agrarian Change* 1 (4): 652–66.

LAPC (Land and Agricultural Policy Centre). 1997. Land Reform in South Africa. Land and Agricultural Policy Centre. Johannesburg, South Africa.

Land Institute Foundation. 2000. Complete Report of the Project to Study Land Holdings, Land Utilisation, Economic Mechanisms and Laws for Optimally Efficient Land Use. Bangkok: National Research Office. In Thai only.

Langevin, Mark S., and Peter Rosset. 1999. "Land Reform from Below: The Landless Worker's Movement in Brazil." In *The Paradox of Plenty: Hunger in a Bountiful World*, ed. Douglas Boucher, 323–329. Oakland: Food First Books.

Lappé, Frances Moore, Joseph Collins, and Peter Rosset. 1998. *World Hunger: Twelve Myths*, 2nd ed. With Luis Esparza. New York: Grove Press.

Lara, Francisco Jr., and Horacio Morales Jr. 1990. The peasant movement and the challenge of democratisation in the Philippines. In The challenge of rural democratisation: Perspectives from Latin America and the Philippines, ed. J. Fox. *Journal of Development Studies* 26 (4):143–62.

Lastarria-Cornhiel, Susana, and Jolyne Melmed-Sanjak. 1998. *Land Tenancy in Asia, Africa and Latin America: A Look at the Past and a View to the Future.* Madison, WI: Land Tenure Center.

Lavadenz, I., and Klaus W. Deininger. 2001. *Mexico Land Policy a Decade After the Ejido Reform.* Report no. 22187 ME. Mexico City: The World Bank, Secretaría de Reforma Agraria.

Lehmann, David, ed. 1974. *Peasants, Landlords and Governments: Agrarian Reform in the Third World.* New York: Holmes and Meier Publishers.

Lemoine, Maurice. 2003. Venezuela: The promise of land for the people. *Le Monde Diplomatique* (October), http://mondediplo.com/2003/10/07venezuela.

Levin, Richard, and Daniel Weiner, eds. 1997. *Struggles for Land in Mpumalanga, South Africa.* Lawrenceville, NJ: Africa World Press.

Lewin, M. 1968. *Russian Peasants and Soviet Power: A Study of Collectivization.* New York: W.W. Norton and Company.

Lipton, Michael. 1974. Towards a Theory on Land Reform. In Lehmann 1974, 269–315.

———. 1993. Land reform as commenced business: The evidence against stopping. *World Development* 21 (4): 641–57.

Llanto, G. M., and M. M. Ballesteros. 2003. Land Issues in Poverty Reduction Strategies and the Development Agenda: The Philippines. In *Land Reform: Land Settlement and Cooperative.* Rome, Italy: FAO.

Lovell, W. George. 1988. Surviving conquest: The Maya of Guatemala in historical perspective. *Latin American Research Review* 23: 25–57.

Lucas, Anton, and Carol Warren. 2003. The state, the people and their mediators: The struggle over agrarian law reform in post new order Indonesia. *Indonesia* no. 76 (October).

Lund, Christian. 1998. *Law, Power and Politics in Niger: Land Struggles and the Rural Code.* Hamburg: LIT Verlag.

MacCannell, Dean. 1998. Industrial agriculture and rural community degradation. In *Agriculture and Community Change in the U.S.: The Congressional Research Reports*, ed. L. E. Swanson, 15–75. Boulder, CO: Westview Press.

Magdoff, Fred, John B. Foster, and Frederick H. Buttel, eds. 2000. *Hungry for Profit: The Agribusiness Threat to Farmers, Food and the Environment*. New York: Monthly Review Press.

Mamdani, Mahmood. 1996. *Citizen and Subject: Contemporary Africa and the Legacy of Late Colonialism*. Princeton: Princeton University Press.

Mançano Fernandes, Bernardo. 2001. The Occupation as a Form of Access to Land. Paper presented at the XXIII Congress of the Latin American Studies Association, Washington, DC, September 6–8.

———. 2002. *A Formação do MST no Brasil*. São Paulo: Editora Voces.

Martins, Mônica Dias. 1994. *Os desafios da cooperação nos assentamentos da reforma agrária*. São Paulo: Peres.

Matondi, Prosper, and Sam Moyo. 2003. Experiences with Market-Based Land Reform in Zimbabwe. In Barros, Sauer, and Schwartzman 2003, 323–402.

McCreery, David. 1990. State Power, Indigenous Communities, and Land in Nineteenth Century Guatemala, 1820–1920. In *Guatemalan Indians and the State: 1540–1988*, ed. Carol Smith. 96–115. Austin: University of Texas Press.

———. 1994. *Rural Guatemala: 1760–1940*. Stanford: Stanford University Press.

Mearns, Robin. 1999. Access to Land in Rural India. World Bank Policy Research Working Paper no. 2123. Social Science Research Network (SSRN), http://ssrn .com/abstract=636208.

Medeiros, Leonilde Servolo de. 1994. *Assentamentos rurais: uma visão multidisciplinar*. São Paulo: Universidade Estadual Paulista (UNESP).

Medeiros, Leonilde Servolo de, and Sérgio Leite, eds. 2002. *Os impactos regionais dos assentamentos rurais: dimensões econômicas, políticas e sociais* (Regional impacts of the rural settlements: Economic, political and social dimensions). Research Report, Convênio CPDA-UFRRJ/FINEP, Rio de Janeiro.

Meer, Shamim. 2003. Some Thoughts on Land Questions: A View from South Africa. Paper presented at the International Seminar on Agrarian Reform and Gender, Global Campaign for Agrarian Reform, Cochabamba, Bolivia.

Merino, L. 2001. Las políticas forestales y de conservación y sus impactos sobre las comunidades forestales. *Estudios Agrarios* 18: 75–115.

Migdal, Joel. 1988. *Strong Societies and Weak States: State-Society Relations and State Capabilities in the Third World*. Princeton: Princeton University Press.

Mihayo, Robert. 2003. 2003: An Unnecessarily Difficult Year. *Business Times* (Dar es Salaam, Tanzania) 23 (May).

Misión de Verificación de las Naciones Unidas en Guatemala. 2000a. Los desafíos para la participación de las mujeres guatemaltecas. Informe de Verificación. Guatemala City: MINUGUA.

———. 2000b. *La situación de los compromisos relativos a la tierra en los Acuerdos de Paz*. Informe de Verificación. Guatemala City: MINUGUA.

Molina C., Javier. 2001. *Acceso a la tierra por medio del Mercado. Experiencias de Bancos de Tierras en Centroamérica.* Oficina Regional de la FAO para América Latina y El Caribe. Santiago, Chile.

Mondragón, Héctor. 2003. Colombia: Either Land Markets or Agrarian Reform. In Barros, Sauer, and Schwarzman 2003, 103–68.

Monsalve Suárez, Sofía. 2004. EU Land Policy Guidelines and the Human Rights Approach to Land. Paper presented at a seminar on the European Union land policies for developing countries, sponsored by FoodFirst Information and Action Network (FIAN), Brussels, April 17.

Moore, Barrington Jr. 1967. *Social Origins of Dictatorship and Democracy: Lord and Peasant in the Modern World.* Harmondsworth: Penguin.

Movimento dos Trabalhadores Rurais Sem Terra. 1993. A cooperacão agrícola nos assentamentos. *Caderno de Formacão no. 20.* Sao Paulo: MST.

———. 1996. Cooperativas de producão: Questoes práticas. *Caderno de Formacão no. 21.* 2nd ed. São Paulo: MST.

———. 1998. CONCRAB: Quatro anos organizando a cooperacão. São Paulo: MST.

———. 2001a. *Construindo o Caminho.* Sao Paolo: MST.

———. 2001b. Os Empreendimentos Sociais do MST. Manuscript. São Paolo: MST.

Moyo, Sam. 2000. The political economy of land acquisition and redistribution in Zimbabwe, 1990–1999. *Journal of Southern African Studies* 26 (1): 5–29.

———. 2001. The interaction of market and compulsory land acquisition processes with social action in Zimbabwe's land reform. Southern African Regional Institute for Policy Studies (SARIPS) Paper presented at the Sapes Trust Annual Colloquium on Regional Integration, Harare.

Moyo, Sam, and Paris Yeros. 2005. Land Occupations and Land Reform in Zimbabwe: Towards the National Democratic Revolution. In *Reclaiming the Land: The Resurgence of Rural Movements in Africa, Asia and Latin America,* ed. Sam Moro and Paris Yeros, chap. 5. London: Zed Books.

Murphy, C. 1999. *Cultivating Havana: Urban Agriculture and Food Security in the Years of Crisis.* Food First Development Report no. 12. Oakland, CA: Institute for Food and Development Policy.

Navarro, Zander. 1998. The "Cédula da Terra" Guiding Project – Comments on the Social and Political-Institutional Conditions of its Recent Development. Porto Alegre: NEAD (mimeo).

Northern Peasants' Federation. 2001. *Voice of the Farmer.* Northern Peasants Federation. In Thai only.

Nuijten, Monique. 2003. Family property and the limits of intervention: The Article 27 reforms and the PROCEDE programme in Mexico. *Development and Change* 34 (3): 475–97.

Oficina Nacional de Estadísticas. 1997. *Estadísticas agropecuarias. Indicadores socioles y demográficos de Cuba.* Havana: ONE.

ole Ndaskoi, Navaya. 2003a. Tanzania: The Maasai predicament. *New African* (June): 44–46.

————. 2003b. Land is becoming a hot issue. *New African* (June): 46.

Ordóñez, César Eduardo. 1998. *Estudio Básico del Altiplano Occidental de Guatemala*. Quetzeltenango, Guatemala: CONSOC; Movimiento Tzuk Kim-Pop.

Paasch, Armin. 2003. The Failure of Market-Assisted Land Reforms and Some Necessary Consequences: Comments on the World Bank's Policy Research Report, www.worldbank.org/landpolicy/.

Paige, Jeffrey. 1975. *Agrarian Revolution: Social Movements, and Export Agriculture in the Underdeveloped World*. New York: Free Press.

Paige, Jeffrey. 1996. Land reform and agrarian revolution in El Salvador. *Latin American Research Review* 31 (2): 1127–39.

Paine, Thomas. 1925. *Agrarian Justice*. Vol. 10 of *The Life and Works of Thomas Paine*, ed. William M. Van der Weyde. New Rochelle, NY: Thomas Paine National Historical Association.

Palma Murga, Gustavo. 1997. *Promised the Earth: Agrarian Reform in the Socio-Economic Agreement*. London: Accord: An International Review of Peace Initiatives.

Palmer, R. 1990. Land reform in Zimbabwe. *African Affairs* 89: 163–81.

Palmer, Robin. 2000. Mugabe's "Land Grab" in Regional Perspective. In *Land Reform in Zimbabwe: Constraints and Prospects*, ed. T. A. S. Bowyer-Bower and C. Stoneman, 15–23. Aldershot, UK: Ashgate.

Patel, Rajeev. 2003. Three cheers for two struggles with one purpose: The conversation between land reformers and trade activists. *Debate Magazine* 9 (August 2003): 36–39.

————. 2006. International agrarian restructuring and the practical ethics of peasant movement solidarity *Journal of Asian and African Studies* 41: 71–93.

Patnaik, Utsa. 2003. Global Capitalism, Deflation and Agrarian Crisis in Developing Countries. In Razavi 2003a.

Peace Brigades. 1996. "The Struggle for Land: Invasions and Evictions." Guatemala City: Peace Brigades.

Pearce, B. 1997. Overview Paper on Land Reform in South Africa. Unpublished mimeograph. December.

Pearce, Jenny. 1998. From civil war to civil society: Has the end of the Cold War brought peace in Central America? *International Affairs* 74 (3): 587–615.

Pengue, Walter. 2005. Agricultura industrial y agricultura familiar en el Mercosur: el pez grande se come al chico . . . siempre? Edición Cono Sur, *Le Monde Diplomatique* 71: 7–9.

Perera, Victor. 1993. *Unfinished Conquest: the Guatemalan Tragedy*. Berkeley: University of California Press.

Petras, James, and Henry Veltmeyer. 2003. The Peasantry and the State in Latin America: A Troubled Past, an Uncertain Future. In *Latin American Peasants*, ed. Tom Brass. Portland, OR: Frank Cass.

Pingali, P. L., M. Hossain, and R. V. Gerpacio. 1997. *Asian Rice Bowls: The Returning Crisis?* Wallingford, UK: CABI Publishing International.

Platteau, Jean-Philippe. 1995. A framework for the analysis of evolving patron-client ties in agrarian economies. *World Development* 23 (5): 767–86.

Polanyi, Karl. 1944. *The Great Transformation*. Boston: Beacon Press.

Pons-Vignon, Nicolas, and Henri-Bernard Solignac Lecomte. 2004. Land, Violent Conflict and Development. Organisation for Economic Co-operation and Development (OECD) Working Paper no. 233.

Ponte, Stefano. 2004. The politics of ownership: Tanzanian coffee policy in the age of liberal reformism. *African Affairs* 103 (413): 615–33.

Prosterman, Roy, and Jeffrey Riedinger. 1987. *Land Reform and Democratic Development*. Baltimore: Johns Hopkins University Press.

PROVEA (Venezuelan Program of Action-Education on Human Rights). 2003/2004. *Informe Annual*, 241, n. 56.

Psacharopoulos, George, and Harry Anthony Patrinos, eds. 1994. *Indigenous People and Poverty in Latin America. An Empirical Analysis*. 206–7. Washington, DC: The World Bank.

Putzel, James. 1992. *A Captive Land: The Politics of Agrarian Reform in the Philippines*. London: Catholic Institute for International Relations / New York: Monthly Review Press / Quezon City: Ateneo de Manila University Press.

———. 2002. The Politics of Partial Reform in the Philippines. In *Agrarian Studies: Essays on Agrarian Relations in Less-Developed Countries*, ed. V. K. Ramachandran and M. Swaminathan, 213–29. New Delhi: Tulika Books (Published in UK by Zed Books, 2003).

Quevedo, Rafael Isidro. 1998. Venezuela: Un perfil general. *Agroalimentaria* no. 6 (June).

Rattanabirabongse, V., R. A. Eddington, A. F. Burns, and K. G. Nettle. 1998. *The Land Titling Project: Thirteen Years of Experience (1984–1996)*. Bangkok: Department of Lands.

Razavi, Shahra, ed. 2003a. *Agrarian Change, Gender and Land Rights*. Geneva: United Nations Research Institute for Social Development / Oxford: Blackwell Publishing.

Repartir a Terra. 2001. Historico da campanha pela emenda constitucional. *Repartir a Terra* (Brazil) 1 (1): 3.

Resnick, Stephen A., and Richard Wolff. 2002 *Class Theory and History: Capitalism and Communism in the USSR*. New York: Routledge.

Reyes, María Eugenia. 1998. Los acuerdos agrarios en Chiapas: øuna política de contención social? In *Transformaciones rurales en Chiapas*, ed. M. E. Reyes, R. Moguel, and G. van der Haar. Mexico City, UAM Xochimilco: Colegio de la Frontera Sur.

Richards, John, ed. 2002. *Land, Property, and the Environment*. Oakland, CA: Institute for Contemporary Studies.

Riedinger, Jeffrey. 1990. Philippine land reform in the 1980s. In *Agrarian Reform and Grassroots Development: Ten Case Studies*, ed. Roy Prosterman, Mary N. Temple, and Timothy M. Hanstad. Boulder, CO: Lynne Rienner Publishers.

———. 1995. *Agrarian Reform in the Philippines: Democratic Transitions and Redistributive Reform*. Stanford: Stanford University Press.

Riedinger, Jeffrey, Wan-Ying Yang, and Karen Brook. 2001. Market-Based Land Reform: An Imperfect Solution. In *Power in the Village: Agrarian Reform, Rural*

Politics, Institutional Change and Globalization, ed. H. Morales Jr. and J. Putzel, 363–78. Quezon City: University of the Philippines Press.

Robles Berlanga, Héctor, and Klaus Deininger. 2000. Procuraduría Agraria and World Bank: Reporte Técnico del Estudio Sectorial Agrario. *Estudios Agrarios* 16.

Rodríguez, J. 1996. Cuba 1990–1995. Reflexiones subre una política económica acertada. *Revista Cuba Socialista* 1: 24.

Ross, Eric. 1998. *The Malthus Factor: Poverty, Politics and Population in Capitalist Development*. London: Zed Books.

———. 2003. Modernisation, Clearance and the Continuum of Violence in Colombia. ISS Working Paper Series no. 383. The Hague: Institute of Social Studies.

Rosset, Peter M. 1995. Understanding Chiapas. In *First World, Ha Ha Ha! The Zapatista Challenge*, ed. Elaine Katzenberger, 157–67. San Francisco: City Lights Books.

———. 1997a. Alternative agriculture and crisis in Cuba. *Technology and Society* 16 (2): 19–25.

———. 1997b. La crisis de la agricultura convencional, la sustitución de insumos, y el enfoque agroecológico. *Agroecología y Desarrollo* (Chile) 11 (12): 2–12.

———. 1997c. Cuba: Ethics, biological control, and crisis. *Agriculture and Human Values* 14: 291–302.

———. 1998. Alternative agriculture works: The case of Cuba. *Monthly Review* 50: 3.

———. 1999. The Multiple Functions and Benefits of Small Farm Agriculture. Food First Policy Brief no.4. Oakland, CA: Institute for Food and Development Policy.

———. 2001a. Access to Land: Land Reform and Security of Tenure. FAO World Food Summit/Five Years Later Civil Society Input/Case Study (October). Food First/Institute for Food and Development Policy, www.landaction.org/display .php?article=179.

———. 2001b. Tides shift on agrarian reform: New movements show the way. *Backgrounder* 7 (1): 1–8. Berkeley: FoodFirst Institute.

———. 2003. Food sovereignty: Global rallying cry of farmer movements. Institute for Food and Development Policy, Food First Backgrounder 9(4): 1–4.

———. 2004. *El Derecho a la Tierra: Cuatro Textos sobre la Reforma Agraria*. Barcelona: Agora Nord-Sud.

Rosset, Peter M., and M. Benjamin, eds. 1994. *The Greening of the Revolution: Cuba's Experiment with Organic Agriculture*. Australia: Ocean Press.

Runge, C. Ford. 1992. Common Property and Collective Action in Economic Development. In *Making the Commons Work*, ed. D. W. Bromley. San Francisco, CA: Institute for Contemporary Studies.

Sachs, Jeffrey D. 1987. Trade and Exchange Rate Policies in Growth Oriented Adjustment Programs. In *Growth-Oriented Adjustment Programs*, ed. Vittorio Corbo, M. Khan, and G. Goldstein, 291–325. Washington, DC: International Monetary Fund and The World Bank.

Saith, Ashwani. 1990. Development strategies and the rural poor. *Journal of Peasant Studies* 17 (2): 171–44.

Salamini, Heather Fowler. 1971. *Agrarian Radicalism in Veracruz, 1920–38*. Lincoln and London: University of Nebraska Press.

SALDRU. 1994. *South African Rich and Poor: Baseline Household Statistics*. Cape Town: SALDRU.

———. 1995. *Key Indicators of Poverty in South Africa*. Document prepared for the Office of the Reconstruction and Development Programme, Cape Town: SALDRU.Sanderson, Susan Walsh. 1984. *Land Reform in Mexico: 1920–1980*. London and New York: Academic Press.

Sanderson, Susan Walsh. 1984. *Land Reform in Mexico: 1920–1980*. London and New York: Academic Press.

Sandoval, Leopoldo. 1987. *Estructura agraria y nuevo régimen constitucional*. Guatemala City: Asociación de Investigación y Estudios Sociales (ASIES).

Sauer, Sérgio. 2002. Terra e Modernidade: A dimensão do espaço na aventura da luta pela terra. PhD diss., Department of Sociology, University of Brasília.

———. 2003. A Ticket to Land: The World Bank's Market-Based Land Reform in Brazil. In Barros, Sauer, and Schwartzman 2003, 45–102.

Schlesinger, Stephen, and Stephen Kinzer. 1982. *Bitter Fruit: The Untold Story of the American Coup in Guatemala*. Garden City, NY: Anchor Press.

———. 1999. *Bitter Fruit: The Story of the American Coup in Guatemala*. Cambridge: Harvard University/David Rockefeller Center for Latin American Studies.

Scofield, Rupert W. 1990. Land Reform in Central America. In *Agrarian Reform and Grassroots Development: Ten Case Studies*, ed. Roy L. Prosterman, Mary N. Temple, and Timothy M. Hanstad. Boulder, CO: Lynne Rienner Publishers.

Scott, James C. 1985. *Weapons of the Weak*. New Haven: Yale University Press.

———. 1998. *Seeing Like a State: How Certain Schemes to Improve the Human Condition Have Failed*. New Haven: Yale University Press.

Scott, James, and Benedict Kerkvliet, eds. 1986. Everyday forms of peasant resistance in Southeast Asia. Special volume, *Journal of Peasant Studies* 13 (2).

Shillinglaw, Geoffrey. 1974. Land Reform and Peasant Mobilization in Southern China, 1947–1950. In *Peasants, Landlords and Governments: Agrarian Reform in the Third World*, ed. D. Lehmann 118–55. New York: Holmes and Meier Publishers.

Shiva, Vandana. 1991. *Ecology and the Politics of Survival: Conflicts over Natural Resources in India*. New Delhi: Sage Publications.

Skarstein, Rune. 2005. Economic liberalization and smallholder productivity in Tanzania: From promised success to real failure, 1985–1998. *Journal of Agrarian Change* 5 (3): 334–62.

Smith, Carol. 1984. Local history in global context: Social and economic transitions in Western Guatemala. *Comparative Studies in Society and History* 26.

Sobhan, Rehman. 1993. *Agrarian Reform and Social Transformation: Preconditions for Development*. London: Zed Books.

Sociedade Rural Brasiliera. 1985. A rural 65 (594): 7–12.

Solimano, Andrés. 2000. Beyond Unequal Development: An Overview. In *Dis-*

tributive Justice and Economic Development: The Case of Chile and Developing Countries, ed. Andres Solimano, Eduardo Aninat, and Nancy Birdsall, chap. 2. Ann Arbor: University of Michigan Press.

South Africa. 1996. Constitution of the Republic of South Africa, Act 108. Pretoria: Government of South Africa.

———. Department of Land Affairs. 1997a. Quarterly Monitoring and Evaluation Report on the Implementation of the Land Reform Programme. Pretoria.

———. Department of Land Affairs. 1997b. White Paper on South Africa Land Policy. Pretoria.

———. Department of Land Affairs. 2000. Annual Report. Pretoria.

South African Institute of Race Relations. 1996. *South Africa Survey, 1995/1996*.

———. 2000. *South African Survey* , 1999/2000.

South African Labour and Development Research Unit. *See* SALDRU.

Spoor, Max, ed. 1997. *The "Market Panacea": Agrarian Transformation in Developing Countries and Former Socialist Economies*. London: Intermediate Technology Publications.

———. 2002. Policy regimes and performance of the agricultural sector in Latin America and the Caribbean during the last three decades. *Journal of Agrarian Change* 2 (3): 381–400.

———, ed. 2003. *Transition, Institutions, and the Rural Sector*. New York: Lexington.

Spoor, Max, and Oane Visser. 2004. Restructuring postponed: Large Russian farm enterprises "coping with the market." *Journal of Peasant Studies* 31 (3–4): 515–51.

Stédile, João Pedro, ed. 1997. *A Reforma Agraria e a Luta do MST*. São Paulo: Editora Voces.

———. 1998. *Questão Agrária No Brasil*. 6th Ed. São Paulo: Editora Atual.

Stiglitz, Joseph. 2002. *Globalization and its Discontents*. London: Penguin Press.

Stringer, Randy, and Virginia Lambert. 1989. *A Profile of Land Markets in Rural Guatemala*. Madison: University of Wisconsin Land Tenure Center.

Tai, Hung-Chao. 1974. *Land Reform and Politics: A Comparative Analysis*. Berkeley: University of California Press.

Tannenbaum, Frank. 1929. *The Mexican Agrarian Revolution*. New York: Archon Books, 1968.

Tannenbaum, F. 1997. The Mexican Agrarian Revolution, 1929. In *Reformando la Reforma Agraria Mexicana*, ed. L. Randall. Mexico City: UAM/El Atajo Ediciones.

Tauli-Corpuz, Victoria, and Joji Cariño, eds. 2004. *Reclaiming Balance: Indigenous Peoples, Conflict Resolution and Sustainable Development*. Baguio City, Philippines: Tebtebba Foundation.

Tellez, Luis. 1994. *La modernización del sector agropecuario y forestal*. Mexico City: Fondo de Cultura Económia (FCE).

Templeton, S. R., and S. J. Scherr. 1999. Effects of demographic and related microeconomic change on land quality in hills and mountains of developing countries. *World Development* 27 (6): 903–18.

Thiesenhusen, William C., ed. 1989. *Searching for Agrarian Reform in Latin America*. Boston: Unwin Hyman.

————. 1995. *Broken Promises: Agrarian Reform and the Latin American Campesino*. Boulder, CO: Westview Press.

Thome, Joseph. 1989. Law, Conflict, and Change: Frei's Law and Allende's Agrarian Reform. In *Searching for Agrarian Reform in Latin America*, ed. William C. Thiesenhusen, 188–215. Boston: Unwin Hyman.

Tiechman, Judith A. 1995. *Privatization and Political Change in Mexico*. Pittsburgh, PA: University of Pittsburgh Press.

Tomaševski, Katarina. 1999. *Women and Human Rights*. London and New York: Zed Books.

Tomich, Thomas P., Peter Kilby, and Bruce F. Johnston. 1995. *Transforming Agrarian Economies: Opportunities Seized, Opportunities Missed*. Ithaca: Cornell University Press.

Toulmin, C., and J. Quan, eds. 2000. *Evolving Land Rights, Policy and Tenure in Africa*. London: Department for International Development (DFID).

Tsikata, Dzodzi. 2003. Securing Women's Interests within Land Tenure Reforms: Recent Debates in Tanzania. In Razavi 2003a.

Tsing, Anna. 2002. Land as Law: Negotiating the meaning of Property in Indonesia. In *Land, Property, and the Environment*, ed. F. Richards, 94–137. Oakland, CA: Institute for Contemporary Studies.

Tuma, Elias. 1965. *Twenty-Six Centuries of Agrarian Reform: A Comparative Analysis*. Berkeley: University of California Press.

Umehara, Hiromitsu, and Germelino M.Bautista, eds. 2004. *Communities at the Margins: Reflections on Social Economic, and Environmental Change in the Philippines*. Manila: Ateneo de Manila University Press.

Unidad de Gestión para la Reforma Agraria. 1998. *Criterios técnicos para la asignación de los recursos DRI para el apoyo de la Reforma Agraria*. Bogotá: UGRA / IICA.

United Nations. 2001. Resolution adopted by the General Assembly on the report of the Third Committee (A/55/602/Add.2 and Corr.1) 55/95. Situation of human rights in Cambodia, UN Document reference: A/RES/55/95, 28 February 2001.

Urioste, Miguel. 2001. Bolivia: Reform and Resistance in the Countryside (1982–2000). Occasional Papers no. 23, Institute of Latin American Studies, University of London.

————. 2003. What is Food Sovereignty? La Via Campesina, www.viacampesina .org/IMG/_article_PDF/article_216.pdf.

Venezuela. 2005. National Assembly of the Republic. *Ley de Tierras y Desarrollo Agrario*. Article 14.

————. 2003. What Is Food Sovereignty? La Via Campesina, www.viacampesina .org/IMG/_article_PDF/article_216.pdf.

Venezuelan Program of Action-Education on Human Rights. *See* PROVEA.

La Via Campesina. 2002. Food Sovereignty. Flyer distributed at the World Food Summit +5, Rome.

Vidal, Aida. 2004. *The Politics and Formation of Indigenous People's Right to Land:*

The Case of Mindanao with Special Reference to the Subanen. Davao, Philippines: AFRIM.

Vilariño, A., and J. Domenech. 1986. *El Sistema de Dirección y Planificación de la Economía Nacional, historia, actividad y perspectiva*. Havana: Editorial Pueblo y Educación.

Vyas, V. S. 1999. *Changing Contours of Indian Agriculture*. New Delhi: National Council of Applied Economic Research (NCAER).

Wagner, Sarah. 2005. Mercal: Reducing Poverty and Creating National Food Sovereignty in Venezuela. Venezuelanalysis.com. June 24, 2005. www.venezuel analysis.com/articles.php?artno=1486.

Walinsky, Louis, ed. 1977. *Agrarian Reform as Unfinished Business: The Selected Papers of Wolf Ladejinsky*. Oxford: Oxford University Press.

Walker, Cherryl. 2002. *Agrarian Change, Gender and Land Reform. A South African Case Study*. Social Policy and Development Programme Paper no. 10, United Nations Research Institute for Social Development, Geneva.

Watts, Michael. 1994. Life Under Contract: Contract Farming, Agrarian Restructuring, and Flexible Accumulation. In *Living Under Contract: Contract Farming and Agrarian Transformation in Sub-Saharan Africa*, ed. P. D. Little and M. Watts, 21–77. Madison: University of Wisconsin Press.

White, Ben. 1997. Agroindustry and Contract Farmers in Upland West Java. *Journal of Peasant Studies* 24 (3): 100–36.

Whitehead, Ann, and Dzodzi Tsikata. 2003. Policy Discourses on Women's Land Rights in Sub-Saharan Africa: The Implications of the Re-turn to the Customary. In Razavi 2003a.

Williams, Donald C. 1996. Reconsidering state and society in Africa: The institutional dimension in land reform policies. *Comparative Politics* 28 (2): 207–24.

Williams, Robert G. 1986. *Export Agriculture and the Crisis in Central America*. Chapel Hill: University of North Carolina Press.

———. 1994. *States and Social Evolution: Coffee and the Rise of National Governments in Central America*. Chapel Hill: University of North Carolina Press.

Wilpert, Gregory. 2006. *Changing Venezuela by Taking Power: The History and Policies of the Chavez Presidency*. New York, London: Verso Books.

Windfuhr, Michael, and Jennie Jonsén. 2005. Food Sovereignty: Towards Democracy in Localised Food Systems. Intermediate Technology Development Group, Working Paper. Warwickshire, UK: ITDG Publishing.

Wolford, Wendy. 2001. Case study: Grassroots-initiated land reform in Brazil; the Rural Landless Workers' Movement. In de Janvry et al., eds., chap. 12.

———. 2003. Producing community: The MST and land reform settlements in Brazil. *Journal of Agrarian Change* 3 (4): 500–20.

Worby, Eric. 2001. A redivided land? New agrarian conflicts and questions in Zimbabwe. *Journal of Agrarian Change* 1 (4): 475–509.

World Bank. 1993. Options for land reform and Rural Restructuring in South Africa. Johannesburg, SA: WB.

———. 1996. Guatemala: Building Peace with Rapid and Equitable Growth. Country Economic Memorandum Report No. 15352-GU. Washington, DC: WB.

——. 1997a. Guatemala Land Fund Project. Natural Resources and Rural Poverty Sector. Washington, DC: WB

——. 1997b. Project Appraisal Document for the Land Reform and Poverty Alleviation Pilot Project. Washington, DC: WB.

——. 1999a. The Irrigation Sector—India, Water Resources Management. *Rural Development Series*. New Delhi: Allied Publishers.

——. 1999b. Operations Evaluation Department. *Land Administration and Rural Development: Two Cases from Thailand*. Precis no. 184, www.worldbank .org.

——. 2003. *Land Policies for Growth and Poverty Reduction*. Washington, DC: WB / Oxford: Oxford University Press.

——. n.d. The Theory Behind Market-Assisted Land Reform. Washington, DC: WB.

World Bank Land Policy and Administration Thematic Group. 2001. *Land Policy and administration: Lessons learned and new challenges for the Bank's development agenda*. Washington, DC. WB, www.worldbank.org/landpolicy/.

World Forum on Agrarian Reform. 2004. *La reforma agraria y los recursos natu- rales. Una exigencia de los pueblos*. Documento final del Foro Mundial sobre Reforma Agraria. Valencia: FMRA Valencia, www.fmra.org/declaracion_final .doc.

World Forum on Food Sovereignty. 2001. Final Declaration. Havana. September 7, www.foodfirst.org/media/news/2001/havanadeclaration.html.

World Resources Institute. 1994. World Resources 1994–95: People and Envi- ronment. Geneva: United Nations Environment Programme and the United Nations Development Program.

Wright, Angus, and Wendy Wolford. 2003. *To Inherit the Earth: The Landless Movement and the Struggle for a New Brazil*. Oakland, CA: Food First Books.

Wurfel, David. 1988. *Filipino Politics: Development and Decay*. Ithaca: Cornell Uni- versity Press.

Young, Iris Marion. 1990. *Justice and the Politics of Difference*. Princeton: Prince- ton University Press.

Zevallos, Jose Vicente. 1989. Agrarian Reform and Structural Change: Ecuador Since 1964. In Thiesenhusen 1989, 42–69.

Ziegler, Jean. 2002. Report of the Special Rapporteur of the Commission on Human Rights on the Right to Food. A/57/150, 27. United Nations General Assembly, New York. August.

——. 2004. Economic, Social and Cultural Rights: The Right to Food. Report submitted by the Special Rapporteur on the Right to Food, in accordance with Commission on Human Rights Resolution 2003/25. E/CN.4/2004/10. Unit- ed Nations Commission on Human Rights, Geneva. February 9.

Zimmerman, F. J. 2000. Barriers to Participation of the Poor in South Africa's Land Redistribution. *World Development* 28 (8): 1439–60.

Zoomers, Annelies, and Gemma van der Haar, eds. 2000. *Current Land Policy in Latin America: Regulating Land Tenure Under Neo-Liberalism*. Amsterdam: Royal Tropical Institute (KIT).

About the Authors

MAVIS ALVAREZ is the retired former director of the International Cooperation of the National Association of Small Farmers (ANAP) in Cuba.

SATURNINO M. BORRAS JR. is a faculty member in Development Studies at the Institute of Social Studies (ISS) in The Hague, Netherlands.

MARTIN BOURQUE is executive director of the Ecology Center in Berkeley, California.

ROSÂNGELA CINTRÃO is a researcher at the Federal Rural University of Rio de Janeiro (UFRRJ) in Brazil.

MICHAEL COURVILLE is an independent writer and researcher in political economy. His work explores the limits of national development and the impact of those limits on resource distribution and human well-being. He holds both an MA in International and Area Studies and a master's in Social Welfare from the University of California, Berkeley.

ANA DE ITA is a rural sociologist and director of the Center for the Study of Rural Change in Mexico (CECCAM).

CARMEN DIANA DEERE is director of the Center for Latin American Studies and professor of Food and Resource Economics at the University of Florida at Gainesville. She is coauthor of *Empowering Women: Land and Property Rights in Latin America* (University of Pittsburgh Press, 2001).

FERNANDO FUNES is an agronomist and retired director of Research at the Institute for Pasture and Forage Research (IIPF) in Cuba. He is coauthor of *Sustainable Agriculture and Resistance: Transforming Food Production in Cuba* (Food First Books, 2002).

SHALMALI GUTTAL is senior associate of the Focus on the Global South in Bangkok, Thailand, and co-coordinator of the Land Research Action Network (www.landaction.org).

BEATRIZ HEREDIA is a professor at the Federal University of Rio de Janeiro / Institute of Philosophy and Social Sciences.

TOM LEBERT is a South Africa–based rural development consultant in the southern Africa region, and former deputy director of the National Land Committee (NLC), a national network of land sector NGOs in South Africa.

REBECA LEONARD is an advisor on community-based natural resource management with the Northern Development Foundation (NDF), a Thai non-governmental organization (NGO) based in Chiang Mai in northern Thailand.

LUCY MARTIN is a sociologist and researcher at the Center for Psychological and Sociological Research (CIPS) in Cuba.

MÔNICA DIAS MARTINS has a PhD in sociology from the Federal University of Ceará, Brazil, where she is a visiting professor. She is also a researcher for the Social Network for Justice and Human Rights.

LEONILDE MEDEIROS is a professor at Rural Federal University of Rio de Janeiro (UFRRJ) in Brazil.

MARIA LUISA MENDONÇA is codirector of the Social Network for Justice and Human Rights (Rede Social) in Brazil, and co-coordinator of the Land Research Action Network.

HÉCTOR MONDRAGÓN is an economic advisor to the National Campesino Council (CNC) of Colombia. He has been an advisor to the National Indigenous Organization of Colombia and the Congress of the Republic, and a consultant to the International Labor Organization, United Nations Development Programme (UNDP) and the Organization of American States.

SOFÍA MONSALVE SUAREZ works for the FoodFirst Information and Action Network (FIAN) International, based in Germany, where she coordinates the participation of FIAN in the Global Campaign for Agrarian Reform of Via Campesina.

KINGKORN NARINTARAKUL NA AYUTTHAYA is the director of the Northern Development Foundation (NDF), a Thai nongovernmental organization (NGO) based in Chiang Mai in northern Thailand, and studies national land rights and natural resource management policies.

ARMANDO NOVA is an economist and teaches at the Agrarian University of Havana (UNAH). He is also researcher at the Center for the Study of the Cuban Economy at the University of Havana.

RAJ PATEL is a postdoctoral fellow at the Centre for Civil Society at the University of KwaZulu-Natal in Durban, South Africa, and is author of *Stuffed and Starved: The Hidden Battle for the World's Food System* (Portobello Books and HarperCollins, 2007).

MOACIR PALMEIRA is a professor in the postgraduate program in Social Anthropology at the Federal University of Rio de Janeiro (UFRJ) in Brazil.

SÉRGIO PEREIRA LEITE is a professor at Federal University of Rio de Janeiro (UFRJ) in Brazil.

PETER M. ROSSET is a researcher at the Center for the Study of Rural Change in Mexico (CECCAM), where he is co-coordinator of the Land Research Action Network. He is also an associate of the Center for the Study of the Americas (CENSA), and visiting scholar at the University of California, both in Berkeley. He is the former executive director and codirector of the Institute for Food and Development Policy (Food First) in Oakland, California.

LAURA SALDIVAR-TANAKA is a researcher who resides in San Cristobal de Las Casas in Chiapas, Mexico, and presently works for the Women in Development project of the Japanese International Cooperation Agency (JICA) and the state government of Chiapas.

SÉRGIO SAUER has an MA in philosophy from the University of Bergen, Norway, and a PhD from the Department of Sociology at the University of Brasilia. He is an aid to Brazilian Senator Heloísa Helena.

MANPREET SETHI is an independent researcher who participated in the Land Research Action Network while working with Focus on the Global South, India.

RODOLFO STAVENHAGEN is a leading Mexican sociologist and currently serves as Special Rapporteur on the Human Rights and Fundamental Freedoms of Indigenous People, for the United Nations Commission on Human Rights.

WELLINGTON DIDIBHUKU THWALA The author was research coordinator at the National Land Committee in Johannesburg, South Africa.

GREGORY WILPERT is a sociologist and is the editor of Venezuelanalysis .com. He is also the author of *Changing Venezuela by Taking Power: The History and Policies of the Chavez Government* (Verso Books, 2006).

HANNAH WITTMAN is an assistant professor in the Department of Sociology and Anthropology at Simon Fraser University in Vancouver, British Columbia. She is actively involved in research on sustainable agriculture, the environment, and social movements in Latin America.

Index